The University of Georgia Press · Athens

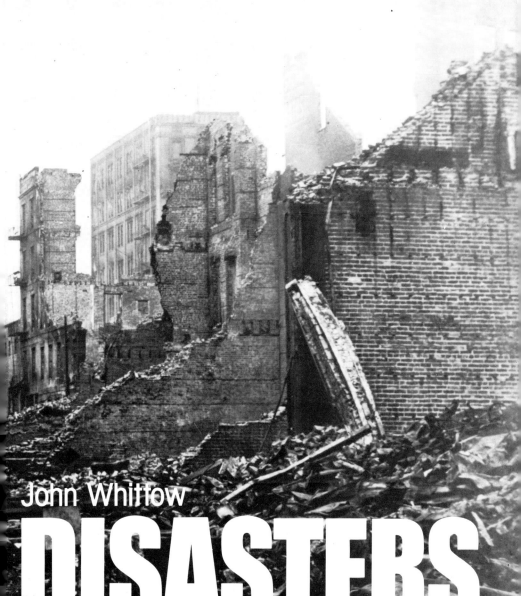

John Whittow

DISASTERS
The Anatomy of Environmental Hazards

International Standard Book Number 0–8203–0499–9
Library of Congress Catalog Card Number 79–5236

The University of Georgia Press
Athens, Georgia 30602

Printed in Great Britain

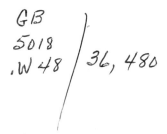

Contents

Acknowledgements

The publishers wish to thank the following for permission to use their photographs: Press Association Photos for plates 1 and 39; Associated Press for Plates 6, 11, 17, 26 34, 36, 37, 38, 41, 48 and 53; Camera Press Ltd for Plates 2 and 33; Central Press Photos Ltd for Plate 35; the Science Museum, London, for Plate 3, Crown Copyright; Institution of Geological Science, London SW7, for Plate 8, N.E.R.C. Copyright, reproduced by permission of the Director; *Sunday Times* for Plates 4, 23, 49 and 52; Rex Features for Plates 45 and 51; United States Geological Survey for Plates 5, 18b, 42, 54 and 55; Radio Times Hulton Picture Library for Plates 7 and 12; Popperfoto for Plates 10, 13, 15, 16, 25, 32, 40, 46 and 50; Frank W. Lane for Plates 9, 18a, 24a, 24b and 43; Richard Costain Ltd for Plate 14; Keystone for Plate 19; United Press International for Plates 20 and 30; Government Information Services, Hong Kong, for Plate 21a; Victor Ho for Plate 21b; British Railways Board for Plate 22; Staffordshire Sentinel Newspapers Ltd for Plate 27; A. F. Calvert for Plate 28; University of Toronto Press for Plate 29; Central Electricity Generating Board for Plate 31; The John Hillelson Agency for Plate 44; the United States Forest Service U.S.D.A. for Plates 47 and 56; the C.P. Agency for Plate 57; all copyrights reserved.

Figures 10, 13 and 80 are based on illustrations in *Geological Hazards* by B. A. Bolt, *et al.*, 1975, by kind permission of Springer-Verlag; Figures 1 and 2 are based on illustrations in *Experiencing the Environment* by S. Wapner, S. B. Cohen and B. Kaplan, 1976, by kind permission of the Plenum Press; Figures 9, 11 and 16 are based on the work of E. R. Oxburgh by kind permission of the Geologists' Association; Figures 22, 24, 25b and 26 are based on illustrations in *Volcanoes* by P. Francis, 1976, by kind permission of Penguin Books; Figures 43, 47 and 109 are based on the work of Q. A. Aune, in *Quick Clays and California's Clays: No Quick Solutions*, Mineral Information Service, 19, No. 8, 1966, by kind permission of the California Division of Mines and Geology; Figure 44 is based on an illustration in *Landslides and their control* by Q. Zaruba and V. Mencl, 1969, by kind permission of Elsevier Scientific Publishing Corporation, Amsterdam and Academia, Publishing House of the Czechoslovak Academy of Sciences, Prague; Figure 57 is based on an illustration in *Permafrost in Canada, Its Influence on Northern Development* by Roger J. E. Brown Copyright © 1970, University of Toronto Press; Figure 60 is based on an illustration in *Natural Hazards: Local, National, Global* by Gilbert F. White *et al.* Copyright © 1974 by Oxford University Press Inc. Reprinted by permission; Figure 81 is based on an illustration in *Flooding and Flood Hazard in the United Kingdom* by M. D. Newson, © Oxford University Press 1975; Figures 101 and 102 are based on illustrations in *Air Pollution* by V. Brodine, 1973, by kind permission of Harcourt Brace Jovanovich Inc.; Figures 104, 110 and 111 are based on illustrations in *The Los Angeles Metropolitan Experience*, Contemporary Metropolitan America Project, by H. J. Nelson and W. A. V. Clark, Copyright 1976, Ballinger Publishing Company. Reprinted with permission; Figure 97 is based on an illustration in *Weather and Climate Modification* by W. N. Hess, 1974, by kind permission of John Wiley and Sons Inc.; Figure 25a is based on an illustration in *Volcanoes* by Fred M. Bullard, © 1962, by kind permission of University of Texas Press, Austin. All rights reserved.

Acknowledgement is gratefully given to Mrs M. Rolley who typed the manuscript, Mrs K. King who drew the diagrams, Mr J. Cater who assisted in the collection of other illustrative material and to Messrs W. T. and I. Fieldhouse who helped in the compilation of certain data.

List of Plates

Disasters

24. (a) and (b) The development of an avalanche in the Swiss Alps.
25. Airolo, Switzerland, in February 1951.
26. Italy's Leaning Tower of Pisa.
27. Coal-mining subsidence damage in Stoke-on-Trent during the mid 1970s.
28. Salt subsidence in Northwich, Cheshire, England, in the nineteenth century.
29. An oil storage tank in Arctic Canada, settled owing to thawing of underlying permafrost.
30. A severe gale in Flensburg, West Germany.
31. The collapse of one of the cooling towers at Ferrybridge power station, Yorkshire, England, in November 1965.
32. Wave damage on the south shore of Long Island, New York, in 1962.
33. A waterspout approaching the Costa Brava, Spain, in 1965.
34. (a–d) Stages in the formation of a tornado in May 1970, in Kansas, U.S.A.
35. A typical tropical cyclone, photographed from space.
36. The flooding of the Bangladesh coastline during the 1970 cyclone.
37. Three freighters swept ashore by Hurricane Camille in the United States in August 1969.
38. The floods in Florence in November 1966.
39. Lynmouth after the Exmoor floods of August 1952.
40. The 1947 snow-melt floods in the Thames valley near Windsor, England.
41. A giant wave, or tsunami, hits the coast of Hawaii.
42. Part of the town of Seward, Alaska, flattened by a tsunami in 1964.
43. Johnstown, Pennsylvania, U.S.A., devastated by floodwaters in 1889.
44. Drought in the Sahel, Africa, 1974.
45. A British reservoir dried up in 1976.
46. The dry River Thames, upstream from London, in 1976.
47. A dust storm approaching a farm in the infamous United States Dust Bowl of the 1930s.
48. The heaviest day's snowfall in the history of New York in February 1978.
49. The British West Country blizzards of February 1978.
50. The sinking *Andrea Doria*, in July 1956, after its collision in sea-fog.
51. The world's worst air disaster at Tenerife airport in March 1977.
52. Patchy fog threatening vehicle pile-ups on a British motorway.
53. Photochemical smog swirling about New York's skyscrapers in November 1966.
54. A newly constructed freeway, damaged by the 1971 earthquake in the San Fernando Valley of Los Angeles.
55. Landslides sometimes block parts of the Pacific Coastal Highway in Los Angeles County.
56. A fire in the Californian brushwood.
57. A policeman stands watch against looters during flooding in Cambridge, Ontario, Canada.

List of Text Figures

Preface

Disasters have always been newsworthy events, whether they be natural, man-made or a mixture of both. The media are constantly responding to the public's unwaning appetite for graphic accounts of sensational phenomena because of the apparently horrific fascination embodied in a catastrophe. Novelists also continue to capitalize on this demand for excitement and on the average person's attempt to escape from the humdrum lifestyle of modern society, a society which, in the developed countries, has been fortified against disease, had much of the hazardousness removed from its everyday labours, and where whole new generations have grown up since the horrors of the Second World War. Psychologists can no doubt explain this human desire for sensation-seeking and why accounts of wartime savagery, of modern cannibalism after an Andean plane-crash, of skyscraper blazes and of giant man-eating sharks, all top the list of best-sellers on the bookstalls.

Throughout the early 1970s rarely a month went by without a major disaster being reported from somewhere in the world – the Bangladesh cyclone of 1970; the Huascaran avalanche in Peru in 1970; the Nicaraguan earthquake of 1972 and the Turkish earthquake of 1975; the Honduras floods spawned by Hurricane Fifi in 1974; the 1972–74 Sahel drought of North Africa. These are just a few of the catastrophic events which took hundreds of thousands of lives and caused property losses of astronomical proportions. The disastrous year of 1976 appeared to be the final cataclysm, when earthquake shocks, volcanic eruptions, tsunamis, hurricanes, floods, blizzards and droughts combined to give the impression that the earth was in a turmoil, and that the day of reckoning was at hand. The present volume is largely a result of the frenetic events of that fateful year. It is an attempt not only to summarize the disasters which have caused such widespread death and destruction, but also to explain, as far as possible, why they occur and to discover whether man is partly to blame. In addition, an effort has been made to show some of the ways in which man can predict the events and also alleviate their effects. Such an investigation has revealed that in the world's developing countries the poorer people are becoming more disaster-prone, whilst the developed world has, in many instances, cushioned itself against some of the worst hazards. Sociologists now speak of the poorest people as having been 'marginalized' – moved onto the marginal lands where increased hazards make their existence more dangerous and unhealthy. We shall see, therefore, how most of the world's greatest death-tolls occur in over-crowded shanty towns on landslide-prone hillsides, flood-plains or coastal lowlands. Paradoxically, even the wealthier inhabitants of some Los Angeles luxury homes will be shown as having the same type of vulnerability, so that things are not always as simple as they first appear. We shall also look at some of the ways in which mankind has triggered-off disasters by an ill-conceived exploitation of the world's natural resources and how, in some cases, this has led to economic and cultural catastrophes.

This is not intended to be a pessimistic book of the *doomsday* variety; if it brings a greater understanding of world hazards to the layman there is every hope that this enlightenment will ultimately result in greater public pressure being brought in order to produce more positive responses in such fields as the prediction, alleviation and relief of disasters.

Whitchurch-on-Thames, August 1978   *J.B.W.*

Part One

Introduction

1. Environmental Hazards

Any study of environmental hazards will necessarily involve an examination of the complex interactions between physical and human systems, since no hazard can exist unless it is perceived and in turn provokes a human response. Thus, human systems of resource utilization, which have often been taken to illustrate the ways in which man has 'controlled' or 'tamed' his environment, have rarely been able to operate independently of atmospheric, hydrological, geomorphological and biological systems. Even slight natural changes in the operation of these physical systems can, under certain circumstances, pose a threat to mankind and as such these fluctuations can be termed hazards. A hazard is a perceived natural event which threatens both life and property – a disaster is the realization of this hazard.

Hazards affect mankind in a variety of ways and by varying degrees, but in general it is true to say that it is only when disasters strike those areas in which man has chosen to settle that they make headline news. When one of the world's great cities is razed by an earthquake, for example, it will be judged to be a much greater catastrophe than, say, the impact of a large meteorite in Siberia, although the energy released by the physical forces involved may be comparable. Nevertheless, it will be seen in the following chapters how the characteristics of hazards can vary considerably, both in their magnitude and in the speed at which they operate. Thus, we shall be examining a number of physical variables which will include such things as differences in energy release, frequencies of occurrence and contrasting periods of duration. Whilst an earthquake may last for only a few seconds, an avalanche for a few minutes and a blizzard for several hours, a flood can last for days or even weeks, and a drought for months or even years. In certain chapters it will be emphasized how man's modification of the environment can have an even longer-term impact and how, in some instances, he may have set in train irreversible processes which could threaten the world with the greatest catastrophe of all time – the destruction of life upon planet Earth. But the present study is not intended to examine in detail the effects

Disasters

Fig. 1. A comparison between natural and man-made disasters, showing magnitude and frequency on a global scale. N.B. For the purposes of this diagram an event is regarded as a disaster when the death-toll exceeds a notional figure of thirty (after S. Wapner, S. B. Cohen and B. Kaplan).

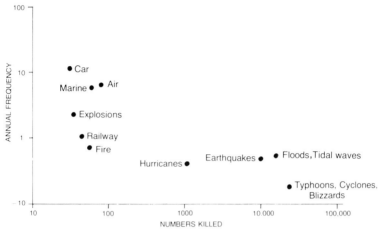

of global environmental pollution or genetic damage, only natural hazards and the ways in which man's interference with the natural physical processes has often served to exacerbate or trigger-off disasters.

Most people would be able to classify disasters into two main categories, those which are natural (sometimes referred to, rather ironically, as 'acts of God') and those which are caused by the thoughtlessness or carelessness of mankind. Such a dichotomy is probably based on two main parameters: the number of people killed, together with the periodicity of the catastrophic event. If these are compared in diagrammatic form (Figure 1) it will be seen how natural hazards claim more lives during world disasters, although man-made hazards kill more often, because of their more frequent occurrence. But what this figure of global disaster does not show is the relationship between deaths from disastrous events and deaths from other causes. The combined mortality from age, disease and malnutrition is thought to account for by far the largest proportion of the world's morbidity rate, although accurate statistics are not always easily obtainable. In a developed country, such as the United States:

Out of slightly less than two million Americans who died in each of recent years, perhaps 500 died as a consequence of natural hazard, 50,000 from the violence of others (war and crime) and of self (suicide), 100,000 in accidents with the made, built and machine environments. More difficult to give quantitative expression to is the effect of environmental events on disease rates: natural and man-made radiation on birth abnormalities and malignancies; the pollutants of the made environment on respiratory diseases and cancer; the hazards of poverty and poor housing on childhood mortality; or the pace of society on cardio-vascular disease. In developing countries, these proportions may be reversed; as many have died from natural hazard in Bangladesh as from heart trouble in the United States.[1]

Possibly because society now realizes the long-term effects which environmental pollution may be having on human health and well-being it is prepared to recognize a third type of hazard. Thus, recent research in Canada has shown that people are currently distinguishing between natural hazards, man-made hazards, social hazards and quasi-natural hazards of air and water pollution (Figure 2). The diagram indicates how the various hazard events have been clustered according to the ways in which people perceived the degree of disruption, and the severity of the threat in terms of their ability to control the event. It is clear from a study of Figure 2, therefore, how people recognize that natural hazards are the most uncontrollable, and it may also explain that whilst expressing a fear of natural hazards a great majority of the population also adopt a fatalistic approach to them. It will

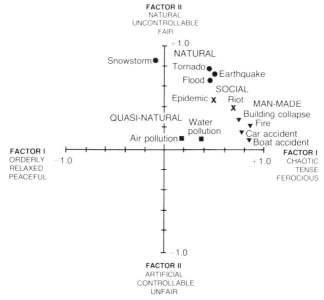

Fig. 2. A classification of hazards into Natural; Quasi-Natural; Social and Man-Made, based on public perception of the degree of disruption and their ability to control the event (after S. Wapner, S. B. Cohen and B. Kaplan).

be seen in Chapter 11 how millions of people in California, for example, are aware of the natural hazards within their environment and of the horrifying death-toll of earlier disasters, but are still prepared to settle in one of the world's most serious hazard zones.

Quasi-natural hazards, on the other hand, are largely the results of man's careless exploitation of his environment and the majority of these can therefore be avoided, alleviated or modified. Only now are we beginning to realize, however, that certain physical changes wrought by man may be irreparable and that future disasters may be precipitated if this erosion of the environment continues. Atmospheric pollution is a case in point and this is touched upon in Chapter 10. But some fresh hazards are inadvertently created by man, sometimes in an attempt to offset existing natural hazards. Who would have thought, for instance, that the construction of some of the world's major dams in an effort to combat drought (amongst other things) could trigger off earthquakes in certain critical seismic zones?

Consequently, the present study is intended to describe and explain all of the major natural hazards, whilst at the same time referring to specific instances where man has exacerbated these in such a way as to trigger disasters such as the Vaiont Dam landslide (Chapter 5). In cases where natural hazards have played a major role in a sudden mechanical disaster, such as an air crash or a motorway pile-up, these will be briefly discussed. Equally, where the works of man have led to a slow but inexorable change in the physical environment which could ultimately result in a cultural, economic or social disaster, these too have been examined, especially in Chapter 6, wherever they fit into the chosen framework. Thus, no attempt has been made to describe such biological hazards as disease and plague, although it is recognized that they are often responsible for a much greater loss of life on a global scale than, say, flooding, which is by far the most widespread and the greatest killer amongst all the natural hazards. Nor is it intended to look at such serious man-made catastrophes as the Soviet nuclear disaster of 1957–58, the Flixborough (U.K.) explosion of 1974, the Seveso (Italy) chemical plant disaster of 1976, and the infamous oceanic oil spillages which have affected many coastlines in recent years.

Classification of Hazards

There are several ways in which hazards may be classified, based on such parameters as magnitude, velocity, duration, death toll, financial cost, etc., but in the present volume it has been decided to categorize them according to their mode of operation. The types of disasters with which man is faced may be grouped into three broad categories: first, those which originate within the earth and are related to internal crustal processes (Chapters 2–4), such as earthquakes and volcanoes; secondly, those which are related to superficial surface processes (Chapters 5–6), including volume changes of surface materials, and these cover such phenomena as landslides, avalanches and surface collapse; and thirdly, there are the disasters which are caused by fluctuations in the atmospheric and hydrological elements (Chapters 7–10), and include violent storms, floods, drought, blizzards and fog. Although the seismic-generated sea wave, known as the tsunami, should strictly be classified as one of the hazards related to internal crustal processes it is described in Chapter 8 because its surface manifestation is that of a coastal flood.

Much of the explanation of the physical causes of disasters is necessarily involved with the scientific laws embodied in physics and will therefore make reference to such disciplines as *soil mechanics, hydrodynamics, thermodynamics* and even *electrodynamics*. But the deeper one gets involved with physical laws and systems the more difficult it becomes to discover simple cause-and-effect relationships. It will be seen, therefore, that the timing and the magnitude of an impending disaster can be extremely difficult to predict, even though the location may be pin-pointed with a fair degree of accuracy. This is particularly true of earthquake behaviour, and this problem is referred to in some detail in the Californian context (Chapter 2 and Chapter 11). Consequently, the best that can be done is to produce a statistical estimate of *risk probability*, which in turn can be used to generate a hazard-zoning map, although it is well known that the laws of nature refuse to be governed by statistical estimates!

It has already been suggested that a disaster will only occur when there is a fluctuation in, or a malfunction of, the physical systems or processes which are said to be governed by the so-called laws of nature, because if the status quo is preserved then no disaster can be triggered-off. Once this state of stability breaks down, however, catastrophic things begin to happen and it is the job of the geologist, geomorphologist, hydrologist, engineer or meteorologist to understand and explain the reasons for the termination of the stable state. They are all aware that the stability of a system can be of two types – static or dynamic – and between them these scientists have established numerous criteria for determining whether a system is statically or dynamically stable or not. These are the criteria which should be used whenever man designs his structures, such as dams, bridges, ocean oil rigs or coastal defence works. But the following chapters catalogue many of the instances where the criteria were either unknown or ignored and where catastrophes were the horrifying outcome either of man's wilful interference with the environment or of his careless miscalculations.

One of the possible consequences of the breakdown of the stability of a physical system is that surface masses become mobilized:

> In many cases, the catastrophe is connected with the motion of large masses of material (soil, rock, water, ice), usually downhill in the gravity field. The course of the mass movement often determines the severity of the catastrophe.
>
> Some catastrophes have their origin in the fluid envelopes of the earth: vortices in an unstable atmosphere lead to 'severe weather'; 'tidal waves' in the sea may impinge upon a coast.[2]

In earlier centuries many millions of lives were lost and much material damage was caused by the inability of man to interpret the world's physical systems and to understand the concept of stability. Today, however, scientists have made in-depth studies of previous disasters and there now exists a greater understanding and awareness of most environmental hazards. One of the more important outcomes from their studies has been in the field of hazard prediction, for it is extremely desirable to know as much as possible about the frequency and severity of disasters in order that we may make suitable contingency plans. Unfortunately, not all disasters exhibit indicative precursors, such as those associated with certain impending volcanic eruptions. Moreover, many of the known precursors are very short-term, so that long-range disaster forecasting has remained generally unsuccessful, as several Californian seismologists have already discovered (see p. 67). Nevertheless, attempts are being made to distinguish linkages between particular catastrophic phenomena in order to establish whether certain global patterns of disaster can be identified. During 1976, for example, many people believed that there must be a causal relationship between the sudden plethora of catastrophic events which captured the world headlines.

Whatever happened in 1976?

By any standards 1976 was a remarkable year for disasters. Record droughts in Britain were matched by those in Western Europe, the American Midwest, Australia and India, where grain harvests were decimated; the volcanic eruptions of La Soufrière (West Indies) and El Sangay (Ecuador) in mid-summer were catastrophic events, whilst tsunamis brought death and destruction to the Philippine island of Mindanao. Above all, it was the high incidence of earthquakes which singled out 1976 as something out of the ordinary, and the following table of seismic events (Figure 3) makes frightening reading:

Fig. 3. World earthquake disasters in 1976. (N.B. For explanation of Richter Scale see p. 38).

4 Feb.	Guatemala, severe earthquake (Richter Scale 7.5), 22,419 killed
19 Feb.	Cuba, minor earthquake, 1 dead
8 Apr.	Ecuador, minor earthquake, 18 dead
6 May	Udine, Italy, major earthquake (Richter Scale 6.9), 850 dead
17 May	Uzbekistan, U.S.S.R., severe earthquake, much damage and loss of life.
3 June	Yunnan, China, severe earthquake
7 June	Acapulco, Mexico, major earthquake (Richter Scale 6). Heavy damage
16 June	Japan, moderate earthquake (Richter scale 5.7)
26 June	New Guinea, major earthquake (Richter Scale 7.1). Many casualties
1 July	Orange Free State, S. Africa, severe earthquake
14 July	Bali, Indonesia, moderate earthquake (Richter Scale 5.8)
28 July	Tangshan, China, very severe earthquake (Richter Scale 8.2), considerable damage and phenomenal death-toll. One of world's worst disasters
29 July	Caucasus, strong earthquake
17 Aug.	Philippines, severe earthquake (Richter Scale 7), tsunamis killed 3,000
17 Aug.	Szechwan, China, severe earthquake (Richter Scale 7.2) Major damage
17 Aug.	Honshu, Japan, moderate earthquake
17 Aug.	Near Naples, Italy, minor earthquake
24 Nov.	Van, Turkey (Richter Scale 7.9), 4,000 dead

As early as May 1976 newspaper correspondents were inquiring whether man himself was causing some of the earthquakes, inspired by the fact that midway between the Udine and Uzbekistan seismic disasters the U.S.S.R. was known to have detonated two underground nuclear explosions:

Shock waves travel round the earth and it is entirely possible that the energy they inject into a deep region under natural stress will cross some critical threshold and trigger a major shock remote from the test area.[3]

Partly because of the unprecedented seismic activity generated by the American underground testing in Nevada during 1968–69 it was significant that the United States government had already decided to transfer its future tests to a remote Aleutian island.

Without speculating on the influence of man the Editor of *Nature* was prompted to seek a more scientific explanation for the high incidence of earthquakes in 1976, when stating that:

> ... among the apparently random occurrences of geophysical phenomena there are some tenuous threads suggesting a grander design than simply isolated games of dice.[4]

By the middle of August, however, the people of Britain were more concerned with their record-breaking drought than with earthquake patterns in remote parts of the world. Having experienced the relatively mild discomforts of water rationing and threatened harvest failures, the British were at last able to grasp the horrifying consequences of the much more severe and prolonged drought conditions which had caused famine and death in the Sahel of Africa (see Chapter 9). Thus, there was not only a gradual realization of the magnitude of the Sahelian disaster, but an awakening to the possibility that harvest failures in the overpopulated tropical countries or even the Russian steppes could generate long-term effects on the stability of world food prices and even ominous political and militaristic consequences. As if to underline the freakish fluctuations of world weather patterns, the severe 1976–77 droughts of Western Europe and North America were followed by unprecedented blizzards and snowfalls during the winter of 1977–78 in virtually the same American and British regions (see Chapter 10). At last the general public was becoming aware of the remarkable oscillations of temperature and rainfall that can occur within our planetary circulation and of their consequences in terms of world food and fuel shortages. More and more people were beginning to ask whether the 'freakish' departures from the apparently normal atmospheric and geophysical systems were in fact the *real* norm – were apparently stable systems becoming unstable? Were natural disasters likely to become more prevalent?

Thus, by 1978, in the aftermath of the Scottish and West Country blizzards (see Chapter 10), some British observers were calling for research into environmental hazards to be given a higher governmental priority in the hope that strategic planning for impending disasters would be woven into future political and social thinking. It was now becoming clear that:

> World agricultural productivity will become less stable: centralized systems will become more vulnerable, and, increasingly, there will be a need to insulate communities – both rural and urban – against the effects of extremes ... It is the short-term violent variation which affects the human condition. And insulation is not just a matter of providing adequate emergency services or of putting 25 cm of expanded polystyrene between you and the weather. It is a far more complicated matter of reappraising all the nation's vital systems from agriculture to energy distribution.[5]

1. Children, knee-deep in flood water, queue for powdered milk in the aftermath of Bangladesh floods.

The ability of any national government to deal with a disaster will depend on a number of factors, including the magnitude of the event, the political ideology and, above all, the availability of capital resources. In some instances the political regime may revert to totalitarianism and find it necessary to introduce martial law in an effort to prevent rioting, looting and the breakdown of law and order. It may become necessary, for example, to fix food prices and to requisition transport services and essential commodities in the aftermath of a disaster. All this calls for a degree of national coordination probably unequalled except in time of war, and it is not surprising that in certain countries a major disaster may be followed by a change of government. During the twentieth century disaster-stricken nations can usually obtain foreign aid, either as a direct gift or from charitable organizations such as Oxfam (Plate 1). More often, however, aid is controlled by international organizations, including the Red Cross, the United Nations Relief and Rehabilitation Administration (U.N.R.R.A.) and the United

Nations Food and Agriculture Organization (F.A.O.). Nevertheless, the effectiveness of a disaster-relief programme will often depend upon the competence of the local-government institutions, and there are many disheartening stories of foreign aid being mismanaged, looted or sold on the black market because of the incompetence or corruption of this local infrastructure.

It is surprising how few nations (with some notable exceptions, such as U.S.A. and Japan) have given a great deal of attention to disaster research and training. In the United Kingdom, some local authorities organize exercises involving the fire brigade, police, medical services, ambulance units, voluntary-aid societies and occasionally the armed forces, but these disaster exercises are by no means mandatory. The Disaster Unit established by the British Government in the early 1970s was somewhat significantly housed in the Ministry of Overseas Development in order to coordinate assistance to other countries, and it was not until the severe drought of 1976 that a government minister was made responsible for disaster planning within the United Kingdom.

There is, today, a growing awareness of environmental hazards and their associated catastrophes and this is reflected by the launching of a new journal in January 1977 – the *International Journal of Disaster Studies and Practice* – by a London-based action group which, in 1978, became the International Disaster Institute. Since 1971 this group has been concerned with most world disasters, explaining their mechanisms, assessing both their impact and how best to alleviate and mitigate the suffering and damage that result:

> Although natural calamities cannot be prevented from happening, the correct application of scientific knowledge before, during, and after their occurrence can minimize their consequences. Chaos, in the past, existed mainly because insufficient resources or expertise were readily available to mitigate the effects of major catastrophes.[6]

Disaster research is now an established discipline in some countries and within the last decade several books have explored such fields as human adaptation in the face of hazards (e.g. *Natural Hazards*, ed. by G. F. White, 1974), economic theory of disasters (e.g. *The Economics of Natural Disasters*, by D. C. Dacy and H. Kunreuther, 1969), and sociological studies of disasters (e.g. *Disasters, Theory and Research*, ed. by E. L. Quarantelli, 1978). Some of the more important results of these research programmes have been incorporated in the following chapters but are especially examined in Chapter 12, in which disaster relief, the economic costs, and remedial and predictive studies are summarized.

Part Two

Subterranean Stress

2. Earthquakes

At precisely 9.22 on the evening of 4 March 1977 the dreams of fulfilling a national economic revolution were rudely shattered for millions of Romanians, as one of Europe's most severe earthquakes devastated the industrial heartland of this Balkan state. Emanating at a depth of some 100 kilometres beneath the thickly forested Carpathian mountains of Transylvania, the shock waves travelled upwards and outwards to be felt as far afield as Rome and Moscow, although the most severe damage occurred in a 500 kilometre crescent along the valley of the Lower Danube as far as the borders of Bulgaria and Yugoslavia (Figure 4). Although an earthquake of similar magnitude had killed a thousand people in the same zone in 1940, the 1977 earthquake was far more devastating (over two thousand deaths) and of greater severity than the other recent Balkan earthquake disaster at Skopje, Yugoslavia, in 1963.

The seriousness of the disaster would have been noteworthy even if it had occurred in a rural community, like that which destroyed many of the foothill towns and villages around Udine, northern Italy, in the early summer of 1976, but the fact that it devastated the Romanian capital of Bucharest (a city of 1.7 million people) made the 1977 earthquake of epic proportions. In Bucharest alone more than 1,100 people were killed and several thousand injured as 20,000 homes were destroyed (Plate 2). Not only were large areas of the old city between the Opera House, Rossetti Square and the Victoria Hotel razed to the ground but nine hospitals, much of the University, the National Physics Centre, the Ministry of Transport Computer Centre and many commercial headquarters were destroyed. In addition, the industrial suburbs were heavily damaged, including one nuclear and three thermal power stations and more than two hundred industrial units, many of which had only been completed a few years previously. It is when such catastrophes occur in major cities (viz. Managua, Nicaragua, December 1972) that world opinion is so horrified, horror that is exemplified by the following anonymous eye-witness report from Bucharest:

Fig. 4. The Romanian earthquake of March 1977.

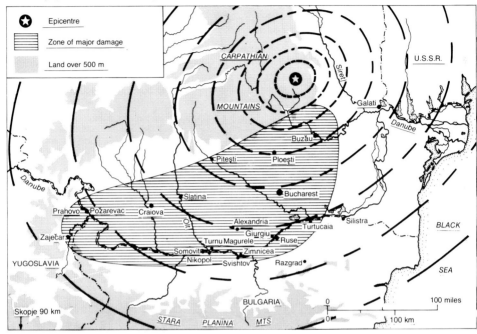

We have many, many buildings, many blocks down. I saw heads, I saw hands, I saw legs. I saw very many parts of bodies in the wreckage of the buildings which collapsed. I think 200 died in one block alone . . . and at least 30 blocks of high rise flats were destroyed. The 'quake also wrecked a city centre restaurant, the Dunarea, and the Nestor cafe, at a time when both were bound to be packed. The Dunarea was in a building which also contained eight storeys of flats – the whole place folded like a concertina.

Elsewhere in Romania, industry was brought to a standstill, especially in the oilfields around Ploeşti where fires raged in the petrochemical plants and refineries. The river port of Zimnicea, on the Danube, was almost totally destroyed, as was neighbouring Svishtov in Bulgaria (Figure 4) whilst in Yugoslavia, river bank collapses brought the docks to a standstill at the Danube port of Prahovo (Figure 4).

In the face of such devastation, in a modern society which boasts unprecedented technological achievements, is it not possible, we ask ourselves, to alleviate or at least predict some of the world's most severe earthquakes?

It is a question which we shall examine in greater depth later in this chapter (p. 67), but at present it is sufficient to note that major research into

32

earthquake forecasting is already underway in countries such as the United States, Japan, the Soviet Union and China. Chinese seismologists, for example, were able to predict an impending earthquake in Liaoning Province early in 1975: the town of Haicheng was evacuated hours before it was devastated by an earthquake. And yet, shortly afterwards, on 28 July 1976 about a million lives were lost when the Chinese mining and industrial centre of Tangshan was flattened and Peking was badly damaged, with very little warning. As if eager to demonstrate that seismic forecasting was still a viable study, Chinese seismologists predicted a further major earthquake in the capital, so that the Government ordered the entire population of Peking to be put under a full earthquake alert. As the citizens crouched fearfully in their tents on the city outskirts, it would be interesting to speculate how many of them believed the party-line that the strength of the masses

2. Part of the devastation in central Bucharest caused by the Romanian earthquake of 4 March 1977.

'can overcome nature' or pondered the events of the year which saw the deaths of Premier Chou-en-lai and of Chairman Mao-tse-tung. For had not the Chinese Government's concern with earthquakes been motivated for many previous centuries largely by the belief that such seismic phenomena portended an imminent change in national leadership? Notwithstanding these earlier idiosyncratic and unscientific beliefs, it is hardly surprising that, in a country renowned for its catastrophic earthquakes (the one in Shensi in 1556 resulted in 830,000 deaths), the world's first seismic measuring device was invented in China during the second century A.D. Despite appearing more like a porcelain vase of the Han dynasty than a scientific instrument, this prototype appears to have been based on the principle of the pendulum (whereby even the slightest tremor could be recorded), the basic rudiments of which have survived today even in our most sophisticated seismographs (Plate 3).

3. The world's first seismograph was shaped like a Chinese vase of the Han dynasty (second century A.D.). A tilting mechanism within the vase projected the balls from the mouths of the dragons to the awaiting frogs.

Meanwhile, in the Western world, the early Greek and Roman civilizations, nurtured in landscapes where volcanic eruptions played so significant a part, saw a natural link between the Aegean and Italian volcanoes and the earthquakes which periodically shattered their towns. It is now known that whilst volcanic eruptions are generally accompanied by earth tremors, the latter are relatively minor phenomena in comparison with the really massive earthquakes, now referred to as tectonic earthquakes. Research has shown that the world's major earthquakes are closely linked with the slow but inexorable deformation of the Earth's crust at specific locations where enormous tectonic strains have built up, but in many instances these regions are also volcanic zones.

The annals of history are littered with references to earthquakes right through the Middle Ages and into modern times, but it was not until the world's most publicized earthquake, the one which devastated San Francisco in 1906, that sufficient funding became available to initiate more serious investigations into the cause of seismic disturbances. No more concise explanation of earthquake mechanisms exists than that of H. F. Reid who, in the official report on the 1906 disaster, stated that:

> It is impossible for rock to rupture without first being subjected to elastic strains greater than it can endure; the only imaginable ways of rapidly setting up these strains are by an explosion or by the rapid withdrawal, or accumulation, of material below a portion of the crust. Since earthquakes occur not associated with volcanic action, we conclude that the crust, in many parts of the Earth, is being slowly displaced, and the difference between the displacements in neighbouring regions sets up elastic strains, which may be greater than the rock can endure; a rupture then takes place.[1]

Such a rupture is known to geologists as a fault, the various types of which can be seen in Figure 5.

An examination of large-scale geology maps will demonstrate the presence of faults in most regions of the world, but it would be foolish to regard all of these as earthquake hazard zones. Many of the faults, especially those in the older rocks, where time has healed the rupture, are now thought to be inactive. Others are found to be releasing the strain by slow differential slippage (termed tectonic creep), thus avoiding the sudden catastrophic lurch. In densely populated regions, such as Japan and Southern California, it has become necessary to monitor even the slightest creep of the major faults by means of a network of sensitive instruments, because it is when the slippage stops that the seismologist begins to worry, for this may imply that tectonic strains are beginning to build up. But seismology remains a complicated science, despite the sophisticated geophysical techniques now

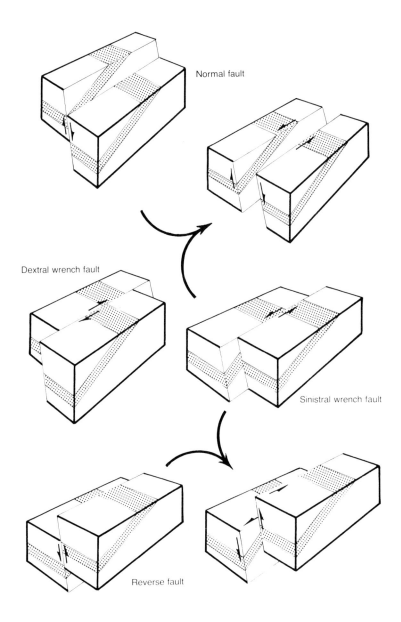

Normal fault

Dextral wrench fault

Sinistral wrench fault

Reverse fault

Fig. 5. Different types of crustal faults.

employed, since it is still difficult to determine whether a fault is truly inactive or merely dormant. It seems something of a paradox, for example, that the Californian earthquake 'risk maps' highlight the possibility that areas of low seismic activity, and thus of potentially minimal risk, which lie along the major faults may be precisely the most likely points for future earthquakes, since they show little evidence of strain release. The 1971 San Fernando Valley earthquake is a case in point, for it was located almost midway between the two high-risk spots of the Los Angeles basin and the Tejon Pass. It is crucial that such 'risk maps' are revised, for not far to the east of San Fernando lies the main aqueduct for Los Angeles's major water supply, a fact which pinpoints yet another hazard faced by urban planners when striving to locate new industrial enterprises such as nuclear reactors or high dams, with their obviously inherent dangers.

In an attempt to identify these types of earthquake hazard zones there has been a concerted effort throughout the 1960s to sponsor seismic research not only in the United States but in other countries with a potentially high earthquake risk such as Japan. One outcome has been the setting up of a global seismographic network (known as the World-Wide Standardized Seismographic Network), ostensibly to cooperate in a data-collection exercise to aid earthquake forecasting but also, in many instances, to assist in surveillance of nuclear tests. It gives cause for regret that two nations which together occupy a large proportion of the Earth's landsurface, namely Russia and China, have shown no desire to participate in the W.W.S.S.N. project. Within the participating nations, however, there are more than 1,000 stations each equipped with its own set of modern seismic instruments.

Earthquakes; Measurement and Explanation

Seismic instrument design has come a long way since the quaint prototype of Chang Hang (second century A.D.) and even from the mid-nineteenth-century Scottish seismometers of Professor J. D. Forbes (p. 62). The first true seismographs were constructed by a group of British scientists who, in the 1880s, had been invited to work in Japan and to assist in establishing research institutions there. It was only after 1896 that the seismographs were sensitive enough to record details of the largest earthquakes. By 1911 the Russian, B. B. Galitzin, had improved the relatively unsophisticated recording methods by the introduction of electromagnetic couplings between the pendulum and the galvanometer, and it is from about this date that we have a reliably accurate measure of earthquake magnitude. Shortly afterwards, Hugo Benioff, of the California Institute of Technology, developed an even more sensitive instrument that could amplify the oscillation by tens of thousands, and it is the latter which is now able to measure with unerring accuracy such important parameters as the earthquake's geographical location, its depth and its energy (magnitude). The most commonly used earthquake severity scale is that devised by an American, Dr C. F. Richter, who computed the magnitude of the tremor from the amplitude of the shock waves. The Richter Scale does not range from 1 to 10 as is commonly supposed but is open-ended (i.e. it is not limited at either end), each numerical magnitude step on the scale representing a tenfold increase in the seismic wave amplitude. Thus, the 1929 Alaskan earthquake of 8.6 magnitude released not twice as much but 100,000 times as much energy as an earthquake of magnitude 4.3. The largest recorded earthquakes have reached a magnitude of 8.9 or even 9.0 on the Richter Scale (e.g. Lisbon, November 1775 – 9.0; Sumba, Indonesia, August 1977 – 8.9), while at the other end a magnitude of 2 is about the smallest tremor that can be perceived by humans without instrumental assistance.

Three types of seismic waves have been recognized (Figure 6). First, the compressional waves or the so-called P waves (P stands for Primary), which spread out from the point of rupture within the crust (known as the focus), with the vibration following the direction in which the wave travels; secondly, the transverse S waves (S = Secondary), whose vibration is at right-angles to the direction of wave-travel and whose speed is always less than that of the P waves. Finally, after the P and S waves have moved *through* the body of the Earth, they are followed by two types of *surface* waves, known as L waves, and it is these which are responsible for much of the destructive shaking away from the earthquake centre, because of their larger amplitude. The point on the Earth's surface immediately above the focus is termed the epicentre.

Although seismic instruments are now able to measure the *magnitude* parameters noted above, additional scales of earthquake *intensity* have long been used to illustrate not only the amount of damage to buildings, but also the alteration of the ground surface and the degrees of human reaction. The first of these intensity scales to be generally accepted was that of de Rossi of Italy and Forel of Switzerland in the 1880s and was the one used to describe the famous San Francisco earthquake of 1906. In Britain C. Davidson modified the Rossi-Forel Scale in order to describe British seismic phenomena (p. 63), although the currently used intensity scale is that named after the Italian, Mercalli, who devised it in 1902, just in time for it to be used to describe his country's worst earthquake, that at Messina, Sicily, in 1908,

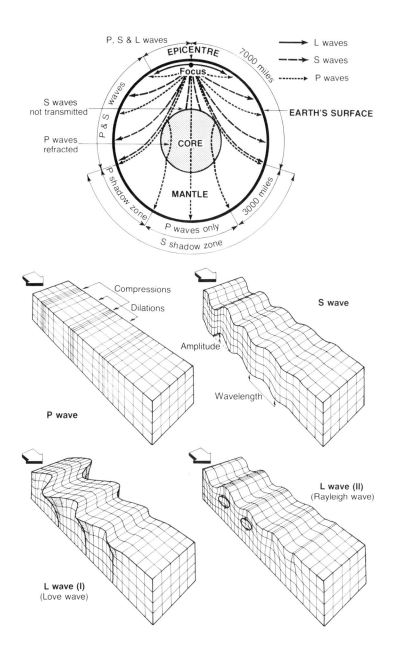

Fig. 6. An explanation of seismic waves.

when one hundred and sixty thousand people died. The modified Mercalli Scale of 1931 is depicted in Figure 7.

Fig. 7. The Modified Mercalli (M.M.) intensity scale of earthquakes (1931).

I   Not felt except by a very few under especially favourable circumstances.

II   Felt only by a few persons at rest, especially on upper floors of buildings. Delicately suspended objects may swing.

III   Felt quite noticeably indoors, especially on upper floors of buildings, but many people do not recognize it as an earthquake. Standing motor cars may rock slightly. Vibration like passing of truck. Duration estimated.

IV   During the day felt indoors by many, outdoors by few. At night some awakened. Dishes, windows, doors disturbed; walls make cracking sound. Sensation like heavy truck striking building. Standing motor cars rocked noticeably.

V   Felt by nearly everyone, many awakened. Some dishes, windows, etc., broken; a few instances of cracked plaster; unstable objects overturned. Disturbances of trees, poles, and other tall objects sometimes noticed. Pendulum clocks may stop.

VI   Felt by all, many frightened and run outdoors. Some heavy furniture moved; a few instances of fallen plaster or damaged chimneys. Damage slight.

VII   Everybody runs outdoors. Damage negligible in buildings of good design and construction; slight to moderate in well-built ordinary structures; considerable in poorly built or badly designed structures; some chimneys broken. Noticed by persons driving motor cars.

VIII   Damage slight in specially designed structures; considerable in ordinary substantial buildings, with partial collapse; great in poorly built structures. Panel walls thrown out of frame structures. Fall of chimneys, factory stacks, columns, monuments, walls. Heavy furniture overturned. Sand and mud ejected in small amounts. Changes in well water. Persons driving motor cars disturbed.

IX   Damage considerable in specially designed structures; well-designed frame structures thrown out of plumb; great in substantial buildings, with partial collapse. Buildings shifted off foundations. Ground cracked conspicuously. Underground pipes broken.

X   Some well-built wooden structures destroyed; most masonry and frame structures destroyed with foundations; ground badly cracked. Rails bent. Landslides considerable from river banks and steep slopes. Shifted sand and mud. Water splashed (slopped) over banks.

XI   Few, if any, (masonry) structures remain standing. Bridges destroyed. Broad fissures in ground. Underground pipelines completely out of service. Earth slumps and land slips in soft ground. Rails bent greatly.

XII   Damage total. Practically all works of construction are damaged greatly or destroyed. Waves seen on ground surface. Lines of sight and level are distorted. Objects are thrown upward into the air.

If we were to examine the locations of the world's major earthquakes, we should find that they all fall within a marked pattern of linear zones between which lie large areas where seismic activity is minimal. Such low frequency areas are known as aseismic regions. Figure 8 shows the plotted epicentres of all the major earthquakes recorded during the year of 1970 and highlights the linearity of the global seismic zones. Clearly, the distribution of the epicentres is not a random one but is concentrated in well-defined belts such as that which marks the mid-Atlantic submarine ridge or that of the Circum-Pacific belt. The recently developed concept of *plate tectonics* explained below leaves little doubt that there is a causal relationship between the geometry of the world's tectonic plates and the geographical distribution of earthquakes.

It has been satisfactorily demonstrated by modern geologists and geophysicists that the Earth's structure is made up of a thin, rigid outer skin (some tens of kilometres thick) known as the *crust*, which is generally thicker under the continents than under the oceans. It has been calculated that below the crust there occurs a dense layer of iron- and magnesium-rich material, termed the *mantle*, which extends towards the Earth's interior to a depth of 2,900 kilometres. Underlying the mantle is the *core* of the Earth, with a radius of 3,490 kilometres, but this need not concern us at this juncture, for it is the composition of the mantle which is of prime importance, so far

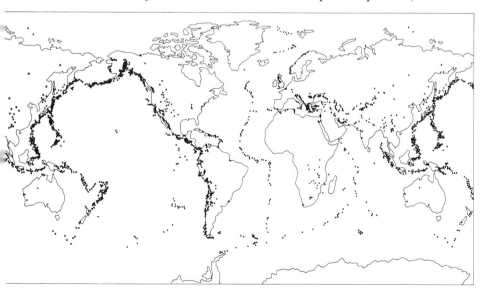

Fig. 8. The location of world earthquakes in 1970 (after R. F. Legget).

as the theory of plate tectonics is concerned. Since it was known that earthquake S waves would pass through solids but not through liquids, the earliest seismic evidence seemed to suggest that the mantle was solid. Further research was able to demonstrate, however, that under certain conditions some solids begin to exhibit a plasticity and become capable of flowing. The best example to illustrate this principle of *rheidity* is that of glacier ice, which appears to possess the properties of a solid, but is also capable of flowing due to the pressure of its own weight. The same is true of the rocks of the mantle, which behave as a solid to suddenly imposed short-term shocks, such as seismic waves, but, under the sustained pressure of overlying material for millions of years, assume the properties of a liquid. Because of variations of both density and temperature within the mantle, circulatory systems similar to convection currents have developed. Thus, as hot, less-dense material rises towards the upper zone of the mantle so it will spread out just below the crust, cool down and eventually sink back into the lower mantle as its density increases.

It is now becoming clear that we have a mechanism operating in the inner layers of the mantle which is capable of carrying both the more solid upper layers of the mantle and the rigid crust horizontally across the surface of our globe. In former years this was referred to as continental drift, but it is now termed Plate Tectonics for the simple reason that it is not only the continents which are moving but the ocean floors as well. Such a mechanism has caused the Earth's crust to break up into a number of discrete plates, the edges of which rarely coincide with continental shorelines. As we shall see below, it is the plate margins which are extremely significant in earthquake studies.

Where a rising, spreading and therefore diverging, convection current occurs it is conjectured that two adjoining plates will move apart, leaving the intervening space, which is marked by a gigantic rift valley, to be filled with molten material ascending from the upper mantle. This type of tectonic movement is known as *extrusion* and the rifting is generally associated with the formation of a volcanic zone. The best example of such a plate boundary is that which forms the so-called Mid-Atlantic Ridge, marking the zone where Africa was formerly joined to South America and where Europe split off from North America some two hundred million years ago. Thus, the Atlantic Ocean has grown progressively wider throughout this period by a process termed ocean-floor spreading. A discontinuous chain of volcanic islands marks the line of the mid-oceanic rift from Tristan da Cunha in the south, through Ascension to Iceland in the north. It stands to reason, however, that if certain of the plates are moving apart then others must be

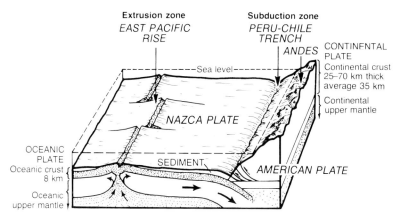

Fig. 9. A diagrammatic representation of the South East Pacific tectonic plates to illustrate the principles of Subduction and Extrusion (after E. R. Oxburgh).

moving towards each other. In order to accommodate such a movement, it becomes necessary for either one plate to over-ride another, or for a head-on collision to take place in which the frontal edge of one plate is shattered into 'flakes'. Since the latter mechanism is not clearly understood, although it may account for much of the complexity of the European Alps, we will consider only the 'over-riding' principle which is termed *subduction* (Figure 9). It is best illustrated on the western margin of South America and also around the western and northern margins of the vast Pacific Tectonic Plate, marked by the Mariana Isles and the Aleutian Isles respectively. In these instances the Pacific Oceanic Plate is being subducted or consumed into the deeper parts of the mantle as it is gradually over-ridden by other surrounding plates. The submarine junction is generally marked by a deep oceanic trench (the Peru-Chile trench of Figure 9) beneath which is a gigantic zone of thrusting known as the Benioff zone after the well-known seismologist. On the landward side of the oceanic trenches in the northern and western Pacific lie the island arcs, so clearly illustrated in the Aleutians and the Kuril Isles. These island-chains represent the belts where the less-dense magma rises from the Benioff zone into the upper layers of the mantle before breaking sporadically through the crust as lava to build volcanic piles on the ocean floor (Figure 10). Such activity is associated with one of the Earth's most active seismic zones.

So far, we have talked only in terms of *oceanic* crust and submarine plates but there are many instances where the tectonic plates coincide with *continental* blocks. When continents collide we find that instead of ocean

43

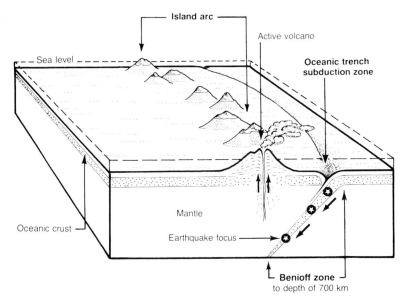

Island arc

Active volcano

Sea level

Oceanic trench
subduction zone

Mantle

Oceanic crust

Earthquake focus

Benioff zone
to depth of 700 km

Fig. 10. The formation of island arcs and oceanic trenches (after B. A. Bolt).

trenches and island arcs we are faced with gigantic ranges of fold mountains. The Himalayas are the best known example, for here the continental leading edge of the partly submerged Indian Plate has moved northwards and driven head-on into the Eurasian Plate. Figure 11 shows that the fold mountains of the Himalayan collision zone can be traced westwards into the Mediterranean basin. It also serves to illustrate the location of the eleven major plates which have so far been recognized.

A comparison between Figure 8 and Figure 11 will indicate that most of the world's major earthquakes are located along the tectonically active plate margins, being related either to the mechanisms known as extrusion and subduction, which we have already considered, or to a third type of tectonic movement known as *transcursion* in which two adjoining plates slide past each other along a series of tear faults or transcurrent faults (Figure 11). The best example of this type of junction is seen where the Pacific Plate is grinding transversely past the North American Plate, largely along the notorious San Andreas Fault of California. It will be something of a surprise to discover, therefore, that the coastal fringes of southern California do not belong to the true American continent, at least from a plate-tectonics point of view. Finally, a word of caution is necessary, for it must not be assumed that major earthquakes are to be experienced only along plate margins. Records show that severe earthquakes have also occurred in zones of weakness within the plates, as witness the severe Tangshan shock (magnitude 8.2) noted above and the damaging Meckering earthquake of 1968 (magnitude 6.8) which destroyed property near Perth in West Australia. Although these are isolated and infrequent instances, they serve to demonstrate that the plates themselves are not entirely rigid or free of locally active faults.

In summary, therefore, scientists are in general agreement that the regions of greatest tectonic instability coincide with the marginal zones of the slowly moving plates, because it is here that the crustal rocks are being subjected to enormous incessant strains as the plates travel in conflicting directions and at differing speeds. Thus, along belts of many thousands of miles, on sea-floor and on continent, rock deformation goes on unendingly, and as the deformation increases so does the stored strain energy. When the stress exceeds the strength of the rock at a particular point or even at a number of points simultaneously, often exploiting some pre-existing lithological weakness, a sudden rupture takes place. The rock on both sides of the fracture snaps back along the tearing fault and it is this sudden release of stored

Fig. 11. The World's tectonic plates (after E. R. Oxburgh).

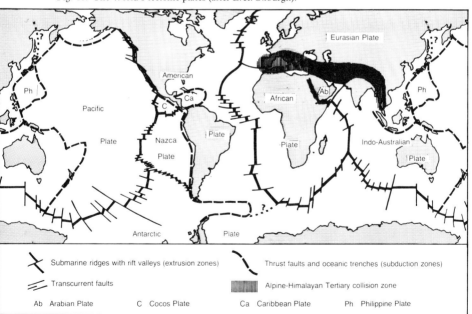

45

strain energy which produces the seismic waves and generates an earth-quake. Such ruptures can occur at any point between the surface and a depth of 700 kilometres. Consequently, we read of *deep-focus* and *shallow-focus* earthquakes, the latter originating within the crust less than 40 kilo-metres below the surface. The shallow-focus earthquakes have been found to produce the most widespread damage and to be responsible for more than three quarters of the world's annual seismic energy release, when judged on the Richter Scale. Having asserted that there is a remarkably close relation-ship between the world distribution of earthquakes and the concept of plate tectonics, it will be useful to examine this geographical pattern by means of a number of case studies.

Since some 75 per cent of the twentieth-century earthquakes have occurred around the margins of the Pacific it would seem appropriate to take our first case studies from this hemisphere. Nowhere has witnessed more highly developed seismic research than along the western seaboard of North America, where one of the Earth's most tectonically active belts happens to coincide with one of America's most prolifically booming settle-ment zones. Such well known cities as San Diego, Los Angeles, San Francisco, Sacramento, Seattle and Vancouver (with a total population of over thirteen million) are located in seismic hazard areas.

The North American Hazard Zone

The North American continent exhibits a remarkably uniform pattern of geological structures in which the nucleus is composed of a stable block of ancient rocks, known as the Canadian Shield, surrounded by broad con-centric belts of rocks which, in general, become progressively younger as they are traced outwards to the continental margins of the south and west. The shield itself is virtually devoid of earthquakes although shocks of intermediate magnitude have been recorded along its south-eastern margins in the St Lawrence – Newfoundland area (viz. the Newfoundland Grand Banks earthquake of 1929 (magnitude 7.2) which disrupted the submarine telephone cables to Europe). Otherwise, the only significant seismic activity away from the Pacific coast is located along the Rocky Mountain ranges from Alberta in the north to New Mexico in the south. Paradoxically, one of the United States's largest earthquakes occurred in none of these areas for in the period December 1811 to February 1812 three major shocks (magnitude about 8) were centred on New Madrid, Missouri, an anomaly difficult to explain in this comparatively aseismic region, away from the tectonic-plate margins. A full list of modern earthquakes in eastern and central North America is given in Figure 12.

Turning now to the Pacific seaboard we can examine the records of some of the world's best documented earthquakes in both the United States and Canada. California is renowned amongst other things for the great rupture known as the San Andreas Fault. Coming on-shore at Cape Mendocino (to the north of San Francisco) this fracture can be traced for 1,000 kilometres southwards through Marin County, across the Golden Gate and into the heart of the city itself. Thence the Fault runs south-eastwards along the Coast Ranges, paralleling the immense Central Valley of California until, in the vicinity of Bakersfield, it swerves eastwards through the San Gabriel and San Bernadino hill-country behind Los Angeles. Finally, it returns to its former south-easterly direction, where its course is marked by a series of depressions such as the Salton Sea and the Imperial Valley, before running out into the Gulf of California. Here, then, is the actual junction between the North American and Pacific Plates, with the latter grinding inexorably north-westwards at an average rate of some 5 centimetres per year. It is almost uncanny to think of such cities as Los Angeles and San Francisco being situated on a slice of land that is being moved relentlessly north-westwards in relation to the remainder of the United States along one of the greatest surface ruptures ever recorded. And yet, despite these quite large lateral displacements it is thought that a great deal of the movement along the San Andreas Fault is dispersed by gradual slippage, for seismic research indicates that there are only a few locations where the strain energy is not being released. These inactive areas are, of course, the hazard zones and they are located where secondary fractures intersect the line of the San Andreas transcurrent fault. One such region is to be found where the east-west submarine fault escarpment of the so-called Murray Fracture Zone leaves the Pacific floor and runs on-shore near Santa Barbara, causing the San Andreas Fault to swing inland and thereby creating a mosaic of cross-faulting in the vicinity of Los Angeles. Another region at risk is that of Oakland near San Francisco, where the famous Berkeley campus of the University of California stands squarely across the Hayward Fault which is an off-shoot of the San Andreas complex. Not only is the university football stadium built right on the fault but also its nuclear reactor!

In 1906 San Francisco was hit by an earthquake of 8.3 magnitude in which seven hundred people died after a sudden lateral shift of the San Andreas Fault of up to 6 metres had caused widespread destruction in the built-up area (Plate 4). A great deal of the $600 million damage resulted from the ensuing fire, which raged virtually unchecked, since all but one of

4. The scene following the 1906 earthquake in San Francisco, showing how certain steel-framed buildings survived the shaking.

the fire hydrants had been put out of action by the jolt. The San Francisco blaze emphasized the severity of the secondary hazards, such as fire, flooding and disease, which in many cases cause a loss of life comparable with that sustained during the tremor itself. As far as the aftermath is concerned, several experts have pointed to the hazardous fire risk of San Francisco's Chinatown in the event of a further earthquake. Despite the specially designed buildings of modern San Francisco, most of which will probably resist future tremors, it has been estimated that the high-rise blocks will generate a new type of hazard, that of glass falling from the shattered windows. Calculations have suggested that although the famous Golden Gate and Bay bridges will probably survive, few of the elevated city freeways will withstand even a moderate tremor. As if this were not enough, the scientists conclude their sobering predictions with a forecast that the greatest damage will occur amongst buildings sited on the unstable foundation of man-made ground. This is expected to be particularly severe in the reclaimed land of the Bay area of San Francisco which, ironically enough, was constructed largely from the rubble of the 1906 disaster! It was conclusively demonstrated in the Good Friday earthquake of Alaska in 1964, and again in the 1971 San Fernando Valley earthquake, that the less consolidated and weaker the bedrock, the greater the degree of ground deformation. In fact, the San Francisco predictions are based partly on the results of the San Fernando tremor which was the first earthquake of any great severity to affect a modern American city. Although the shock was only classed as a moderate one (magnitude 6.5), it provided a good opportunity to judge the effects of ground shaking on such reinforced concrete structures as tower blocks and elevated roads, in addition to the hazards of fractured gas, water and electricity mains (see also Plate 5 and Plate 54).

Fig. 12. Major earthquakes of Western North America (> 6.0 magnitude).

Date	Epicentre	Richter Magnitude Scale	Comments
1857, 9 Jan.	Fort Tejon, California	c. 8.0	
1865, 8 Oct.	San Francisco, California	< 7.0	Extensive damage.
1868, 21 Oct.	Hayward, California	7.0	30 killed.
1872, 26 Mar.	Lone Pine, California	c. 7.5	27 killed, 7 m fault scarp formed.
1872, 14 Dec.	Puget Sound, Washington	unknown	
1899, 3–10 Sep.	Yakutat Bay	8.5	14 m of horizontal displacement.
1901, 13 Dec.	Andreanof Islands, Alaska	7.8	
1902, 1 Jan.	Unimak Islands, Alaska	7.8	
1903, 2 Jun.	Alaska Peninsula, Alaska	8.3	Deep focus.
1904, 27 Aug.	Alaska Range, Alaska	8.3	
1905, 14 Feb.	Andreanof Islands, Alaska	7.9	
1906, 18 Apr.	San Francisco, California	8.3	700 killed, 6 m of horizontal displacement. $600 million damage.
1906, 17 Aug.	Rat Islands, Alaska	8.3	
1907, 2 Sep.	Near Islands, Alaska	7.8	

Fig. 12. (*continued*)

Date	Epicentre	Richter Magnitude Scale	Comments
1915, 22 Jun.	Imperial Valley, California	<7.0	6 killed, $1 million damage.
1915, 2 Oct.	Pleasant Valley, Nevada	7.6	
1925, 29 Jun.	Santa Barbara, California	6.3	13 killed, $13 million damage.
1927, 4 Nov.	Santa Barbara, California	7.5	Off-shore epicentre.
1929, 7 Mar.	Fox Islands, Alaska	8.6	Greatest magnitude for N. America.
1932, 20 Dec.	Cedar Mountains, Nevada	7.3	1 m horizontal displacement.
1933, 10 Mar.	Long Beach, California	6.3	120 killed, $41 million damage.
1934	Excelsior Mountains, Nevada	6.5	
1934, 30–31 Dec.	Baja, California	7.1	
1940, 18 May	El Centro, California	7.1	$6 million damage in Imperial Valley.
1940, 14 Jul.	Rat Islands, Alaska	7.8	Deep focus.
1947	Manix, California	6.2	
1949, 13 Apr.	Puget Sound, Washington	7.1	$25 million damage in Seattle area.
1949, 22 Aug.	Queen Charlotte Islands, British Columbia	8.1	
1952, 21 Jul.	Kern County, California	7.7	12 killed, $60 million damage.
1954, Jul.–Dec.	Fallon/Dixie Valley, Nevada	6.9	2 m horizontal displacement.
1954, 21 Dec.	Eureka, California	6.6	
1956, Feb.–Mar.	Baja, California	6.8	
1958, 10 Jul.	Lituya Bay, Alaska	8.0	6 m horizontal displacement.
1964, 27 Mar.	Prince William Sound, Alaska	8.5	130 dead, $500 million damage.
1965, 4 Feb.	Rat Islands, Alaska	7.9	
1965, 30 Mar.	Amchitka Islands, Alaska	7.5	
1965, 29 Apr.	Puget Sound, Washington	6.5	$12 million damage in Seattle area.
1971, 9 Feb.	San Fernando Valley, California	6.5	65 killed, $500 million damage.

The seismic activity of western Alaska and the Aleutian Isles, although falling within the North American earthquake-hazard zone, differs from that of the other American and Canadian Pacific states because its earthquakes are generated in a different way. Whilst the major earthquakes farther south were seen to be triggered-off by massive lateral movements between the Pacific and North American tectonic plates (i.e. by transcursion), a glance at Figure 11 will show that the Aleutian Isles mark a different type of plate boundary. Here is an excellent example of subduction, as noted earlier, in which the Pacific Plate is being overthrust from the north by the Bering Sea section of the North American Plate. The perfect arc of the Aleutian Isles is followed on its southern flank by the sweeping curve of the Aleutian Trench and it is this zone, near to the deep sea trench, where the major seismic activity is found. The Aleutians are rated as one of the Earth's most important seismic regions, since their earthquakes are all of high magnitude (see Figure 12). Fortunately, the recorded shocks prior to 1964 occurred mainly on the sparsely peopled, remote islands, but finally, on Good Friday 1964, the towns of the west Alaskan coast were hit by a severe earthquake (magnitude 8.5). It has become notorious not so much for its loss of life which, by Asian standards, was relatively low, but for the widespread destruction of buildings, roads, railways, bridges, docks and public utilities (Plate 5). Such devastation was caused because of the

5. Citizens of Anchorage, Alaska, attempt to salvage possessions from the severely damaged properties in 4th Street after the Good Friday earthquake of 1964.

unprecedented degree of ground disturbance. The deformation of the Earth's crust was on a greater scale than anything yet recorded in a single earthquake, for the land surface changed its level over a broad 1,000 kilometre tract of western Alaska. Figure 13 illustrates how the entire coastal

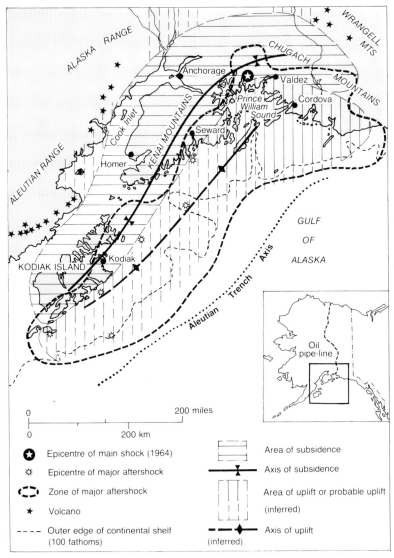

Fig. 13. The Alaska earthquake of Good Friday 1964 (after B. A. Bolt).

6. The deep fissures and landslips generated by Alaska's Good Friday earthquake caused considerable damage to the residential suburb of Turnagain Heights, located on unstable quickclays (see also Figs. 43 and 47).

belt from Kodiak Island to Prince William Sound was uplifted, sometimes by as much as 11 metres. At the same time a broad zone of subsidence occurred on the landward side of the epicentre, where mountain ranges were suddenly lowered by 2 metres. Presumably, the overriding Northern Plate had lurched forwards across the downward-plunging Pacific Plate and had created a crumple along its leading edge. Figure 13 also shows the location of the major settlements of West Alaska, with Anchorage being the largest city affected. Because of the nature of the local bedrock (soft, easily deformed clays) some of the ground disturbance in Anchorage was quite spectacular as the unconsolidated material cracked, heaved or slipped into a crazy mosaic (Plate 6). One final point of interest relating to the 1964 earthquake concerns the little port of Valdez, located at the head of Prince William Sound. Since it was only 70 kilometres from the epicentre (Anchorage was 130 kilometres away) the devastation was immense, especially in the waterfront area, where sea waves up to 9 metres high swept on shore destroying everything in their path. Suffice it to say that Valdez has subsequently been selected as the terminal of the Trans-Alaska oil pipeline!

The Japanese Hazard Zone

It is little wonder that the Japanese islands bear the dubious honour of being the world's most active seismic area when it is realized that they are the meeting place of no less than five island arcs (Figure 14). Thus, not only is Japan located at the margin of the vast Eurasian and Pacific Plates, but also at the fringes of the smaller Philippine Plate and possibly that of a conjectural one beneath the Sea of Okhotsk. The differential stresses set up by these moving plates give rise to virtually continuous seismic activity within the archipelago of Japan and account for almost one fifth of the world's seismicity. Japan, with a population double that of the United Kingdom in a territory only one-and-a-half times the size of the United Kingdom, is particularly at risk from natural disasters due to the frequency and magnitude of destructive phenomena; in addition to earthquakes and their related seismic sea waves (tsunamis) this is a land of volcanoes, landslides, floods and typhoons, and a man-made smog. Amongst these natural hazards, however, earthquakes are the most fearsome, striking without warning and creating lasting changes in the terrain. Because of the complexity of the plate tectonics noted above, Japan exhibits an intricate pattern of differential warping of the landsurface. Whilst the southern island of Kyushu, for example, is being uplifted, the area to the north of Tokyo is sinking at a measurable rate, although some of this is due to other causes (p. 187).

The tectonics of the Japanese archipelago are similar to those of the Aleutians, for the Pacific Plate is being subducted beneath the Eurasian Plate in a head-on collision. Like the Alaskan earthquakes, those experienced in Japan are also of a great severity (Figure 14); indeed, the world's greatest shock was recorded off north Honshu in 1933 (Richter Scale magnitude 8.9). Several of the epicentres of the most destructive earthquakes (including

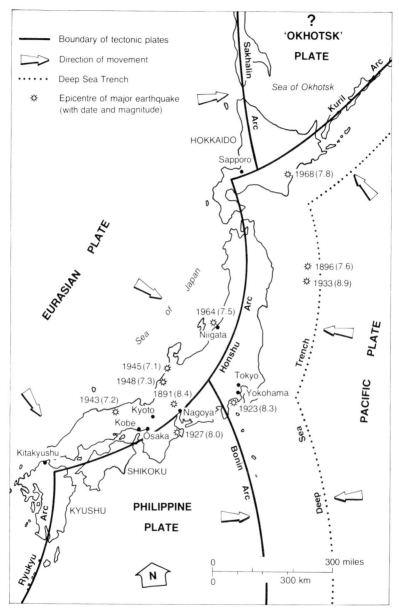

Fig. 14. The location of Japan's major earthquakes (1891–1968). Note the island arcs and the oceanic trench (compare Figure 10).

55

the Kwanto earthquake of 1923 when over 156,000 died) occur on the main island of Honshu itself, although examination of Figure 14 will show that seismic activity is also quite marked off the eastern coastline near the deep-sea trench. This is precisely the same type of pattern which we saw in the Aleutians, for here is the location of the deep-thrusting Benioff zone (see Figure 10).

The most devastating earthquake of the twentieth century was that of 1 September 1923 when both Tokyo and its neighbouring port of Yokohama were destroyed, very largely in an ensuing conflagration (Figure 15). Because Tokyo's great fire resulted from the traditional wooden house-design and the method of open-hearth cooking, legislation was passed to ensure that new public buildings would be designed to withstand seismic shaking and would also be constructed in non-combustible materials. Furthermore, Japanese urban planners were enjoined to locate settlements away from poorly consolidated bedrock, such as river alluvium, because of its inability to withstand great earth-movement. But the lack of alternative sites has meant that in some Japanese cities it has been impossible to implement this particular recommendation. Niigata is a case in point, for although every attempt was made to reduce earthquake hazards by designing blocks of flats on concrete rafts, the 1964 earthquake witnessed a wholesale tilting due to liquefaction of the unconsolidated ground in the newly reclaimed land along the Shinana River. Nevertheless, the implementation of new building codes and other protective measures meant that the sizeable Niigata earthquake (magnitude 7.5) had a death-toll of only twenty-five.

Enormous amounts of capital are being set aside by the Tokyo city authorities to fund earthquake-alleviation programmes, which is hardly surprising in a city that suffers a recorded earth-tremor on one day out of every three. New building codes are being introduced where possible; open spaces are included in urban plans as potential disaster evacuation areas; great wall-like office and apartment blocks are being built as fire-breaks; emergency services have been brought to a high degree of efficiency, awaiting the fateful day when the next major earthquake jolts the city.

The Mediterranean and Western Europe

Although there are many regions of the world where more severe earthquakes are experienced (e.g. Pacific coast of South America, the East Indies and China), the last case study has been chosen to illustrate a different type of tectonic-plate activity from those already examined, and because there

Fig. 15. Japan's historic earthquakes (after B. A. Bolt).

Date	Epicentre	M	Comments
684, 29 Nov.	Nankaido	8.4	
745, 5 Jun.	Mino	7.9	
818, 10 Aug.	Tokyo	7.9	
869, 13 Jul.	Osju	8.6	
887, 26 Aug.	Mino	8.6	
1293, 27 May	Kamakura	7.1	
1361, 3 Aug.	Kinai	8.4	
1498, 20 Sep.	Totomi	8.6	tsunami
1596, 4 Sept.	Kyushu	6.9	
1605, 31 Jan.	Shikoku	7.9	tsunami
1611, 2 Dec.	Sendai	8.1	tsunami
1614, 26 Nov.	Central Japan	7.7	tsunami
1677, 13 Apr.	Tsugaru	8.1	
1703, 31 Dec.	Tokyo	8.2	5,233 dead
1707, 28 Oct.	Shikoku	8.4	4,900 dead; tsunami
1751, 20 May	Echigo	6.6	2,000 dead
1843, 25 Apr.	Yedo	8.4	tsunami
1847, 8 May	Zenkoji	7.4	12,000 dead
1854, 23, 24 Dec.	Simoda	8.4, 8.4	3,000 dead; tsunami
1855, 11 Nov.	Sagami	6.9	6,757 dead
1891, 28 Oct.	Mino-Owari	8.4	7,273 dead
1896, 15 Jun.	North Japan	7.6	27,122 dead; tsunami
1923, 1 Sep.	Tokyo (Kwanto)	8.3	156,000 dead
1927, 7 Mar.	Tango	8.0	3,017 dead
1933, 2 Mar.	North Honshu	8.9	2,986 dead; tsunami
1943, 10 Sep.	Tottori	7.2	1,190 dead
1944, 7 Dec.	Tonankai	8.3	998 dead; tsunami
1945, 12 Jan.	Mikawa	7.1	1,901 dead (aftershock of 7 Dec. 1944)
1946, 20 Dec.	Nankaido	8.5	1,330 dead; tsunami
1948, 28 Jun.	Fukui	7.3	5,386 dead
1952, 4 Mar.	South East Hokkaido	8.6	600 dead
1964, 16 Jun.	Niigata	7.5	25 dead; tsunami
1968, 16 May	Tokachi-Oki	7.8	48 dead; tsunami

exists a lengthy historic record of seismic activity in this heavily populated region.

Earthquake activity in Europe, North Africa and the Middle East is related essentially to the broad zone of Tertiary fold-mountains that sweep in great arcs from the Himalayas through the Caucasus and the Alps to the Pyrenees and the Atlas. This is known as the Alpine system of fold-mountains (see Figure 11), where thousands of metres of former ocean-floor sediments have been crumpled and uplifted by the collision of the African, Arabian and Indian Plates on the one hand with the relatively stable Eurasian Plate on the other. Nowhere is the plate system more complicated than around the eastern Mediterranean, a fact exemplified by the intricate patterns of mountain chains in Italy, Greece and Turkey (Figure 16). Some

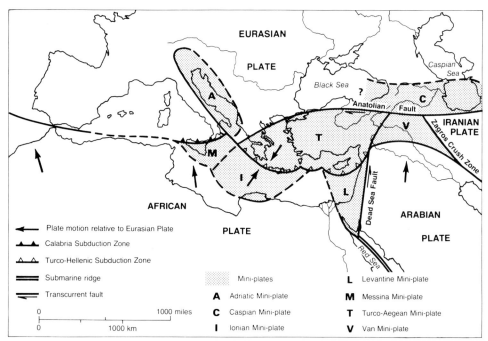

Fig. 16. The complexity of the Mediterranean and Middle East Mini-plates in the Alpine *Collision Zone* (after E. R. Oxburgh). Compare with Figure 11.

geologists have suggested that several mini-plates may exist in this complex mosaic; the Turco-Aegean sub-Plate, for example, moving south-westwards at the sizeable speed of 10 centimetres a year. But the Mediterranean jig-saw remains as bewildering as ever and although the concept of:

. . . plate tectonics has allowed great insights into tectonic processes, the Mediterranean demonstrates that our understanding is far from complete . . . we must either assume that the Alps are atypical in their complexity, or recognize that pre-Tertiary analysis of [mountain] belts, where the evidence is less complete, may be wildly incorrect.[2]

So far as the seismicity is concerned, many of the tremors are from shallow focii except in southern Italy, Sicily, Crete and Cyprus, where deeper focus earthquakes also occur. This line may well mark a type of subduction zone between the Eurasian and African Plates, but we must realize that the boundary is not a simple one as in the Aleutians; Cyprus, for example, is unique in the northern hemisphere, for it is the only landsurface where *oceanic* crust is currently revealed.

It will be seen from Figure 17 that although earthquakes occur fairly frequently around the Mediterranean they are not often of very great magnitude on the Richter Scale. Nevertheless, because of the density of the settlements in this historic region, long-term records illustrate how many horrific disasters have struck over the centuries. Some of the greatest losses of life have occurred in southern Italy, Greece and Turkey, but it is interesting to note that in the Holy Land archaeologists now believe that many of the cataclysmic events recorded in the Bible may have seismic explanations. The destruction of the walls of Jericho in 1250 B.C. is a case in point, and future research may soon be able to establish whether Sodom and Gomorrah were destroyed by an earthquake 4,000 years ago. By drilling deep into the floor of the Dead Sea, Israeli scientists have obtained samples of mud dating back to the first century B.C. Layers of white material in these sediment cores have been equated with the activity of springs which are triggered-off by earthquakes. The matching of the distinctive white layers with known seismic events has enabled the scientists to identify, for example, the earthquake of 746 A.D. which damaged the Temple in Jerusalem.

No account of European earthquakes would be complete without reference to the disastrous earthquake, fire and tsunami which wrecked Lisbon in November 1755. Over 60,000 perished in one of Europe's worst natural catastrophes. The epicentre lay offshore and though the shock waves could not be monitored effectively because of the lack of seismic instruments at that time, it has subsequently been suggested that the Lisbon earthquake may have been the greatest of all time, with a Richter magnitude of 9.0. This would have released more than 10,000 megatons of energy (a hundred times greater than the largest nuclear explosion); sea waves reached southern England five hours after the shock causing a sudden sea-level rise of > 2 metres on the coast. Lakes as far away as Norway and Scotland were

Fig. 17. Major twentieth-century earthquakes of Europe and the Mediterranean.

Date	Epicentre	Richter Magnitude Scale	Comments
1903, 11 Aug.	Off South Peloponnese	8.3	
1904, 4 Apr.	Pirin Mts, Bulgaria	7.5	
1908, 28 Dec.	Messina, Sicily	7.5	160,000 killed
1909, 9 Feb.	Kelkit, Turkey	6.7	
1909, 11 Jun.	Provence, South France	—	40 killed
1911, 16 Nov.	Swabia, Germany	6.2	
1912, 9 Aug.	Dardanelles, Turkey	7.7	
1913, 14 Jun.	Byela, Bulgaria	6.7	
1914, 3 Oct.	Taurus Mts, South Turkey	—	
1915, 13 Jan.	Avezzano, Italy	7.5	30,000 killed
1915, 11 Jul.	Tunis	6.2	
1916, 24 Jan.	Samsun, central Turkey	7.8	
1920, 7 Sep.	Reggio, South Italy	—	1,400 killed
1922, 13 Aug.	Rhodes	6.8	
1926, 18 Mar.	off Rhodes	6.9	
1926, 26 Jun.	Rhodes	8.3	Deep focus
1927, 11 Jul.	Jordan Valley	6.2	
1927, 11 Sep.	Yalta, Crimea	6.5	
1928, 31 Mar.	Izmir, West Turkey	6.3	
1928, 14–18 Apr.	Rhodope Mts, Bulgaria	6.7	
1930, 6 May	East Turkey	7.2	
1930, 23 Jul.	South Italy	6.5	
1930, 30 Oct.	Abruzzi, Italy	6.0	1,500 killed
1931, 8 Mar.	Valandovo, Yugoslavia	6.7	
1932, 26 Sep.	Aegean Sea	6.9	
1933, 23 Apr.	Cos Islands, Aegean Sea	6.8	
1935, 19 Apr.	Coast of Libya	7.1	
1936, 18 Oct.	Venetian Alps, Italy	—	
1938, 19 Apr.	Kirsehir, central Turkey	6.7	800 killed
1939, 21 Nov.	Tercan, central Turkey	6.0	
1939, 26 Dec.	Erizincan, East Turkey	8.0	40,000 killed
1940, 10 Nov.	Transylvania, Romania	7.4	1,000 killed, deep focus
1941, 10 Sep.	Van, East Turkey	6.0	500 killed
1941, 25 Nov.	off coast of Portugal	8.4	
1941, 27 Dec.	Tunis	6.8	
1942, 20 Dec.	Erbaa, central Turkey	7.3	

1943, 20 Jun.	Igeyve, West Turkey	6.3	
1943, 26 Nov.	Central Turkey	7.6	
1944, 1 Feb.	Cerkes, Bolu, central Turkey	7.6	5,000 killed
1944, 6 Oct.	off West Turkey	7.2	
1946, 12 Feb.	East Algeria	—	264 killed
1947, 6 Oct.	South Peloponnese	7.0	
1948, 9 Feb.	Carpathos Islands, Aegean Sea	7.1	
1948, 30 Jun.	Levkas Islands, Ionian Sea	—	6 killed
1951, 13 Aug.	Cankiri, West Turkey	6.8	50 killed
1952, 3 Jan.	Hasankale, East Turkey	5.5	94 killed
1953, 18 Mar.	Yenice, West Turkey	7.4	1,200 killed
1953, 12 Aug.	Cephalonia, Ionian Sea	7.1	435 killed
1953, 10 Sep.	West Cyprus	6.2	40 killed
1954, 29 Mar.	off South Spain	7.0	Very deep focus
1954, 20 Apr.	Thessaly, Greece	7.0	25 killed
1954, 9 Sep.	North Algeria	6.8	1,600 killed
1955, 19 Feb.	North Sicily	5.5	Very deep focus
1955, 12 Sep.	off North Egypt	6.7	20 killed
1956, 12 Jan.	Budapest, Hungary	5.8	2 killed
1956, 16 Mar.	South Lebanon	5.5	138 killed
1956, 9 Jul.	Santorini Islands, Aegean Sea	7.8	48 killed, tsunami
1957, 20 Feb.	Tunisia	5.3	
1957, 8 Mar.	Thessaly, Greece	7.0	2 killed
1957, 25 Apr.	off Rhodes	7.1	18 killed
1957, 26 May	Abant, West Anatolia	7.1	66 killed
1959, 1 Sep.	South Albania	6.3	
1960, 21 Feb.	Jebel Chukot, Algeria	5.7	
1960, 29 Feb.	Agadir, Morocco	5.9	14,000 killed
1960, 26 May	Albania–Greece border	6.5	90 killed
1962, 11 Jan.	Makarska	6.0	
1962, 18 Mar.	South Albania	6.0	15 killed
1962, 21 Aug.	Apennine Mts, Italy	6.0	
1963, 26 Jul.	Skopje, Yugoslavia	5.8	1,200 killed
1966, 19 Aug.	Varto, East Turkey	6.8	2,529 killed
1967, 22 Jul.	Mudurno, West Turkey	7.1	86 killed
1968, 15 Jan.	Sicily	5.4	252 killed
1970, 8 Mar.	Gediz, West Turkey	7.1	1,087 killed
1975, 6 Sep.	Lice, East Turkey	6.8	2,300 killed
1976, 6 May	Udine, North Italy	6.9	850 killed
1976	Turkey	7.9	5,000 killed
1977, 4 Mar.	Transylvania, Romania	7.2	> 2,000 killed, deep focus

disturbed – Loch Lomond exhibited almost 1 metre of oscillation (termed a seiche).

There have been no major earthquakes in Britain during the twentieth century, although the Hereford earthquake of 17 December 1896 may have been equivalent to about magnitude 6.2 on the Richter Scale, whilst that at Colchester some twelve years earlier may have been about magnitude 6.9. Britain is well away from the Mediterranean seismic zone so that catastrophic earthquakes are missing from the historic records. Nevertheless, as Figure 18 demonstrates, numerous small tremors have been recorded (probably between magnitude 2 and 5). During 1975, 1976 and 1977, for example, a series of unexplained tremors rocked the southern suburbs of Stoke-on-Trent. These were subsequently classified as tremors associated with coal-mining, similar to those in the Rhondda Valley and those of Pendleton (1905) and Barnsley (1903). Britain's greatest tectonic earthquakes, however, are generally linked with movement along major faults. The majority are related to the Great Glen Fault which slices northeastwards through the Scottish Highlands from Oban and Fort William to Inverness. Strong earthquakes have caused structural damage in the Loch Ness area on several occasions, with those of 1769, 1816 and 1901 being the most severe. Indeed, that of 18 September 1901 created an earth fissure 550 metres in length along the towpath of the Caledonian Canal at Dochgarroch Locks. The Inverness earthquake of 1816 and that at Oban in 1880 each affected areas of some 130,000 square kilometres (50,000 square miles). In the region of Kintail, near the Kyle of Lochalsh, no less than eleven shocks up to magnitude 5 were recorded during 1975, but these are related to a different fault system.

The two other highly seismic regions of Scotland are also associated with major fault-lines: the Highland Border Fault in Perthshire and the Ochil Fault of the Midland Valley. In the former case, hundreds of earthquakes have been recorded between Crieff and St Fillans, but especially at Comrie, where one of Professor J. D. Forbes's prototype seismometers was first erected in the church steeple. Strong shocks were experienced in this district in 1801 and again between 1839 and 1848, during which 20 metres of road collapsed near Perth itself. The damaging tremors associated with the Ochil Fault have always been strongest in the hillfoot towns between Blairlogie and Dollar where, despite the magnitude of the local shaking, the effects were not felt very far afield, in contrast with the Inverness, Oban and Comrie earthquakes.

Although more than three quarters of Britain's seismicity is located in Scotland several important earthquakes have been recorded south of the

Fig. 18. Major British earthquakes (after C. Davison). (N.B. Davison Scale = Rossi-Forel Scale in which Intensities 7, 8, 9 = Richter Scale Magnitude 5 to 6)

Date	Epicentre	Davison Intensity Scale	Comments
1120, 28 Sep.	Vale of Trent	?8–9	Many houses fell, burying their inhabitants
1180, 25 Apr.	Nottingham	8	Many houses were thrown down
1185, 15 Apr.	Lincoln	8	Lincoln Cathedral damaged
1246, 1 Jun.	Canterbury	8–9	'Several churches overturn'd'
1248, 21 Dec.	Wells	8	Cathedral roof collapsed (Matthew Paris)
1248, 19 Feb.	South Wales	8	
1275, 11 Sep.	Glastonbury	8	Church of St Michael's destroyed
1349, Lent	Yorkshire	?7	People shaken from their seats
1382, 21 May	Canterbury	8	'It suncke some Churches and threwe them down'
1480, 28 Dec.	Norfolk	8	Buildings destroyed at Norwich
? 1573	York	?8	'A severe earthquake at York'
1575, 26 Feb.	Central England	8	Part of Ruthin Castle, Wales, fell
1480, 6 Apr.	London	8	1 killed; churches damaged
1581, Apr.	York	?8	'It strook the very stones out of Buildings'
? 1600	York	?8	'A very serious earthquake at York'
1608, 8 Nov.	North Fife, Scotland	?	
1736, 30 Apr.	Menstrie, Clackman	8	
1750, 19 Feb. 1750, 19 Mar.	London	7–8	Westminster Abbey damaged; houses fell
1750, 29 Mar.	Chichester	7	1750 noted as the 'year of the earthquakes' by W. Stukeley
1750, 11 Oct.	Northampton	7	
1769, 14 Nov.	Inverness	8–9	Several killed; houses thrown down
1777, 14 Sep.	Rochdale	7	Recorded by Boswell at Ashbourne (Derbyshire)
1782, 5 Oct.	Caernarvon	?7	
1786, 11 Aug.	Carlisle	7	Damage at Whitehaven and Egremont; felt over 70,000 km² area
1795, 18 Nov.	Derbyshire	8	Felt in Bristol, London, York
1801, 7 Sep.	Comrie, Perths.	7	
1802, Aug.	Menstrie, Clackman.	?7	Damage in Clackmannan town
1816, 17 Mar.	Mansfield	7	
1816, 13 Aug.	Inverness	8–9	Strongest Scottish earthquake; affected 130,000 km²

Fig. 18. (*Continued*)

Date	Epicentre	Davison Intensity Scale	Comments
1839, 23 Oct.	Comrie, Perths.	8	Damage in Earn valley; affected 68,000 km^2
1841, 29 Jul.	Comrie, Perths.	8	323 minor shocks.
1843, 17 Mar.	Kendal	7	
1863, 6 Oct.	Hereford	8	Houses damaged at Ross; affected 221,000 km^2
1871, 17 Mar.	Kendal	7	Affected 130,000 km^2
1880, 28 Nov.	Oban	6–7	Affected 130,000 km^2
1884, 22 Apr.	Colchester	9	4 killed; most severe British earthquake; Affected 137,250 km^2. (Possibly Richter Scale 6.9)
1888, 2 Feb.	Inverness	7	
1890, 15 Nov.	Inverness	7	
1892, 18 Aug.	Pembroke	7	Affected 114,000 km^2
1893, 2 Nov.	Carmarthen	7	Affected 36,000 km^2
1896, 17 Dec.	Hereford	8–9	Cathedral and 217 buildings damaged; affected 254,800 km^2. (Possibly Richter Scale 6.2)
1901, 18 Sep.	Inverness	8	Affected 86,000 km^2
1901, 30 Sep.	Inverness	7	
1903, 24 Mar.	Derby	7–8	
1903, 19 Jun.	Caernarvon	7	Damage at Clynnog and Pentir
1904, 3 Jul.	Derby	7	
1905, 23 Apr.	Doncaster	7	Affected 28,000 km^2
1906, 27 Jun.	Swansea	8	40 towns and villages damaged; affected 98,000 km^2
1908, 20 Oct.	Menstrie, Clackman.	7	
1912, 3 May	Menstrie, Clackman.	7	
1916, 14 Jan.	Stafford	7	Affected 130,000 km^2
1946, 25 Dec.	Spean Bridge, Inverness	6–7	
1956, 11 Jan.	Sedbergh, West Riding	7	Movement of Dent Fault
1957, 11 Feb.	Leicestershire	8	Injuries and damage in Derby and Loughborough; affected 156,000 km^2
1963, 25 Oct.	Portsmouth	7	
1975–76	Kintail, Scotland	maximum 7	Eleven shocks recorded

N.B. The km^2 refer to the size of the areas over which the earthquake was felt

Border (see Figure 18). That at Colchester on 22 April 1884 was the most destructive British earthquake when four people were killed and four hundred buildings damaged in the town (Plate 7). In an area of 390 square kilometres (150 square miles) more than 1,200 buildings were damaged, including the town of Wivenhoe where some 70 per cent of the houses suffered. Fissures which were opened in the ground at West Mersea were measured as being 2 metres deep. The shock was felt over an area of 137,250 square kilometres (53,000 square miles) and was one of the few British earthquakes to be felt on the mainland of Europe. The noise of the earthquake was heard as far west as Oxford. Although no major faults exist in East Anglia, the shock may have been generated by slumping of fairly young rocks around the perimeter of the North Sea basin, with the shaking being exaggerated by the unconsolidated nature of the local clays and sands.

Although not as damaging as the Colchester earthquake, that at Hereford in 1896 was certainly more widespread, for it was felt over an area of 254,800 square kilometres (98,000 square miles) and heard as far away as Liverpool, Lincoln and Exeter. There is a record that horses were disturbed up to 133 kilometres away and that dogs reacted up to 174 kilometres away. The shock was apparently caused by two almost simultaneous slips along a transverse fault in the Old Red Sandstone. An earthquake which struck central England in 1575 may have had an even greater severity, whilst one in London in 1580 caused damage to several churches and one fatality. It is interesting to speculate whether it might have been these two earthquakes which influenced Shakespeare to write his famous description:

Diseased nature oftentimes breaks forth in strange eruptions; oft the teeming earth is with a kind of colic pinch'd and vex'd by the imprisoning of unruly wind within her womb; which, for enlargement striving, shakes the old beldame earth, and topples down steeples and moss-grown towers.[3]

Earthquakes: Frequency, Prediction and Alleviation

Although it has been possible to explain the geographical patterns of earthquake activity and to offer a working hypothesis to elucidate their mechanisms, nobody has yet been able to account for the periodicity of seismic phenomena or to say why certain years have greater earthquake frequency than others.

Since seismographs were refined to an acceptable accuracy in 1896 some faint patterns of frequency and severity have begun to emerge. The decade from 1896 to 1906, for example, was one in which the annual frequency of

Some of the labels within the illustration:

COTTAGE, ABBERTON.

AT ABBERTON.

PUBLIC-HOUSE, PELDON ROSE.

PARISH CHURCH, PELDON.

MR. CHARLES HARVEY'S HOUSE, WIGBOROUGH.

COTTAGE, PELDON ROSE.

DOORWAY OF COTTAGE, PELDON ROSE.

MR. NELSON'S, WIG FARM, LANGENHOE.

7. Some of the effects of Britain's most severe earthquake in the vicinity of Colchester, April 1884.

very severe earthquakes (> 8 magnitude) was higher than in subsequent years. 1906 was an exceptional year, with five shocks surpassing 8 on the Richter Scale, including the major disasters of San Francisco and Valparaiso. There followed a period of almost fifty years when events of such magnitude occurred less frequently, averaging only one or two a year until 1953. That year there was a severe earthquake in Tibet and several other notable ones within a few months, followed by a decade in which very large earthquakes were again less frequent. The Alaskan earthquake of 1964 was an exceptional event, for seismic activity has remained relatively low until the 1970s, when it began to increase gradually until the fateful year of 1976. This seems to mark a return to the earthquake level of the early years of the twentieth century, with the 1976 earthquakes in China and the Philippines surpassing magnitude 8, and that of Sumba, Indonesia (1977), attaining a magnitude of 8.9.

From such short-term records it would be impossible to predict with any accuracy the likely occurrence of major earthquakes in future years. One is tempted to draw a comparison with long-range weather forecasting which, despite the advantage of lengthier weather records, has achieved only a modest success by the use of analogues. Even if one was able to predict a year of increased seismic activity, the precise date, location and magnitude would still be unknown. Nevertheless, 'risk maps' have been devised for earthquake-prone regions such as California, where the activity of known surface faults can be monitored. But at present this is only possible in *transcursion* zones, for in *subduction* zones the study of fault-mechanics is made more difficult by the fact that much of the seismic activity is generated deep in the Benioff zone and cannot easily be correlated with surface structures. Thus statistical testing of earthquake periodicity is the only reasonable method in attempting to produce a probability model for a given region. Unfortunately, nature has a way of confounding such exercises, which has led one American scientist to summarize his earthquake prediction studies with the wry comment that '. . . the longer it's been since the last one, the closer we are to the next.'

Despite such scepticism, in April 1976 Dr J. H. Whitcomb announced to a scientific meeting in Washington that an earthquake of magnitude 5.5 to 6.5 (the San Fernando Valley earthquake was 6.5) could be expected in the Los Angeles area possibly within a year. This was based partly on the crustal upwarping that has been measured over an area of some 60,000 square kilometres around the town of Palmdale, California. The area of uplift, ironically termed the 'Palmdale Pimple', is not only located astride the San Andreas Fault but marks a zone where there has been no strain-release since 1932. Research in the Soviet Union has recently suggested that some time before an earthquake the interval between the arrival of the P and S waves at a recording station gradually decreases, then shortly before the shock itself, it returns quite suddenly to normal. The Russians also maintain that where strain begins to build up, a multitude of tiny cracks appear in the rock, causing it to bulge and leading to the decrease in the arrival-time interval of the seismic waves. Palmdale not only exhibits the premonitory bulge of this so-called *Dilation theory* but also the decreasing interval between arrival of seismic waves. Only time will tell whether this prediction is proved correct.

In the opening pages of this chapter we noted that the Chinese had made their historic prediction of the 1975 Haicheng earthquake. In this case thousands of people had been instructed to watch for changes in wildlife behaviour and for unusual natural phenomena. This is nothing new, because for centuries both the Chinese and Japanese had observed such occurrences in attempts to predict earthquakes. There are numerous records of these bizarre phenomena, but only the following are noteworthy: the unusual behaviour of fish in both sea and fresh-water pools, especially the catfish; the frenzied activity and disappearance of small animals such as rats and weasels prior to the tremor; the emergence of reptiles from holes in the ground; the restlessness of birds, horses, dogs, etc.; the appearance of curious meteorological phenomena such as rainbows and unseasonal fogs; the bubbling of wells: the behaviour of mentally disturbed people.

At an international conference on theoretical physics held in 1977 it was disclosed that the Chinese have made significant progress in the field of seismic prediction. Of the five major earthquakes which occurred in China in the few years prior to 1977 four of them (including that at Haicheng) were successfully forecast. Thus, not only were long-term warnings issued, but in each of the four successful cases imminent alarms were given within hours of the event. The exception to this otherwise satisfactory record of seismic prediction was the fearful 'quake of July 1976 (see p. 33) near to Peking, but even this event had been monitored in the build-up stage, only the more immediate precursory phenomena had been missed – hence the lack of a final warning. The success has been attributed to the Government's policy of encouraging thousands of amateurs to make simple measurements at regular intervals – a blanket coverage which, it is claimed, ensures that most of the precursory phenomena are monitored.

In view of the seismicity of Japan, the Japanese obsession with amateur earthquake prediction is highly understandable, but it took some time before strong public demand led to a government-supported long-term programme based on a more scientific footing. The Niigata earthquake of 1964, in one of Japan's most industrialized regions, provided the necessary spur, and a programme was immediately initiated, consisting of the following disciplines:

(1) Detection of premonitory crustal movement by geodetic ground survey
(2) Detection of premonitory crustal movement by tide-gauge observation
(3) Continuous observation of crustal deformation by strainmeters and tiltmeters.
(4) Observation of overall seismic activity in Japan
(5) Observation of changes in travel-time of seismic waves
(6) Detailed survey of active faults and folds
(7) Geomagnetic observation to monitor changes in the Earth's magnetic field
(8) Laboratory tests on rock-strength and rock-failure
(9) Establishment of data-processing centres

The Japanese programme created a great deal of interest amongst American seismologists who, in 1965, presented a long-term programme of their own, aimed not only at earthquake prediction but also at prevention of earthquake hazards. The estimated 1965 cost of implementing such a ten-year research programme in California and Nevada alone was over $30 million, which is probably the main reason why the United States Government failed to give formal support until the late 1970s. Nevertheless, American seismic research has been stepped up, especially in many Pacific coast universities, finally resulting in the establishment of the Earthquake Hazards Reduction Program (E.H.R.P.) in 1973 under the auspices of the United States Geological Survey. All of the Japanese disciplines were included together with such techniques as deep-drilling at fault zones and the introduction of multibeam lasers for high-precision distance measurement. Cooperation between United States and Japanese seismologists has long existed and it is noteworthy that international cooperation in earthquake prediction research received a much-needed boost when exchanges took place between American and Russian seismologists in 1973 and between the Americans and the Chinese in the following year.

These promising research programmes have been praised by Dr Charles Richter but he also sounds a note of caution when he emphasizes that we are

... still a long way from the point of being able to say we know enough to issue definite predictions. Large earthquakes often happen with no detectable forewarning phenomena at all. In rare instances, definitely the exception not the rule, there will be increasing activity of small earthquakes building up to the main event over a period of days or weeks. [4]

Thus, we are left with a suspicion that even the experts are uncertain whether current earthquake prediction studies have reached a stage where they can be of any practical use.

The most useful earthquake-warning period would, of course, be one of sufficient duration to implement an orderly evacuation of an urban area in, say, a day or two, thus avoiding panic, traffic jams and road accidents. But it is precisely the very short-range prediction which is the most difficult to monitor, despite the fragmentary evidence which suggests that impending earthquakes are heralded by anomalous sea retreats, sudden changes in ground tilt and in electric resistivity. Consequently, on the one hand it has been claimed by some that earthquake-prediction research would be more usefully aimed at assisting in shock-proof building design. This in turn would help to lower the amount of subsequent damage and the very high insurance cover, being based on the premise that since it appears impossible to reduce the magnitude of the hazard itself it is better to lessen the impact of the after-effects. On the other hand, there are those who believe that every attempt must be made to save lives should a highly damaging earthquake (> magnitude 7) be forecast by seismologists as likely to occur within a certain period of time, say several months. Nevertheless, the costs of long-term evacuation and temporary re-housing of the population of Tokyo or Los Angeles, for example, would be prohibitive. Equally, the financial losses would be astronomical if the authorities ordered a long-term shut-down of nuclear power stations, oil refineries, blast furnaces and the like, in the interests of safety. Government compensation for loss of output would be enormous and lead to complex disputes, especially if the prediction failed.

Recent research relating to hazard perception studies has demonstrated that the citizens of San Francisco, for instance, whilst fully aware of earthquake hazards, gave them a fairly low priority and expected future seismic damage to be relatively slight. Many of the respondents in the San Francisco study exhibited a fatalistic approach, regarding an earthquake as an act of God, about which little could be done. Whilst the majority of the sample believed that shock-proof structural changes in their homes, allied with increased insurance cover, were 'good things', few had bothered to implement such adjustments. Thus, as in most other seismic-risk regions, precautions have been left largely to the local authorities, often bound by government legislation to strengthen buildings such as schools and hospitals. In addition, attention has generally been paid to the potential hazards of high-dam fracture, landslide danger zones, gas, water, and electricity-supply problems, together with a whole host of other emergency measures.

Finally, amidst all this preparation, is it not possible, we ask ourselves, to modify the magnitude of the hazard itself? With our current technological expertise can we do nothing to control earthquakes by gradual release of the strain energy?

It is generally admitted that there is probably very little one can do to modify deep-focus earthquakes, especially those which originate off-shore. On land, however, some remedial measures have been attempted in the United States and Japan. As often happens, the first seismic modification was something of an accident, following the injection of waste water into a deep well near Denver, Colorado, in 1962. Although this is an aseismic area, the injection of water triggered-off a number of earthquakes, which decreased when the injection stopped only to increase on resumption of the experiment. The earthquakes ranged in magnitude from 0 to 3.7 and were of shallow-focus origin (< 5.5 kilometres). It appeared that the water lubricated the rupture planes, decreased the friction and allowed slips to take place. Similar results occurred when water-injection experiments were carried out in 1970 at Matsushiro, Japan, and in 1972 at the Rangely oil field, Colorado. It now remains for these experiments to be tested along a critical stretch of the San Andreas Fault but, bearing in mind that they might trigger-off a devastating earthquake, no attempt has yet been made.

A more drastic measure for releasing strain energy has been examined during the last decade, but to date there is no record of anyone daring to experiment. This concerns the possibility of inducing an earthquake by a controlled underground nuclear explosion, where the triggering mechanism would be the increase in pore-pressure of the rocks due to the movement of underground water associated with the explosion. If the experiment took place in a high-risk area, it seems likely that an earthquake of great magnitude would be induced. The advantages are obvious: the evacuation of inhabitants could be effectively carried out, because the timing of the explosion could be gauged with some precision. The disadvantage remains, however, that one would be unable to predict the severity of the induced earthquake or the number of severe after-shocks which might result over an unknown period of time. But, whilst the Americans hesitate, it has been suggested that the Russians may have already taken such a drastic step. In the early summer of 1976 the U.S.S.R. detonated two underground nuclear explosions in Siberia. Shortly afterwards, on 17 May, a massive earthquake devastated the city of Tashkent some 4,000 kilometres away in southern U.S.S.R. Admittedly, the link is a very tenuous one, but how do we know that the man-made earthquakes did not trigger off the Tashkent tremor? The evidence from the American and Japanese experiments demonstrates that we are in a position to modify seismic activity and this discovery has been highlighted, following the inadvertent induction of earthquakes by the impounding of water in artificial reservoirs. Destructive shocks up to magnitude 6.4 have resulted from the building of major reservoirs in several world localities, some of which were previously aseismic areas. First noticed in 1939, following the construction of the Hoover Dam in south-west U.S.A. (magnitude 5), such induced earthquakes have subsequently been recorded as follows:

1962	Hsinfengkiang, China	Magnitude 6.1
1963	Monteynard, France	Magnitude 4.9
1963	Kariba, Rhodesia	Magnitude 6.1
1964	Kremasta, Greece	Magnitude 6.2
1967	Koyna, India	Magnitude 6.4

It appears that it is not the absolute volume of stored water, but rather the height of the dam which correlates with the seismic activity. Reservoir-associated earthquakes seem to be related to dams more than 100 metres in height.

In addition to the man-made seismic triggers noted above there are, of course, a number of natural events which are believed to trigger off earthquakes at the point when strain has reached breaking-point and needs only a minor natural phenomenon to act as a final straw. These trigger processes have been listed by the scientists at Griffith Observatory, California, and include minor changes of barometric pressure in addition to lunar-induced tidal variations. Thus, earthquakes appear to be more frequent at new or full phases of the Moon, and when the Moon is either furthest away from or closest to the Earth. It has been claimed that a Russian scientist, Professor A. I. Yelkin, used this type of lunar relationship to predict a Turkish earthquake in November 1976. Above all, a search of past records appears to leave little doubt that there is a distinct correlation between periods of major volcanic outbursts and maximum phases of seismic activity and that these, in turn, are also related to the Earth's wobble (termed the Chandler Wobble) as it rotates on its axis, to the wandering of the poles and to the changes in the Earth's magnetic field. The question remains, however, do the earthquakes stimulate the volcanoes or do the volcanic explosions trigger off some of the world's earthquakes? Furthermore, do the Earth's occasional phases of major axial wobble cause sudden bursts of seismic activity or is it the other way round? Professor D. L. Anderson of California sees a very complex but nevertheless significant relationship between many of the Earth's geo-physical and meteorological phenomena which may, perhaps, explain why there was an apparent increase in the magnitude and the frequency of natural disasters in the period 1976–77. The changing periodicity of solar activity (sunspots and flares) is now known to have a fairly close rhythmical relationship to outbursts of seismic activity, and we cannot fail to be impressed by the similar grouping of natural disasters at the beginning of the present century:

The turn of the century, roughly following the Krakatoa eruption, was a period of major unrest. It was also a period of rapid climatic change, changes in the drift pattern of the magnetic field and changes in the explosive volcanic activity of the earth. Between 1897 and 1914 there were 71 earthquakes of magnitude greater than 8; or roughly 4 per year; of these, 10 were giant earthquakes, magnitude greater than 8.5 . . . To complicate matters, during this same period of time the global mean temperature rose by 1°C, sea level rose, the westward drift of the magnetic field accelerated, the earth's rotation slowed down at an unprecedented rate and the Chandler Wobble was growing to a peak value.[5]

Another period of major solar activity has been predicted for the early 1980s. Will it bring with it a new phase of severe earthquakes, including the dreaded rupture of the San Andreas Fault?

3. Volcanoes

Because of the difficulties involved in earthquake forecasting it has been seen how the inhabitants of seismic regions have largely adopted a fatalistic attitude. The same may be said, to a certain extent, of the people who dwell in areas of volcanic hazard, but there is one major difference. Whereas earthquake zones have few visible manifestations of their former activity, regions of active vulcanicity usually exhibit many examples of earlier eruptions. Thus the local population is left in little doubt that by living in the vicinity of an active volcano they are taking a calculated risk. Only occasionally do volcanic eruptions occur in areas where the volcano was thought to be extinct or in regions where no previous vulcanicity has been recorded in historical times, and in these instances the perils are completely unforeseen. Why, then, do people choose to dwell on the flanks of volcanoes? The answer appears to lie, in part, in the fertility of volcanic soils, particularly if they are well watered, so that in the hope of substantial agricultural rewards some farmers are prepared to tolerate the volcanic hazard. In other instances population pressure dictates that all available land must be utilized, which means that in some parts of the world, such as Indonesia, people are left with little choice.

In the case of the volcanic islands of the West Indies it seems probable that both soil fertility and population pressure have been responsible for the reclamation and settlement of the thickly forested foothills of the volcanic peaks. One such island is Martinique, an attractive and prosperous place, famed for its luxuriant vegetation, profusion of tropical flowers, bananas and sugar cane. Little wonder that at the beginning of the twentieth century it was a favourite resort for summer visitors from France who came to holiday in the two major towns of Fort de France and St Pierre. The latter settlement (28,000 population in 1902) nestles on the coast at the foot of the island's highest peak, Mont Pelée (1,463 metres, 4,798 feet), reputedly named from the baldness of its volcanic peak protruding above the skirts of tropical forest. Since the initial French colonization of Martinique in 1635, only two eruptions had been recorded prior to 1902, but these were of only minor proportions. During the 1851 outburst it is noteworthy that the tiny crater lake, termed L'Étang Sec, in a separate depression below the main summit crater, dried up. Of further significance was the fact that the depression in question was flanked on all sides, except the south-west, by precipitous cliffs. It was on the south-western slopes that a great chasm terminated in a stream gorge known as the Rivière Blanche, and it was this breached south-western slope which overlooked St Pierre (Figure 19).

In early April 1902 the idyllic existence of St Pierre's inhabitants was interrupted by the ejection of great volumes of steam accompanied by violent hissing noises from the subsidiary crater which held the dried-up lake. Three weeks later there were light falls of ash in the foothills, accompanied by rumblings and a strong smell of sulphur in St Pierre itself. A scientific mission was immediately dispatched to the summit of Mt Pelée and its members returned to report that the crater of L'Étang Sec had refilled with water after an interval of fifty years and that alongside the lake a small cinder cone was building, from which a column of steam was being ejected. The signs looked ominous and as the rumblings grew louder and the ash falls in St Pierre more prolific the inhabitants became increasingly alarmed. By 3 May the more prudent of them had left the town as the sulphur fumes had become almost unbearable, but their places were taken by people fleeing from the volcano's lower slopes. A graphic account of the conditions prior to the disaster is given in a letter written by the wife of the American consul in St Pierre:

> The smell of sulphur is so strong that horses in the street stop and snort, and some of them drop in their harness and die of suffocation. Many of the people are obliged to wear wet handkerchiefs to protect themselves from the strong fumes of sulphur.[1]

This lady had the opportunity of leaving St Pierre, but like many others, she believed that the crisis would soon pass, lulled into a sense of false security by the local newspaper reports and the pronouncements of a certain Professor Landes who stated that Mt Pelée presented '. . . no more danger to the inhabitants of St Pierre than does Vesuvius to those of Naples' – an unfortunate analogy in view of Vesuvius's destructive record. On 5 May the volcano gave a final warning when the boiling lake-waters of L'Étang Sec burst through the rim and spewed a scalding deluge of mud and boulders down the Rivière Blanche. Travelling at a phenomenal speed the mudflow overwhelmed a sugar-cane factory at Guérin, a mere kilometre to the north of St Pierre, thereby killing its thirty employees. In the town panic set in, but even now the warnings were ignored by the municipal authorities and

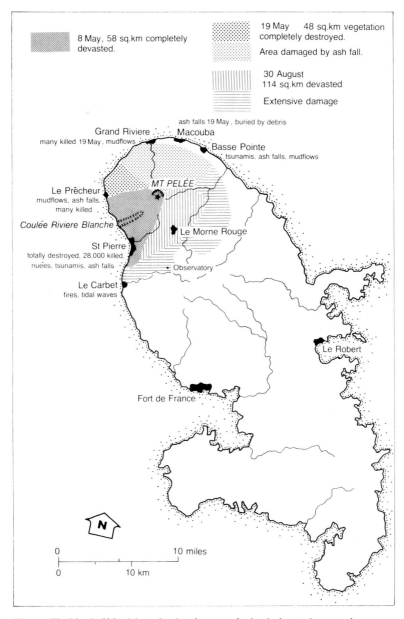

Fig. 19. The island of Martinique showing the areas of volcanic devastation around Mt Pelée in 1902.

8. The ruins of St Pierre, Martinique, after the volcanic eruption of Mt Pelée, May 1902. Note the lava spine of Mt Pelée in the distance.

the local newspaper confessed that '. . . we cannot understand this panic. Where could one be better off than at St Pierre?' To halt the exodus the governor is reputed to have sent troops to guard the roads – the catastrophe was now inevitable and the folly of mankind has rarely been illustrated so clearly.

At 7.49 a.m. on 8 May 1902 Mt Pelée exploded with the force of a nuclear bomb – by 7.52 a.m. St Pierre had ceased to exist (Plate 8). Of its 28,000 citizens there were only two survivors, the remainder had been blotted out in a great flash of searing heat. Of eighteen vessels lying at anchor in the bay only two remained, but these were severely damaged and most of their passengers and crew were killed. A survivor from one of the ships speaks of the prelude to the explosion and of the holocaust itself:

We could distinguish the rolling and leaping red flames that belched from the mountain in huge volume and gushed high in the sky. Enormous clouds of black smoke hung over the volcano . . . There was a constant muffled roar. It was like the biggest oil refinery in the world burning up on the mountain top . . . [Then] The mountain was blown to pieces . . . The side of the volcano was ripped out, and there hurled straight towards us a solid wall of flame . . . The wave of fire was on us and over us like a lightning flash. It was like a hurricane of fire, which rolled in mass straight down on St Pierre and the shipping.[2]

St Pierre was set alight in an instant, with its numerous casks of stored rum exploding and running in blazing torrents through the gutted streets. One of the most valuable eye-witness accounts is that of Monsieur Arnoux, a French scientist who was watching the eruption from a neighbouring hill, well away from the hazard zone. The significance of the following account lies in the fact that it describes a volcanic phenomenon hitherto unknown to science – a turbulent mass of superheated gas, incandescent ash and pulverized lava fragments, now termed a *nuée ardente* or 'glowing cloud'; and probably the most fearsome type of all volcanic eruptions (Plate 9):

. . . while still watching the crater, I noticed a small cloud pass out, followed two seconds later by a considerable cloud. This latter cloud rolled swiftly down towards St Pierre, hugging the ground, but extending upwards at the same time, so that it was almost as high as it was long.[3]

Not one of the eye-witness accounts refers to flows of lava and it is interesting to contrast the Mt Pelée eruption with other famous volcanic disasters where damage and casualties appear to have resulted largely from lava flows and ash falls. In St Pierre most victims appear to have been killed by inhaling the searing hot gas or by the blast. Because of its swiftness the *nuée ardente* which struck St Pierre (travelling at an estimated speed of 33 metres per second) must rank as the greatest vulcanological horror of all time, for it appears to have been utterly relentless and totally irresistible. Estimates of its temperature vary from 1,200°C at the centre of the explosion to 700°C in St Pierre itself, where glassware was partially melted, some 6 kilometres away. Peter Francis in his book *Volcanoes* likens the St Pierre conflagration to the 'fire storm' condition which developed in such German cities as Hamburg when they experienced saturation bombing during the Second World War. In that episode the multitude of separate fires amalgamated into one gigantic fire which itself generated an enormous vortex of hurricane-force winds that sucked in fresh oxygen to fuel the inferno.

If we pause to ask ourselves the question: How does one measure the severity of a volcanic disaster? we are immediately faced with the problems of classifying volcanic eruptions. In drawing up our table of magnitude, should

9. Sightseers at St Pierre, Martinique, soon after the catastrophic eruption of 1902, are startled by the appearance of a hazardous *nuée ardente*, similar to that which destroyed the town.

we be governed by the number of deaths? by the loudness of the explosion? by the amount of fall-out? or simply by the cost of rehabilitation? One answer is to construct a table which shows the magnitude of the potential hazard and this is illustrated in Figure 20.

Fig. 20. Classification of Volcanic eruptions (after A. E. Scheidegger).

HAZARD	Low Risk ——————————— High Risk		
	Lava Fluidity	Gas Pressure		
Low Risk		Low	Medium	High
	Most Fluid	Icelandic Hawaiian	Strombolian	Vesuvian
	Intermediate	—	Vulcanian	Perretian[3]
High Risk	Viscous Least fluid	Merapian[1]	Vincentian[2]	Peléean

Note 1. Merapian is named after the Merapi volcano in central Java.
     2. Vincentian is named after Soufrière volcano in St Vincent, West Indies.
     3. Perretian is named after F. A. Perret, a distinguished American vulcanologist.

It is clear from a study of Figure 20 that the character of any eruption is determined by two main factors – its gas pressure and the fluidity of its lava. Vulcanologists use the term *viscosity* to describe the ability of a lava to flow; at its most viscous the lava is least fluid and because of its stiffness is unable to flow far from the vent, if at all, and this type is often referred to as 'block lava'. The lava which is most fluid is termed 'pahoehoe (or ropy) lava' from a Hawaiian name, whilst lava of intermediate fluidity is given another Hawaiian name – 'aa lava'. Similarly, gas quantity and pressure vary so that we can distinguish volcanoes where the explosive forces are relatively high from those where the ejection of material will be less violent. This is a very generalized ordering of magnitude, for even in Hawaiian and Icelandic eruptions there are occasional bouts of severe detonations, but it is the Vesuvian type of eruption which produces some of the most violent explosions. The reader will soon appreciate, however, that the more viscous the lava the more choked the volcanic vent will become; the extreme condition is reached in the Peléean type of eruption where the lava 'stopper' was so viscous in 1902 that it was pushed to a height of 600 metres above the crater as a narrow spire-like tower. Thus the most frightful explosions and the most severe hazards are produced by a combination of high viscosity and high gas pressure (Figure 20). It is interesting to note that the fearful *nuées ardentes* produced by the laterally directed explosion of the Peléean type become rather less dangerous in the Vincentian type in which the *nuées* result from the copious gravity fall-back into an open vent, following a vertically directed explosion. The Merapian type, with a low gas pressure, is characterized by a vent which is virtually blocked by the spine, so that the *nuées* are in part composed of collapsing fragments of the crumbling spine.

There have been numerous attempts at classification of volcanoes, including that of the widely accepted version outlined by Professor A. Lacroix, a French geologist. He distinguishes four types: Hawaiian, Strombolian, Vulcanian and Peléean. To these, later geologists have added the Icelandic type and Katmaian type, although there remains the difficulty, inherent in a classification of this kind, that a volcano may change the character of its activity and hence its classification over a period of time and even during a single eruption. Thus, whilst retaining the well-established terms noted above, it will be prudent to remember the relationships outlined in Figure 20, when reading the following descriptions of volcanic hazards, in which an attempt is made to explain the varying character and different mechanisms of volcanic eruptions.

Despite the variety of volcanic eruptions it is possible to recognize three major hazards to human life and property: lava flows; pyroclastic falls; pyroclastic flows; of these the lava flows are the least hazardous and the pyroclastic flows the most hazardous. In addition, we shall examine other types of volcanic hazard, such as mudflows, poisonous gases and ice-melting.

Hazards from Lava Flows

Outpourings of lava will occur when a weakness in the surface of the crust allows molten rock material from depth to combine with varying amounts of gas to form a magma. While the magma remains confined beneath the surface in a lava chamber it is under pressure so that the gaseous constituents remain in solution. As the lava rises up the vent or fissure, however, pressure is released, allowing gases to escape, often with great violence; much of the energy generated during an eruption is due to this gas pressure being suddenly released. The analogy of uncorking a bottle of champagne is one that is frequently used to describe the eruption of a volcano, with the liquid being analogous with the lava and the froth with the pumice. To continue the analogy further, should the cork (lava plug) become jammed and the pressure unreleased there is a danger of the bottle (volcano) being shattered in a violent (Vesuvian or Peléean) explosion.

The fluidity or viscosity of a lava generally reflects its chemical composition and is intimately related to the amount of SiO_2 (silicon dioxide) present. Thus, lavas which contain more than 66 per cent SiO_2 (termed acid lavas) are extremely viscous, stiff and reluctant to release their gases; lavas with 52 per cent to 66 per cent SiO_2 content are termed intermediate, whilst those with less than 52 per cent SiO_2 are referred to as basic and very fluid lavas from which the gases are easily liberated. Readers will now begin to understand why the Hawaiian and Icelandic types of eruptions, noted in Figure 20, are least hazardous to mankind for they are generally associated with basic and fluid lavas which are poured out relatively quietly without a great deal of explosive activity. In fact the great volcanic island of Hawaii itself is made up almost entirely of thousands of metres of basic lava, with less than 1 per cent of its rocks composed of ash or other fragmental material related to explosive activity.

Nevertheless, even in the absence of catastrophic explosions, because of its low viscosity, basic lava can flow at considerable speeds (48 kilometres per hour have been recorded) and also cover very large areas. Long before man appeared on the earth many basic lava flows appear to have covered thousands of square kilometres in places such as Northern Ireland, the Scottish Hebrides, Iceland and the Columbia River region of North West U.S.A. The longest recorded flows of historic times relate to Mauna Loa volcano on Hawaii: that of 1859 ran downslope for 53 kilometres before crossing the coast and continuing an unknown distance beneath the sea; the 1881 flow reached the outskirts of the city of Hilo after a journey of 46 kilometres. If we are to believe the writings of a Roman scribe a lava flow from Mt Etna in Sicily, more than 38 kilometres long and 3 kilometres wide, halted the advance of the Carthaginian army in 396 B.C. The worst of Etna's lava flows, however, was a 16 kilometre flow which, in 1669, destroyed the city of Catania and blocked its harbour. The same flow is said to have engulfed no less than fourteen other neighbouring towns, some with a population of 3,000 to 4,000. If this were so, then it is the world's most disastrous record of lava inundation. Other noteworthy modern lava flow catastrophes include the destruction of Mascali (Sicily) in 1928 (Plate 10); the frequent overrunning of the town of Torre Annunziata by lava flows from Vesuvius, the last occasion being in 1906; the partial destruction of the towns of San Sebastiano and Massa by Vesuvian lavas in 1944; the complete obliteration of two Mexican towns by floods of lava from the new volcano of Paricutín in 1943–44; the swamping of the entire settlement of Kapoho by Hawaiian

10. A stream of lava from Mt Etna overwhelms the church and civic buildings at Mascali, Sicily, during the eruption of November 1928.

lavas from Kilauea volcano in 1960; finally the gradual overwhelming of the suburbs of the Icelandic town of Vestmannaeyjar, the capital of the Westmann Isles, in 1973.

The most widespread devastation from lava inundation has, in the past, resulted not from central-vent volcanoes, as described above, but from so-called fissure eruptions during which enormous floods of very fluid lava (generally basalt) have poured out rapidly from lengthy fissures, or cracks in the earth's crust. The fissure eruption is typical of the Icelandic type of vulcanicity, and most of the lava plains of that country have been created by former activity of this kind. The most famous on record is the Laki eruption of 1783 when 12.25 cubic kilometres of lava flooded out of a fissure 24 kilometres in length for a period of more than five months, by which time no less than 558 square kilometres of land had been over-run – an area the size of the Isle of Man. The eruption took place along the flanks of Mt Skaptar (its first eruption in historic time), which lies 320 kilometres east of Iceland's capital, Reykjavik. The lava flows, almost 180 metres thick in places, not only caused melting of the neighbouring glaciers but also a considerable disruption of the local drainage network. The outcome was severe flooding of many farmsteads as the lava-impounded lakes overflowed. Thus, although few casualties were caused directly by the lavas themselves the death-roll began to rise from drowning. But worse was yet to come, for a pall of sulphurous fumes enveloped the countryside over an area of hundreds of square kilometres and this appears to have severely damaged grazing lands, crops and hayfields alike. So serious was the effect on the food supply that famine slowly took its toll of both man and beast, ultimately leading to the greatest natural disaster in Iceland's history. The Haze Famine, as it came to be called (from the bluish haze of the sulphur dioxide fumes), was an indirect result of the fissure eruption and it cost the country dearly – 20 per cent of Iceland's population died, as did 50 per cent of its cattle and some 75 per cent of its sheep and horses. It is interesting to speculate whether this ranks amongst the world's greatest natural disasters, as far as a single nation is concerned. Only the terrible Indian famine of 1770, when over 30 per cent of the population is reputed to have died, is of greater proportions, but the Irish Potato Famine of 1845 is claimed by some to have caused the deaths of some 20 per cent of Ireland's population.

Hazards from Pyroclastic Falls

Pyroclastic materials (or tephra) are those constituents of a volcanic eruption which have been fragmented and blown into the atmosphere by its explosive activity (*pyro* = fire; *clastic* = broken; *pyroclastic* = broken by fire). We have already noted that generally speaking, the more viscous the lava and the higher the gas pressure, the greater will be the magnitude of the explosion and therefore the volume of pyroclastic material produced. It must be remembered, however, that explosively ejected material during an eruption can be of two major categories: first, that which has been thrown out as solid material, merely fractured by the blast, and, secondly, that which, having been thrown out of the vent as liquid-lava globules, has solidified in the air and hit the ground as solid material. Tephra comprises all this fragmented material ejected by all types of volcano, whether its lava is acid or basic (or intermediate between the two). Consequently, pyroclastic falls *can* be associated with the fluid lavas of the Hawaiian and Icelandic types of eruption almost as much as with the Strombolian, Vulcanian and Vincentian types (see Figure 20). Before looking in detail at some case studies of tephra as a volcanic hazard it is important to note that geologists subdivide this pyroclastic fall-out according to the size of its fragments. Thus, *Ashes* are particles less than 4 millimetres across; *Lapilli* are 4–32 millimetres in diameter, whilst *Bombs* and *Blocks* are greater than 32 millimetres across.

On reflection it will be realized that the dangers from tephra will vary according to the intensity of the explosion, the quantity and density of the material ejected, the turbulence of the air and the direction of the wind. At one extreme, for example, the mildest, least explosive eruption of heavier, basic tephra in relatively windless conditions would create less of a hazard than, say, a violent eruption of less-dense material where ash and pumice may be wind-borne over tremendous distances. Light ash falls may be injurious to grazing animals only if the tephra is toxic, but heavy ash falls will destroy the vegetation altogether. One metre of ash is usually considered to be the minimum required to produce catastrophic results not only on vegetation, when leaves and branches are stripped from the trees by its burden, but also in the case of flat-roofed buildings, which collapse unless they are of special construction. Much of the damage caused during pyroclastic falls results from fires generated by the hot tephra – forested country is severely hit in this way, whilst buildings of wooden construction, like those in Vestmannaeyjar (page 83), are extremely prone to total destruction.

In the most violent eruptions (often referred to as the Plinian type – see below) the upward blast is so violent that vast quantities of tephra are shot to remarkable heights in relatively short periods, so that heavy ash falls become a serious hazard over comparatively large areas. Two of the most famous examples relate to the eruptions of Vesuvius in 79 A.D. and Mt Hekla in 1947.

During the first century A.D., at a time when the Roman Empire was still flourishing, the coastal area now known as the Bay of Naples was an especially favoured one in which to live. Vineyards and farmsteads thrived on the warm, fertile volcanic soils of the well-drained sunny slopes of the dormant Mt Vesuvius. Even though some Roman scholars knew that it was a volcano there was no record of any eruption. Thus, unaware of any hazard, the inhabitants of Pompeii and Herculaneum, for example, carried on their day to day activities and disregarded the earth tremors and rumblings which warned of the fearful cataclysm about to break. The first major earthquake to be associated with the renewal of Vesuvian activity came in 63 A.D., during which both Pompeii and Herculaneum were severely damaged. After a further sixteen years of tremors a final warning shock occurred on the night of 24 August 79 A.D. The next day almost 50 per cent of the volcanic cone was destroyed by a fearful explosion – the remnant of the former cone, which now partly circles the northern slopes of the modern cone, is known as Monte Somma (Figure 21).

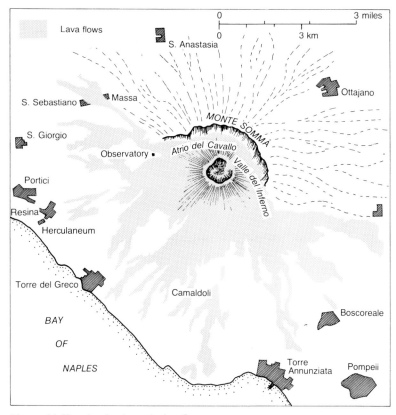

Fig. 21. Mt Vesuvius showing major lava flows.

One of the most famous eye-witness accounts of a natural disaster is that of Pliny the Younger in his letters to Tacitus, in which he recounts the death of his uncle whilst visiting Stabiae (now Castellammare) during the eruption. Today the type of eruption described by Pliny is termed a Plinian eruption, whilst his description of the eruption cloud as resembling a pine tree has given us the scientific term *pino* (Italian: *pino* = pine tree). Curiously,

Pliny makes no reference to the destruction of Pompeii and Herculaneum and we are forced to depend on the writings of a later author, Dion Cassius, and on subsequent archaeological excavations to unravel the history of the disaster. It seems clear, however, that the inhabitants of the two towns did not die from inundation by lava flows, but rather by a combination of toxic gases and pyroclastic fall-out. Cassius states, for example, that

... an inexpressible quantity of dust was blown out, which filled land, sea and air; which did much other mischief to men, fields and cattle, ... and besides buried two entire cities, Herculaneum and Pompeii ...[4]

Geological analysis has demonstrated that the 3 metres of debris which buried Pompeii was mainly ash and pumice derived from the newly emerging lava rather than shattered rock material from the former cone (Monte Somma). In which case, it would appear most likely that the old cone disappeared not so much from explosive disintegration but largely from collapse into the newly evacuated magma chamber. Since many of the bodies excavated at Pompeii appeared to have been attempting to cover their faces with their hands or with cloths, asphyxiation is the most likely cause of death, but others have manifestly been killed by buildings collapsing under the weight of tephra. At Herculaneum, however, things seem to have been rather different. Here, the city was overwhelmed not simply by tephra fall but also by a final, devastating mudflow, exceeding 20 metres in thickness in some areas. Once the mudflow had dried out it became extremely tenacious so that only a small part of Herculaneum has subsequently been excavated owing to the hardness of the material and to its excessive thickness. We shall examine the mechanisms relating to volcanic mudflow later in the chapter (pp. 97–8); suffice to say that in contrast to Pompeii the majority of the inhabitants of Herculaneum appear to have escaped, a fact which suggests that the wind direction was more favourable, so far as pyroclastic fall-out was concerned (Figure 22), and that the mudflow came at a fairly late stage in the eruption.

The eruption of Mt Hekla, Iceland's most renowned volcano, on 30 March 1947, produced one of the largest Plinian-type eruptions of the twentieth century, although this type of activity lasted for only a few hours. Nevertheless, in the first hour eye-witnesses describe how the ash-laden 'pino' had risen to 27,000 metres (about three times the height of Everest), covering the countryside in a thick tephra fall-out and blotting out the sun for many hours (Plate 11). The rate at which ash was ejected in the first half hour reached the astonishing proportions of 100,000 cubic metres per second, and so extensive was the area of fall-out that ash falls occurred as

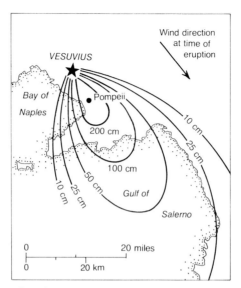

Fig. 22. Ash fall-out from the Vesuvius eruption of 79 A.D. Contours illustrate the depth of tephra (after P. Francis).

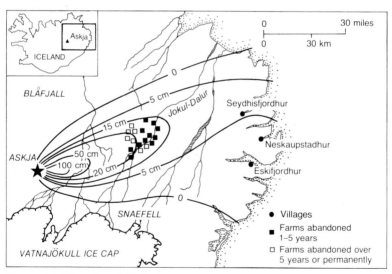

Fig. 23. Ash fall-out from Askja (Iceland) eruption of 1875 (after S. Thorarinsson).

far away as Finland some two days later. The Laki eruption of 1783 (see p. 83) resulted in a rain of ash in both Norway and Scotland, in sufficient quantities to damage crops, whilst the 1875 ash fallout from Askja caused many farms to be buried and abandoned (Figure 23). Fortunately, there was minimal loss of life associated with the 1947 Hekla eruption, although thousands of hectares of grazing land were ruined and livestock were severely affected.

The effects of the high flung ash-clouds from Plinian-type eruptions have prompted some scientists to seek links between the far-spreading volcanic dust veils and climatic modification. During the summer and autumn of

11. The eruption of Mt Hekla, Iceland, in March 1947 produced one of the highest ash-laden explosion clouds on record when it reached 27,000 metres above the snow-covered landscape.

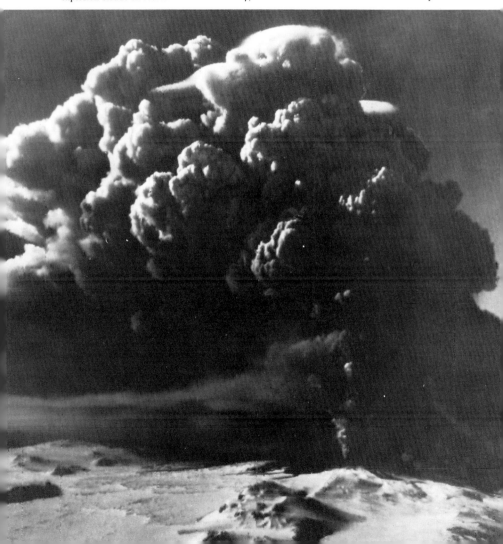

1815, for example, London experienced a lengthy series of remarkably brilliant sunsets, which has even led to the claim by certain critics that the greatest work of J. M. W. Turner, one of Britain's finest artists, may have been inspired by these phenomena. But this example of luminous twilights, together with the abysmally wet and cloudy British summer of the following year, might be quite coincidental with the fact that in April 1815, the world's greatest recorded eruption is known to have taken place. Estimates have suggested that when Tambora volcano, on the island of Sumbawa, Indonesia, exploded some 151 cubic kilometres of material were ejected, during which the cone was lowered by 1,250 metres in height (almost the height of Scotland's highest peak) and a caldera 11 kilometres in diameter was formed. We must look now at the question of caldera formation, for it is this particular volcanic landform which is associated with two of the world's best known volcanic disasters, both of which can be examined under the heading of pyroclastic falls.

Scientists have been able to demonstrate that at the close of some eruptions such massive quantities of lava have been ejected from the volcanic vent that a hollow space is left behind in the former magma chamber, deep down beneath the cone. In certain instances the weight of the volcanic overburden is such that the volcano itself collapses into the underground cavity, thus creating a caldera (see the discussion relating to Monte Somma on p. 87). Some of the world's greatest calderas are perfectly circular, such as Ngorongoro in East Africa and Crater Lake, Oregon – both wrongly described as craters rather than calderas. The two most remarkable calderas, however, are submarine and are now represented only by groups of islands, the first being at Santorini in the eastern Mediterranean and the second at Krakatoa in the Sunda Straits, Indonesia. Before examining the formation of these two features in more detail a few statistics on their respective dimensions will be of interest. Santorini caldera has a diameter of about 16 kilometres and the eruption which led to its collapse is thought to have produced 62.5 cubic kilometres of ejected material; Krakatoa caldera has a diameter of about 11 kilometres and the volume of material associated with its historic eruption is estimated at 18 cubic kilometres (N.B. various estimates of the volume of material ejected during the 1835 eruption of Coseguina, Nicaragua, fall between 50 cubic kilometres and 10 cubic kilometres).

The Santorini group of islands in the Aegean Sea has been shown to be the partly submerged ruin of a volcanic caldera, created as the result of a gigantic eruption of the volcano known as Thera in about 1500 B.C. The late Bronze Age civilization in the eastern Mediterranean had, by that time, split into two groups – the Minoans in Crete and the Mycenaeans in mainland

Greece. Archaeologists have claimed that in 1450 B.C. a major catastrophe struck the island of Crete, bringing the Minoan culture to an abrupt end. The suggestion that the disaster was the result of the Thera eruption had become fairly widely accepted by the mid-twentieth century. The hypothesis proposed that the destruction had been wrought by a combination of heavy pyroclastic fall-out and a series of tsunamis (phenomenal shock-generated sea-waves, wrongly referred to as tidal waves, see p. 265) and that the explosion and partial disappearance of Thera may also have given rise to the ancient legend of the drowned continent of Atlantis, referred to by Plato. There seems little doubt that prior to the volcanic eruption Thera had been dormant for several thousand years, and that after the explosion the outpost of Minoan culture on the flanks of the volcano (now Santorini) was buried by a thick fall of tephra. Significantly, however, unlike Pompeii, no bodies have been found in the buried city of Akrotiri on Santorini, leading experts to the conclusion that, warned by the initial earth tremors, the 30,000 inhabitants must have seized all their movable objects and fled, just before the eruption destroyed their city. It was very tempting to broaden the hypothesis to incorporate the total destruction of the main Minoan civilization on Crete some 130 kilometres away, but unfortunately the latter demise appears to have occurred not in 1500 B.C., as in Santorini, but fifty years later, in 1450 B.C.

Because of this discrepancy in the dates an alternative hypothesis was then devised which, at first sight, appeared to accord more closely with the geological facts. It was suggested that in 1500 B.C. Thera's initial eruption wiped out Santorini but that, fifty years later, a second eruption caused the volcanic cone to collapse into the underlying cavity to form a caldera, thus generating gigantic tsunamis which destroyed the Cretan towns. Recent research by two German scientists, H. Pichler and W. Schiering, has suggested, however, that the volcano collapsed *immediately* after the initial explosion in 1500 B.C. and that there was no further eruption of Thera, certainly not with a magnitude sufficient to destroy the Minoan civilization in Crete. In conclusion, therefore, the German scientists suggest that a more likely explanation for the sudden termination of Minoan Crete would be found in a disastrous earthquake – after all, is this not a fairly active seismic zone?

No speculation is needed in the case of Krakatoa for many eye-witnesses have left a detailed record of the events which accompanied one of the world's greatest natural explosions. It has been suggested that Krakatoa's explosion released twenty-six times the energy of the greatest hydrogen bomb so far detonated, but it still remained only one fifth as powerful as the

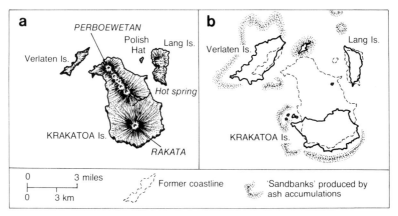

Fig. 24. Krakatoa (a) before and (b) after the eruption of 1883 (after P. Francis).

Santorini explosion. In the narrow Sunda Straits, between Java and Sumatra, a tiny group of uninhabited islands today marks the site of the Krakatoa caldera, all that remains of a larger volcanic island which stood here prior to 1883. Since the eruption in 1681 no volcanic activity had been recorded on Krakatoa for more than two hundred years, although earth tremors had grown in intensity during the late 1870s. On 20 May 1883 eruptions began in the Perboewetan cone of the island and by the middle of August Krakatoa had three of its central volcanic vents in full eruption (Figure 24). By midday on 26 August a series of deafening explosions began to occur at regular intervals and by 17.00 hours the sound could be heard all over Java and Sumatra. By the following morning, 27 August, the explosions had grown even louder, the stupendous detonation of 10.02 hours being heard no less than 4,811 kilometres away on Rodriguez Island in the Indian Ocean, whilst at Elsey Creek in South Australia, 3,224 kilometres distant, people were awakened from their sleep (Figure 25). To appreciate the magnitude of the explosion it has been demonstrated that if, for the sake of argument, Pike's Peak in Colorado, U.S.A., had been an exploding volcano of similar violence the noise would have been heard all over the mainland of the United States!

The Krakatoa ash cloud rose to a phenomenal height of 80 kilometres, with the dust being carried several times around the earth by the upper air-currents, until it covered the entire globe. The sunsets of 1883 were, if anything, even more brilliant than those of 1815 (see p. 90) owing to the reflection of sunlight from the dust particles. Ash falling in Western Europe

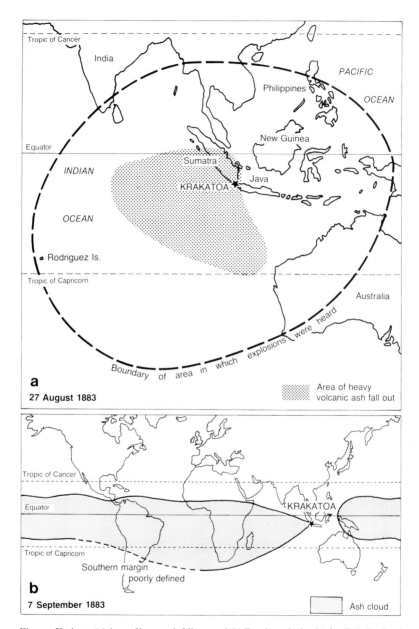

Fig. 25. Krakatoa (a) Area of heavy ash fall-out and (b) Ensuing ash cloud (after F. Bullard and P. Francis).

was analysed and found to be derived from Krakatoa, whilst on the eastern seaboard of the United States fire engines were summoned on 30 October to 'quench the burning skies', so bright was the flaming sunset. Closer to the explosion, however, the spectacle was less appealing, for the ash cloud was so extensive that the Sunda Straits had two days of total darkness. Even in Batavia (now Djakarta), 160 kilometres away, the sun was blotted out for almost two hours on 27 August, but this city was upwind, so it escaped relatively lightly (Figure 25). Most of the ash fall was over the Indian Ocean, although crops and vegetation were destroyed by fall-out over wide areas of Java and especially of Sumatra. Surprisingly, few people were killed by the pyroclastic fall or by the blast, but the accompanying tsunamis, generated as the cone collapsed into the caldera, wreaked fearful havoc along the coasts of the Sunda Straits. In some locations the sea waves swept up to heights of 36 metres, destroying or damaging well over 250 towns and drowning the majority of the 36,417 people who lost their lives as a result of the Krakatoa eruption. In 1927, after forty-four years of calm, a new volcanic cone, termed Anak Krakatoa, commenced submarine activity until it emerged from the sea at the centre of the old caldera in 1952. Small eruptions are still continuing from this new centre, so that the Indonesian authorities are keeping a wary eye on this 'child of Krakatoa'.

Hazards from Pyroclastic Flows

In the opening pages of the chapter we have described one of the most horrific case studies of a pyroclastic flow, that of Mt Pelée on 8 May 1902. Few people realize that the initial *nuée ardente* may be succeeded by several subsequent flows, some of which may be just as devastating as the first *nuée*. This was, in fact, the outcome in Martinique where further pyroclastic flows and mudflows laid waste to much of the northern end of the island for several months after the St Pierre disaster (Figure 19). By this time, however, most of the inhabitants had taken refuge elsewhere so that casualties were far fewer than on 8 May 1902. Nevertheless, because the soil can be restored so rapidly after the passage of a *nuée ardente* there is a dangerous tendency for the population to reoccupy the hazard zone before the eruption has completely ceased. Only when the lava spine of Mt Pelée had ceased to grow upwards could it be said that the area was becoming less hazardous, although the danger had not really passed until the spine itself had crumbled and weathered away, which it did within the space of a few years. A further period of eruption took place on Mt Pelée between 1929 and 1932, but despite the accompanying *nuées* there was no loss of life, because of evacuation and the lower intensity of the flows. A new lava dome arose in the 1902 crater and this is thought to have effectively sealed the vent once and for all. Whether Mt Pelée is now extinct or merely dormant, only time will tell. Other recent disasters resulting from *nuées ardentes* are recorded from Hibokhibok in the Philippines in 1951 when five hundred deaths occurred; from the unsuspected volcano of Mt Lamington, New Guinea, in the same year, when three thousand were killed; and from Mt Mayon in the Philippines in 1968, when early evacuation avoided a major loss of life.

The 1902 eruption of Mt Pelée produced what we may term a *pyroclastic surge* which is only one, albeit the most destructive, of three types of pyroclastic flow. The surge, travelling at the speed of a nuclear blast, is composed of a relatively low density ash/gas mixture so that it can flow over valleys and hills regardless of the topography. No living thing can survive in its path, death resulting from severe external burns and/or internal burns because of inhalation of the searing hot *nuée*. The blast is generally severe enough to topple buildings, so that falling masonry is a further cause of death. Lower down the scale of intensity come the small-scale pyroclastic flows which normally follow topographic depressions, because their constituent materials are somewhat denser – these are more typical of the Vincentian type of activity (see Figure 20). Nevertheless, they are equally as devastating over small areas as the surges. Scientists are still uncertain of the actual mechanisms which cause the *nuées* to flow so rapidly downslope – various hypotheses have been suggested including that of a turbidity current in air; the boundary-layer concept of fluid dynamics, with a low-viscosity layer developing between the flow and the ground; finally, the idea that the *nuée* moves forward along a layer of trapped and compressed air, almost like a hovercraft.

The final type of pyroclastic flow is that which produces the so-called *ignimbrite* (Latin: *ignis* = fire, *imbris* = rain), which is a sort of incandescent lava drizzle, which extends over very wide areas. Following the eruption of Mt Katmai in Alaska in 1912 this type has sometimes been referred to as the Katmaian type of eruption, although this is not referred to in Figure 20, for there it is a sub-classification of the Peléean. Ignimbrites are composed largely of pumice fragments, similar in many ways to that which results from a pyroclastic fall. There is evidence to show, however, that ignimbrite sheets were laid down by high-speed ground-surface flows, similar to those of *nuées ardentes*, although because of their extreme fluidity the masses of ignimbrite dust can travel many kilometres farther than the true *nuées ardentes*. Ignimbrite sheets were laid down in earlier geological episodes in places such as North Wales, the Taupo area of New Zealand and Nevada, U.S.A. Since the ignimbrite flow material is so similar to that of the pyroclastic fall, the question has often been asked as to how two equally explosive types of eruptions, such as the Plinian (Vesuvian) and the Katmaian (Peléean), differ in their actual mechanisms. The most satisfactory explanation is given by Peter Francis in his book *Volcanoes*, in which he claims that during a Plinian eruption:

As the magma approaches the surface, the pressure on it decreases, the gas expands, and a violently self-accelerating process takes place, blasting the fragmented magma up out of the vent. The basic difference between a Plinian eruption and an ignimbrite-producing eruption seems to be the site at which the de-gassing takes place. In the Plinian case it must occur deep down in the throat of the volcano, so that the pumice is blasted upwards like shot from a gun, whereas when ignimbrites are erupted, the de-gassing takes place near the surface, so that the whole mass froths out sideways rather than upwards.[5] (Figure 26).

Fig. 26. Comparison between Plinian and Ignimbrite eruptions (after P. Francis).

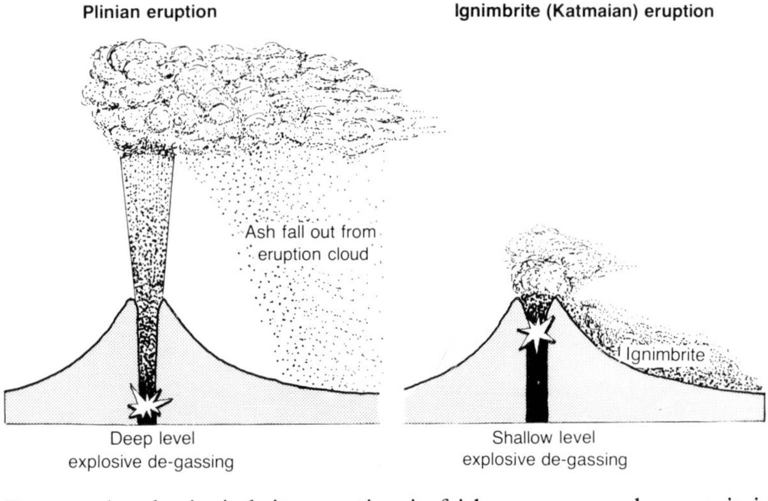

Plinian eruption   Ignimbrite (Katmaian) eruption

Ash fall out from eruption cloud

Ignimbrite

Deep level explosive de-gassing   Shallow level explosive de-gassing

Fortunately, the ignimbrite eruption is fairly uncommon because it is potentially the most devastating of all eruptions. Both of the twentieth-century examples have occurred in isolated and virtually uninhabited parts of the world – Mt Katmai (1912) in Alaska and Mt Bezymianny (1956) in Kamchatka, U.S.S.R. The latter eruption is claimed to be the largest volcanic explosion this century, when 1 cubic kilometre of material was ejected (sufficient to cover Paris to a depth of 15 metres, according to Haroun Tazieff, the famous vulcanologist). More importantly, it has been shown how the ignimbrite flow from Mt Bezymianny stripped vegetation up to 30 kilometres away, whilst its accompanying mudflows ran for distances of some 90 kilometres – all without loss of life.

Other Volcanic Hazards

In several of the case studies described above mention has been made of accompanying hazards which are only indirectly related to the volcanic eruption itself. Of these the most important are mudflows, glacier melts, tsunamis and toxic gases. Tsunamis are usually associated with large-scale submarine or coastal earthquakes but can also be produced by gigantic volcanic explosions, such as that of Krakatoa (p. 92). But since the hazard results from coastal flooding and may have no connection with a volcanic eruption the tsunami is dealt with in Chapter 8.

Among the remainder the mudflow is the hazard which generally produces the greatest loss of life and damage to property. Mudflows can be caused in several ways but their danger lies in their considerable velocity, owing to excessive fluidity. The majority of mudflows (sometimes termed 'lahars') result from heavy rainfall during an eruption, so that the precipitation mixes with the thick volcanic ash on the slopes of the cone, producing a lethal and unstable mixture. On occasion a similar 'brew' is created when a *nuée ardente* is influenced by a deluge of rain or when a *nuée* crosses a lake or river; in the latter case the *nuée* would turn the river course into a gigantic mudflow following the existing river valley. The most disastrous mudflow on record is one which killed 5,500 people during an eruption of Kelut volcano, Java, in 1919.

One of the most destructive types of mudflow is that caused by the rupturing of a crater lake either during an eruption or for other reasons (possibly an earthquake). On Christmas Eve, 1953, for example, the crater lake of Mt Ruapehu, New Zealand, burst, possibly by crevassing in one of its supporting ice-barriers. The resulting mudflow plunged down the mountain side, tearing out huge boulders en route, and finally swept away a railway bridge two minutes before an express train was due. In the ensuing rail disaster of Tangiwai Bridge 151 people died in the cauldron of mud and volcanic débris in the gorge below. This was New Zealand's second catastrophe caused by a mudflow, since eleven workmen had been killed whilst mining sulphur on White Island in 1914. At present the Ruapehu crater lake is full of sulphuric acid, a potential hazard to the neighbouring winter sports centre in the event of a future eruption beneath the lake. A similar eruption occurred at the

Kawah Idjen volcano in Java in 1936 and resulted in severe acid burns for those unfortunate enough to be caught in the fall-out zone. Scalding from hot-water during geyser eruptions is a hazard which has rarely caused loss of life. But very hot mudflows are known to have wrecked nine towns on the slopes of Vesuvius during its 1631 eruption, including those of Portico, S. Giorgio a Cremono and Resina (site of ancient Herculaneum). The entire death toll during that eruption was four thousand, although it was not recorded how many died directly from mudflows. Geologists have demonstrated that some of the world's largest mudflows occurred on the slopes of Mt Rainier, Washington State, U.S.A., some five thousand years ago. Several towns have subsequently grown up above Tacoma on the flanks of Mt Rainier, located on the prehistoric mudflows themselves, so that they now stand in potential hazard zones.

In a few areas of the world, such as Iceland, Alaska and the southern Andes, volcanoes are associated with ice-caps and glaciers – even the ice-capped dormant cone of Kilimanjaro, East Africa, has its sulphur fumes. If there are major sub-glacial eruptions, as in the Vatnajökull of Iceland, vast quantities of meltwater can be generated in a relatively short period and once these break out of the encompassing ice-barrier a potentially dangerous flood will result. Such 'glacier-bursts' are termed *jökulhlaups* and are described more fully in Chapter 8. Fortunately, the majority of these occurrences are located in sparsely populated regions so that losses of life are relatively uncommon. The same is true of the final volcanic hazard, that associated with the slow seepage of toxic fumes. The greatest damage has been caused to crops, such as the case in Nicaragua, Central America, where the Masaya volcano emitted such toxic sulphur fumes between 1946 and 1951 that almost six million coffee trees were blighted in an area of 130 square kilometres, resulting in a loss of production worth almost $10 million. In other instances, especially in Iceland, livestock have been poisoned by grazing in hollows where odourless and colourless carbon dioxide had accumulated. Fluorine and cobalt poisoning of livestock has also been reported on several occasions, from Iceland and New Zealand for example, where toxic fall-out from volcanic eruptions has poisoned the surrounding pastures.

Prediction and Alleviation of Volcanic Hazards

In the previous chapter we have noted how a certain number of countries, especially those bordering the Pacific, have set up earthquake research centres and forecasting units. Since earthquakes and volcanoes are related to each other in many ways it is not surprising to discover that almost all of these countries are also seriously concerned with vulcanological research, because the world distribution map of active volcanoes (Figure 27) is extremely similar to that of the seismic zones, but with a few major exceptions (compare Figures 8 and 27). It soon becomes clear that much of the earth's vulcanicity occurs along the margins of the major tectonic plates, so that the Pacific 'Ring of Fire' (as it is popularly called), the Mid-Atlantic Ridge, the West Indian island arc and the eastern Mediterranean are all well known volcanic earthquake zones, because they all coincide with plate margins. The three major exceptions to the almost perfect correlation are found in the Himalayas, East Africa and Hawaii; in the first case the seismically active mountains of north India, Nepal and Pakistan are remarkably non-volcanic, whilst in the case of East Africa there are some very active volcanoes in the Rift Valley, a zone not normally associated with major earthquakes; finally in Hawaii, a very active area of vulcanicity lies in a non-seismic (aseismic) zone.

An explanation of these three major anomalies is obviously called for since they do not fit easily into the concept of plate tectonics outlined in Chapter 2. The East African volcanoes are the simplest to explain for they are all associated with the well-known Rift Valley whose tectonics are similar in some ways to those of the Mid-Atlantic Ridge where hot magma is rising to the surface in a zone of tensional fractures. Some geologists believe that East Africa is in fact a mini-plate and is slowly parting from the remainder of the African Plate along the line now marked by the Rift Valley. Hawaiian vulcanicity, too, has a relatively simple explanation, despite its location at the centre of the Pacific Plate, far away from the active plate margins. Some scientists believe that Hawaii (like the equally anomalous extinct Saharan volcanoes of Tibesti and Ahaggar) represents a site in the crust which is located immediately above a particularly 'hot spot' in the mantle. Here a rising plume of hot material is thought to be burning a hole in the overlying crustal plate. The case of the Himalayas is the most complex anomaly of all and no one has satisfactorily explained the absence of modern vulcanicity along this particular plate-margin collision zone. There is evidence that volcanoes existed here in the geological past, but the tectonics are not as simple as, say, those of the Andes, so that no easy explanation is forthcoming. Perhaps it is fortuitous that India and Pakistan do not have to contend with additional volcanic hazards in view of their existing problems related to earthquakes, floods, droughts and famines!

In the past, prediction of volcanic eruptions has been based solely on

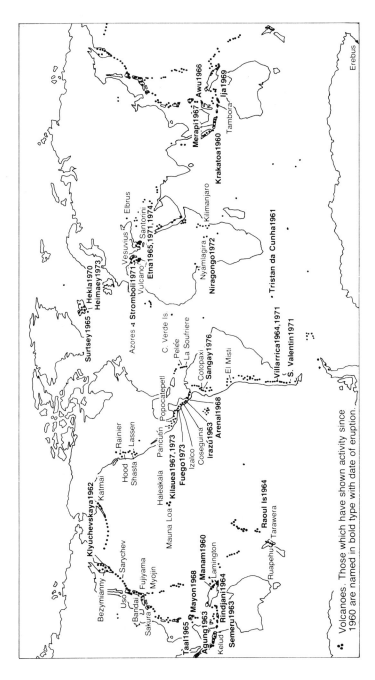

Fig. 27. Distribution of World Volcanoes, showing recent eruptions.

surveillance of known volcanoes, but we have already noted that in the cases of Mt Lamington and Mt Bezymianny no one knew that they actually *were* volcanoes. In other cases volcanoes which were thought to be extinct (Bandaisan, Japan, 1888; Tristan da Cunha, 1961) suddenly burst into life, so that in all these instances no predictions could be made. Of the remaining 760 active volcanoes known to science, only a handful are monitored sufficiently well to be useful in the field of volcanic prediction. Furthermore, apart from surveillance for purely scientific research, it is generally agreed that monitoring of volcanoes in sparsely populated zones is not worthwhile, for most hazard prediction is geared to the saving of life and property. Thus, only where a few notorious volcanoes lie in regions of high population density have there been serious attempts to establish observatories and other vulcanological research centres. For, make no mistake, like seismic forecasting, volcanic eruption prediction is expensive in terms of both equipment and manpower. Before looking at the detailed methods employed, however, let us look briefly at a recent case study where vulcanologists made a confident prediction of an impending eruption.

During the summer of 1976 the volcano of La Soufrière, on the West Indian island of Guadeloupe, began to exhibit signs of a major eruption. By 17 August it was belching forth *nuées ardentes* accompanied by severe earth tremors, so that bearing in mind the 1902 disaster of neighbouring Martinique, the vulcanologists, who had been observing the volcano over a period of time, ordered an evacuation of 70,000 people from the towns in the predicted hazard zone covering a radius of 10 kilometres. So certain were the scientists of the impending eruption that they went so far as to predict the magnitude of the explosion – equivalent to thirty million tonnes of T.N.T. or several atomic bombs. Despite the official evacuation some inhabitants were reluctant to leave and had to be evicted from the hazard zone. Imagine the embarrassment, therefore, when after a few final flashes and bangs La Soufrière ceased its eruption without a major explosion. This exemplifies the difficulties which face the scientist attempting to predict a natural disaster and highlights one of the reasons for the scepticism and the fatalism behind the attitudes of many of the local inhabitants.

Unless a volcano is monitored by sophisticated equipment it only remains possible to calculate a rough periodicity of future eruptions by a geological analysis of the products of its former eruptions. Nevertheless, this latter type of research has distinct advantages, for not only can the character and the volume of past eruptions be calculated (i.e. magnitude of lava flows, ash falls or *nuées ardentes*), but it also becomes possible to construct maps of potential hazard zones based on analogues. These maps illustrate that in addition to such obvious examples as Naples (Italy), Catania (Sicily), Bandung (Java), Basse-Terre (Guadeloupe), Georgetown (St Vincent) and Thera (Santorini) such unexpected places as Portland (U.S.A.), at the foot of Mt Hood, and Arequipa City (Peru), below El Misti, together with Moshi (Tanzania), overshadowed by Kilimanjaro, might well lie in future hazard zones. Some authorities have even suggested that Rome is within the reach of future volcanic activity, surrounded as it is by prehistoric pyroclastic-flow deposits. This sort of prediction really depends on a recognition of the length of the cycle of volcanic activity, for some volcanoes may exhibit a periodicity of a few thousand years, which means that there is no record of an eruption within historic time.

A much more precise degree of prediction will be achieved if instrumentation is introduced into the exercise, although these more sophisticated methods are generally used to complement the visual surveillance. One of the most commonly used instruments is the tilt-meter which is based on the principle of the spirit-level. It is known that in certain types of volcanic eruptions, the activity is preceded by a gradual upwarping of the surface, known as *tumescence*, quickly followed by a deflation of the swelling as the eruption gets under way. Perhaps the most remarkable record of a swelling of this type is that monitored by Japanese scientists in Hokkaido between 1943 and 1945, during the birth of a new volcano – Syowa Sin-Zan. An enormous tumescence lifted villages, roads and paddy fields to 50 metres above their former level, in a dome 4 kilometres across, before volcanic eruptions began. But the tilt-meter is sensitive enough to measure a warping much smaller than this, even one as little as one millimetre per kilometre. In some places, such as Hawaii and Japan, the introduction of laser-beam geodetic surveying techniques has brought the measurement of tumescence to a highly sophisticated level. These types of instrumentation enabled vulcanologists to make a remarkably accurate prediction of a lava eruption on the flank of Kilauea volcano in January 1960, even to forecasting the site at which the outburst would occur.

Much use is also made of the seismograph to detect volcanic earth tremors, which occur at much shallower depths than the deep-focus tectonic earthquakes noted in the previous chapter. During the period of tumescence, as magma ascends towards the surface, the frequency of the earth tremors is found to exhibit a marked increase. On the well-instrumented Kilauea volcano in Hawaii, for example, the frequency of shocks was seen to increase by a factor of fifty in the four weeks preceding an eruption in 1955. Other types of instrumental measurement include the use of magnetometers to measure changes in the magnetic field of some volcanoes, changes induced by magmatic heating of the surface rock strata from below. The same magma may also cause changes in the local gravitational field, fluctuations which may themselves be monitored by gravimeters. Finally, future methods of prediction may be extended by the use of instruments carried in the numerous satellites now circling the Earth; infra-red radiometers, for example, could measure widespread changes of thermal activity in volcanic regions, pin-pointing specific sites where ground survey could most usefully be carried out. In conclusion it has to be said, however, that none of the above methods is reliably predictive, with the notable exception of the tilt-meter measurements. Even the increasing frequency of tremors, recorded by seismographs, has not always led to an actual eruption, thus producing the embarrassment of a false alarm.

The ability to predict the location, the timing, the character and the magnitude of an eruption is simply to give warning of an impending hazard so that orderly evacuation may proceed. Once the eruption has started, however, the emphasis frequently swings away from concern about human life to a desire for preservation of property, crops, roads and railways, etc. It is at this stage that various methods of alleviating the damage from an eruption are appraised and finally implemented. It must be realized that since there is no chance of altering the violence of the eruption itself the only means left open to the threatened population is to divert the mud and/or lava flows or to halt them. In the case of pyroclastic falls and flows there is virtually nothing that can be done to mitigate the hazard, although strengthening of roof tops may prevent collapse from overloading by ash. To avoid widespread loss of life, evacuation may be essential, even if material damage cannot be prevented. During the eruption of Mt Usu, North Japan, in August 1977, for example, more than 10,000 residents and countless numbers of tourists were evacuated from the thriving holiday resort of Toyako Onsen. The hazard in this instance was tephra fall-out, which affected some 120 towns and cities and caused damage of £32 million.

There is a lengthy historical record of attempts to prevent lava flows from damaging property in places as far afield as Italy, Japan and Iceland. This has usually taken the form of throwing up earthen embankments in order to deflect the lava streams, but this method has met with only limited success. More than three hundred years ago, in order to protect their city from Mt Etna's lava streams, the people of Catania increased the height of the city walls – all to no avail, it seems, since the flow of 1669 overtopped the walls and destroyed the city. An interesting attempt to divert one of the 1669 flows had previously been tried when the flank of the flow itself had been artificially breached, allowing a new tongue of lava to escape laterally, thus releasing the pressure on the main flow heading for Catania. Working on similar assumptions, i.e., that breaking the walls of the lava flow would dissipate its energy into several subsidiary streams, modern vulcanologists in Hawaii arranged for aircraft to bomb a lava flow which threatened the city of Hilo in 1935. Within thirty hours of the bombing the flow ceased altogether, but whether this was coincidental remained to be proved. Reasonable proof came in 1942 when a similar bombing mission was carried out on another threatening flow in the same location. Since the results were comparable, there is reason to believe that artificial breaking of the lava 'skin' dissipates the energy of the flow. One of the most recent attempts to halt a lava flow was that at the Icelandic town of Vestmannaeyjar during the 1973 eruption of Helgafell volcano. Here millions of litres of sea water were pumped on to various parts of the lava flow in an attempt to slow it by chilling and solidifying the 'skin'. Following some two weeks of continuous hosing of the snout the lava temperature was reduced from over 1,000°C to less than 100°C, at which point the lava ceased to steam and 'coagulation' stemmed the flow. This was the first time that such a method had ever been attempted and the results were quite spectacular.

The final method of alleviation from volcanic hazards concerns the danger of mudflows which, like lava flows, can sometimes be diverted by artificial barriers and channels. On occasion, however, the magnitude of the flow is such that these sorts of preventive measures are futile, as was the case in the Kelut mudflow (Java) in 1919, referred to on p. 97. In this instance a crater lake was the villain of the piece, leading to catastrophic mudflows at fairly frequent intervals. The remedial measures included the excavation of numerous drainage channels through the crater wall to enable the lake waters to escape slowly instead of suddenly, as the lake refilled following an eruption. For thirty years the suite of tunnels appeared to have successfully solved the problem but a 1951 eruption damaged the tunnels, reducing their efficiency quite considerably. Despite scientific warnings that a new set of tunnels was required no effective action was taken so that an eruption of 1966 caused a series of catastrophic mudflows once more, killing hundreds of unsuspecting villagers.

4. Sinking Coastlines

Referring to the River Thames in London, Samuel Pepys wrote in his famous diary on 7 December 1663: 'There was last night the greatest tide that ever was remembered in England to have been in this River all Whitehall having been drowned.' On a different occasion it was Pepys who commented on the presence of hazel nuts in a peat layer, which had been exposed some metres below sea level during the excavation of Tilbury docks in the seventeenth century. Both observations suggest that the landsurface around the Thames estuary is probably sinking in relation to the level of the ocean, although three hundred years ago it was not possible to prove conclusively whether it was as a result of a sinking landmass or a rising sea level.

The scientists of the seventeenth century, whilst searching for more rational explanations of earth history, were still dominated by biblical teachings so that all rock structures and landforms were seen as products of the Flood in Genesis. Thomas Burnet, for example, saw the Flood as a catastrophe occurring when the sun's rays cracked the shell of our egg-like globe, thus allowing a deluge of water to escape from a central abyss. His contemporary, John Woodward, saw the emerging flood waters carrying off all the rocks, minerals, flora and fauna, before finally depositing them in stratigraphic, fossiliferous layers of mud, peat, rock, etc., after God had relented and allowed the waters to subside. With almost unbelievable authority biblical scholars of that time dated the biblical Flood as 2348 B.C., whilst no less a personage than the Vice Chancellor of Cambridge University categorically stated in 1654 that the Earth was created on the 26 October 4004 B.C. at 9 o'clock in the morning! Even as late as the nineteenth century some of the leading English geologists were still clinging to the ideas of a biblical Flood in order. . . 'to explain the phenomena of diluvian action which are universally presented to us, and which are unintelligible without recourse to a deluge exerting its ravages at a period not more ancient than that announced in the Book of Genesis.'[1]

Not surprisingly, if the church leaders and the scientists of earlier centuries were in such close accord it is little wonder that the numerous legends of great coastal inundations and of drowned kingdoms have persisted in British literature. Almost every stretch of coastline in the British Isles is associated with stories of catastrophic sea floods in which countless hectares of land had been lost beneath the ocean waves in times gone by. Foremost among the tales is the Legend of Lyonesse which relates to the sea area between Land's End and the Isles of Scilly, but which was once reputed to have been a land of great fertility with prosperous towns and no less than one hundred and forty churches. Even though it is difficult to substantiate such a claim it is noteworthy that modern archaeologists and geologists are agreed that in the neighbouring Isles of Scilly, lines of prehistoric field walls are now submerged beneath the ocean. Equally, there seems little doubt that the notorious reefs of the near-by Severn Stones (on which the Torrey Canyon oil tanker precipitated a different kind of disaster) were once an island in their own right. The 'lost Welsh kingdom' of Cantref-y-Gwaelod in Cardigan Bay provides another example of such a legend, but when we have there the associated evidence of submerged coastal peats (former land surfaces) and tidal inundation of prehistoric earthworks we are forced to pause and reconsider the facts. Could it be possible that such legends are based on stories of actual marine incursions in the not-too-far-distant past? To answer such a question it will first be necessary to understand the mechanisms involved in the fluctuation of land and sea levels.

Variations in land and sea level

At the outset it is important to distinguish between those cases where coastal losses are due to wearing away of the land by marine waves and those instances where there has been an actual change of level – in which the sea has risen or the land has subsided. There are many examples along the Holderness coast of Yorkshire, for example, where villages have been lost simply by cliff retreat resulting from marine erosion. We shall return to this phenomenon in Chapter 7, but at the moment only vertical changes of level will be examined. We have already noted the difficulty of determining to which cause the change of level is due, for a rise of sea level or a subsidence of the land will produce the same end-product. So too will a lowering of sea level or an elevation of the land. But one clue is furnished by the fact that in general a progressive fluctuation of sea level will affect all ocean margins equally; a tectonic change of land level, on the other hand, is rarely uniform over long distances, with some tracts rising or falling more than others. Such

Fig. 28. Temple of Serapis, Pozzuoli, Italy showing evidence of fluctuating land surface.

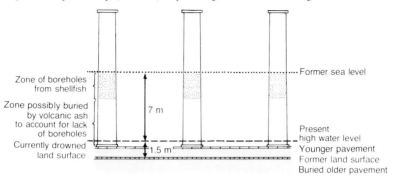

tectonic differences are known as crustal warping, and this may be upon a local scale, covering a small area of a few kilometres, or it may involve widespread continental margins or ocean basins.

One of the most famous examples of local change of land level is provided by the so-called Temple of Serapis at Pozzuoli on the Gulf of Naples. Here, there is evidence of a landsurface oscillation of some 8 metres (from 1.5 metres above to 7 metres below sea level) after the building was constructed in Roman times (Figure 28). In 1832 the eminent geologist Charles Lyell described this changing level at Pozzuoli, illustrating the way in which the boring of numerous holes in the columns by inter-tidal shellfish had facilitated the measurement of a fluctuating sea level. But since other classical monuments along the Italian coastline show no comparable evidence of submergence, it has been suggested that Pozzuoli was elevated and depressed by crustal warping probably connected with the volcanic activity of the neighbouring Phlegrian Fields and Vesuvius. To what extent such an oscillation was catastrophic is not on record.

A much more widespread change of level has been recorded around the shores of the Baltic Sea. Early in the eighteenth century the scientist Celsius concluded that the waters of this land-locked sea were slowly falling. His critics pointed out, however, that if this were so, why had the ancient port of Danzig continued to function unhindered for over seven hundred years? Long-term measurements around the Baltic coasts vindicated the observations of Celsius, but since the southern shorelines have remained virtually static and those in Finland and Sweden (i.e. around the Gulf of Bosnia) have exhibited steady uplift, this was clearly a case of regional land elevation. Stockholm, for example, was found to have been rising at about half a metre per century, coastlines farther north at twice that rate, whilst those in southern Sweden rose at only about half that rate. Consequently many of the Swedish and Finnish coastlands are composed of uplifted beach shingle, in places elevated to 275 metres above present sea level (Figure 29). Similar 'raised beaches', as they are termed, have been recognized in northern Britain and Ireland, with the Scottish examples being especially well known, particularly those in the Hebridean isles of Jura and Islay.

Fig. 29. Crustal uplift in Scandinavia due to removal of Pleistocene ice-sheet loading (after R. A. Daly), N.B. Contours are in metres.

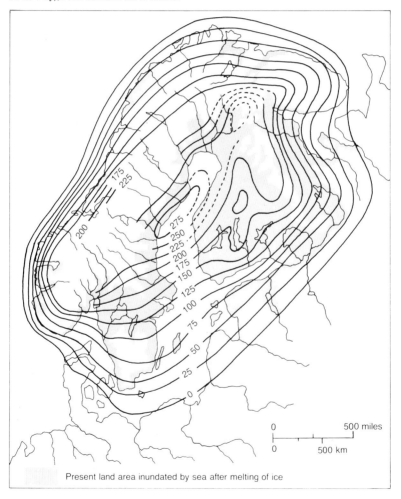

Present land area inundated by sea after melting of ice

Before investigating the reasons for these widespread crustal upwarps it is important to realize that in an area midway between the raised shorelines of Scandinavia and those of northern Britain there lies the basin of the North Sea and the adjacent Low Countries of Holland and Belgium. In this region a very contrasting coastal scene is encountered, for instead of raised beaches the countryside is famous for its polderland which is little more than reclaimed sea floor at an elevation below mean sea level. The Low Countries have a long history of coastal inundation and their inhabitants still continue to wage a constant war against the encroachment of the North Sea. Much of their land has been reclaimed from coastal marshland and has had to be carefully drained and embanked before it could be utilized as farmland. Like the English Fenlands on the other side of the North Sea, these low coastal tracts of Holland and Flanders are hazard zones, as far as coastal flooding is concerned, for they flank a basin of land subsidence, a basin wherein the North Sea floor is slowly sinking. In prehistoric times, for instance, the Dogger Bank was dry land, judging by the flint tools and other artifacts occasionally dredged up in the nets of fishing trawlers. Thus we can deduce that some nine thousand years B.P. (Before Present) early man lived on what is now the floor of the North Sea, although his former hunting grounds currently lie beneath some 35 metres of sea water. Part of this submergence has resulted from a positive rise in sea level, a rise which is known to have inundated the coastal tract of Flanders some six thousand years ago and which has been termed the Flandrian Transgression. But some of the submergence can be attributed to a crustal downwarping of the land, a tectonic subsidence which has been underway for many millions of years.

It is now time to explain the mechanisms which result in crustal warping of the type described above and to introduce the concepts of *isostasy* and *glacio-eustasy*.

In Chapter 2 we have already noted that the earth's structure is made up of three main units: the core, the mantle and the crust, and it is the latter, the relatively thin crustal layer, with which we are primarily concerned. Geophysical studies have demonstrated that the crust is probably composed of two parts – the upper layer, termed *sial*, of broadly granitic composition, and the underlying layer, termed *sima*, of basaltic composition. The sial is thought to be rigid and to possess considerable strength, whereas the underlying sima is thought to be denser, hotter and of lesser strength and rigidity. Experiments carried out since the eighteenth century have enabled scientists to postulate that beneath the deep oceans, such as the Pacific, sima is exposed on the sea floor, because the sial is missing, whereas the sial not only forms the continents but thickens considerably beneath the high mountain masses. One such experiment was carried out in 1855 by Sir George Airy (Figure 30a) who floated a series of wooden blocks of differing dimensions in water, noting that they protruded at varying heights above the surface consistent with the dimensions of the individual blocks. If we regard the blocks as sial 'floating' in sima (the water) we have a rough analogy with the concept of *isostasy*, a term introduced by C. E. Dutton in 1899. In this model we see that there is a state of isostatic balance maintained between topographical masses and the underlying supporting material. If we now examine Figure 30b, we shall see why geologists talk about a large mountain range, such as the Himalayas, having 'roots', because the elastic resistance of the crust is so small that any extra load added to it, such as a mountain mass, pushes it down until the load becomes balanced by the upward pressure of the underlying material.

Fig. 30. The principles of Isostasy. (a) Sir George Airy's model of wooden blocks floating in water; (b) idealized section of the earth's crust, showing continents 'floating' isostatically in sima.

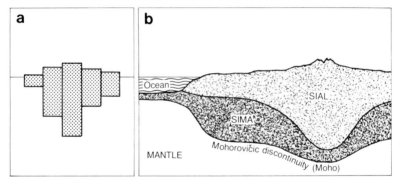

Those regions of the earth which exhibit the characteristics of Figure 30b are said to be in a state of *isostatic equilibrium*, but studies have shown that in some areas such geophysical concepts are not borne out. Instead we are faced with narrow zones of *isostatic inequilibrium*, such as that which underlies the plains of the Indian Ganges, where a down-buckling of the crust is not compensated by a mountain range. Here, a great weight of lighter density siallic material is pushing down into the denser sima, largely as a result of the accumulation of overlying sedimentary material being constantly deposited by rivers at the foot of the Himalayas, as this vast mountain range is eroded. In other words this transference of load from one place to another tends to upset the isostatic equilibrium, which must be restored by the 'flow' in the underlying sima from regions of increasing load to those of diminishing load. Thus, as the crust is downwarped beneath the Ganges plain, so the Himalayan range becomes isostatically uplifted. In certain regions of the world, however, the topographic contrast between the downwarped and upwarped zones is not as marked as in the Himalayas. Such is the case in the North Sea basin which we shall examine in more detail below. Here is a smaller area of inequilibrium, with the down-buckling a result of lengthy periods of sediment deposition throughout the last two hundred million years of geological time, but where there is currently no major flanking mountain mass.

Having outlined the principles of *isostasy* it will be easier to understand the concept of *glacio-eustasy*. In this instance the load which induces the downwarping is not a basin of sedimentary material but an excessively thick ice-sheet, similar in magnitude to that of the present Greenland ice-cap. During the Pleistocene Ice Age (which terminated some ten thousand years ago) many of the northern fringes of Eur-Asia and North America were covered by ice-sheets several kilometres in thickness. One such ice-mass was centred in Labrador, another in Scandinavia; a third, of smaller dimensions, had its centre in western Scotland. It hardly needs emphasizing that the water which was 'locked up' in the ice-sheets became temporarily abstracted from the hydrological cycle (see p. 253), since it failed to return to the oceans. Consequently there was a worldwide lowering of sea level during the Ice Age, which meant that in some areas former shallow sea floors became dry land. This may well have been the case in Cardigan Bay, the Scilly Isles and parts of the North Sea (see p. 109). Such a lowering of sea level is termed a *glacio-eustatic* lowering. But at the same time the weight of the neighbouring ice-caps caused parts of the adjoining continental crust to be downwarped due to *isostatic* depression.

As the ice-sheets began to melt at the close of the Pleistocene Period so the crustal loading would gradually decrease, although some ice-caps are still persisting. The results were twofold: first, there was a eustatic rise of sea level throughout the world as water returned to the oceans, and secondly, there came a gradual isostatic uplift of the land which had been glaciated – an uplift so slow that it is continuing today in some places. The areas where the ice had been thickest exhibited the greatest degree of uplift, but those zones beyond the limits of the former ice-sheets showed no isostatic recoil and therefore became slowly drowned by the rising sea level. We can now begin to understand why Scotland, Labrador and Scandinavia (see Figure 29) have raised strandlines. In areas far removed from the former ice-centres, however, the post-glacial rise of sea level gradually overwhelmed low-lying coastlands – the Flandrian Transgression (p. 109), which, at its maximum some eight thousand to nine thousand years ago, exhibited a rise of sea level at a rate of 5 to 6 millimetres per year. Even in modern times the accelerated melting of glaciers between 1900 and 1950 was accompanied by a eustatic rise of 1.2 millimetres per year. We are now in a position to examine the first of our case studies, that of the North Sea basin, for in its southern half the remorseless but slow post-glacial rise of sea level is being exacerbated by the equally slow but irresistible isostatic crustal sinking due to sediment loading. The combination of these forces has meant that such cities as London and Rotterdam are now in serious danger of coastal flooding, especially when extreme meteorological and tidal conditions coincide, as they did in 1953.

The North Sea basin

Some seven million years ago the North Sea began to assume something of the outline with which we are now familiar. This was the geological period termed the Pliocene, which immediately preceded that of the Pleistocene Ice Age, and which witnessed the gradual accumulation of sediments, known as the Crags, in the slowly evolving basin. In England the sedimentary rocks belonging to the Pliocene and early Pleistocene periods are found only in East Anglia, stretching along the coastal fringes from Cromer (Norfolk) to Walton (Essex). The Crags are little more than loosely cemented shell banks, interspersed with current-bedded sands, and are thought to have been formed largely beneath a shallow sea into which a massive delta belonging to the combined Rhine-Thames drainage systems had formed. Here, then, was the major source of the latest mass of sediments which was to continue the long-term history of subsidence in the southern half of the North Sea basin, a subsidence which appears to be continuing even today.

Geophysical surveys and boreholes have shown that the ancient surface upon which the Crags were deposited exhibits a marked downward tilt along the perimeter of the North Sea downwarp (Figure 31). Thus, the buried sub-Pliocene floor to the north-east of London stands at an elevation of about 30 metres *above* sea level at Ipswich, but at neighbouring Lowestoft it has already plunged to a depth of 60 metres *below* sea level. In the Netherlands this downwarping along the edge of the North Sea basin is even more marked for the sub-Pliocene floor declines northwards from about sea level along the Belgian border to 365 metres below sea level at Utrecht. This sudden structural downturn along the edges of the North Sea basin implies an isostatic instability in these zones which may manifest itself by occasional

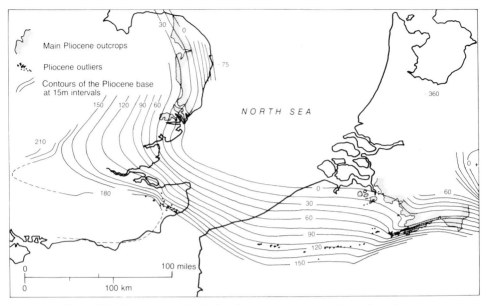

Fig. 31. The downwarping of the land surface around the southern North Sea in the last seven million years (after S. W. Wooldridge and D. L. Linton).

faulting and slumping of the submarine sediments – a possible explanation of the remarkable Colchester earthquake (see p. 65) in what is generally regarded as an earthquake-free area.

Studies of the fossil marine shells within the Crags have enabled geologists to draw up a record of progressive climatic deterioration during the latter phases of the Pliocene Period. The growth of the Pleistocene ice-sheets was soon to follow, setting in train the complex series of isostatic and glacio-eustatic movements outlined above (pp. 109–111). The outcome of the Ice Age in Britain has left, amongst other things, a marked isostatic recovery in western Scotland and a slow rise of world sea level at an average rate of between 1 and 2 millimetres per year. Taking both movements into account it is possible to construct a tentative map, based on geodetic levelling and studies of tide-gauge data, which suggests that, whilst north-western Britain is still rising, the south-eastern corner is experiencing a gradual submergence (Figure 32). If we add to this the effects of the slow tectonic subsidence of the North Sea basin we can begin to realize the seriousness of the long-term effects, for the likelihood of serious coastal flooding will increase as time goes on.

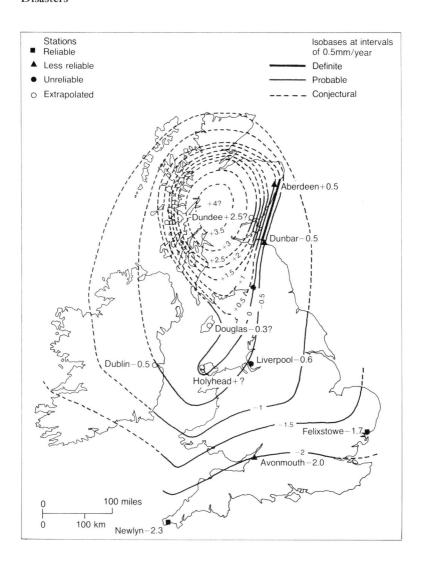

Fig. 32. Present vertical movements of the British Isles in relation to mean sea level, showing the relative uplift in the North and relative subsidence in the South (after H. Valentin). N.B. The true crustal movement can be obtained by adding the current sea-level rise of about 1 mm/year. Thus, land within the − 1 mm isobase is rising.

Inundations of the coastlands in south-east England and the Netherlands are commonplace in historical records and it has recently been demonstrated how a storm surge in 1287 flooded medieval peat workings to form the Norfolk Broads. Moreover, the peat beds which Samuel Pepys saw in the Thames estuary are now known to have been formed at sea level some six thousand five hundred years ago and, like those of similar age in the Humber and the Rhine delta, have now subsided to depths of some 6 metres below sea level.

Following centuries of sporadic flood activity, the overtopping of the East Anglian sea defences in November 1897 finally spurred the British Government into action for, although no lives were lost, many coastal farmers were ruined and many farmlands became permanently abandoned. The outcome was the very belated Royal Commission on Coastal Erosion and Reclamation of Tidal Lands, which concluded in 1906 that either these coastal tracts were sinking or that the tides were higher. But even at this late date very little action was taken and the maintenance of sea embankments remained almost entirely the responsibility of private landowners. Then, on the night of 6–7 January 1928, a particularly high tide overtopped the Thames Embankment in London and drowned fourteen people in basement flats of Westminster, Fulham and Hammersmith (Plate 12). The tide was almost half a metre higher than anything previously recorded in the Thames estuary and both the Government and the general public were at last alerted to the dangers of tidal flooding. Research was inaugurated jointly by the Tidal Institute and the Meteorological Office in an attempt to understand the reasons behind the 'storm surge', as it was now termed, for both in 1897 and 1928 an occurrence of a high 'spring' tide together with a deep atmospheric depression centred over the North Sea had combined to cause a pile-up of sea water along the east coast of Britain. Shortly afterwards a systematic survey of the state of the dykes and sea walls in East Anglia showed that some two thirds of them were dilapidated and in need of repair and in 1930 the costs of maintaining these embankments were moved partly out of private hands and onto the local rates. But it was not only the sea walls which were at risk for in February 1938 the coastal dunes at Horsey in Norfolk were breached by storm waves, allowing the sea to overflow several thousand hectares of farmland around the Norfolk Broads. Again no lives were lost but the night of reckoning was now approaching.

At noon on Thursday 29 January 1953, a typical atmospheric depression was reported by Britain's Atlantic weather ships to be slow-moving midway between Iceland and the Azores. A small current of warm air broke away from it, quickly followed by a mass of cold air – thus was 'Low Z' formed on

12. One of the houses where several people were drowned in the London borough of Westminster, when the Thames burst its banks during the storm surge of January 1928.

the Atlantic weather chart. This was to be the villain of the piece, for it continued to deepen all through Friday 30 January at the remarkable rate of 10 millibars every two hours. By early on Saturday 31 January, it was centred over the Orkneys with a central pressure of 968 millibars – one of the deepest depressions ever recorded in Britain. A strong ridge of high pressure had already begun to build over the Atlantic, thus creating a remarkably steep 'pressure gradient' which generated unprecedented hurricane force northerly winds straight into the North Sea (Figure 33). The average wind

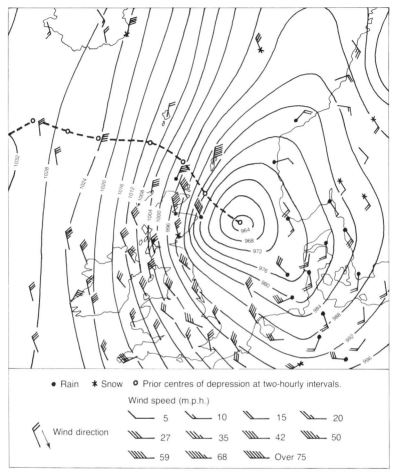

Fig. 33. Weather chart for 31 January 1953 during the disastrous North Sea coastal floods.
N.B. Windspeeds are in m.p.h.

speed measured in the Orkneys between 09.30 and 10.30 on 31 January was
144 kilometres per hour (90 m.p.h.) with gusts of up to 200 kilometres per
hour (125 m.p.h.). Off the Hebrides two merchant ships sank and the
Ullapool trawler fleet dragged its anchors and was blown ashore in Loch
Broom. Altogether, 28 per cent of the entire Scottish fishing fleet was lost
that day, but the most tragic loss of life at sea was the British Rail car ferry,
the Princess Victoria, which foundered in the North Channel en route from
Stranraer to Larne, with 132 deaths.

The effect of this hurricane was to build up a gigantic bank of water which drove southwards into the bottleneck of the North Sea, coinciding as it did with a predicted spring tide of 3 metres above normal. The storm surge, however, had forced an extra 4 billion cubic metres (m^3) of Atlantic water into the North Sea, thus adding a further 2.5 metres to this tidal figure. So great was the rise of water that many of the east-coast tide gauges in Britain were destroyed, and the waves began to tear remorselessly at the natural protections of the shingle banks and sand dunes, to say nothing of the artificial defences. The catalogue of death and destruction soon began to unfold from Yorkshire to Kent: the shingle spit of Spurn Head was the first to be breached, followed by the Lincolnshire coastal dunes, causing 2-metre floods in Sutton-on-Sea, Boston and Mablethorpe. The embankments around The Wash were not breached but overtopped, drowning fifteen people in King's Lynn and another sixty-five between there and Hunstanton. Because the tide reached its zenith during the night and the wind had destroyed many telephone lines, there were virtually no warnings passed on from Lincolnshire and Norfolk to Suffolk and Essex until it was too late, and these were the counties which were to bear the brunt of the disaster.

By late on Saturday night, Felixstowe, Harwich and Maldon were flooded, with tragic loss of life, and by midnight the tide had overtopped the majority of the sea defences in Essex, including those of Canvey Island whose 11,500 inhabitants lived entirely below spring-tide level. It is not surprising, therefore, that the majority of the British casualties occurred here (fifty-eight drowned) after the sea walls collapsed at 01.00 hours on Sunday, 1 February (Plate 13). But the disaster was just as severe elsewhere in Essex for the sea rose almost 1 metre in fifteen minutes at Jaywick housing estate in Clacton, drowning thirty-five people – some 5 per cent of its population. The catastrophe cannot be measured only in terms of the fatalities, however, since the flooding affected large areas of the Thames estuary's major industrial complex which is located in a zone from Southend through Tilbury to London's dockland. Here the oil refineries of Thames Haven, the cement works, factories, gasworks and electricity generating stations were inundated and brought to a standstill. On the Kentish side of the estuary the damage was also severe: the B.P. oil refinery on the Isle of Grain was flooded, as was the Naval Dockyard at Sheerness, where two ships were sunk; the Margate lighthouse was destroyed; the so-called 'Isle' of Thanet lost all its road and rail links as it became insular again. When 100 metres of sea wall collapsed in London's East End, some 1,100 houses were flooded as 640,000 cubic metres (142 million gallons) of Thames water flowed into the streets of West Ham. On the other side of the river the Embankment was

13. Most of the British casualties of the 1953 North Sea flood disaster occurred in Canvey Island, Essex. Note the breaches in the sea walls (bottom).

overtopped between London Bridge and Greenwich Pier, but in central London the tidal surge halted at the very brink of the Embankment between Westminster and Chelsea, since the river flow was low after a dry spell. This was the highest tide ever recorded in London (almost 2 metres above the predicted level) and a major disaster was averted by a matter of only a few centimetres.

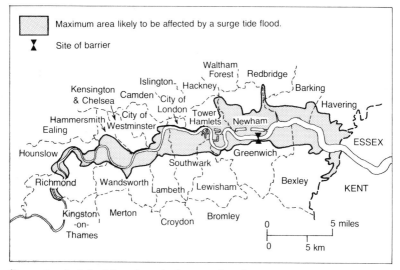

Fig. 34. London's flood-hazard zone in the event of a major storm surge.

In 1976, in his novel *Deluge*, Richard Doyle postulated what the effects of a somewhat greater storm surge would be on the London of 1977 and his predictions make frightening reading, since they cannot be far from reality. His belief is that 150 square kilometres (60 square miles) would be inundated (Figure 34), putting one and a half million people at risk in homes and offices. The water would probably flood six hospitals, fifteen power stations, fifty-six telecommunications buildings and, most fearsome of all, some seventy underground stations, where the carnage would be frightful. The associated hazards of sewage pollution, power station and gas explosions, together with fire perils are all chronicled in chilling detail, leading to a postulated death toll of over 100,000.

In fact London came within a hairsbreadth of such a disaster during the night of 12–13 January 1978 when a storm surge generated by 130 kilometres per hour winds coincided with a period of high North Sea tides. The synoptic conditions were an almost exact replica of those which produced the 1953 storm surge, but by now the East Coast sea defences were stronger, the early warnings more efficient and the evacuation more disciplined. Thus the loss of life from flooding was restricted to one person despite the exceptionally high costs of the damage (estimated at £20 million). The piers at Skegness, Hunstanton and Margate were destroyed and thousands of homes inundated by 1-metre deep floodwaters in King's Lynn, Wisbech and Cleethorpes. The stricken town of Cleethorpes was suffering its second bout of tidal flooding within a year, for the little publicized storm surge of January 1976 was if anything slightly higher on the Lincolnshire coast than that of 1953. In the Thames estuary the 1978 flood tide rose to within half a metre of the top of the sea walls, which had been increased in height only four years previously. For the first time since they were built in 1972 the enormous steel and rubber floodgates, constructed by order of the Greater London Council, were closed to seal off the five major London docks. Staff at London's flood emergency centres went on full alert and at one stage Londoners were warned by a series of T.V. flashes that the Thames was in danger of bursting its banks. The increasing frequency of tidal flooding in eastern England within the last few decades highlights the necessity of a Thames Flood Barrier to protect Britain's capital city. Until this is completed (see p. 131) Londoners are being given warnings of the flood dangers, notably by means of hazard maps posted not only in the city's Underground stations but also in some of British Rail's main commuter stations outside the capital.

14. An artist's impression of the completed Thames Flood Barrier.

Were an inundation, on the scale envisaged by Doyle, to occur there seems little doubt that the Thames would revert to its ancient channels, many of which, such as that at Deptford, are now covered by London's streets. Professor Steers, in tracing the changes of London's river since Roman times, highlights how some of the well known districts of Central London were little more than islands (termed 'eyots') at that time, similar to the modern Chiswick Eyot and Eel Pie Eyot:

> We need only mention Putney, Chelsea (Chesil or Shingle Island), Battersea (St Peter's Island) and Westminster (Thorney Island). The Isle of Dogs was then, and for some centuries later, a more or less isolated mudbank.[2]

In conclusion it is noteworthy that the landsurface of Roman London has now subsided by almost 5 metres.

On the eastern shores of the North Sea, the 1953 storm surge created even more chaos, for we have already noted the greater vulnerability of the Netherlands. Here the nation's history is written:

> . . . in terms of the endless struggle against the sea, as the tale of gains of land and losses of land, of dyke building and dyke breaches, of inundation and reclamation.[3]

During the last hundred and fifty years, for example, five major coastal floods have occurred, with Zeeland being particularly badly affected in 1906, followed in 1916 by the over-running of 60,000 hectares of agricultural land around the Zuider Zee. This last disaster was instrumental in the formulation of plans to close off the Zuider Zee from the North Sea by the construction of a phenomenal enclosing dyke – the famous Afsluitdjik between Friesland and Noord Holland. But whilst giving greater protection to the polderland of the northern Netherlands the Afsluitdjik has increased the area of land below normal high-tide level to almost 50 per cent of the entire Dutch homeland, a hazard region occupied by no less than six million people.

In the south of the country, no such protective measures were taken, certainly not on the scale of the Afsluitdjik Here a gigantic delta has been formed from the combined estuaries of the Rhine, Maas and Schelde, thus creating the complex mosaic of islands, channels, mudbanks and marshes of Zuid Holland and Zeeland (Figure 35). In this area several engineering studies had been undertaken in the 1930s, first to improve the shipping lanes of the Dutch waterways, but later to investigate the hazards of coastal flooding. In almost all instances it was found that the dykes were not high enough for the empirically predicted flood levels of the next half century. The implementation of remedial measures was held up during the Second World War and only in the early 1950s was attention turned again to the

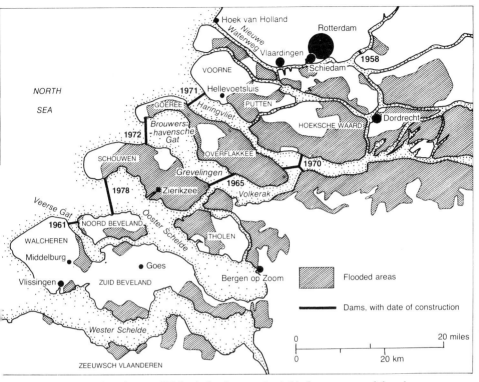

Fig. 35. The Delta area of Holland, showing areas flooded in January 1953 and the subsequent remedial measures.

vulnerable lands of the delta. But it was too late, for the 1953 storm surge caused the tide to exceed all previous heights and to achieve the extreme water level that was not expected to occur until the year 2000.

An examination of Figure 35 will illustrate the extent of the flooding but it will not convey the full horrors of the disaster. The area ravaged by the sea contained a population of 580,000, of whom 1,800 lost their lives and 65,000 were evacuated. In addition, some 50,000 head of livestock were lost and 133,000 hectares of agricultural land inundated. All the islands of the delta suffered to some degree, and some, like Schouwen and Goeree-Overflakkee, were virtually obliterated. Many houses were destroyed in the towns which were completely inundated (Plate 15) whilst the extensive oil refineries and port industries around Rotterdam were severely hit. Even the coastal dunes were insufficient to protect the well-known holiday resorts along the North Sea beaches from the waves and high winds generated by the hurricane. Sea-front hotels from Zandvoort to Scheveningen were severely battered but fortunately the Hondsbossche sea wall, which protects Noord Holland, withstood the enormous pressure as did the main dykes of the Delfland district. Had these been breached the seawaters would have put a further three million people at risk and would have advanced as far as Amsterdam. As it was, the damage was enormous, for of the 1,100 kilometres of dykes more than 500 kilometres were damaged, with sixty-seven major gaps and five hundred smaller breaches. In addition 2,600 homes were destroyed and 50,000 damaged, leading to an overall disaster cost of over £100 million (Plate 16).

15. Many of the houses in the Dutch village of Kortgene (Noord Beveland) were destroyed by the 1953 flood disaster, during the North Sea storm surge.

16. The damage and heart-breaking losses in the wake of the Dutch coastal floods of 1953 are graphically summarized in this picture of a Dutch household.

Venice

The setting of Venice, amidst the coastal marshes and sand spits at the head of the Adriatic Sea, is similar in many ways to that of the Low Countries. Instead of the North Sea basin we have the Plain of Lombardy underlain by an enormous thickness of geologically youthful sediments; in place of the delta complex of the Rhine, Maas and Schelde, Venice is situated a few kilometres to the north of the combined deltas of the Po, Adige and Brenta; replacing the famous dykes of Holland are the great Venetian sea-walls, termed Murazzi, completed in 1782, although no part of the Venetian urban area is below mean sea level, as is the case in Holland. A final comparison with the Netherlands is exemplified by the extensive land reclamation schemes in the famous Venetian Lagoon. Here, in an effort to provide economic stability for the area, three large industrial zones have been constructed during the latter part of the twentieth century on areas won back from the sea by artificial filling (Figure 36). Not surprisingly the introduction of new land areas, vastly greater in size than the historic nucleus, has had serious repercussions on the local hydrology and crustal stability, to say nothing of the atmospheric pollution which they have generated. Widespread coastal flooding has been periodically recorded in the long history of Venice, but nothing to compare with the inundation which occurred on 4 November 1966, the same date on which Florence was devastated by the Arno river floods (see pp. 248–9). On that fateful day the waters of the Adriatic overflowed the city to a record depth of almost 2 metres and in doing so severely damaged the sea defences (Plate 17). Such a catastrophe merely highlighted that this cultural treasure-house is in severe danger of gradual destruction – not a cataclysmic disaster but a slow and inexorable one. In order to explain the reasons for this sad state of affairs it will be necessary to trace the history of this coastal zone.

On a greatly reduced scale the Plain of Lombardy is analogous to that of the Ganges, with the Alps replacing the Himalayas as the fringing mountain chain. Thus the isostatic principles outlined on page 110 are manifest in northern Italy also, albeit with an order of magnitude different from that of the Indian example. Thus, since Miocene times material eroded from the Alps has been carried by rivers (and latterly by glaciers) down to the Lombardy lowlands, there to be dumped as a series of enormous *piedmont* fans (the type-site for this depositional landform). Isostatic instability has been operative in the Lombardy basin for several million years as the enormous weight of alluvial sediments has caused a marked crustal down-warp along the axis of the basin and into the delta itself (Figure 37). Never-

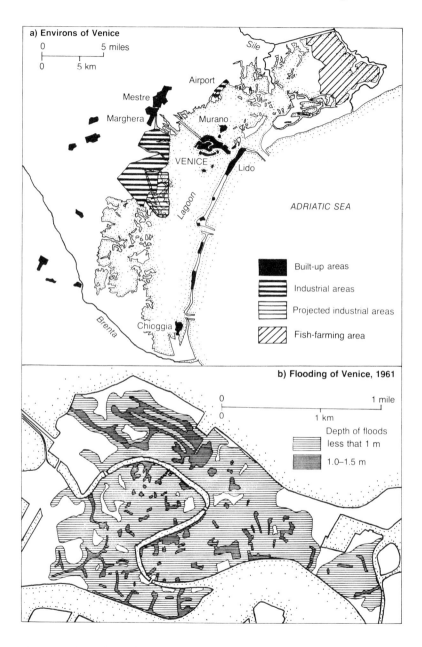

a) Environs of Venice

0   5 miles

0   5 km

Sile

Airport

Mestre

Marghera   Murano

VENICE   Lido

Lagoon

ADRIATIC SEA

Built-up areas

Industrial areas

Projected industrial areas

Fish-farming area

Brenta

Chioggia

b) Flooding of Venice, 1961

0   1 mile

0   1 km

Depth of floods
less that 1 m

1.0–1.5 m

Fig. 36. (a) The Environs of Venice (b) Flooding of Venice, 1961.

theless a very delicate physical balance came to be achieved, where the effects of the long-term crustal sinking were to a large extent offset by the systematic removal of silt by the river channels and a slight but critical raising of the landsurface by the gradual build-up of mudbanks in the delta region at the head of the Adriatic. Thus was created the well-known coastline

17. The historic buildings of Venice were deeply inundated by floodwaters when the level of the Lagoon rose to unprecedented heights in November 1966.

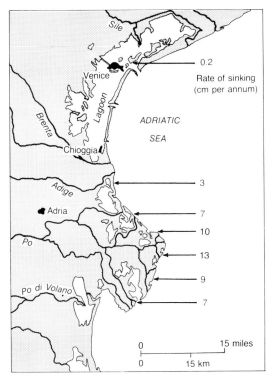

Fig. 37. Rates of coastal sinking around the Po delta, Italy (after H. W. Menard).

of protecting sandbars, such as the Lido, fashioned by the waves of the Adriatic, behind which lay the sheltered waters of the Lagoon and its cluster of islands (Figure 36). But two factors have combined to upset the delicate balance: first, the influence of the worldwide rise of sea level following the melting of the Pleistocene ice-sheets (see p. 110); secondly, the influence of man-made structures which, above all, have turned the magnificent City of the Doges into a major hazard area.

The glacio-eustatic rise of sea level (1–2 millimetres per year) has been graphically illustrated by the recent discovery of an ancient Roman coastal resort, now located beneath the waters of the Adriatic some 9 kilometres offshore. As in the case of the North Sea, the Adriatic too has its storm surges, during which periodic high tides are pushed northwards into the Gulf of Venice by strong 'sirocco' winds. Of greater consequence, however, has been the enormous weight of masonry which has slowly accumulated on the islands over the centuries, for this burden is now much greater than the original wooden foundations were intended to support. Furthermore, because the silting-up of the river channels was beginning to threaten their economic prosperity, the early Venetians diverted the River Brenta and the River Sile around the perimeter of the Lagoon (Figure 36). What had not been realized was that by so doing they had cut off the supply of silt which had till then renewed the deltaic mudflats and to some extent offset the gradual settlement of the existing sediments; once the supply had ceased the sinking of the city became more marked over the succeeding centuries.

Several other factors have been responsible for the gradual decay in the city's fabric, including the constant wetting and rotting of the stone and brickwork of the ground floors due to the increasing periodicity of sea flooding. This has not been helped by the neglect of the sea defences and the erosion caused by the wash of high-speed modern motor boats – the traditional gondola never created such problems. Above all, the abstraction of water by the neighbouring industrial districts during the last few decades has led to an accelerated crustal subsidence and this, more than anything, has put Venice in dire peril.

The newly constructed industrial zones of Marghera on the neighbouring mainland shore of the Lagoon have generated a voracious demand for water, both for cooling and other purposes. Such requirements have been met not by the construction of pipe lines from elsewhere but by the sinking of thousands of artesian wells into the deep water-bearing sands of the deltaic sediments. Water abstraction on this sort of scale has caused a lowering of the water-table by an average of 10 metres during the twentieth century. This in turn has led to a compaction of the sediments themselves and to an accelerated sinking of the landsurface, reaching a rate of 10 millimetres per year in the worst affected parts of the Lagoon. In addition, to facilitate the passage of merchant shipping through the shallow Lagoon to the industrial wharves, new deepwater channels have been excavated. The increased tidal scour which has resulted has removed large quantities of silt from the islands and exposed the city's ancient foundations to increased erosion from both tides and the wake of passing craft.

In summary, if we combine the various factors of a glacio-eustatic rise of sea level, ground-water abstraction, tectonic downwarping and compaction of sediments, removal of silt and neglect of sea defences, it is not difficult to predict that unless swift remedial measures are undertaken the magnificent piazzas, palaces and churches of Venice are doomed. Calculations have shown that in the seventy years since the turn of the century Venetian sea level has risen more than 20 centimetres, so that every high tide becomes more menacing than the last. On 30 October 1976, almost ten years to the day after Venice's worst flood, the city was engulfed again (see Plate 17), underlining the fact that in the last decade no fundamental action has been taken.

Remedial Measures

To combat the problems posed by sinking coastlines calls for massive feats of technological ingenuity and enormous capital outlay. When the hazard zone is as extensive as that of the Netherlands there is no alternative except to implement lengthy programmes of coastal protection and hydraulic engineering, since permanent evacuation and relocation of the population is unthinkable. The same philosophy is true in the case of London and its coastal flood hazards but here, somewhat surprisingly, there has been an apparent reluctance to take major remedial action until the 1970s. It is probably true, however, that hardly any of London's citizens think of themselves as living in a hazard zone. Equally, the majority of Venetians see the periodic inundations of their island city as little more than a nuisance. Nevertheless, the population drift from Venice to the mainland has accelerated in recent years – no less than 33 per cent of the Venetian residents left the city between 1951 and 1971, with their main reason for leaving being stated as 'inconvenience', according to a U.N.E.S.C.O. report. This was not only the inconvenience of continuing to live in a crumbling and unhealthy city but that of mounting unemployment, lack of amenity and of incentive. Above all there is an increasing feeling of frustration tinged with despair among those Venetians who remain, for there appears to be a reluctance by the Italian Government to tackle the enormous job of rehabilitation. Despite a gigantic $500 million 'Venice Loan' raised by international bankers in 1973, no fundamental action has yet been taken, whilst some authorities state that the loan was immediately used by the Italian Government to reduce a heavy deficit in the country's balance of payments.

Financial problems have also been uppermost in the minds of the Treasury officials of the British Government, when faced with the funding of measures to prevent the future flooding of London. Finally convinced that drastic remedial action had to be taken, the Greater London Council have agreed to the building of a massive storm-surge barrier, which is now being installed in the tidal waters of the Thames at Woolwich (see Plate 14). Construction commenced in 1974 at an estimated cost of £54 million, but inflation and labour disputes had already escalated the estimate to

£360 million by 1976 and this figure is expected to rise to £441 million before the scheduled completion date in 1981. The Thames Barrier has been designed to allow the passage of shipping through to London Docks, so that it is not simply a solid wall of steel. Large concrete islands have been constructed in midstream and these will house the hydraulic machinery to power the enormous steel sluices and gates, some of which are being constructed in Teeside factories. Not surprisingly the contractors are an Anglo-Dutch consortium, for the engineers from the Netherlands have unsurpassed expertise in this type of venture. In fact the overall design of the Thames Barrier is based largely on the dams which are being systematically installed in the estuaries of the vulnerable countryside of south Holland.

In contrast to the British scheme on the Thames estuary, which has received surprisingly little publicity, the coastal defence project of the Dutch Delta Plan has been highlighted as a model of unparalleled achievement in the world of hydraulic engineering. After its approval in 1957, a mere four years after the disastrous storm surge of 1953, the Delta Plan was implemented and will ultimately provide for four major barriers at the Veerse Gat, the Oosterschelde, the Brouwershavense Gat and the Haringvliet (see Figure 35). In addition, before the estuaries could be closed, three secondary dams had first to be built, namely the Zandkreek Dam, the Grevelingen Dam and the Volkerak Dam (Figure 35), in order to separate the estuaries from each other. Of these barriers and dams only that of the Oosterschelde remains uncompleted and that is expected to be operative by 1978–79. It will be noted that of the Dutch flood hazard areas no provision has been made for barriers across the Westerschelde or the Nieuwe Waterweg (the southern and northern estuaries of the delta respectively), because of interference with shipping entering the ports of Antwerp and Rotterdam. Nevertheless these vulnerable areas have not been ignored and their sea walls have been raised in height where necessary. Similarly, in the Thames estuary, outside the Barrier the sea defences have been considerably strengthened.

To a much greater extent than the Thames Barrier the Delta dams must make due allowance for the navigational interests of river traffic farther upstream, for it must not be forgotten that water levels in the delta are critical to shipping on the Rhine, one of Europe's greatest inland waterways. Thus the Haringvliet Dam has been constructed with very large flood sluices not only to serve as outlets for the excess waters of both the Waal and Maas (the Dutch names for the Rhine and Meuse) but also to maintain optimum water levels for Rhine barges farther upstream.

Turning finally to the coastal flooding problems of Venice we find that the

Italian Government announced in September 1975 an international competition for a suitable flood-control plan. In essence this really involves discovering a method of closing the three entrances to the Lagoon whilst maintaining shipping access to the industrial districts. If the Lagoon were ultimately to be closed-off during flood alerts, this would create a 2-metre difference in water levels between the Adriatic and the Lagoon itself, which would entail major reinforcement of the sea walls on the Lido and the other protecting sandbars. But the problem posed by the design of the barriers is the one which is causing the greatest concern, for no construction work has yet been started. One proposed design necessitates a sluice-gate system for the shallow entrances and a series of caissons for the deepwater channel. The caissons (enormous hollow metal tanks) would normally be submerged to allow the passage of shipping, but could be raised by compressed air to form a flood barrier when storm surges were forecast in the Adriatic.

Alongside the plans for closing off the Lagoon it has been realized that other remedial measures must also be taken if Venice is to be saved. The first of these has been a complete ban on the abstraction of groundwater for industrial purposes in the vicinity of Venice. The results were immediate, for measurements have shown a gradual return of the water-table to former levels in the Venetian artesian wells. Such a rise in groundwater pressure suggests that the settlement rate of the sediments will be reduced ultimately from the 5 millimetres per year figures of the 1960s to that of 1 millimetre per year, which largely represents the degree of crustal downwarping due to isostasy and which is impossible to stop. By banning ground-water abstraction it has been necessary to plan to bring industrial water to the Marghera complex by means of lengthy pipelines from outlying districts. Other necessities include the reinforcement of the foundations of many of Venice's buildings, some of which will need to be jacked up in order to bring them back to a level above the high waters of the Lagoon. Furthermore, a complete new sewage system will have to be installed, since the closing of the Lagoon entrances will mean that the tidal scouring and removal of the city's waste from its historic canals will be seriously curtailed.

In conclusion it is important not to forget the problems faced by the Japanese along the sinking coastline of Tokyo Bay. Although most of the land subsidence here has resulted from groundwater abstraction, no less than 115 square kilometres of eastern Tokyo have now sunk below sea level. For centuries the area has suffered periodic inundation from exceptionally high tides, despite its tidal embankments. The record high tide of 1917 in Tokyo Bay, for example, was associated with a very severe typhoon, but the Tokyo Metropolitan Authorities were slow to heed the warning, largely because the city's land subsidence was not discovered until 1924, as a result of a precise geodetic levelling programme following the Kwanto earthquake of 1923. The catastrophic typhoon of 1959, however, galvanized the Tokyo officials into action for they noted how the city of Nagoya, some 240 kilometres away, had lost almost two thousand lives when a 5-metre storm-surge tide had swept over the harbour defences. Thus, in 1963 a major building programme of substantial tidal embankments, giant flood gates and pumping stations was implemented in the Koto Delta district of Tokyo's built-up area. In the first four years following their completion the flood gates were closed against predicted typhoonal storm surges on no less than thirty-five occasions!

Part Three

Surface Instability

5. Landslides and Avalanches

Movement of material downslope, in response to gravity, is often thought to be one of the most dangerous of the world's natural hazards because of its rapidity and lack of warning. Of the other geological hazards, with the notable exception of the *nuée ardente* (p. 78), only earthquakes strike with such rapid violence and without forewarning.

Strictly speaking, a landslide can be defined as a downslope movement of material which has become separated from the underlying static part of the slope by a plane of separation usually referred to as the *slip surface*. In this respect the term 'avalanche' could be regarded as a type of landslide, although its use is generally reserved for describing the downslope movement of ice and snow *en masse*.

A considerable amount of research has been undertaken by geologists, glaciologists and civil engineers in an endeavour to ascertain in advance the proneness of slopes to collapse (i.e. predictive studies) and also to develop methods of controlling slope stability (i.e. corrective and preventive studies). Nevertheless, the chronicles of history are littered with references to catastrophic events resulting from landslides and avalanches (see Figure 38). Even a cursory glance at this list of disasters is sufficient to illustrate the considerable death-toll from this cause but it fails to convey the enormous costs of the damage. During the winter of 1950–51, for example, when avalanches caused between six hundred and seven hundred fatalities in the European Alps, Switzerland alone suffered damage estimated at £2.2 million and was faced with a further expenditure of £1.25 million related to remedial measures. In Austria the sums were £1.75 million and £1 million, respectively. Although these bald statistics may give some measure of the loss of livestock, the cost of rehabilitating agricultural and forest land and the outlay on new housing, communications, power lines, etc., they cannot convey the cost in human suffering or the horror of the disaster itself.

The world's most horrendous disaster relating to a sudden downslope movement of material was caused in part by an ice-avalanche and in part by

Fig. 38. List of the World's major landslide and avalanche disasters.

Date	Location	Character	Comments	Deaths
218 B.C.	European Alps	Avalanches	Hannibal's army	c. 18,000
1478 A.D.	St Gothard Pass, Alps	Avalanches	Swiss Troops	60
1499	St Bernard Pass, Alps	Avalanches	French Troops	100
1499	Ofen Pass, Alps	Avalanches	Austrian Troops	400
1512	Biasco, Alps	Landslide	Temporary lake burst	>600
1518	Leukerbad, Switzerland	Avalanche		61
1556	Hsian, Shensi, China	Landslides	Earthquake triggered	c. 1 million
1584	Yvorne, Switzerland	Landslide		>300
1598	Graubunden, Switzerland	Avalanche		>100
1648	Göteborg, Sweden	Landslide	Quickclays	85
1689	Saas, Switzerland	Avalanche		57
1689	Montafon Valley, Austria	Avalanche		>300
1718	Leukerbad, Switzerland	Avalanche		55
1720	Obergesteln, Switzerland	Avalanche		88
1720	Rueras, Switzerland	Avalanche		100
1720	Brig, Switzerland	Avalanche		40
1806	Goldau, Switzerland	Rock slide	14 million m³ volume	457
1881	Elm, Switzerland	Rockfall	10 million m³ volume	115
1885	Alta, Utah, U.S.A.	Avalanche		16
1892	Haute-Savoie, France	Icefall, Mudflow		150
1893	Vaerdalen, Norway	Rockfall, Landslide	55 million m³ volume	111
1902	Telluride, Colo., U.S.A.	Avalanche		19
1903	Frank, Alberta, Canada	Rockfall		70
1910	Wellington, Wash., U.S.A.	Avalanche	Two trains swept away	96
1910	Rogers Pass, B.C., Canada	Avalanche		62
1911	Usoy, Pamir Mts. Russia	Landslide	Earthquake triggered	54
1915	Brittania Mine, B.C., Canada	Avalanche		57
1916	Marmolada, Dolomites, Italy	Avalanches	Italian & Austrian troops	253
1916–18	Dolomites, Italy	Avalanches	Italian & Austrian troops	c. 40,000
1920	Kansu, China	Landslides	Earthquake triggered	c. 200,000
1926	Bingham Canyon, Utah, U.S.A.	Avalanche		40
1936	Loen, Norway	Rockfall into fjord	'Tsunami' flood wave	73
1941	Huaraz, Peru	Avalanche & Mudflow		7,000

1951	Andermatt, Switzerland	Avalanche		20
1951	Vals, Switzerland	Avalanche		11
1951	Airolo, Switzerland	Avalanche		10
1954	Vorarlberg, Austria	Avalanches		125
1956	Santos, Brazil	Landslides		> 100
1959	Madison Canyon, Montana, U.S.A.	Landslide	Earthquake triggered	26
1962	Mt Huascaran, Peru	Ice Avalanche & Mudflow	13 million m³ volume	c. 4,000
1963	Vaiont Dam, Italy	Landslide	250 million m³. Subsequent flood	c. 2,000
1965	Mattmark, Switzerland	Ice Fall	1 million m³ volume	88
1965	Camp Leduc, British Columbia, Canada	Avalanche		27
1966	Rio de Janeiro, Brazil	Landslides	Shanty towns	279
1966	Hong Kong	Landslides		64
1966	Aberfan, South Wales, U.K.	Debris flow	Colliery waste tip	144
1967	E. Switzerland	Avalanches		23
1970	Mt Huascaran, Peru	Ice & Rockfall, Debris flow	Earthquake triggered	25,000
1971	St Jean-Vianney, Quebec, Canada	Landslide	Quickclays	31
1971	Certj-Sacarimb, Romania	Mudslide	Mining village	45
1972	Hong Kong	Landslides		> 80
1972	W. Virginia, U.S.A.	Landslide & Mudflow	Mining waste tip	400
1974	Mayunmarca, Peru	Rockslide and Debris flow	1,000 million m³ volume	450
1976	Pahire-Phedi, Nepal	Landslide		150
1976	Hong Kong	Landslide		22
1977	Göteborg, Sweden	Landslide	40 houses destroyed	8
1978	Col des Mosses, Switzerland	Avalanche	Ski lift overwhelmed	c. 60
1978	Myoko Kogen Machi, Japan	Mudflow	Ski resort overwhelmed	12

a rockfall. It occurred in the high mountains of Peru on 31 May 1970 when one of the strongest earthquake shocks on record triggered off a collapse of the summit ice-cap on the lofty north peak of Huascaran (6,654 metres). Thousands of tonnes of rocks were displaced by the falling ice and as these crashed down into the glacier-filled basin below the summit, a gigantic debris flow was generated. Travelling at a speed of over 320 kilometres per hour this mass of snow, rock and pulverized ice burst out through the narrow gorge below the glacier and roared down-valley as an unstoppable surge. As it crossed the glacial moraines it scooped up vast quantities of

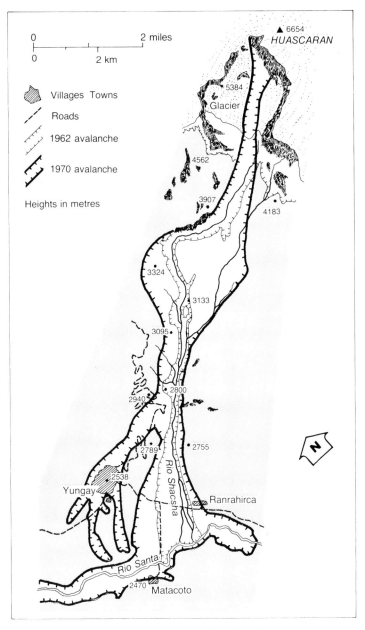

Fig. 39. Map to illustrate the Mt Huascaran disasters in 1962 and 1970.

finer-grained material and by the time it reached the meltwater stream of the Rio Shacsha it had changed into a mudflow more than 1 kilometre in width. The increased fluidity and the tremendous energy of this phenomenal debris flow were capable of moving gigantic boulders – individual rocks were afterwards measured at 15 cubic metres (bigger than an average house) – so it is not surprising to find that no obstacle was able to stand in the path of this terrible wave of destruction. Within a few minutes the wave had plunged the 15 kilometres down the fertile valley of the Rio Shacsha to the point where it joined the larger trunk valley of the Rio Santa (Figure 39).

This was not the first occasion that a devastating mudflow had swept down the Rio Shacsha valley, for in 1962 the small town of Ranrahirca had narrowly escaped destruction. Nevertheless four thousand people died in the devastated valley in the 1962 disaster (Figure 39). Few inhabitants believed that there would be a repetition of this terrible event, but in fact the 1970 catastrophe proved to be of an even greater magnitude, both in its area of destruction and in its death-toll. Not only were Ranrahirca and neighbouring Matacoto partly overrun but the large town of Yungay was completely obliterated (Figure 39).

In the annals of natural disasters there are very few instances when settlements of the size of Yungay have been wiped off the map. One can think of Herculaneum and Pompeii in the Vesuvian eruption of 79 A.D., the town of Longarone in the Vaiont Dam disaster of 1963, or St Pierre in the Martinique volcanic catastrophe of 1902, but in each of these cases some of the buildings survived – at Yungay there was no evidence that this flourishing ski-resort had ever existed, for it was buried under millions of tonnes of mud and rock (Plate 18a and 18b). Indeed, two members of the visiting United Nations investigation team said that the destruction was

. . . almost unbelievable, possibly surpassing in magnitude such catastrophic events as the Mount Pelée eruption of 1902 on the island of Martinique, and the eruption of Vesuvius in A.D. 79 that buried the city of Pompeii.[1]

Ironically the only part of Yungay to escape was Cemetery Hill, on whose small eminence ninety-two people saved their lives by running to the hill top. But since the debris flow reached Yungay in less than four minutes, it is not surprising that so few of its inhabitants survived. In total the Huascaran disaster claimed 25,000 victims. The most vivid eye-witness account of the rapid debris flow came from a Peruvian geophysicist:

The crest of the wave had a curl, like a huge breaker coming in from the ocean. I estimated the wave to be at least 80 metres high. I observed hundreds of people in Yungay running in all directions and many of them towards Cemetery Hill. All the while, there was a continuous loud roar and rumble. I reached the upper level of the

18. (a) The Huascaran avalanche and debris flow of 1970 obliterated the Peruvian towns of Ranrahirca and Yungay.

(b) Cemetery Hill in Yungay was severely damaged by the earthquake which triggered the 1970 avalanche, but since it stood above the debris flow it proved to be a haven for ninety-two survivors.

cemetery near the top just as the debris flow struck the base of the hill and I was probably only 10 seconds ahead of it . . . It was the most horrible thing I have ever experienced and I will never forget it.[2]

The foregoing account of the Huascaran disaster highlights the rapidity of the movement, although it must be appreciated that catastrophic events which take place on slopes need not necessarily be rapid. The gradual down-slope movements of both property and lines of communication, even if unaccompanied by loss of life, may be equally catastrophic in terms of their long-term economic consequences. The notable British example of the slippage of the M6 motorway at Walton's Wood, Staffordshire, England, during the construction phase, not only held up the completion date, but also incurred considerable excess expenditure related to the remedial measures. Consequently the slow but inexorable 'creep' type of phenomenon is usually included in any classification of landslides, although for the purposes of the present chapter we shall only briefly examine the outcome of such gradual events. In the main we shall concentrate on the more rapid phenomena of rock-falls, landslips, earth and debris flows, together with the separate circumstances of the avalanche. Before turning to an examination of each of these features in detail, however, it is important to explain some of the fundamental mechanisms involved in the field of slope instability.

In the first instance we have to distinguish between *soil* and *rock* for these two materials exhibit entirely different types of behaviour, leading to a distinction being made between the disciplines of 'soil mechanics' and 'rock mechanics'. An understanding of the character of the soil or rock components is of the utmost importance for it is upon such factors as the particle size, the porosity and the degree of jointing that the *cohesion* of the material will depend. It is well known that particular soils or rocks are more prone to landslipping than others (see p. 147). If *stresses* are brought to bear on these materials, either generated naturally by frost, rainstorms or seismic events or generated artificially by human interference such as quarrying, then material changes will ultimately take place. If the stress is relatively small the response may only be of an 'elastic' fashion; greater stress, however, will lead to eventual fracture, when a discontinuity appears in the material and 'failure' is said to have occurred. Thus, civil engineers introduce the term rock and soil 'strength' and speak of the *'tensile strength'* and *'shearing strength'* of materials, which differ markedly according to the various rock and soil types involved. In addition to the inherent qualities of the materials themselves, it is equally important to have some knowledge of the slope character, especially its normal angle, as well as of the type and magnitude of the stress involved. All these critical factors are illustrated in Figure 40a, which shows the geometry of a soil slope and the development of a potential plane of sliding or *'slip surface'*. If the other relevant factors are known – viz. the shearing strength, the stress, the cohesion and the angle of internal friction – it becomes possible to demonstrate empirically the critical height at which the slope will 'fail' along the potential slip surface as the stress is increased, and to trace the collapse of the potentially unstable slice A.B.C. shown in Figure 40a. In many instances, however, the potential slip surface is curvilinear, not planar, so that the geometry is considerably more complicated (Figure 40b). This type of slope failure produces a landslide which is characterized by a rotational movement around the centre of gravity and hence is frequently referred to as a rotational slip (Figure 40c). In soils and rocks containing complex patterns of joint planes there may be a combination of both planar and rotational slips.

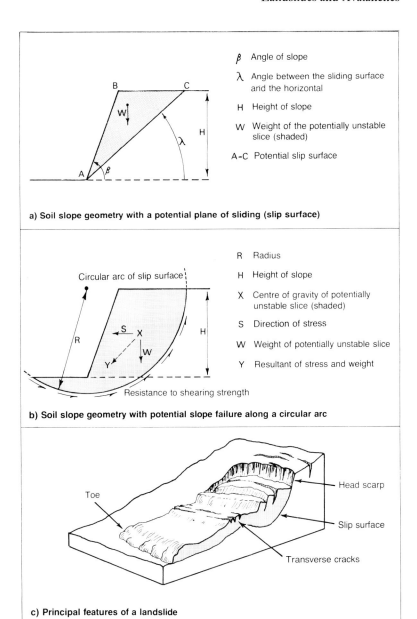

a) Soil slope geometry with a potential plane of sliding (slip surface)

β   Angle of slope

λ   Angle between the sliding surface and the horizontal

H   Height of slope

W   Weight of the potentially unstable slice (shaded)

A–C   Potential slip surface

b) Soil slope geometry with potential slope failure along a circular arc

R   Radius

H   Height of slope

X   Centre of gravity of potentially unstable slice (shaded)

S   Direction of stress

W   Weight of potentially unstable slice

Y   Resultant of stress and weight

Circular arc of slip surface

Resistance to shearing strength

c) Principal features of a landslide

Toe

Head scarp

Slip surface

Transverse cracks

Fig. 40. The mechanisms of slope failure: (a) Soil-slope geometry with a potential plane of sliding (slip surface); (b) Soil-slope geometry with potential slope failure along a circular arc; (c) Principal features of a landslide.

A further important factor to be examined in our study of landslide mechanisms relates to that of the so-called '*pore pressure*'. In the majority of soils spaces occur between the individual grains and these are referred to as 'pores' or 'voids'. As far as rocks are concerned the pore spaces may be linear fissures or cracks. Simple experiments enable us to show that if, on the one hand, the pores are moisture free, i.e. filled only with highly compressible air, then the application of external pressure on the soil or rock will cause a volume change in the mass. The soil grains or rock fragments will be pressed more tightly together and will at the outset become stronger. If, on the other hand, the pores are saturated with water, external pressure will meet considerable resistance from the incompressible water content and the pore pressure will increase accordingly. If there is no means of escape to a region of low pore pressures in the soil or rock mass, the introduction of an external *shearing stress*, such as an earthquake, can lead to distortion of the mass, when the solid grains tend to move by slipping over each other. Continued shearing stress will ultimately lead to 'failure' along a slip surface, at which point the mass of material will move bodily in the direction of least resistance – on a slope this will be outwards and gravitationally downwards. Thus, as pore pressures fluctuate according to groundwater conditions, they are seen to play a significant role in the ability of a soil or a rock mass to withstand suddenly imposed stresses such as earthquakes. As pore-pressure changes take place unseen, many of the world's catastrophic landslides occur unexpectedly, since the build-up to the critical point of failure takes place without any surface manifestation.

We have already noted that slope failure can be caused by the introduction of natural stresses, but it can also be induced by abnormal loading. In many instances interference by mankind creates this type of instability as, for instance, when buildings or large quantities of earth are placed at or near the top of slopes. The excessive loading will immediately cause an increase in pore pressures and will lead to potential slope failure. Landslide tendencies on formerly stable slopes may also be initiated when the normal drainage pattern of the surrounding area is changed, either by weather fluctuations or by man's activities. One of the most notable examples of such a change is that which caused the horrifying disaster at Aberfan, South Wales, in October 1966, when a colliery spoil heap slipped, following decades of tipping across the spring-line of the valley slopes (see p. 161). Even the seemingly harmless introduction of artificial watering of gardens in a formerly semi-arid environment is thought to have exacerbated slope instability in some of the Los Angeles suburbs (Chapter 11). Two further factors which have to be taken into account when examining potential slope instability also relate to human interference. One is the alteration of the slope gradient by quarrying or other earth removal; the other relates to removal of vegetation, which not only has a binding effect on the soils but also helps to maintain a balanced groundwater regime.

A final word is necessary on the effect of earthquake vibrations on certain types of soils. It has already been shown how increased loading will build up pore pressures, whilst we now discover that experiments have further demonstrated how intermittent or cyclic loading (similar to the pulsatory vibrations of earthquake waves) leads to incremental increases in pore pressure. In certain soils this rise of pore pressure will eventually exceed a critical threshold, at which point the soil is said to have suddenly *liquefied*. Liquefaction of soil, when the material assumes the characteristics of a dense liquid rather than those of a solid, will only occur in certain soil types: coarse grained, freely draining gravels and sands will not usually liquefy during an earthquake; nor will silts and most clays which are too cohesive and whose particles will become more closely bonded; medium to fine-grained sands and certain sensitive clays, however, are particularly prone to liquefaction during seismic stress (see below, p. 159). Slope instability due to lique-faction caused a great deal of the damage inflicted during the Alaskan earthquake of 1964 (see p. 51) and also during the Japanese earthquake at Niigata in the same year (see p. 56).

Having discussed the fundamental mechanisms of slope instability, it is now possible to examine more fully certain case studies to illustrate the four categories of slope movements which often cause disasters. First, there are the rockfalls and rockslides which often occur along predisposed joint and bedding planes. Secondly, the landslips and slumps which result from instability in clayey rocks (clays, marls, etc.) will be examined. Thirdly, we shall describe slope movements in superficial deposits and finally turn our attention to the special case of snow avalanches.

Rockfalls and Rockslides

The annihilation of the Peruvian town of Yungay and its neighbouring villages by the gigantic landslide and debris flow from the near-by peak of Huascaran in May 1970 is thought to have been initiated by massive falls of rock and ice from the upper slopes, triggered off by earthquake shocks. Internal stresses must already have prepared the rock mass to the point of failure and the additional external seismic stress was sufficient to cause a rock fall, which is no more than a simple gravitational response. It remains

Disasters

possible that the internal stresses may have been imposed by the overloading created by the burden of the summit ice-cap of Huascaran, but the joint pattern and disposition of the rock-bedding planes may also have led to potential instability.

Anyone who has visited glaciated valleys or rocky coastlines may have noted that, where the bedding planes are not far removed from the horizontal, the mountain precipices and sea cliffs are capable of standing vertically to very great heights. In many instances, however, the bedding planes are not horizontal and in certain cases may tilt or dip downwards and outwards towards the valley or cliff foot. Such locations are notorious hazard zones and rockfalls or rockslides are commonplace in all the world's high fold-mountain ranges such as the Himalayas, Andes, Rockies and Alps, particularly where frost-shattering is one of the dominant geomorphological processes. These types of areas are characterized by naturally unstable slopes, but where there is a record of human interference the hazard may be considerably increased. At Goldau, in Switzerland, for example, the steeply dipping rock strata of the Rossberg peak were always potentially unstable and in 1806 they 'failed' of their own accord, sweeping an enormous mass of sandstone and conglomerate onto the unsuspecting village and burying 457 people (Figure 41). By contrast, at Elm, also in Switzerland, the disaster of

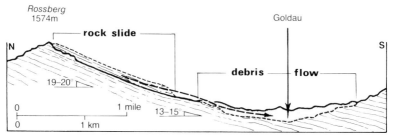

Fig. 41. The Goldau landslide, Switzerland (1806) (after A. Heim).

1881 was induced by man. Because of its steeply sloping valley walls, oversteepened by former glaciers, the village stood in a potential hazard zone in any event, but by systematically removing the slate from the valley side the quarry workers gradually undermined the upper cliffs and provoked a spectacular series of rockfalls. During a period of some twenty minutes more than 10 million cubic metres of rocks collapsed, burying an area of 90 hectares, killing 115 inhabitants and running as a debris flow 100 metres up the opposite slope of the valley.

148

19. A gigantic rockslide (a) caused the waters of the Vaiont Reservoir to overflow the retaining dam (b) in October 1963. Towns in the Piave valley (foreground) were completely destroyed as the wall of water swept out of the gorge.

Perhaps one of the greatest follies of mankind, as far as landslides are concerned, is illustrated by the Vaiont Dam disaster in the Italian Alps in 1963 (Plate 19). Here, despite the manifestly unstable bedding planes of the surrounding rocks (as shown by former landslide evidence), a large dam was constructed to impound a sizeable reservoir. Gaping fissures in the slopes above the reservoir suggested that new landslides were imminent and that these might be induced by a seismic shock. Whatever the ultimate cause, on 9 October 1963 a massive rockslide, estimated at 260 million cubic metres in volume, crashed into the reservoir to create a water wave 100 metres in height which overflowed the dam and drowned almost two thousand people in the Piave valley below (Figure 42). Deaths from drowning, connected indirectly

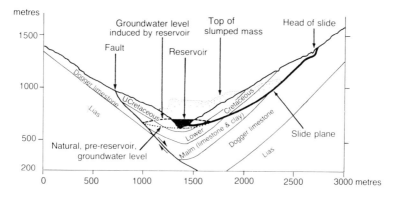

Fig. 42. The Vaiont landslide of northern Italy (1963) which caused the disastrous flooding of the Piave valley.

with a rockfall into water, also featured in the Leon disaster in Norway in 1936. In this case 1 million cubic metres of rock fell into the Nordfjord, generating a water wave 75 metres in height which claimed seventy-three victims. Drowning disasters of this sort can also occur long after the land-slide has taken place, as witness the 1893 rockfall which blocked the head-waters of the Ganges in a Himalayan valley, thus forming an ephemeral lake. The following year the temporary 'dam' collapsed and allowed the flood-waters to devastate the upper Ganges valley. In 1911 another rockfall, this time in the Pamir Mountains, caused a similar lake to form which claimed fifty-four lives at Usoy in the Bartanga river valley. There have been many other instances of large rockfalls in central Asia, described by Russian scientists, many of them having been triggered off by earthquakes. The most massive rockslide on record, however, occurred as recently as April 1974 in the Peruvian Andes, in which several villages were buried and 450 people lost their lives. This disaster at Mayunmarca, in the Mantaro valley, occurred when a great mass of sandstones and marls slid along bedding planes from the crest of a steep slope. The volume of the rockslide has been calculated at 1,000 million cubic metres and since it descended a vertical distance of 1,500 metres in less than four minutes its estimated velocity of

120–140 kilometres per hour will give some idea of the rapidity of the catastrophe. A temporary lake was impounded, but by the time it overflowed, the population had been evacuated, so that further casualties were avoided.

One of the best chronicled rockfalls in the present century is that which occurred at the coal-mining town of Frank, Alberta, Canada, in 1903. The account of the disaster, published by the Geological Survey of Canada, was the first comprehensive investigation of a man-induced landslide. In their official report the geologists emphasized that 'Of the various causes which were responsible for the big slide there can be no question but that mining of the coal was a prime one.'[3] Although the bedding planes of the Turtle Mountain rock strata dip *away* from the mining valley and at first glance appear to present no hazard, the joint pattern trends steeply *towards* the valley, virtually parallel with the slope gradient itself. If one adds to this the generally weak nature of the underlying limestones and shales, it is little wonder that human interference precipitated a catastrophe. Coal mining at the foot of the valley side not only removed some of the supporting rocks but altered the groundwater characteristics of the overlying rocks by changing their drainage attributes. The resulting rockfall of 1903 partly buried the town of Frank, killed seventy people, and so oversteepened the valley wall that an even more dangerous rockfall has been predicted which could have even graver consequences:

A [further] larger slide would cut off all railway communication and close the mines west of Frank. It might permanently close the pass. The town of Frank would be wiped out with a fearful toll of life. These are some of the risks that are being taken by tampering with the foundation of this mountain. It was unsafe to do what has recently been done in the way of mining. This was pointed out before this work was started and the present unfavourable condition of Turtle mountain as compared to that of last year shows that the opinion then expressed was well founded. No further mining of the seams near the base of Turtle mountain can safely be done.[4]

To date, this predicted rockfall has not occurred, but it seems to be only a matter of time.

Landslips in Clayey Rocks (Slumps)

A distinction has already been made between the behaviour of solid rocks and of soils, when affected by loading and stress. We have noted that in most instances the rockfalls and rockslides described above have taken place along pre-existing bedding planes, jointing patterns or lines of fracture. When we turn to an examination of landslides in clays, marls and clayey shales, however, it will be seen how movement occurs mainly along newly initiated slip surfaces within the clayey rocks themselves, rather than along pre-existing bedding planes or joints, although there are a few instances where the disposition of the clay beds causes landslides to descend along simple slide surfaces within the rock strata.

In the majority of cases landslides in clayey rocks exhibit mechanisms similar to those which cause slips in superficial materials (such as glacial drift or mining waste) and in soils (see below). Once the shear strength of unconsolidated or poorly consolidated clayey rocks is surpassed, curvilinear slip surfaces will form on the slope, down which large slices of material, known as slumps, will descend at varying speeds. Since the slip surface is curved, the movement becomes a rotational one, as illustrated in Figure 40c, and as the transverse cracks are gradually filled with water the slope equilibrium becomes further disturbed. It is when the 'tongue' of the flow becomes waterlogged that it takes on the character of an earth flow or debris flow, and it is this increased fluidity which increases the magnitude of the hazard because of its greater mobility (see below).

The addition of rainwater or groundwater to clays and clayey rocks serves not only to affect their pore pressures but also to lubricate the slip surfaces. Thus many records of catastrophic landslips make reference to periods of increased rainfall or interference with the groundwater flow. In Portland, Oregon, for example, the landslides which affected the city zoo showed a marked relationship between periods of excessive rainfall and renewed sliding movements. In this example there was no disastrous loss of life, unlike the following case studies of Rio de Janeiro and Hong Kong, where rainfall-triggered landslides took a severe toll.

The prosperous city of Rio de Janeiro, located in a relatively cramped position between the precipitous slopes of its 'sugar loaf' mountains, has witnessed the undignified spectacle of its growing population being forced to build their shanty towns on the steep, unstable hillsides at the city boundaries. In January and March 1966 the heaviest recorded rainfall in the city's history triggered off catastrophic landslides (Plate 20), killing 239 people in the first episode and almost destroying the hillside shanty town of Petropolis (death toll – forty) on the second occasion. A similar situation has developed on the over-crowded island of Hong Kong where population pressure is just as great as that of Rio de Janeiro. In August 1976, following a tropical cyclone which released more than 500 millimetres (20 inches) of rainfall on Hong Kong in two days – the heaviest downpour for fifty years – a series of landslips killed twenty-two, injured sixty-five and left thousands homeless. Since this was a repetition of a similar disaster which claimed more

20. A landslip destroyed a large section of the Rio de Janciro–Sao Paulo highway during heavy rainstorms in January 1966.

21. (a) A 1972 landslide in Hong Kong claimed more than seventy lives when a high-rise block of flats was swept away.

(b) A 1977 photograph shows the site of the 1972 slide and the artificial terraces which were constructed to prevent further slope failure.

than eighty lives in 1972 (Plates 21a and 21b) the Hong Kong Government set up a special inquiry in the hope of avoiding a further catastrophe on this scale. This is a good example of very belated action, for in 1966 landslides had claimed sixty-four lives and caused the evacuation of over eight thousand people. Subsequent research has shown that many of the landslips were associated with new road cuttings and artificially modified slopes. Of more significance, however, was the conclusion that the rapidly growing tropical vegetation on the hillslopes can be misleading.

Its presence often imparts to the slope it covers a temporary measure of stability; it serves to hold back creep, but in doing so it may set the stage for subsequent large-scale slope deformation. In Hong Kong . . . over-reliance on the vegetation cover for stabilization of slopes may turn a mere accident in nature into a great man-made disaster.[5]

On the other side of the Pacific Ocean, along the coasts of southern California, the climate is characterized by aridity, although on the few occasions when the winter rainfall does occur it may fall in only two or three severe storms, during which up to 500 millimetres of rain can be dumped in a few hours. Over large tracts of southern California the geology comprises a series of alluvial gravels, sands and silts held together largely by natural water-soluble cements which are, therefore, extremely vulnerable to the seasonal rainfall. This combination of circumstances would, in itself, be sufficient to cause severe landslipping, but when we add to this the tectonic instability created by earthquake shocks and the heedless development of property on hillslopes and in canyons, irrespective of the hazards involved, it is little wonder that there is a long record of slope failure, property damage and substantial insurance claims in that region. In view of the fact that the hazard problems of Los Angeles are treated more fully in Chapter 11, however, there will be no further discussion of Californian landslides at this juncture.

In Britain, although there is a lengthy history of landslipping in clayey rocks, the death-toll has been minimal, largely because the landslides have in general been relatively slow affairs, by comparison with those so far described in other parts of the world. One of the first places where landslips proved to be a major constraint to urban development in Britain was at Bath. Cramped in a narrow gorge, which has been carved by the River Avon through bedded layers of Liassic Clays and overlying Jurassic Limestones, the city had faced few urban building problems until its rapid expansion in Georgian times. In 1790 a major slippage of the Liassic Clays stopped the completion of Camden Crescent and serious slumping continued in the Hedgemead area throughout the nineteenth and twentieth centuries. Despite remedial measures, such as draining and tree planting, certain parts of Bath have had to be retained as open spaces in view of the landslip hazards, whilst the subsequent construction of tower blocks beneath the notorious Beacon Hill slip required very special foundations. The largest British landslips, however, are to be found around the coasts, in localities where marine erosion has undermined the unstable clayey rocks and induced major slides. In north-eastern Skye, one of the larger Hebridean Isles, the whole of the landscape is dominated by the jumbled terrain of gigantic rotational landslips, where Liassic Clays have once again proved incapable of sustaining the overlying burden of sedimentary rocks and in this case thick volcanic basalts.

On the south coast of England there are several examples of major landslips in clayey rocks, the largest being found in the Downland landslide between Lyme Regis and Axmouth. Here, after a long period of heavy rainfall, a great mass of chalk and sandstone (40 million cubic metres in volume) suddenly slid seawards on Christmas Day 1839, carrying with it several houses. The chasm opened up by the failure of the underlying clay beds was 400 metres wide and almost 1 kilometre in length whilst the toe of the slide pushed up a linear ridge of sandstone rocks just offshore to a height of some 12 metres above the sea. Landslips are also a feature of the holiday resort of Ventnor and neighbouring Blackgang in the Isle of Wight where several homes were destroyed in March 1978, but the most famous English example of slope instability is that of Folkestone Warren in Kent, just below the well-known chalk cliffs of the Channel coast. Because of the persistent failure of the underlying Gault Clay, the overlying beds of Lower and Middle Chalk have a lengthy history of collapse, thus forming the complex jumble of The Warren at the cliff-foot. The most famous landslip occurred in 1915 when many thousands of tonnes of chalk foundered:

> The weight of the mass which fell caused ridges of land below the tide-mark to rise through the shallow water, and the railway track was affected as by an earthquake. Considerable lengths of the line were twisted or raised or sunk.[6]

As a result, some 3 kilometres of the main south-coast railway track had to be rebuilt, at the not unsubstantial cost for those days of £310,000 (Plate 22). Remedial measures have been undertaken constantly over several decades at this notorious site which, in the words of a notable civil engineer, '. . . constitutes probably the worst individual landslide situation ever to be faced and solved by civil engineers'.[7]

Few of the British landslides noted above were associated with loss of life, so it comes as something of a shock to read how enormous landslides resulted

22. The landslip at Folkestone Warrèn, England, in 1915 deformed the main railway track as if by an earthquake.

in a death-toll of 200,000 during the 1920 earthquake in Kansu province, China. Figure 38 illustrates that this was by no means the largest number of casualties associated with a Chinese earthquake, for in 1556 about one million are reputed to have died in Shensi province, due mainly to the collapse of loess hillslopes. In both of these tragic examples it appears as though the shearing resistance of the silty particles of the loess soils was insufficient to withstand the enormous stress of the seismic shaking. Loess is composed of very fine wind-blown silt that has accumulated to consider-able depths in certain parts of central Asia and North America, its formation generally being attributed to the winnowing effect of the ice-cap winds on the terminal moraines and glacio-fluvial outwash, laid down during the Ice Age. The fine-grained loessic particles have been gradually cemented by

Fig. 43. The geological structure of the Anchorage region, Alaska. Note the quickclays represented by the Bootlegger Cove Clay (after Q. A. Aune).

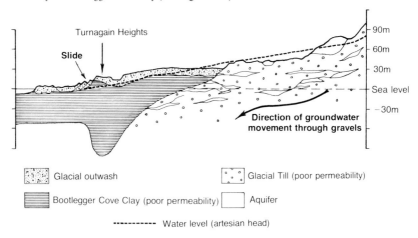

material which is highly water soluble, thus leading to excessive instability
during periods of exceptional rainfall or when seismic vibrations cause soil
liquefaction (see p. 147). Detailed descriptions of these Chinese landslips,
however, are not available so that the most detailed account of land-slipping
by soil liquefaction due to earthquake vibration is that of the famous Alaskan
earthquake of 1964 (see also Chapter 2).

At the City of Anchorage, Alaska, seismic-generated landslides were
responsible for much of the substantial damage, especially in the phenomenal
landslide of Turnagain Heights (see Plate 6). It is now known that the earthquake shocks caused many cycles of shearing stress in the so-called Bootlegger Cove Clay and its overlying glacial outwash sands, culminating in a
series of gigantic slides in the coastal bluffs which supported a flourishing
residential housing estate. Figure 43 illustrates the geology of Anchorage,
where the disposition of the critical, impermeable Bootlegger Cove Clay can
be seen. Furthermore, it becomes clear from Figure 43 how the seaward
flow of groundwater through the underlying glacial tills is faced with this
impermeable barrier which obstructs its free passage to the sea, thus building
up considerable hydraulic pressure behind the clay formation. If the particles
of this clay barrier had been able to remain coherent, its shearing strength
would have been sufficient to hold back the groundwater pressure from
inland. Unfortunately, the clay formation in question also contained
saturated lenses of sand and silt and it was in these that liquefaction occurred
during the Good Friday earthquake in 1964. Consequently, a gigantic
landslip, measuring 2.5 kilometres by 0.5 kilometres, broke away and slid
towards the coast, precipitating the disaster at Turnagain Heights.

The sand seams within the Bootlegger Cove Clay had rapidly changed into a liquid state when disturbed by sudden vibration and therefore they provide us with a good example of *quicksands*, which have no cohesive strength whatsoever. Some clays exhibit analogous behaviour and as such have been termed *quickclays* – indeed some of the clay bands in the notorious Bootlegger Cove Clay formation had already assumed the properties of a quickclay. Quickclays have a limited world distribution, since they are products of glaciation in which the fine silt and clay particles have been produced by the grinding action of ice. The sensitivity of quickclays has generally been attributed to their peculiar mineralogy plus the degree of leaching or 'flushing' by groundwater which has occurred since their deposition. There seems little doubt that the gradual dissolution of the natural cement by groundwater 'flushing' remains a very important factor in the promotion of potential slope failure, but there is now some doubt as to whether the quickclay composition need necessarily be dominated solely by *clay minerals*, as had formerly been supposed. Recent research has suggested, in fact, that the propensity of quickclays to liquefy depends more on the predominance of *non-clay minerals* such as quartz and feldspar.

One of the most serious aspects of quickclay sensitivity is that catastrophic landslipping can be induced in virtually flat areas (slopes of less than $5°$) and usually occurs at very great speeds. Quickclay slides have been reported in Scandinavia and Canada in which the death-toll reached very serious proportions, due to the lack of warning and the unawareness of the public that they were living in a potential hazard zone. The slip at Vaerdael, near Trondheim, Norway, in 1893 claimed 111 victims, as 55 million cubic metres of liquefied clay overwhelmed an area of 8.5 square kilometres in less than half an hour. At near-by Skjelstadmark in 1962 a smaller slide of 2.1 million cubic metres was far less catastrophic but the Göteborg disasters of 1648 and 1977 caused loss of life in an unstable Swedish area of quickclays. In the St Lawrence Valley of eastern Canada several quickclay landslides have occurred in recent years, one of the worst being that at Nicolet, Quebec, in which three people were killed and in which the cathedral narrowly escaped destruction.

Earth Flows and Debris Flows in Superficial Materials

When we turn away from examining landslide phenomena in solid rocks we are left with a few case studies relating to instability in surface soils, glacial tills (boulder clays), peat deposits and artificially dumped quarry or mine waste. In all instances the mechanisms are very similar to those described above and illustrated in Figures 40b and 40c. Numerous examples of earth flows have been described from central Europe by the Czech geologists Q. Zaruba and C. Mencl, including one of the largest which took place near Handlová in Czechoslovakia in 1960. Reaching a length of 1,800 metres over a period of several weeks some 20 million cubic metres of superficial material not only destroyed 150 houses and disrupted communications but dammed the adjoining river valley. Two years later, following a period of unusually heavy rainfall, a smaller but equally spectacular earth flow destroyed the Czechoslovakian village of Liesková, dammed up the river Riečnica and impounded a lake which threatened several other villages (Figure 44).

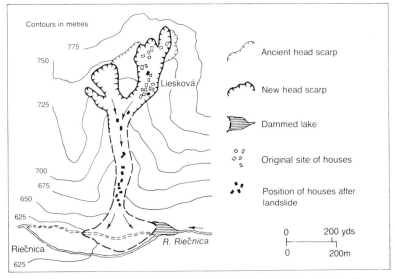

Fig. 44. The Liesková landslip, Czechoslovakia (1962) (after Q. Zaruba and V. Mencl).

The two earth flows described above were characterized by relatively slow downslope movements so that few casualties occurred despite the large amount of damage sustained. Similar slow-velocity flows have been described in Northern Ireland, Kent (England), Stoss (Switzerland) and Slumgullian, Colorado (U.S.A.), in which their average rate of movement ranged up to 600 metres per year. A comparison between earth flows and glaciers will show that they have many similarities, not least in their velocities, their sharp boundaries and their linear form (see Figure 44). Various explanations have been suggested to account for these flow phenomena, ranging from a theory of plasticity to one which draws on an analogy with the flow of a viscous lava. When we turn to examine rapid earth flows and debris flows, however, the mechanical explanations become more dependent on river-flow formulae, since these high velocity flows are composed of dense, porridge-like mixtures of earth, mud and water.

One of the most horrifying examples of a rapid superficial earth flow is that which devastated the tiny coal-mining town of Aberfan in South Wales in 1966. Just as the townsfolk were starting the day's work on 21 October, the 250 metres high, rain-soaked tip of mining waste which stood on the valley side above the town collapsed and flowed downslope with a thunderous roar, engulfing a row of houses and the school, before coming to a halt 800 metres from the tip itself. Under the obscene black sludge of the flow 144 people were suffocated, including 116 children in the school, virtually the entire juvenile population of Aberfan (Plate 23). The grief-stricken parents, joined by thousands of volunteers, including miners from neighbouring coal mines, dug frenziedly in the ruins of the school and the houses, some with their bare hands, but to little avail. Apparently, ample warnings had been given about the potential hazard, for the tip had moved forward on two previous occasions and a former headmaster of the buried school had repeatedly drawn attention to the danger. Yet mining debris was still being dumped on the tip when the catastrophe occurred. One outcome of the disaster was the introduction of special safety and remedial measures on the other South Wales coal tips – an immediate examination disclosed that more than 25 per cent of them were in a dangerous condition at that time. A national relief fund raised well over £1.5 million and this was donated in part to the bereaved families and in part towards the rehabilitation of the town of Aberfan. The most heart-rending feature of the disaster was that virtually every family lost a relative in the buried school and, despite the relief fund and the world-wide sympathy, the traumatic experience has continued to scar the lives of this community. No less than 158 people have subsequently undergone voluntary psychiatric treatment because of the shock.

The official investigation disclosed that for thirty years the colliery waste at Aberfan had been tipped on the hillside across a line of natural springs or groundwater seepages. Thus, the foundations of the tip had long been saturated with water, so that, when the granular material suddenly failed, high-pore pressures rapidly developed and the entire foundation liquefied like a quickclay:

23. The debris flow of Aberfan, S. Wales, in 1966, during which 116 children perished in a school when a coal-mining waste tip collapsed, was one of the most horrifying disasters in Britain. The photograph was taken from above the offending tip and illustrates how the stream of black sludge overwhelmed part of the mining town.

The upper part of the tip, not being saturated, did not liquefy but some of it would be carried forward floating on the liquefied material . . . Being of the nature of a liquid the whole mass then moved very rapidly down the hillside, spreading out sideways into a layer of substantially uniform thickness. As this happened, water was escaping from the mass so that the particles of soil regained their contact [cohesion] and the soil mass returned to its solid nature.[8]

Not long afterwards a similar incident occurred on the other side of the Atlantic when the failure of a dam, which held up coal-mining waste, caused the deaths of 118 people in West Virginia, U.S.A., as a very fluid mudflow swept downvalley in 1972.

Avalanches

Snow and ice are, in a way, also superficial materials, albeit of a transient nature, so that when they are rendered unstable on steep mountain slopes they often create devastating gravity movements known as avalanches. Although some of the basic laws of stress/strain behaviour of snow and ice are different from those that govern the behaviour of rocks and soils, their associated mechanical problems, together with the resulting catastrophes and the subsequent research into remedial measures, have a lot in common.

Like landslides, snow and ice avalanches cause vast amounts of damage and claim many lives each year but are, of course, limited to areas of the world which exhibit high snow-covered mountain ranges. Probably the greatest avalanches occur in the Himalayas, the Andes and in Alaska, but because of their relatively high population density it is the European Alps which suffer the greatest death-toll, year in, year out, with dozens being killed in the worst winters. Switzerland, for example, has an average death rate from avalanches of twenty-five per year. By comparison the figures for Norway are twelve per year, although it should be noted that many of the Swiss fatalities are tourist skiers, whilst those in Norway are local inhabitants. Yet despite the regular loss of life and property the Alpine villagers are of stoic character, shrugging off the disasters of the previous winter and reconstructing their villages in the same hazard zones as before. Nevertheless, in recent decades the avalanche-warning systems of the Alps have achieved a high degree of success, so that latterly deaths have been largely confined to the ranks of visiting skiers, some of whom have foolishly ignored the warning signs. It is only when some unforeseen circumstance, like a sudden rise of temperature, triggers off a massive ice fall, glacier surge or snow avalanche, that the unsuspecting inhabitants are themselves caught unawares. Such was the case in the Mattmark disaster in Switzerland in 1965 when eighty-eight people were killed, and in the first of the Huascaran catastrophes (see also p. 141) in which a prodigious ice-fall and subsequent mudflow killed some four thousand Peruvian villagers in 1962. Because snow avalanches are more commonplace, however, we shall concentrate largely on these and look first at the factors which are instrumental in producing their potential hazard (Plate 24a and b).

The first important factor relates to the influence of the terrain, especially its degree of slope steepness. Avalanches are rarely initiated on slopes with a gradient of less than 22°, a figure which is derived from the friction angles of granular snow. It is true that during the melt season, when great volumes of water have turned the snow into a mushy fluid, wet-snow avalanches can occur on lesser gradients, but these are special cases. What we must remember, however, is that, once initiated, the momentum of an avalanche frequently carries its destructive power across the low-angled slopes of the valley floor before coming to rest. This ability to continue down gentler gradients is more marked if the avalanche becomes channelled into a gully (see below).

Aspect or slope-orientation is another important factor in avalanche susceptibility. As far as the northern hemisphere is concerned, strong spring sunshine, for example, causes many wet-snow avalanches on south-facing slopes, but in winter on the same slopes, the sunshine may have a stabilizing effect on the snow surface. On the whole, therefore, it is the northerly and easterly slopes which are the most dangerous, for snow stabilizes more slowly in the lower temperatures of these shaded slopes. It has been calculated, for instance, that in the Alps about 90 per cent of avalanche accidents involving skiers occur on the northern and eastern slopes.

The stability of the snow in mountainous areas changes constantly throughout the winter, depending on fluctuations of temperature and on constant renewals of the surface snow. Thus, the depth of the newly fallen snow is another significant factor in the understanding of a potential hazard. Generally speaking, the following amounts of newly fallen snow create different degrees of avalanche hazard: less than 30 centimetres, no risk; 30–50 centimetres, only local risks; 50–75 centimetres, threats of blocked roads and railways; 75–125 centimetres, villages in danger of structural damage; more than 125 centimetres, major disasters possible. Fortunately, rapid snowfalls of more than 125 centimetres in depth are rare occurrences so that major disasters occur infrequently in the Alps. But when they do occur, the avalanches strike both swiftly and silently, burying settlements in a matter of minutes. One expert, Colin Fraser, has concluded that 'Anyone

24. (a) and (b) The development of an avalanche in the Swiss Alps.

who falls into the merciless clutches of an avalanche is subjected to one of the most terrifying experiences that man can endure.'

In his book *The Avalanche Enigma* Colin Fraser recounts several graphic stories of the Swiss avalanches which took a grim toll during the winter of 1950–51, one of the worst on record. There were as many as six hundred and fifty avalanches in one canton alone, that of Graubünden in N.E. Switzerland, where fifty-four people died and damage ran into millions of francs. During one period of January 1951 all the Graubünden roads and the main railway line were blocked whilst the famous ski resort of Davos was completely cut off for five days. In central Switzerland, however, the snowfall of that fateful January was even heavier and at Vals 120 centimetres of snow fell in a mere four days. In the darkness of the night of 20 January several enormous avalanches flattened a number of houses in the village of Vals and claimed nineteen lives. Some 50 kilometres to the west lay the little village of Andermatt, near the famous St Gothard Pass, and it, too, experienced unprecedented snowfalls during the same period of

January 1951. By 20 January almost 110 centimetres of fresh snow had accumulated in only three days and this was destined to collapse swiftly into the valley in a series of catastrophic avalanches throughout that day. At breakfast time a small avalanche swept into the military hospital as a fore-taste of what was to come. In mid morning two more blocked the main road, destroyed the river bridge and tore down the railway's overhead power lines. But it was in the early afternoon that the first catastrophic slide took place for this one plunged into the village itself, destroying several houses and so damaging the famous Drei Könige hotel that it had to be demolished. Nine people died in this avalanche and two others in a later one which buried the army barracks.

The devastating frequency of the Andermatt avalanches on 20 January 1951 was nowhere surpassed in Switzerland, so that the inhabitants were still shocked and frightened when further avalanches plunged into their village three weeks later, following an extraordinary snowfall of almost 2 metres in less than two weeks! In the neighbouring Bedretto Valley there was an Alpine record snowfall of 125 centimetres in twenty-four hours on 12 February – little wonder that it triggered twenty-six major avalanches in a space of three days in this one valley alone, amazingly without causing any loss of life. On the southern side of the St Gothard Pass, however, the villagers of Airolo were not so fortunate, for the same February blizzard led to ten avalanche deaths and considerable damage (Plate 25). By the end of that unforgettable winter 279 people had been killed in the Swiss Alps alone, together with a further 285 who had been seriously injured.

Other nations, too, have had their casualties from avalanches: Norway has records to show that in the entire country between four hundred and five hundred people died from this cause in 1679, with 200 more in 1755 and a further 161 in 1886. Since those fearful losses of earlier centuries the annual death toll from Norwegian avalanches has rarely risen above thirty, pre-sumably as stringent safety measures have been introduced. The Vorarlberg region of Austria suffered 125 avalanche deaths in 1954 despite the warning-system installed that very year. Even Britain has recorded a serious accident from an avalanche but this occurred not in the highlands of Wales or Scot-land, as one might expect, but in the Sussex town of Lewes. Here on 27 December 1836 a row of cottages was crushed by a mass of snow which fell from the adjoining slope of the chalk downland. Of the fifteen people who were buried only seven were rescued alive.

Because of their different characteristics, avalanches have been variously classified over the years, but the most widely accepted classification is that proposed by Professor R. Haefli and Dr M. de Quervain of the Swiss Federal

25. The devastation caused by avalanches at Airolo, Switzerland, in February 1951, when ten people were killed.

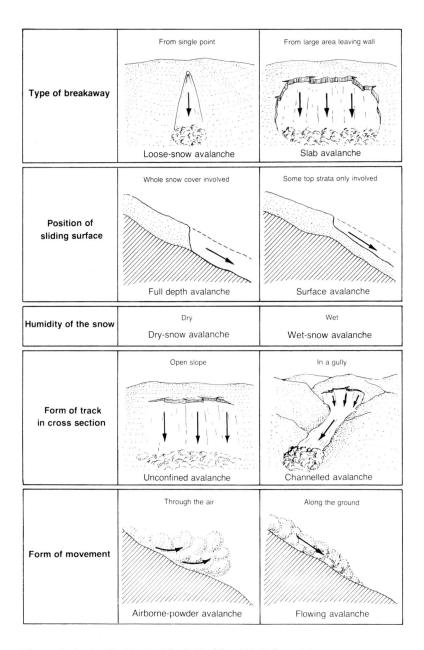

Fig. 45. Avalanche Classification (after R. Haefeli and M. de Quervain).

Snow and Avalanche Research Institute (Figure 45). Five major criteria
have been recognized relating to: the form of the initial fracture or break-
away; the depth of snow involved; the snow humidity; the form of the
avalanche track; and finally, whether the avalanche is airborne or not. Each
of the different avalanche types illustrated in Figure 45 has its own special
features but two of the most catastrophic are the airborne-powder-snow
avalanches and the wet loose-snow avalanches. In the first case, the devastation of the airborne-powder-snow avalanche is largely the work of the
associated shock-waves, which are powerful enough to decimate mature
forests and explode buildings. Not only does a wave of snow-free air precede
the actual avalanche, but within the following mass of airborne-powder-
snow a whole series of violent swirls, created by internal turbulence, move
faster than the mass itself (Figure 46). It is these phenomenal internal gusts,

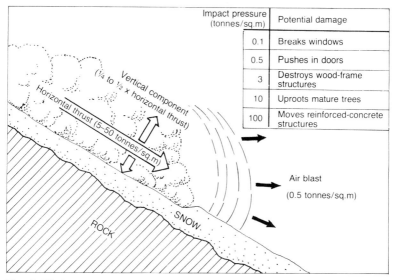

Fig. 46. The impact of an avalanche.

travelling at speeds in excess of 300 kilometres per hour, which create the
greatest damage to property, for when a building is buffeted from several
sides by these destructive blasts it simply disintegrates. Skiers who have
survived accidents involving airborne-powder avalanches have spoken of the
violence of these turbulent gusts and how the rapid change of air pressure
had almost ruptured their lungs. If, in the case of the airborne-powder-snow

avalanche, it is the violent air movement which creates the most damage, when we turn to examine the wet loose-snow avalanche we shall discover that it is the weight of the snow that causes the devastation. So great is the energy of the wet snow avalanche that it is capable of uprooting trees and incorporating massive boulders into the maelstrom so that the final product has a considerably increased potential for destruction. Such an avalanche is termed a *grundlawine* by the people of Switzerland and Austria and it is this type of phenomenon which causes the greatest Alpine disasters. Calculations have suggested that one colossal wet-snow avalanche, which crashed into a valley of the Italian Alps in 1885, comprised no less than 2.5 million tonnes of snow and was equivalent to the generation of about 300 million horse-power. Compare this figure with the mere 168,000 horsepower developed by the world's most powerful ocean liner, the former *Queen Elizabeth*!

Prediction and Mitigation of Slope Instability

It is very clear from the foregoing accounts of landslides and avalanches that for all mankind's technical progress there is little likelihood of it ever being possible to stop completely these accidents related to slope instability. At the best man can modify the hazards by a variety of positive actions or, alternatively, take a fatalistic, negative approach and continue to live with the constant threat of impending disaster. In the majority of cases mankind has learned to judge the relative costs and benefits of remedial action or of putting up with the hazard. But before such action can be planned it is essential to recognize the nature of the hazard, the size of the hazard zone and the periodicity of the destructive event.

Turning first to the study of landslides we find that civil engineers and geologists have long had an eye for troublesome ground or landslide-prone terrain, despite a few significant cases where the evidence has been ignored and the penalty has had to be paid (e.g. Folkestone Warren and the M.6 Motorway at Walton's Wood – see above). In general, however, where there is good evidence of former landslide activity the prudent civil engineer has relocated his structure or, if relocation has proved to be impossible, has introduced corrective and preventive measures. In order to make this decision the civil engineer will have drawn heavily on both geological and geomorphological evidence. For instance, he will have needed to know not only the character and disposition of the solid rocks, the whereabouts of faults and the pattern of the groundwater regime, but he will also have had to be familiar with the surface drainage, the critical slope-angles and the character of the superficial deposits including the soils. To accumulate this knowledge the engineers of earlier centuries were dependent almost entirely on field survey, together with a few additional laboratory tests to show the shearing strength of rocks. Today, however, the civil engineer is able to draw upon a vastly superior collection of technological aids, which include the use of air photographs, sophisticated field-survey instruments (including geophysical equipment) and a plethora of laboratory equipment relating to both soil and rock mechanics.

Having collected all the available data the engineer must now turn to theoretical calculations which will ultimately determine whether the unstable slope in question can be successfully treated or whether it should be avoided at all costs. This theoretical approach is part of the all-important cost-benefit exercise, for there will always be a constraining cost factor. By being able to determine a numerical value relating to the *safety factor*, it should now be possible to estimate how much it will cost to increase this safety factor by a predetermined amount. It will then become a matter for the local authorities to decide the minimal degree of risk which will be acceptable for each particular set of circumstances. In certain instances, where the hazard may only threaten disruption of roads or power lines, for example, the requirement may be one with only a relatively low degree of safety, thus involving a correspondingly small amount of investment in remedial measures. At the other extreme, however, it may be decided that a catastrophic event, such as that at Aberfan, must never happen again, in which case the maximum safety factor will have to be introduced. In general this will entail very costly remedial action, such as flattening of slopes, building of revetments or construction of drainage channels – in exceptional circumstances it may even involve the abandonment of a village and its relocation elsewhere, as has happened in some mountain valleys. Where destructive landslides threaten human settlements, many of the local planning authorities have produced various 'hazard maps' which may illustrate the degrees of liability to damage for each building in a village, or merely the location of potentially hazardous quickclays and unstable slopes (Figure 47).

Prediction is, of course, the most important aspect of landslide prevention and, as population pressures have led to greater spreads of urban development into hazard zones, there has been an increasing interest in the prevention of landslides by careful zoning and ground treatment *before* the area is built over. Expenses incurred in competent site-investigation prior to construction will save not only considerable capital outlay in subsequent remedial measures but also possible loss of life, severe disruption and hard-

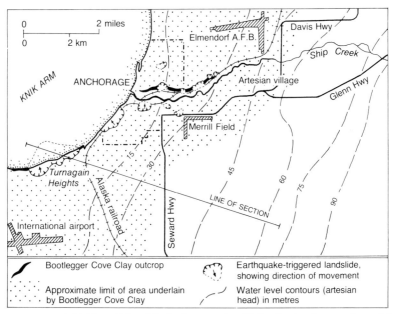

Fig. 47. Landslide Hazard Map of the Anchorage region, Alaska, showing the zone of potential slope failure (dotted). Note: the line of section refers to Figure 43 (after Q. A. Aune).

ship, to say nothing of the heavy insurance claims which would result from the landslide catastrophe. Nevertheless, there are still innumerable examples where it is a case of being wise after the event and where expensive corrective measures have finally had to be employed in order to stabilize the landslides and ensure that there is no repetition of the disaster.

Corrective measures for landslide control can be grouped into five main categories: surface drainage modification; groundwater modification; alteration of slope gradient; installation of artificial structures; re-vegetation of hill slopes. In the present volume it will be possible to look only briefly at each of these measures and to explain the reasons for their implementation.

At the outset it will be essential to divert any surface water flowing into the slide area, not only because of its intrinsic danger, but also because it will continue to exacerbate the slope instability by increasing pore pressures, etc. Following the Aberfan disaster, much of the initial relief work was involved in diverting the surface streams before it became safe to uncover the buried school. Once the surface water has been cleared, the next step will be to de-water the slide itself by constructing subterranean horizontal drains and by drilling deeply into the slumped mass. As soon as the surface water and groundwater have been reduced to manageable proportions the emphasis can be switched to slope modification and to the introduction of artificial structures and tree planting.

The stability of a slope may be substantially increased either by reducing the mass of material at the head of the slide or by enlargement of the mass at the landslide toe. Research has shown, for example, that by transferring a mere 4 per cent of the mass from the head to the toe of the slide, the slope stability is increased by 10 per cent. In such a displacement, however, care must be taken not to disturb the new equilibrium of the upper part of the slope, thus triggering-off a further landslide. To retain slope stability it has often been found necessary to construct a number of steps or 'berms' on a hillside. Alternatively one is forced to introduce artificial structures or methods of fixing the slope, of which the following are the most widely practised: retaining walls; over-bridging; pile-driving; grouting; rock bolting. More rarely, two methods of soil hardening – by electro-osmosis and by thermic treatment – are used in special cases.

Over the years a great variety of concrete, steel and wooden retaining walls has been constructed at different landslip locations in attempts to prevent further movement of the landslide toe, with varying degrees of success. For example, it took almost half a century of trial and error with different structures before the Folkestone Warren landslip was finally conquered. In some cases the slope instability is such that overbridging of the slide area becomes necessary, although this solution is considerably more expensive. One of the best British examples is to be found on a precipitous sea coast near Barmouth, Wales. Here, following an extensive landslide which swept a railway track into the sea, in March 1933, a concrete structure was built in order to overbridge the track. There were no casualties from the Barmouth landslip, in contrast to the two disastrous railway landslips which had occurred elsewhere in Britain in earlier years. The first involved a chalk landslip in Sonning cutting, near Reading, on Christmas Eve 1841, when the London-Bristol express train ran into the toe of the slide, killing eight people. The second, at Little Salkeld near Penrith, on 19 January 1918, caused seven deaths when the London-Glasgow express ploughed into a landslide caused by a sudden thaw. In deep mountain valleys, especially those prone to rock falls, there may be few alternatives to overbridging. One of the oldest methods in the treatment of landslides is that of pile-driving, but in general only shallow landslides have been satisfactorily treated in this way. Where more deep-seated slides are involved the piles cannot achieve sufficient depth to overcome the instability, whilst very fluid sands or clays, because of their mobility, are unlikely to be retained by such methods. In these latter instances success may only be achieved by grouting or by hardening the soil by artificial means. The process of grouting involves the displacement of moisture from the rock or soil fissures and its replacement by a cement mixture which will ultimately harden to provide a rigid framework within the unstable material. The exclusion of groundwater by electro-osmosis or by thermic drying is also the major aim in cases where normal drainage methods of the slumped mass have proved to be inadequate. Because of their considerable expense, however, these two methods are used only in limited areas where drainage is critical. One such example was in Ontario, Canada, when slope instability threatened the foundations of an important road bridge. The moisture content of the superficial material, on which the bridge supports rested, was successfully reduced by electro-osmosis. Loessic soils, which are notoriously unstable (see p. 157), have occasionally been treated by oil-generated thermic drying in both Czechoslovakia and Romania, but with limited success.

When dealing with rock falls and rock slides most of the remedial measures outlined above will be of little avail so that methods of rock-bolting and steel-netting installation may have to be introduced in order to ameliorate the hazard. The practice of rock-bolting to stabilize cliffs has grown from a limited to a widespread use in recent years. Great success has been achieved in Australia, France and in the United States, where rock bolts were extensively used to avert rock falls at dam sites in the states of Arizona and Washington. In Britain similar remedial work has been carried out on the cliffs of the Avon Gorge, Bristol, the Tremadoc cliffs, Snowdonia and on the famous chalk cliffs at Dover, Kent, where rockfalls were proving dangerous to the townsfolk. On the new Kyle of Lochalsh road-improvement schemes in the Highlands of Scotland, several of the rock cliffs have been stabilized by means of enormous nets of steel mesh bolted against the rock face.

We have already noted that in certain instances vegetation on an unstable slope may give a false sense of security (see p. 155) but in general careful re-vegetation of a landslip will often assist in its stabilization, with the notable exception of the very deep-seated landslides. Tree-growth has two major functions in the context of remedial measures: first, the transference of soil moisture to the atmosphere by transpiration, and, secondly, the stabilization of the soil by means of its root network. Since most deciduous trees have a greater capacity than conifers for transpiration they are preferable; furthermore, some conifers have notoriously shallow root spreads and do not, therefore, anchor the soil so successfully.

When we turn to examine the problems associated with avalanche protection schemes, they can be grouped under three headings, similar to those relating to landslide mitigation. In the first instance, it is important to establish research centres which can concentrate on predictive studies, thereby producing Avalanche Warning Systems and Risk Maps. Secondly, there are studies which can suggest methods of avalanche prevention and finally there are those relating to avalanche protection, largely in the form of corrective measures, such as reinforced building construction and the installation of special avalanche remedial structures.

Since there is a close relationship between meteorological conditions and avalanche frequency it is clear that avalanche activity will vary both from place to place and over time. Thus it is essential for particular regions or countries to have an adequate network of data-collection centres, all coordinated by one or more research institutes. After a period of time these coordinating centres are able to establish, with a fair degree of accuracy, the probability that a given number of avalanches will be exceeded at a particular location over a specific time interval. From such probability studies it is possible to delimit avalanche-hazard zones and to produce Risk Maps for individual valleys or villages (Figure 48). Once the estimated periodicity is computed then appropriate corrective measures can be implemented, as illustrated on the Avalanche Risk Map. It must be remembered, however, that avalanche predictive studies cannot deal successfully with the freak event which is related to other external forces such as an earthquake or a volcanic eruption.

The leading avalanche research unit in Europe is the Swiss Federal Snow and Avalanche Research Institute, which is located high on a mountain top above Davos. Here, the predictive studies have reached such advanced levels that the Swiss authorities pride themselves on the excellent record of their Avalanche Warning System. Although it is by no means 100 per cent fool-proof, it has facilitated a substantial number of village evacuations over the last decade which have undoubtedly saved hundreds of lives. Nevertheless, despite this degree of success, there has been a continuing rise in the number of ski accidents, as winter sports have gained rapidly in popularity. Thus the research into avalanche prevention goes on. The Swiss Avalanche Warning System has been in existence for forty years, although it was originally based on only twenty-five data collection stations. The severe snowfalls of January–February 1951, however, demonstrated that the measurement network in Switzerland was inadequate, leading to a doubling in the number of stations from that date onwards. Of the other warning systems throughout the world, that in the United States is one of the best known. Whereas the flexible Swiss system bases a great deal of its forecasting on personal experiences of avalanche behaviour, the American system

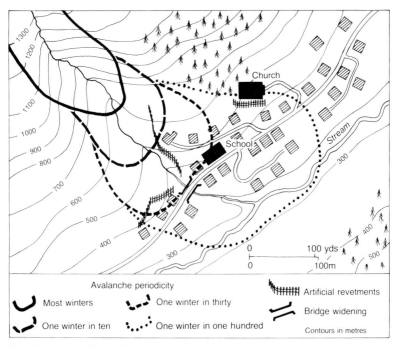

Fig. 48. Avalanche Hazard Map.

is much more rigid, because of its greater dependence on statistical criteria. Thus, when any of the ten significant factors relating to avalanches attains a critical statistical threshold the United States experts begin to calculate the magnitude of the potential hazard by a careful statistical analysis aided by computers. Both systems, however, have produced adequate warnings and are being constantly refined as new avalanche prediction methods are developed, either at Davos or at such places as the Institute of Arctic and Alpine Research at the University of Colorado, U.S.A. Japan, too, has its Snow Research Station where, amongst other achievements, the Japanese scientists have developed an avalanche intensity scale, similar to the well-known Richter Scale for earthquake magnitude (Chapter 2). The avalanche scale is based on measurements of a factor known as Mass Magnitude: the smallest avalanches are classified as M.M. < 1; the large ones as M.M. 3 to 5 with occasional occurrences as high as M.M. 7.

All the research centres are concerned with methods of avalanche prevention, either by the construction of metal fences high up on the steep slopes where deeper snow accumulates or by artificial triggering of avalanches by controlled explosions. In most regions both methods have been employed but the former method, which attempts to stabilize the snow on metal supporting structures, is extremely expensive, because to achieve success the structures have to be virtually continuous walls. Thus the use of explosives is more common, so that a number of small, harmless avalanches can be artificially induced, in order to forestall a much larger destructive event. Although a variety of methods of controlled explosions has been tried, two major ones remain superior: hand thrown projectiles, known as *sprengbüchsen*, and mortar bombs. In some instances, however, even conrolled explosions generate larger avalanches than expected. A final method of avalanche prevention that has recently been developed is one which attempts to stabilize the snow mass by treating it with chemical aldehydes. These are found to affect the metamorphism of the snow flakes and inhibit the growth of the more unstable of the snow crystals.

Since most high mountain regions experience avalanches at some time or another, much of the research and investment has been geared to the development of successful corrective measures. Such measures are based largely on the Risk Map probability zones (see Figure 48) and are intended to deflect avalanches away from vulnerable buildings or lines of communication. One of the earliest methods was the planting of woodlands in attempts to shield villages in avalanche hazard zones, but it has subsequently been shown how some of these plantations can give a false sense of security. Some airborne-powder-snow avalanches are capable of flattening even mature stands of trees and then incorporating the trunks as battering rams. Thus, the most successful of the remedial measures have been either the construction of enormous stone-built splitting wedges, termed *spaltkeile*, which act like the prow of a boat, or the building of stone retaining walls and revetments to divert the avalanches into less vulnerable areas (see Figure 48). In addition, there has been a widespread introduction of stricter building codes in the avalanche-prone villages. Based on the zoning of the Risk Map, the endangered buildings can now be constructed or converted to withstand varying degrees of pressure. Even in the zones where avalanches can be expected once in every thirty years, buildings are permitted as long as they conform to the regulation whereby they are able to withstand pressures up to 3 tonnes per square metre. But it is not only the roofs and proximal walls which are critical, for provision should also be made to give the buildings firm anchorage in order to counteract the outward drag of the avalanche and to prevent the houses from being toppled.

6. Ground Surface Collapse

In a previous chapter we have already explained how the inexorable sinking of certain coastal and deltaic regions of the world is the outcome of gradual crustal warping whose origins can be traced back for millions of years. Such tectonic movements are impossible to stop, although it has been shown how human interference has often exacerbated the subsidence to the point where it has become a severe hazard. It is important to distinguish, therefore, between those instances where a widespread downward movement of the land surface is the result of natural mechanisms and processes, as in the case of the Alaskan earthquake of 1964 (see Figure 13), and those examples where man has induced ground surface subsidence or even collapse. Since the majority of the case studies of ground subsidence relate to the latter cause, the present chapter is devoted, in the main, to an examination of the ways in which human intervention has frequently interfered with the natural order of things, sometimes by accelerating the normal physical process and at other times by stopping or reversing the natural process altogether, occasionally with disastrous consequences.

Most of the crustal movements which act in the vertical plane and which are related to natural events generally do so over a lengthy time period and because of their slowness are less likely to lead to sudden disasters. But there are a few notable exceptions, in which natural ground displacement may be very rapid, as exemplified in earthquake disturbance and limestone solution collapse. On turning to the numerous examples of artificially induced subsidence, we discover that the legacy of man's former interference with the land surface can provoke a sudden disaster, such as that in April 1945, when an abandoned coal-mining shaft near Wigan, England, unexpectedly caved in, engulfing a freight train and its crew. An even greater catastrophe was only narrowly averted when the entire carriageway of a major trunk road suddenly disappeared into a derelict mine shaft on the outskirts of Birmingham, England, in November 1977. In general, however, the works of man provoke only a very limited response, for in most instances the degree of surface subsidence is relatively small and takes place very gradually. Nevertheless, it will be realized that in certain cases there will come a critical point in time when the sustained sinking of the surface is of such magnitude that important buildings and other structures have become so badly damaged that they are in imminent danger of collapse. If the threatened structures are of a particularly hazardous type (i.e. a dam or a nuclear reactor) then a major disaster may be triggered; if they are of great historical importance then a cultural disaster may be threatened.

As the majority of modern buildings and allied structures have been sited and designed to withstand ground instability they are unlikely to face major problems, but in earlier centuries, when engineering skills were less sophisticated than those of today, there was a lengthy record of collapse due to unstable ground conditions. It is little wonder, therefore, that some of the world's most historic cities are now facing severe subsidence hazards due to a combination of poor foundations and subsurface abstraction of water and/or mineral wealth. Ravenna and Copenhagen are two such cities.

The north Italian town of Ravenna possesses some of the world's finest Byzantine mosaics, dating back to the Early Christian period of the fifth and sixth centuries A.D. But many of these mosaics, together with the fabric of the ancient buildings, are threatened with destruction as the city continues to sink at an ever-increasing rate. Because Ravenna was built on marshes at the southern edge of the Plain of Lombardy, the city has been sinking very slowly ever since Roman times, largely for the same reasons as those affecting Venice, namely a gradual crustal warping around the head of the Adriatic. Unlike Venice, however, Ravenna has not been threatened by flooding from marine inundation and so its problems have given less cause for concern, despite the fact that the original floor of the famous San Vitale church has subsided more than 2 metres in fifteen centuries. But all this complacency changed after 1953 when the rate of subsidence was seen to be increasing at an alarming rate until it became ten times faster than that of Venice.

By 1976 the sinking had increased from a mere 2 millimetres per year to 100 millimetres per year, giving rise to a forecast that within a decade Ravenna would probably be under water. Pumps have been installed in the basements of all the important buildings, but the continual pumping is washing away some of the foundations, thus weakening the threatened structures to an even greater extent. The reasons for the dramatic increase in the rate of sinking are not far to seek, since, as in the case of Venice, the voracious demands for water by the city's expanding industries have caused a sinking of the built-up area during the last twenty years by drastically reducing the groundwater supply, abstracted at the rate of 1.5 million cubic

metres per annum, from the 2,500 wells and boreholes. After lengthy nego-
tiations a pipe line has now been constructed in order to provide alternative
industrial water supplies, but even this remedial measure may not be
sufficient, for some of the subsidence is also linked with the abstraction of
natural gas from the underlying strata. Since Ravenna is one of Italy's major
gas producers, it may be more difficult to resolve this part of the dilemma.

In a more northerly latitude yet another of Europe's historic cities is facing
subsidence problems not dissimilar to those of Ravenna. Copenhagen, like
Stockholm and Amsterdam, was built on marshland which then became
systematically drained and reclaimed during the succeeding centuries. By
canalizing their surface water and continuing to abstract their groundwater,
Copenhagen's citizens have hastened the falling groundwater table, and in
so doing have quite unwittingly sown the seeds for a future cultural tragedy.
Not that the ground surface will subside sufficiently to place Copenhagen
into a potential hazard zone from marine flooding for, unlike London,
Amsterdam and Venice, the Danish capital lies on the perimeter of the
Scandinavian region of isostatic uplift (see Figure 29). Nevertheless, parts
of the old city exhibit signs of local subsidence and it is these which are in
greatest danger.

The Roman dramatist, Plautus, once wrote of Ravenna that 'the corpses
float on the water and the living die of thirst'. This seeming paradox is also
apposite in the case of modern Copenhagen which has surface water everywhere but not enough in the ground itself. As the water table continues to
drop, the massive wooden piles, which support Copenhagen's ancient
buildings, are becoming increasingly exposed to the air. Once this happens
the timbers begin to dry out and become vulnerable to an insidious attack by
a mysterious fungus which rapidly rots the wood, thus finally undermining
the overlying buildings. Remedial measures to save the Royal Theatre have
already started at a cost of some $3 million. But further action is urgently
needed to save the royal palace of Amalienborg, at an estimated cost of over
$4 million, leaving the reader free to judge for himself what the total costs
might be if the entire urban fabric of Copenhagen's historic city centre is to
be rescued from ultimate collapse. Such costs would be the measure of a
cultural disaster.

It was almost certainly the sudden industrialization of Ravenna which
brought its subsidence problems to a head; in the case of Copenhagen the
difficulties have been linked with its massive programme of post-war
modernization. Taller buildings not only require deeper foundations and
better drainage but also underground car parks and more sophisticated
stormwater systems. Because the surface water has been led more effectively

straight into the sewer outfalls; because the city's ground surface has been coated with asphalt and concrete and because its subsoil has been more efficiently drained, the water table has fallen dramatically in its elevation. This decrease in the level of the groundwater has been accelerated by the substantial increase in the demands for domestic and industrial water. It would appear, therefore, that Denmark's technological expertise will now have to be turned to the problem of saving the architectural heritage of its capital city – the alternative might be to have to accept that much of Copenhagen's urban fabric will ultimately decay and collapse in the not too far distant future.

In an attempt to explain the general problems associated with surface subsidence and collapse it becomes possible to identify four major causes: (1) surface loading; (2) extraction of fluids; (3) extraction of solids; (4) volume changes of superficial materials. Any sinking due to tectonic movements has been referred to elsewhere (see Chapter 4).

Surface Loading

The stability of any building will depend, for the most part, on the ability of the civil engineer to produce satisfactory foundations. The degree of success will depend in turn on the character of the soil and the depth of the underlying bedrock which, if occurring near to the surface, will pose few problems, as far as foundation engineering is concerned.

> If, however, solid ground cannot be found, but the place proves to be nothing but a heap of loose earth to the very bottom, or a marsh, then it must be dug up and cleared out and set with piles . . .[1]

In the case of Copenhagen, quoted above, as in many other ancient cities, the use of wooden piles to carry the loads of major structures was widely practised in earlier centuries. Today, steel and concrete piles are more commonly used in any foundations deeper than 10 metres below the surface. Whatever their composition, however, the piles will have to be sufficiently strong to transmit the load of the building to the underlying strata (or foundation beds), which in turn must be able to withstand the load.

Because of the great varieties of soils, superficial deposits and solid rocks which exist in the world, there is a wide range of figures relating to the basic parameter of *load-bearing capacity*. But in general it can be said that to achieve success the foundation depth must be equal to at least twice the width of the foundation itself, in order to offset the compressibility of the

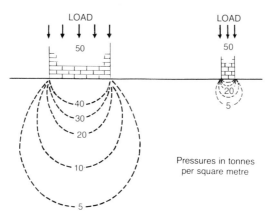

Fig. 49. The so-called Bulb of Pressure (after R. F. Legget).

underlying soil and subsoil. Figure 49 illustrates this fundamental concept and shows the way in which the loading stress at the surface will gradually be dissipated through the underlying subsoil. When a soil or subsoil is subjected to loading it will be compressed, so that varying degrees of *consolidation* will take place, with the rate of consolidation being dependent on the *permeability* of the soil (see p. 147). Such terms belong to the science of soil mechanics, which is an integral part of civil engineering, and it is from research in these allied fields that we know how soil permeability depends on the grain-size of the material. When dealing with clays and silts, for example, the permeability is said to be low, since excess water can only escape very slowly from these fine-grained sediments. Thus, there will be a relatively lengthy interval before the foundations have settled or subsided to their final resting place in a foundation bed of clay or silt. Sands and gravels, on the other hand, have large grain sizes, are extremely permeable and allow excess water to escape fairly rapidly. As a result, surface settlement will take place as soon as the loading is applied.

From the above it will be appreciated how lack of adequate information about complex soil formations can easily lead to an unreliable calculation of the load-bearing capacity of their constituent materials, since the latter may vary quite considerably from place to place. Although errors of this sort are occasionally made today, the majority of the cases which exemplify surface loading, subsidence and building collapse through insufficient knowledge of the underlying geology, belong to earlier centuries. Perhaps the most famous example of loading and differential subsidence is that of the Leaning Tower of Pisa (Plate 26). Although construction started in the year 1174, the

26. Italy's famous Leaning Tower of Pisa illustrates building subsidence due to insufficient knowledge of the underlying geology in the thirteenth century. Here, the Director of the Institute of Geophysics at the local university measures the increased tilt of 1.2 millimetres that occurred during 1965–66.

underlying mixture of clays and sands soon resulted in differential settlement of its foundations. As work progressed the builders continued to construct in the vertical plane so that by the time of its completion in 1350 the tower exhibited an extraordinary tilt and a curiously 'dislocated' appearance. If the tower had settled evenly there would have been no major problem; but since the tilting has continued at a rate of about 1 millimetre per year it would not be surprising to hear predictions of its imminent collapse, were it not for the remedial measures that have now been devised to maintain the famous tower for posterity. A lesser known example of this type of differential settlement is to be found in the city of Bristol, England, where the tower of Temple Church is remarkably out of true. Shortly before completion in 1390 work on the tower ceased for a period of seventy years, after which time the structure had tilted some 1.2 metres from the vertical (Pisa's Leaning Tower is an amazing 4.2 metres out of true). When building was resumed in 1460 the remainder of the tower was built vertically and it has survived until the present day despite its perilous appearance.

Many of England's medieval cathedrals were not as fortunate as Temple Church, for there is a long list of major catastrophes arising partly from insecure foundations. The towers of Winchester, Gloucester and Worcester collapsed during the twelfth century; that of Lincoln fell in the thirteenth century and those of Ely and Norwich in the fourteenth century. It is true that some of these collapses may have been triggered by earthquakes (see Figure 18), especially in the case of Wells cathedral where the roof collapsed during the earthquake of 21 December 1248. Despite this setback, Wells cathedral tower was constructed shortly afterwards, but still without sufficient knowledge of the underlying subsoil, with the immediate result that serious subsidence occurred due to excessive surface loading. Nevertheless, by an ingenious use of gigantic inverted arches beneath the tower the situation was rectified so that by 1338, this central tower had been saved and the interior bestowed with a feature of unique architectural merit. Finally, mention must be made of York Minister whose famous edifice was threatened by a settlement of 2.6 centimetres, detected during the 1960s. Happily, the threat of future collapse has been averted by costly remedial measures.

Extraction of Fluids

Some of the world's most serious ground subsidence has resulted from the withdrawal of fluids which occur naturally in subterranean 'reservoirs'. The most common of the fluids in question is that of water, but extraction of both oil and natural gas can have equally injurious consequences. All of these fluids are contained in layers of permeable rocks at varying depths below the surface and are therefore maintained under differing degrees of pressure from the overlying strata. In certain instances the pressure is sufficient to cause the fluid to rise naturally to the surface by *artesian* mechanisms, once a well has been bored down into the permeable layer. In most cases, however, the fluid has to be pumped to the surface, but in any event the overall effect will be to lower the level of the fluid in question – in the case of water this is referred to as a *lowering of the water table*. By lowering the fluid pressure at depth, the permeable layer becomes subjected to an ever-increasing stress from the overlying burden, thus causing the de-watered layer to compress. As in the case of surface loading, noted above, the amount of compression is reflected by a gradual subsidence of the ground surface, and since most granular materials exhibit an irreversible behaviour, as far as compression is concerned, there is no way in which the ground surface can be returned to its former level. Nevertheless, a cessation of fluid extraction will at least re-establish the subterranean fluid pressure and terminate the subsidence. Only in a few instances will the subsoil materials expand when groundwater is returned to the permeable layer, but even this expansion is usually minimal. Examples of such dilation will be examined below.

Turning first to an examination of the subsidence problems relating to groundwater withdrawal, it is instructive to note that at the U.N.E.S.C.O. symposium on land subsidence held in Tokyo during September 1969, it was concluded that, because of the increasingly worldwide exploitation of groundwater resources, there is likely to be a very rapid growth both in the number and in the size of the areas affected by surface subsidence. Some of the more serious areas are listed in Figure 50.

It is not by chance that the U.N.E.S.C.O. symposium was located in Tokyo, for the Japanese nation faces some of the most widespread problems relating to ground surface subsidence. Brief reference has already been made in an earlier chapter (p. 133) to the hazards of severe coastal flooding which threatened large tracts of Tokyo in the Koto Delta district and how the subsidence was only discovered during the precise surveying programme following the Kwanto Earthquake of 1923.

The recognition of this major ground subsidence and its detailed monitoring in succeeding years is said to be the first example not only in Japan but anywhere in the world. Measurements have demonstrated that in the period 1938–40 parts of Tokyo had subsided by amounts of 10–20 centimetres, mainly in the Koto district (Figure 51). Although the pre-war Japanese hydrologists were uncertain of the causes of this severe sinking an interesting

Fig. 50. Areas of major land subsidence due to groundwater extraction (after T. Nakano).

Location	Depositional environment and age	Depth range of compacting beds below land surface (metres)	Maximum subsidence (metres)	Area of subsidence (sq. km)	Time of principal occurrence
Japan, Osaka, and Tokyo	Alluvial (?) Quaternary (?)	10–200 (?)	3–4	?	1928–43 1948–65+
Mexico, Mexico City	Alluvial and lacustrine; late Cenozoic	Chiefly 10–50	8	25+	1938–68+
Taiwan, Taipei Basin	Alluvial, late Cenozoic	30–200 (?)	1	100±	?–1966+
Arizona, central	Alluvial and lacustrine (?) late Cenozoic	100–300+	2.3	?	1952–67+
California, Santa Clara Valley	Alluvial; late Cenozoic	50–300	4	600	1920–67+
California, San Joaquin Valley (three areas)	Alluvial and lacustrine; late Cenozoic	90–900	8	9,000	1935–66+
Nevada, Las Vegas	Alluvial; late Cenozoic	60–300 (?)	1	500	1935–63+
Texas, Houston-Galveston area	Fluviatile and shallow marine; late Cenozoic	50–600+	1–2	10,000	1943–64+
Louisiana, Baton Rouge	Fluviatile and shallow marine; Miocene to Holocene	40–900 (?)	0.3	500	1934–65+

correlation was then discovered, almost inadvertently, between ground-water abstraction and surface subsidence. Following the increasing subsidence trends which were recorded between 1938 and 1944, the time period from 1944 to 1950 was found to coincide with negligible subsidence. This pause in the surface sinking could only be ascribed to the almost total stoppage of industrial water extraction following the United States' bombing raids towards the close of the Second World War in which Tokyo's industrial zone was virtually destroyed. The correlation was confirmed when major ground subsidence re-commenced in the early 1950s, once the Japanese industry had begun to recover. By 1961 the factories of Tokyo's Koto district were extracting water at the rate of 190,000 cubic metres per day and the land surface had been lowered a further 2 metres. By this time, however, the

Fig. 51. Land subsidence in Tokyo (1938–40).

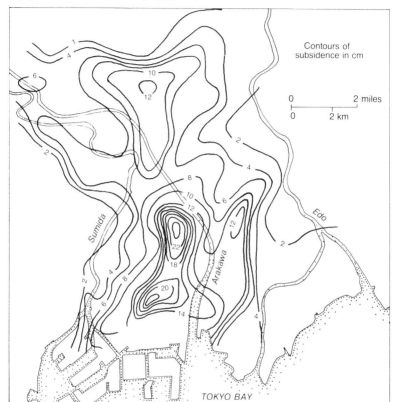

Tokyo authorities had already installed twenty-five observation wells and had been dismayed by the catastrophic flooding of their docklands during a series of major typhoons. Legislation to limit groundwater withdrawal was rapidly introduced and the rate of land subsidence began to decrease from 1965 as the water table rose once again. Nevertheless, there remains no room for complacency since the damage had already been done and the rate of sinking had only been slowed down – it had not been stopped completely.

The Japanese city of Osaka exhibits a very similar history to that of Tokyo, as far as its hydrogeology is concerned, and there, likewise, the military bombing of the Second World War, having caused a destruction of the city's industrial fabric, had also led to a concomitant replenishment of the groundwater supply and a virtual halt in the land subsidence (Figure 52).

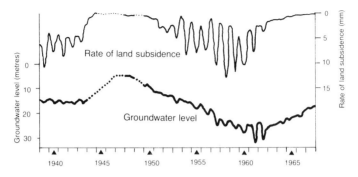

Fig. 52. Variations in groundwater level and land subsidence in Osaka, Japan (1938–68), showing effect of Second World War bombing.

In California, land subsidence due to excessive groundwater extraction was first noticed in 1932–33 in the Santa Clara Valley on the southern outskirts of San Francisco. By 1967 the water table had fallen 75 metres in a period of some fifty years during which time the land surface itself had subsided by almost 4 metres. In the neighbouring San Joaquin section of the well-known Central Valley of California land subsidence became even more widespread and is now affecting an area of over 9,000 square kilometres, including some of California's most productive agricultural land, and is equal to about one third of the entire valley (Figure 53). In addition to the dislocation of thousands of deep well-casings, roads and transmission lines, the continuing subsidence has severely affected both canals and aqueducts, including the major California Aqueduct. In contrast to the industrial water extraction of Tokyo and Osaka, the water withdrawal in central California is concerned almost entirely with the irrigation requirements of the Santa Clara and San Joaquin agricultural enterprises.

Bearing in mind the pronounced subsidence of central California, it is therefore surprising to discover that the even longer-term pumping of groundwater from the artesian basin of south-east England, known as the London Basin, has had virtually no effect on the land surface. In fact, during a century of pumping since 1865 the maximum subsidence in central London has been measured as a mere 2.4 centimetres (around Hyde Park), with the ground surface of the northern and southern suburbs having been affected hardly at all. And all this in one of the world's major cities which has been extracting enormous volumes of water from the underlying permeable rocks

Fig. 53. Land subsidence in the Central Valley of California (after B. E. Lofgren).

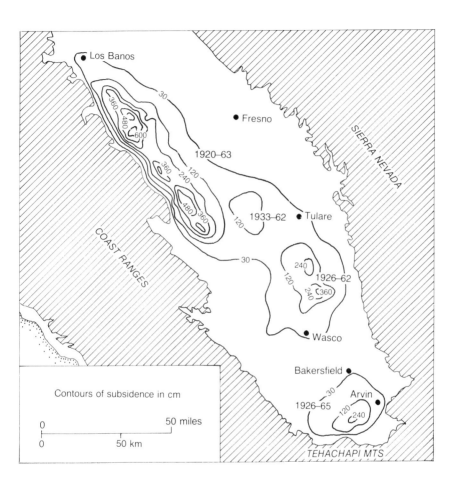

for several centuries. These permeable water-bearing strata (termed an *aquifer*) of chalk rocks are overlain by a thick layer of so-called London Clay. London's negligible subsidence due to groundwater abstraction, therefore, is a fair measure of the relative incompressibility of these overlying clay rocks, although the incessant pumping has lead to a lowering of the water table in the aquifer by about 100 metres during the last 150 years.

Even if Britain's largest city has suffered no ill-effects from its water extraction policy the same cannot be said of Mexico City. In this case parts of the Mexican capital have subsided to depths of some 8 metres (see Figure 50). Having been located on the mixed sediments of a former lake, known to the Aztecs as Lake Texcoco, some of the city's older buildings have suffered varying degrees of damage due to differential settlement following underground water extraction. Foremost of these is the Palacio de Bellas Artes, weighing, together with its concrete raft foundation, a total of 103,000 tonnes. Since the building was commenced in 1904 it has settled unequally by more than 3 metres and is continuing to sink at the rate of 3.7 centimetres per year. Water is now brought to Mexico City from elsewhere, which has served to alleviate the severe de-watering of the underlying clays and sands. Thus, subsidence has slowed down from an annual rate of 30 centimetres to almost one tenth of that amount, but not before serious damage had already been done to the public buildings and utilities. Nevertheless, with correct foundation engineering, it has been demonstrated how even skyscrapers can be constructed in this apparently hazardous terrain of Mexico City. Opposite to the renowned Palacio de Bellas Artes the forty-three-storey Tower Latino Americana has successfully survived for some twenty-five years, because of a careful preliminary investigation of the geology and the introduction of appropriate safety measures. 'Probably nowhere in the world is there such a juxtaposition of two great buildings that illustrate foundation engineering at its worst and at its best.'[2]

On turning to an examination of the results of oil and natural gas withdrawal, we discover that although the mechanisms involved are similar to those of water extraction the surface sinking is generally on a smaller scale. This is because these fluids are usually drawn from considerably greater depths where the strata are less compressible. Only where the oil and gas deposits lie near to the surface will there be land subsidence on a scale comparable to that caused by de-watering. The most severe sinking in the oil-mining history of the United States has occurred in the Los Angeles region, but this will be referred to in more detail in Chapter 11. Suffice to say that of the nineteen Californian oilfields only four (Buena Vista, Huntington Beach, Inglewood and Wilmington) have exhibited more than 1 metre of subsidence. In the well-known Texas oilfields the greatest problems have been produced by a combination of both water and oil extraction in the Houston-Galveston region. Although the amount of subsidence (maximum 1.5 metres between 1943 and 1964) is small in comparison with the Long Beach sinking of Los Angeles (which had about 9 metres displacement between 1928 and 1966) the detrimental effect of the subsidence has been considerable in this Gulf region of low relief. In addition to the usual damage to buildings, wells, sewers and city streets there is evidence of fracturing of the runways at Houston International Airport and of an isolated case of rupturing in a gas-supply pipe – either of which could have caused a major catastrophe.

Pumping of natural gas from beneath the city of Ravenna has already been mentioned, for the methane gas of the Po delta is exploited on a large scale nowadays. Another city which has experienced severe land subsidence due to natural gas extraction is the earthquake-prone city of Niigata, Japan (Figure 54). Here, during 1958–59 the rate of settlement averaged 53 centimetres per year and by 1968 parts of the waterfront had sunk by amounts of 2 metres in less than a decade. Before long, the harbour facilities had been rendered almost useless, the roads, factories and farmlands threatened by invasion of the sea, to say nothing of the widespread structural damage. Although important countermeasures have been introduced, the local authorities are reluctant to lose the benefits of this natural fuel supply.

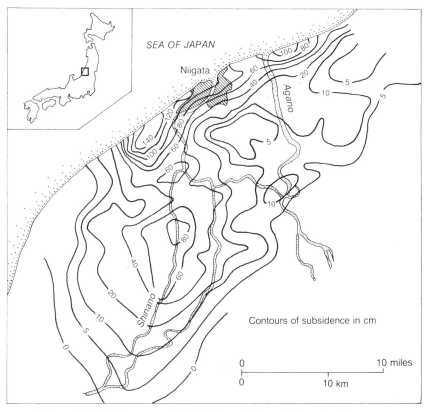

Fig. 54. Land subsidence around Niigata, Japan, due to natural gas extraction (after Y. Yamanoshita).

Subsidence from oil and gas extraction has been observed in other areas of the world, with one especially remarkable example being that around Lake Maracaibo, Venezuela, where sinking at the rate of more than 1 metre per decade is not uncommon. It remains to be seen what sort of results the long-term programme of oil and natural gas withdrawal will have on the North Sea basin. Chances are that it will have very little effect on surface settlement, partly because the oil and gas are pumped from considerable depths, and partly from the fact that sea water is constantly being injected into the critical sediments in order to maintain the pressure necessary to keep the oil flowing.

Extraction of Solids

Twentieth-century mining technology has improved quite markedly from that of earlier centuries, so that surface disturbance is much less common than hitherto. Nevertheless, despite all modern precautions, sudden collapses of underground workings still occur, often leading to substantial and rapid surface subsidence. A recent example of this took place in South Africa where, on 21 January 1960, in a mere five minutes, no less than 3 square kilometres of Coalbrook Colliery collapsed at a depth of 143 metres below ground. More catastrophic than the accompanying surface settlement, however, was the death-toll of 437 underground workers. Later in the chapter (p. 193) we shall examine the method of mining known as the *pillar-and-stall* principle – suffice to say that the Coalbrook disaster was apparently caused by the failure of a single pillar, thus setting off a chain reaction, because of the increasing loads placed on the remaining pillars. Collapse of a whole pillar district is, fortunately, an uncommon occurrence and has never been a significant problem in Britain.

The removal of bulky materials by underground mining probably produces a greater potential for ground movement, and a consequential surface deformation, than does the withdrawal of fluids, because of the greater voids which are left behind. Prediction of land-surface subsidence has by necessity reached its greatest development in the coal-mining industry, for not only is it a labour-intensive industry, but it normally requires that large areas be undermined if there is to be a significant coal production. A combination of these factors means that coal-mining areas are usually heavily urbanized and that the environmental impact of subsidence is often considerable. Not only does the damage cause personal hardship and business inconvenience; it can also occasionally lead to a disaster. Because of the controversial nature of coal-mining subsidence, a former president of the Royal Institute of Chartered Surveyors in U.K. was stimulated into saying that:

Coal mines are costly and it is in the national interest that coal should not be needlessly sterilised. It is therefore important that, especially in urban areas, the effects of working should be as accurately estimated as possible so that the balance of advantage between the working of coal and the damage to property can be fairly assessed in advance.[3]

As far as underground working is concerned two principal methods of coal-mining can be identified. First, that known as pillar-and-stall working, where intersecting galleries are separated by intervening pillars. But since this method involves the abandonment of much valuable coal the second method, known as *longwall* mining, has gradually become more common-place. This latter method is able to remove the entire coal seam but in so doing produces a greater vulnerability to ground-surface subsidence.

Fig. 55. Coal-mining subsidence (after B. Wohlrab).

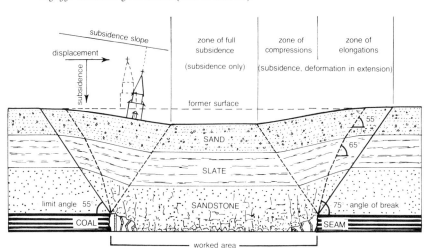

The essential components of longwall mining subsidence are illustrated in Figure 55, where it will be seen how the *angle of break* varies according to the different rock lithologies and how both the amount and the character of the ground movement changes with distance from the central zone of maximum subsidence. The figure also illustrates the principle known as *caving*, in which the roof is allowed to collapse immediately after working, in order to occupy the potentially dangerous void. Such a method leads to a degree of surface settlement equivalent to as much as 90 per cent of the thickness of the worked seam (i.e. a 'caved' coal seam 1 metre thick could result in a surface subsidence of 90 centimetres), but this is the least efficient method of packing the worked-out seam. Two alternative methods are also employed: *strip packing*, in which rubble is hand stored between solid stone walls; and *solid stowing*, in which crushed and wetted stone is forced into the cavities by pneumatic pressure. The former of these reduces surface subsidence by a mere 10 per cent whilst the much more successful pneumatic stowing method reduces ground disturbance to about half of that which results from the caving principle.

From the foregoing description of contrasting degrees of surface settlement it will be appreciated that disturbance from underground coal mining can be categorized according to the magnitude of the damage. In Britain the National Coal Board has produced a table of subsidence damage (Figure 56), in which analogies are drawn with the modified Mercalli Earthquake Scale (see Figure 7). It is interesting to note that the so-called 'earthquake tremors' which caused a substantial amount of damage, inconvenience and

Fig. 56. Categories of subsidence damage (after National Coal Board 1975).

Change of length of structure	Class of Damage	Description of Typical Damage	Mercalli et al Earthquake Scale
<31 mm	1. Very slight or negligible	Hair cracks in plaster . Isolated crack in building not visible on exterior.	1–4
31–61 mm	2. Slight	Several slight cracks showing on interior of building. Doors and windows stick slightly. Repairs to decor probably necessary.	5
61–122 mm	3. Appreciable	Slight fractures showing on exterior of building (or one main fracture). Doors and windows stick. Fracture of service pipes.	6–7
122–183 mm	4. Severe	Service pipes disrupted. Open fractures need rebonding. Window and door frames distorted. Floors slope noticeably. Some loss of bearing in beams. Lifting of brickwork.	8
>183 mm	5. Very severe	As above but worse. Requires partial or complete rebuilding. Roof and floor beams collapse. Walls lean and require shoring up. Windows broken by distortion. Buckling of walls and roofs.	9–10

27. The so-called earthquake tremors in Stoke-on-Trent during the mid 1970s were finally confirmed as coal-mining subsidence phenomena. Here the local Member of Parliament is seen talking to a family whose home has been severely damaged.

fear in parts of Stoke-on-Trent, England, in the mid 1970s were finally attributed to coal-mining disturbance (Plate 27). After a lengthy period of geophysical research it was discovered that the earth movements could be terminated only by a total ban on working of the offending coal seam.

A short distance from the Stoke-on-Trent coalfield is the highly concentrated region of salt working in the county of Cheshire, from which the bulk of the British output is produced. Salt extraction can be carried on in two ways, either by direct mining or by brine pumping, both of which methods have produced significant ground-surface subsidence. Although the majority of the sinking can be attributed to human intervention there is reason to believe that the small pools of water, known as meres, which dot the Cheshire countryside are the result of natural subsidence over a lengthy time period (possibly more than one million years) as groundwater has slowly dissolved the saliferous beds. More importantly, however, the greatest damage to property has occurred in recent centuries, particularly during the period towards the end of the nineteenth century when brine pumping from abandoned mines was carried out with reckless abandon.

The earliest production of salt was by simple mining techniques, not unlike those of the pillar-and-stall methods of the coal industry. Occasionally, vast chambers were hollowed out, one reputedly capable of housing London's St Paul's Cathedral. Miscalculations of the load-bearing capacity of the pillars led to frequent roof collapse which in turn allowed subterranean water into the workings. Once this flooding occurred the mine would have to be abandoned and as the water dissolved the remaining pillars, so further collapse of the workings took place. Consequently, parts of the surface became prone to sudden and sporadic sinking, often with disastrous consequences (Plate 28). During the period when brine pumping replaced mining there was a time when 'wild' brine pumping caused unpredictable surface collapse, since subsidence may occur several kilometres from the point of extraction. Even today, when brine pumping is strictly controlled, ground subsidence continues to be an inhibiting factor, as far as residential and industrial development is concerned, because of this unpredictability. Thus, such well-known English salt towns as Northwich, Winsford and Middlewich have been restricted in their urban expansion plans, for subsidence is still continuing and the water-filled hollows, known as 'flashes', are expanding in area.

Records of surface collapse from salt extraction exist in other parts of the world, one of the most famous being the disaster at Windsor, Ontario, in 1954 when a disused working caved in, destroying two buildings and causing widespread damage. Elsewhere in Canada, however, the salt-subsidence hollows, one of which is now occupied by Crater Lake near Yorkton, Saskatchewan, are natural phenomena similar to those of the Cheshire meres. Likewise, the rapid subsidence of the 'Meade salt sink', Kansas, U.S.A., in March 1879 has also been explained as due to natural solution of deep saliferous beds.

Subsidence has also resulted from extraction of solids other than coal or salt, notably during the mining of limestone and gypsum. In general, because of its high load-bearing capacity, limestone is a competent rock, so that its removal at depth rarely gives rise to significant subsidence. One major exception, however, proved to be in the city of Paris, the historic fabric of which is built almost entirely of limestone quarried from beneath the city streets. In addition to the beds of limestone an extensive deposit of gypsum

28. During the nineteenth century it was common to see the timber-framed houses of Northwich, Cheshire, England, up-ended by salt subsidence.

occurs and this was for long a source of the renowned 'plaster of Paris'. During the earliest periods of extraction sufficient roof cover was left to support the weight of the overlying buildings. By the eighteenth century, however, whilst the thickness of the cover had decreased, the weight of the urban structures had increased so substantially that catastrophic subsidences and collapses began to occur. After the fatalities accompanying the disasters of 1774 and 1776 a special commission was appointed to investigate the feasibility of remedial measures. Probably as a result of the commission's findings, all extraction of both limestone and gypsum from beneath the Parisian boulevards ceased in 1813, by decree of Napoleon himself. The extraction legacy left some 10 per cent of the city under-mined with a honeycomb of workings – 835 hectares in the limestone and 65 hectares in the gypsum beds. Since gypsum is more readily soluble than limestone, extensive surface subsidence can occur fairly rapidly due to subterranean collapse, as in the American states of Oklahoma and New Mexico. Equally serious is the fact that gypsum in solution produces a sulphate capable of weakening concrete foundations, which is a hazard to civil engineering projects.

It is reported that the northern suburbs of Reading, England, have been built unknowingly above some large underground quarries in the chalk, fortunately without any recorded subsidence. In contrast, a new housing estate in Bury St Edmunds, England, had to be abandoned in July 1966, when so-called 'crown holes', associated with former underground chalk mining, began to subside, as the ground instability had been accelerated by interference with the underground drainage regime during the modern site development.

Metaliferous mineral extraction generally produces very few examples of surface subsidence and collapse, largely due to the fact that in most cases the ore bodies are associated with competent rocks. Thus, such metals as copper, tin, lead and iron rarely produce a landscape of subsidence pools, damaged buildings and unstable ground. Nevertheless, their abandoned mine shafts still provide a hazard of sorts and there are occasional reports of fatalities in formerly mined districts. Thus there have been widespread attempts to locate and infill old workings, especially in such well-known British tourist areas as Cornwall and the Peak District.

A final word is necessary about 'pseudo-mining damage', especially in view of the escalation of insurance claims related to property damage in Britain in recent years. This was particularly prevalent following the British drought years of 1975–76 (see Chapter 9), when a natural lowering of the water table led to shrinkage of clay soils and differential movement of buildings. Although the movements were generally slight, they were usually sufficient to cause significant damage to walls, plasterwork, etc., and although the ground returned to normal in the ensuing rainy season the damage had already been done. The problem of ground shrinkage will be examined in more detail below, but it is noteworthy that 'pseudo-mining damage' from ground-movement is exacerbated during a drought season by vegetation, which absorbs water from the soil at an increasing rate. A large tree, for example, can cause a subsidence of 7.5 centimetres during a drought, whilst even a garden hedge has been known to cause 2 centimetres of shrinkage!

Volume Changes in Superficial Materials

Mention has already been made of the capacity of certain clay minerals to absorb and discharge water in such quantities as to have a significant effect on the volume of the soils themselves. In some instances even the bedrock components, especially clay shales and mudstones, may look like rocks but behave like soils. These particular rock formations together with the great varieties of clay soils often contain a high percentage of the mineral known as montmorillonite, which has a considerable capability of water absorption. When such a rock or soil swells, it is because the absorption of water produces pore pressures high enough to overcome its inherent strength. Conversely, when the same soil or rock becomes desiccated, there will be a negative change of volume or shrinkage leading to consolidation. It will be clear to the reader that changes of this sort can produce ground instability, particularly in those instances where large quantities of water are concerned.

Organic soils, such as peat, are generally the most hazardous in this respect, for they do not provide good sites for the construction of roads or buildings. This has proved to be a seriously inhibiting factor in the development plans of all those countries which possess extensive peat deposits. Parts of Scandinavia, U.S.S.R., Ireland and Canada fall into this category, with the latter country possessing no less than 130 million hectares of troublesome organic terrain, locally termed 'muskeg'. Peat is the most unstable of soils, because of its incoherent structure and its very high water content, so that it has virtually no load-bearing capacity. Considerable use must therefore be made of pile-driving in order to achieve stable foundations for buildings, but we have already noted in the case of Copenhagen (p. 180) what happens when the water table falls and the piles become exposed. Similarly, drainage of peatlands invariably leads to shrinkage and subsidence, as demonstrated in the Fenlands of England, after some four hundred years of artificial draining. Variations in the level of the water table in organic deposits were also responsible for the slow subsidence and threatened collapse of one of England's most famous cathedrals, that of Winchester, wherein 7.6 centimetres of differential sinking was discovered at the beginning of the present century. Excavation showed that the enormous weight of masonry was carried merely on a raft of logs and a number of wooden piles driven into an underlying peat bed. Shrinkage, rotting and settlement had all combined to threaten the building, although, happily, the renovation has proved to be entirely successful.

Lengthy periods of artificial drainage in the Dutch polderlands have also led to considerable shrinkage of the peaty clays, causing amounts of consolidation of up to 35 per cent in a century. In a nation where even a slight degree of subsidence or change of water level is of the utmost significance, this critical shrinkage has given rise to official concern. Consequently, it has become very important to predict as accurately as possible the amount of any further subsidence which may be expected, for this will have a considerable bearing on the design of the local pumping stations, sluices and other drainage structures. Although polder subsidence due to shrinkage of the reclaimed subaqueous sediments is no more than 1.5 metres, it will be realized that in a country like the Netherlands, which is also undergoing tectonic sinking, even this amount is substantial. Thus, close monitoring of polder subsidence continues to play an important role in the Dutch national programme of flood protection.

Dykes or levees built on organic soils are notoriously unstable and may collapse without warning at any time. Although the Dutch engineers have long been aware of this potential flood hazard, it is somewhat surprising to learn that a disaster occurred in California in 1972 due entirely to undue reliance on shoddy engineering structures. At the eastern end of San Francisco Bay a large number of artificially-created islands were reclaimed from the deltaic region of the Sacramento River during the late nineteenth century. As in the case of the English Fenlands and the Dutch polders, subsequent shrinkage of their peaty clays meant that the land surface of the islands has gradually subsided below sea level, leading to the ultimate necessity of levee construction as a safeguard against flooding. The collapse of such a badly built levee in 1972 led to catastrophic flooding of the town of Isleton on Andrus-Brannan Island. Not only was there an enormous financial loss, estimated at some $40 million, but in addition the invasion of salt water destroyed the island's fresh water supplies and left 50,000 tonnes of saline residue spread across its farmlands. At other locations in the United States, shrinkage and subsidence of organic soils has proved to be less of a hazard than of an inconvenience. Nevertheless, predictive studies have suggested that the currently farmed peaty soils of the Florida Everglades will probably be too shallow for agricultural use by the year 2000, because of continual shrinkage.

One of the major problems facing engineers in countries which extend into Arctic latitudes is that of swelling and shrinking soils due to expansion and contraction by freezing and thawing. Although most inhabitants of high latitudes have experienced localized frost-heaving of soils during very cold winters, this is of very little significance in comparison with the substantial surface movement which takes place in the regions which have perennially frozen ground. The term *permafrost* has been coined to describe such a phenomenon and it is somewhat surprising to discover the magnitude of the permafrost zone in the northern hemisphere. About one third of the U.S.S.R., about one half of Canada and virtually all of Alaska are underlain by perennially frozen ground. In such areas the seasonal surface thawing together with the differential ground heaving and subsidence play havoc with all construction attempts. After years of structural failures and costly

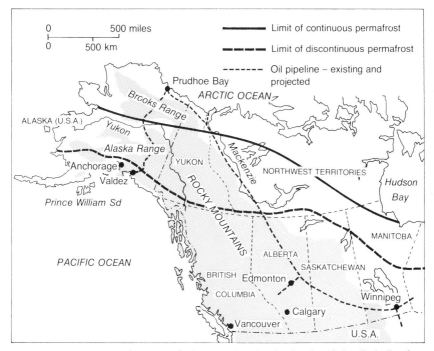

Fig. 57. The Permafrost zone of Alaska and Canada, showing the Alaska oil pipeline from Prudhoe Bay to Valdez. The Mackenzie River pipeline is a projected route (after W.R.D. Sewell).

maintenance, civil engineers have come to realize that special techniques are needed in this zone whilst at the same time recognizing the extreme sensitivity of the ground surface to man-induced disturbance.

Scientists have introduced the term *active layer* to describe the critical surface 'skin' of the permafrost in which the summer thaw activates about 3 metres of its upper layers. When great volumes of water are seasonally released in this way, they cannot escape by percolation in the normal way because of the frozen subsoil, so that extensive pools, marshes and tracts of unstable ground inhibit much of the human activity. Because of its in-hospitable environment the Arctic tundra has long been allowed to remain a wilderness unsullied by man's permanent settlements and communications. But all this has suddenly changed, as far as Alaska is concerned, for in 1968 it was announced that North America's largest oilfield had been discovered at Prudhoe Bay on the barren and virtually ice-bound coast of the Arctic Ocean (Figure 57).

In order to export the enormous output of two million barrels per day the oil company has had to construct a pipeline for a distance of 1,270 kilo-metres southwards to the ice-free port of Valdez on the Pacific coast. Such a mammoth undertaking has not only entailed the building of permanent large-scale industrial structures, but has also resulted in a considerable environmental impact on the 'fragile' tundra land surface noted above. To avoid any repetition of the seemingly endless catalogue of collapsed buildings and severely damaged sewers and water mains which characterizes the permafrost regime, the engineers have had to call on all their ingenuity and technological expertise. In a zone of such marked ground-surface instability it is not surprising to discover the widespread concern for the hazards related to an oil-pipeline fracture. Plate 29 illustrates how oil storage tanks in northern Canada have already been damaged by permafrost rupture and it needs little stretch of the imagination to forecast either an ecological disaster or a catastrophic oil fire were this to happen in the case of the Alaska pipeline.

29. This oil tank in Arctic Canada has settled owing to thawing of the underlying permafrost. Because of buckled plates the leaking oil constitutes a hazard.

Let us first examine the measures that have been taken to offset the likelihood of an ecological disaster in which the vegetation could be irreparably damaged and the local fauna thoroughly disrupted if not destroyed. Even the construction phase posed a threat, for the mosses and lichens that protect and insulate the permafrost are so prone to damage that special wide-tracked vehicles were designed in order to exert less pressure on the surface than that of a man. To repair those areas where it became essential to remove the ground cover, biologists developed new strains of rapidly growing grasses, while to allow free passage for the large herds of caribou which migrate annually across its route the pipeline was raised onto piers at critical locations. For all the merits of this carefully planned conservation exercise it remains, regretfully, one of the very few attempts that have been made to safeguard the Arctic's delicately balanced ecosystem. Indeed, ecologists are claiming that man's recent exploitation of the natural resources of Arctic Canada has already done irreparable damage by increasing the depth of the active layer, thereby exacerbating surface instability.

Doomsday statements of this type were often difficult to substantiate until the advent of the Alaska pipeline, which demonstrated that the fears were justified. Calculations showed that when an oil pipeline is buried at a depth of 2 metres in permafrost the 80°C temperature of the oil would probably increase the depth of the active layer by a factor of three (i.e. down to 9 metres below the surface). To avoid such a probability it became necessary to place the entire pipeline within brine-filled conduits in which, paradoxically, the brine had first to be refrigerated to inhibit heat transfer. Such loss of heat would, of course, result in permafrost melt, differential ground movement due to alternate freezing and thawing and ultimate pipeline fracture. But permafrost rupture is not the only hazard dreaded by the conservationists, for in Chapter 2 we have already noted how sections of the pipeline traverse active seismic areas in Alaska. To prevent oil leakages from earthquake damage the pipeline has been raised on to specially designed mountings throughout the hazard zones, thus allowing some 6 metres of horizontal displacement and 1.5 metres of vertical movement. Finally, as a last precaution against excessive spillage the pipeline is monitored constantly by a computerized control centre at Valdez, from which the entire system can be shut down within seven minutes.

Prediction and Mitigation of Ground Surface Instability

At various points in the foregoing narrative it has been noted how in some instances remedial measures have had to be introduced in an attempt to rectify some of the most critical problems arising from ground instability. But it is not sufficient to be wise after the event and in order to determine both the magnitude and the frequency of any future hazards it remains imperative for research to continue in the field of prediction. All efforts should be made to offset the likelihood of future disasters by forestalling, or at least minimizing, differential ground movement and its accompanying social hardship and structural damage.

As far as subsidence resulting from extraction of solids is concerned, most predictive studies rely primarily on an empirical approach, although there is a parallel research effort which is attempting to base forecasting upon experimental considerations. Not surprisingly, most of the current research is using techniques developed in the coal-mining industry, in which the predictive methodology involves a thorough understanding of the principles of soil and rock mechanics. Such methods involve data collection in four specific fields. First, that which defines the resource geometry i.e. the size and shape of the projected cavity; secondly, that which relates to the properties of the materials involved e.g. their load-bearing capacity; thirdly, that which gives a detailed specification of any load which may be introduced at the surface; finally, that relating to the boundary conditions, i.e. the character of the ground surface and the roof and face of the void itself. Generally speaking, a fair measure of success has been achieved in the prediction of coal-mining subsidence, as befits the most common of the world's extractive industries, but we have seen how this success has not been shared by the salt industry, in which unpredictable degrees of subsidence both in space and in time are common.

When dealing with ground sinking due to water and oil extraction, both empirical and experimental techniques have produced excellent correlations between the degree of subsidence and the magnitude of the exploitation, so that in these cases quite reliable forecasts can be made. It is when engineers move into unfamiliar territory, however, that they sometimes fail to grasp some of the fundamental principles and it is in these rare cases that mistakes occur. A misunderstanding of the properties of materials, for example, can lead to a basic weakness in the design of a protective structure or a remedial measure, leading to a possible disaster – be it of a physical, cultural or ecological nature. In the case of the Alaska pipeline, where scientists and engineers were faced with a set of unusual problems in an unfamiliar permafrost environment, a gigantic predictive exercise was launched long before the construction phase began. Indeed, the U.S. Department of the Interior was obliged by law to prepare what is known as an Environmental Impact Statement, before permission for pipeline construction could be obtained.

In this specific instance the preventive measures could therefore be implemented from the outset, but in the majority of case studies we have seen how substantial damage had already been done before steps were taken to introduce remedial action.

It is one thing to predict the hazards of ground instability, it is quite another to implement measures which will mitigate the impact of these hazards. One of the simplest methods is to introduce legislation banning further exploitation of the underground resource, and we have noted how such draconian action has been essential in the cases of water extraction from beneath Venice, Ravenna, Copenhagen, Tokyo and large tracts of California's Central Valley. On turning to the question of coal-mining subsidence, it has also become necessary in a few critical localities to cease the exploitation of the underground seams, albeit with much reluctance on behalf of the mining authorities. By means of modern cost-benefit analysis, however, it has become possible to discover the point at which compensation for mining damage may well exceed the computed value of the exploited mineral, but in some instances public outrage at the environmental hazards has outweighed all other considerations.

There are many examples in which predictive studies have assisted in the formulation of preventive measures, whereby new building development could be specially designed to withstand any future surface movement. At Heanor in Derbyshire, England, for example, a school which was scheduled to be constructed in an area of severe coal-mining subsidence was eventually built on an articulated concrete raft which allowed significant differential settlement, but without any resulting damage to the specially jointed building itself. On a much larger scale than that of a single building was the collaborative scheme between the National Coal Board and a new-town development corporation in north east England. Here, in the newly planned town of Peterlee a wide range of special construction techniques was introduced, together with a carefully phased extraction programme. By 1970 some 500,000 tonnes of coal had been removed from underlying seams without creating major surface damage. Such a scheme provided a valuable blueprint for future coalfield development plans, as hitherto many thousands of hectares of potential building land had been sterilized by underground mining. Furthermore, land disturbed by open-cast (surface) mineral mining has also been avoided for permanent building sites, because of the lengthy period required for compaction of the infill material. Depending on the depth of loose fill, which averages about 30 metres, this period of surface settlement can last up to twenty-five years. In the open-cast iron-mining area of eastern England, however, experiments are currently being carried out in another new town, that of Corby, where *dynamic consolidation* is being attempted. Several methods of compaction are being tried out, including that of dropping gigantic weights onto the surface from specified heights, in addition to the more novel method of surface loading by water flooding. It is hoped to speed up the rate of surface compaction, thereby releasing many hectares of building land prematurely for the expanding new town of Corby.

Preventive measures are only possible, of course, in areas where mining has not yet commenced, or where new building programmes need to be located in subsidence-risk areas. Elsewhere, in places where the damage has already been done, one can only introduce alleviating measures in order to mitigate the hardship. On the assumption that the mining authorities are playing their role in effective underground packing, the remaining remedial works must be carried out on the surface, generally on the structures themselves.

In former years the method of strapping or banding a threatened building, in which numerous iron ties and bands were inserted in an effort to hold the fabric together, was most commonplace. In severe subsidence zones houses were sometimes built with jacking-points as part of their integral design. Thus, in the salt town of Northwich, for example, houses could be jacked back into the horizontal plane whenever necessary. Jacking of buildings has also been used very successfully in California, where many of the Long Beach harbour installations were saved from either severe damage or flooding by this method. It has also proved possible to release some of the ground surface-tensions by a programme of trench excavation parallel with the walls of endangered buildings, a method which is both effective and inexpensive.

The most costly remedial measures are those which involve the introduction of sophisticated structures such as articulated steel frames or the laborious technique of underpinning by the insertion of reinforced concrete rafts and piles beneath existing buildings. Such methods have finally been adopted by the Danish Government in their fight to save the historic buildings of Copenhagen. Prior to this the city engineers had tried a number of other methods to control the rotting of the wooden foundations. For example, one proposal to kill the critical fungus entailed the pumping of vast quantities of natural gas into the ground – a method which had been successfully tried in Holland. This idea was quickly abandoned not only because of the prohibitive expense and the loss of valuable energy resources, but also because of the new environmental hazards which would be generated. Although natural gas is non-toxic to man and his animals, it can still create a dangerous explosive mixture, as many have discovered to their cost. Gas explosions resulting from leaks due to differential ground movements are not uncommon in mining areas or in regions of perenially frozen ground. Moreover, in some localities underlain by particular types of clay soils, alternating shrinkage and expansion can lead to catastrophic fracture of gas pipes. The notorious British drought of 1975–76, for example, has been blamed for the spate of gas explosions which followed in its wake when desiccated soils again expanded in response to the renewed rainfall. Whenever gas and oil pipelines have to be constructed in zones of high-fracture risk from ground instability, the authorities have endeavoured to fit flexible couplings and expansion joints to obviate the hazard.

Part Four

The Restless Atmosphere

7. High Winds

So far, in our study of disasters, we have concentrated essentially on the interaction between man and the various natural systems which contribute to the make-up and the functioning of the earth's crust or lithosphere. But we have been constantly reminded that many of the geomorphic processes which take place on the earth's land surface are closely related to and are often energized by the natural systems of the atmosphere and hydrosphere. This was particularly true in our examination of the effects of ocean flooding on sinking coastal areas and of the mechanics of avalanche and landslide phenomena, in which oceanic storms, snowfall and excessive rainfall were each seen to play their respective parts in the triggering of the ensuing disasters. Indeed, because the atmosphere is capable of transporting water vapour and heat quite rapidly across the earth's surface, it has sometimes been suggested that atmospheric processes are the most dominant of the world's environmental controls. This is an oversimplification, however, for the landmasses and the oceans have vital roles to play in the modification of atmospheric processes, a modification which is reflected in the seasonal changes of our world-weather patterns.

Modern scientists have been able to demonstrate in great detail how most of the earth's environmental phenomena can be explained within the framework of a unified planetary system, which in turn is composed of two closely integrated systems of energy transfer, namely the global *heat balance* and the global *water balance*. The mobility of our atmosphere and our oceans allows them to act as mechanisms of heat transfer, exporting heat from areas of excess and carrying it to regions of deficiency. Similarly, moisture can be transported, but in this case not only through the atmosphere and the hydrosphere, but also across the landmasses themselves, in the form of rivers (or even glaciers). Such are the ways in which the earth's heat and water balance are normally maintained, but in this chapter and the succeeding chapters we shall examine some of the catastrophes which eventuate from fluctuations in our planetary system of air and water circulation. We

Year	Country	Death Toll	Comments
1959	Japan	5,098	Typhoon Ise Bay
1960	East Pakistan	> 5,000	2 Cyclones
1960	U.S.A.	50	Hurricane Donna
1961	U.S.A.	46	Hurricane Carla
1961	Japan	202	Typhoon Muroto II
1963	East Pakistan	15,000	Cyclone
1963	Cuba–Haiti	> 7,000	Hurricane Flora
1964	U.S.A.	3	Hurricane Cleo
1964	U.S.A.	38	Hurricane Hilda
1964	U.S.A.	5	Hurricane Dora
1964	East Pakistan (May)	35,000	Cyclone
1964	East Pakistan (Dec)	15,000	Cyclone
1965	East Pakistan	> 19,000	Cyclone
1965	U.S.A.	75	Hurricane Betsy
1966	U.S.A.	48	Hurricane Inez
1966	Haiti	750	Hurricane Inez
1966	Mexico	65	Hurricane Inez
1967	U.S.A.	6	Hurricane
1967	U.S.A.	15	Hurricane Beulah
1967	East Pakistan	> 130	Cyclone
1968	Scotland	20	Hurricane
1968	East Pakistan	> 1,000	Cyclone
1969	U.S.A.	256	Hurricane Camille
1970	U.S.A.	11	Hurricane Celia
1970	Bangladesh–India	? c. 1,000,000	Cyclone
1970	Australia	13	Cyclone
1970	India	20,000	Cyclone
1972	U.S.A.	—	Hurricane Agnes
1973	Mexico	200	Hurricane Brenda
1974	Japan	103	Typhoon Gilda
1974	Honduras	8,000	Hurricane Fifi
1974	Australia	47	Cyclone
1976	Mexico	> 700	Hurricane
1977	India	100,000	Cyclone

Fig. 58. The world's most severe tropical storms (1959–77) (after G. F. White).

shall see how excessive transfer of moisture often results in flooding (Chapter 8) and how a protracted deficiency of moisture culminates in drought (Chapter 9). A combination of excessive moisture and a deficiency of heat can lead to a disastrous snowfall or sometimes a fog (Chapter 10). The instrument that assists in the global transfer of heat and moisture is known as a planetary wind, which in turn activates the ocean current. Broadly speaking, a wind may be defined as any air motion which occurs, relative to the earth's surface, and we shall now explore some of the ways in which excessive wind speeds play their part in the fashioning of disasters.

With the notable exception of the Chinese floods of 1931 in which the Hwang Ho river is reputed to have been responsible for 3,700,000 deaths, storms with violent wind velocities have caused higher death-tolls than those emanating from other natural hazards. Even earthquake casualties rarely exceed the annual totals of victims resulting from hurricanes, typhoons and cyclones when judged on a global scale. Figure 58 illustrates the 1959–77 period during which about 1.25 million people died in a series of tropical cyclones, although this period does include the most disastrous storm on record, when India and Bangladesh lost about 1 million people in a matter of days. Needless to say, the death-toll is not the only problem to be faced, for often the amounts of damage reach astronomical proportions. In the United States, for example, the estimated cost of hurricane damage between 1960 and 1970 totalled no less than $4,848 million. Very often the less developed countries have little means of assessing the monetary value of damage, especially where the property or the crops have been uninsured, so that the financial costs of some of the world's greatest storm disasters remain unknown. Despite the variations in the extent of destruction from year to year, it has been calculated that storm-damage trends are probably rising as world population pressure and land hunger are driving more and more people into the earth's hazard zones. Little wonder that the fearful tropical cyclone of 12–13 November 1970 killed well over half of the population of the over-crowded and storm-prone Ganges Delta, wiping out 65 per cent of the coastal fishing capacity and thus seriously depleting the major protein supply of Bangladesh for many years (Figure 59).

In some parts of the world the storm-warning systems are sophisticated enough to avoid catastrophic loss of life and it is instructive to learn that in the United States, whilst the costs of damage from hurricanes have risen sharply in the last half century, the number of deaths associated with these disasters has steadily declined. Statistics such as these illustrate not only the efficiency of the United States' storm-warning systems and the high degree of mobility of its large automobile-owning public, but also the increasing

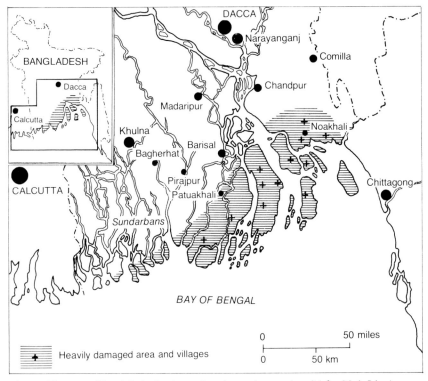

Fig. 59. The coast of Bangladesh, showing cyclone devastation area (1970) (after M. A. Islam).

number of expensive structures which are being built in the vulnerable coastal areas. Indeed, it is known that over half of the American public now lives on or near its coastlines and that this proportion is increasing. By 1971 hurricane forecasters in the United States were predicting '. . . that the death-toll might move sharply upward in the future if a severe hurricane were to make a direct hit on a crowded coastal area and evacuation routes became clogged'.[1] Ironically, in the following year (1972) Hurricane Agnes lashed the eastern seaboard of the United States and although 500,000 people were left temporarily homeless, rapid evacuation kept the loss of life to minimal proportions. Again, in 1974, but this time in northern Australia, a tropical cyclone scored a direct hit on a large urban area, totally destroying the city of Darwin but killing only forty-seven people, since more than 20,000 had been rapidly evacuated by private transport. It is when a storm strikes a heavily populated, underdeveloped country that the greatest disasters occur, for even if adequate warnings are given there is very little chance of evacuating the bulk of the population when road networks are poor and transport facilities virtually non-existent.

Such was the case in south-eastern India in 1977 when a tropical cyclone of frightful intensity struck the Indian coast of the Bay of Bengal. A warning was given forty-eight hours before the cataclysm, but to no avail since the vast majority of the population either ignored the warning or were unable to take evasive action. Thus, one of the most severe Indian Ocean cyclones ever recorded took its fearsome toll in November 1977, when winds gusting up to speeds of 160 kilometres per hour tore down trees, swept away dwellings and even buckled steel structures. In addition to the great amount of damage caused by the winds themselves, enormous 6-metre tidal waves were driven far inland by the pile-up of water along the low-lying coastline of Andhra Pradesh. Here, in the fertile deltas of the Kistna and Godavari rivers, entire villages were wiped off the map and even the coastal towns were severely damaged, most casualties having been caused by collapsing buildings. In some rural areas more than 90 per cent of the population perished, with some reports giving the final death-toll at over 100,000. Those few who survived were faced with starvation, despite the Indian government's initial relief grant of $6 million, but with no homes, no possessions, no livestock and 50,000 square kilometres of their agricultural land devastated, the outlook was bleak.

It is difficult for an outsider to conceive the degree of destruction and the utter despair of the survivors who had lost their all. But, as relief helicopters dropped supplies to the stricken villagers, an eyewitness account conveys something of the horror:

As the aircraft gains height leaving the outskirts of the isolated hamlet, its crew see that almost all the huts are completely flattened and a once protecting circle of palm trees is down. Bloated carcasses are dotted all along the edges of the inundated fields. Every now and then there are human corpses . . . You get the stink from 50 feet to 100 feet above the ground. As we fly towards the sea the lines of the big rice fields of the rich agricultural region disappear and for about 25 miles the landscape is completely waterlogged, often only a dirty brown except for the foliage of uprooted trees.[2]

Despite the appalling nature of the 1977 cyclone it is disturbing to discover that this type of disaster is not uncommon in the Indian sub-continent, for rarely a year goes by without a major catastrophe of this sort (see Figure 58).

The sheer physical impact of a hurricane-force wind is capable of much destruction by itself, such as the lifting of roofs and the breakage of glass windows, thus causing deaths and serious injuries from airborne objects and flying glass (Plate 30). Furthermore, sudden gusts have been known to cause

30. The physical impact of strong winds is capable of lifting roofs and causing injury from flying debris, as illustrated in this scene of a gale in Flensburg, West Germany.

the destruction of a building which up till then had been able to withstand the strong but relatively unwavering impact of the wind. Collapse from gustiness is usually the outcome of unequally imposed pressures being suddenly generated on different sides of a building simultaneously, the cause being similar in some respects to the differential stresses set up by a tornado, as a result of which buildings are said to 'explode' (Plate 31). In other instances, tall structures, such as church spires and radio towers, may be so stressed by severe gustiness that an oscillation develops, leading to ultimate structural failure and disintegration. There is a long history of structural damage caused by high winds, ranging from the collapse of the spire on Lincoln Cathedral's central tower to the destruction of a 490-metre T.V. mast in New Mexico, U.S.A., during a 1960 gale. One of the most sensational rail disasters in Britain occurred when the newly completed rail bridge over Scotland's River Tay was blown down during a winter storm in 1879, carrying with it a trainload of passengers. More recently, the destruction of the Tacoma suspension bridge in Washington State, U.S.A., graphically illustrated the hazard of wind-induced oscillation.

31. The collapse of one of the cooling towers at Ferrybridge power station, Yorkshire, England, during a period of gusty winds in November 1965.

One of the most bizarre examples of the effects of wind impact on modern structures comes from the American city of Boston. Here, the well-known Hancock Tower (240 metres), the tallest of the city's skyscrapers, has consistently rained glass into the surrounding streets as its windows have dropped out. The magnitude of the hazard will be appreciated when it is realized that the 5 square metres sheets of glass each weighed 180 kilograms and that there are no less than 10,348 windows! So much glass fell in 1972 that the neighbourhood was cordoned off, and since the gaping holes had to be boarded up against the elements one of Boston's most prestigious buildings became known as the Plywood Palace. Experts who were hastily enlisted admitted that 'the phenomenology was too complicated to give a simple answer' but admitted that high winds made the tower bend and twist simultaneously. Newly designed toughened glass was then fitted at a cost of $8 million, but this too fell out shortly afterwards. To counteract the tower's swaying and twisting motions, gigantic shock absorbers have now been installed, together with a strengthening of the building's steel frame, at a combined cost of a further $8 million. It remains to be seen what degree of success has been achieved, but it is a sobering thought that the remedial measures have already totalled well over one quarter of the initial building costs.

Wind impact is not the only hazard associated with violent storms for it has already been seen how the accompanying 'tidal waves' or 'storm surges' can cause extensive devastation on exposed coastlines. This is not simply a matter of the depredations caused by marine flooding, but it is also because of the havoc produced on unprotected foreshores by the battering of storm waves (Plate 32). In the worst instances beaches may be totally combed away and large sections of the cliffs so undermined that they collapse into the sea, sometimes taking with them houses, roads and railways. Finally, it is commonplace for the heavy and prolonged rainfall which accompanies a severe storm to lead to extensive river flooding. The various types of damage that ensue from a storm of great intensity are illustrated in Figure 60, in which the separate hazards can be identified and the potential destruction projected by means of this cyclonic impact diagram.

Elementary Wind Physics and the Origin of Storms

In order to understand the mechanisms which generate the earth's atmospheric storms it will be necessary to look briefly at the history of scientific research into the origin of winds.

32. *right* A violent storm in March 1962 brought havoc to these American homes on the south shore of Long Island, New York.

Fig. 60. Model of potential damage from tropical cyclones (after A. U. White).

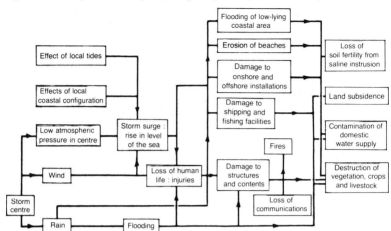

Once mankind had chosen to regard windstorms as something more than the wrath of God, several simple gadgets were devised to measure the wind. The earliest wind vanes, for example, were known to the ancient Egyptians and Chinese, although in Europe it seems likely that the prototype was located on the Tower of the Winds, built in Athens in the second-century B.C. Even before this Aristotle had written his famous *Meteorologica*, in which he realized the important relationships that existed between the four elements of air, water, fire and earth. Nevertheless, because he was unable to master the basic principles of physics, he gave unsatisfactory explanations of atmospheric processes. Yet, despite its failings, Aristotelian theory remained the inspiration behind most meteorological thinking until the end of the sixteenth century, when the invention of a number of scientific instruments during the Renaissance heralded a revolution in the study of the atmosphere.

In the forefront was Galileo, who invented the thermometer, closely followed by his pupil Torricelli, who constructed the earliest barometer. Henceforth, the changes in barometric pressure were found to coincide with fluctuations in wind velocity and direction, and these observations have continued to form the basis of weather forecasting to this day. By the end of the seventeenth century Sir Isaac Newton had propounded several classical theories relating to the physical laws which govern the universe. Two of these, the *Law of Conservation of Mass* and the *Second Law of Motion*, constitute the foundations of atmospheric physics, for they relate mass, force and changes in velocity to each other. The fundamental principles of meteo-rology were virtually completed within the next century, thanks to the work of Robert Boyle and Jacques Charles, from whose laws scientists were able to calculate the expansion and contraction of air during heating and cooling. After the discovery of the *Law of Partial Pressures* by John Dalton in 1790, meteorologists were in a position to determine the amount of water vapour in the atmosphere and therefore to account for cloud formation. The last of the basic principles in the science of atmospheric physics was discovered by James Joule, and was ultimately to become the *First Law of Thermodynamics*, in which the fundamental relationships were explained between the heating of a gas and the work done during its expansion. The term *Joule* is now used universally as a measure of kinetic energy. It was left to two nineteenth-century scientists, Coriolis and Ferrell, to add some final principles by explaining the pattern of the earth's prevailing winds in relation to its rotational movement.

Despite the enormous scientific achievements of the twentieth century, the study of atmospheric physics has progressed very largely in terms of new instrumentation and data-collection techniques rather than in the field of meteorological theory. Satellite photography, high-speed computers and a world-wide network of weather stations have allowed more consistent and more sophisticated weather forecasting, and this has been particularly true as far as storm prediction is concerned.

Fig. 61. The principles of air turbulence.

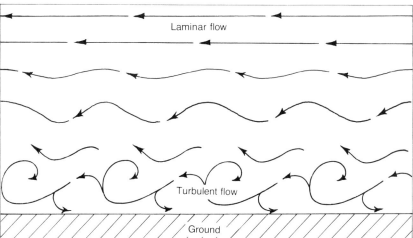

We have already noted that at its simplest the term wind may be defined as air in horizontal motion, with such motion tending to equalize lateral differences in temperature, humidity and pressure. Consequently, wind may be regarded as a very important regulator of atmospheric inequalities. A distinction must be made at the outset between the horizontal air movement – or wind – and the vertical air movement, termed a current. When air moves horizontally across the earth's surface its lower layers will be affected in two ways: first, by the roughness of the underlying terrain, which generates friction, and, secondly, by thermal convection, if the earth's surface is warmer than the air itself. The upper layers of the air are not affected by these surface influences so that at higher elevations in the atmosphere there exists a smooth, sheetlike flow of air known as *laminar flow*. At lower levels, however, surface interference produces eddy motions, referred to as *turbulence*, which manifest themselves as gusts and lulls in the wind stream (Figure 61). Turbulence increases not only as a function of the roughness of the land surface, but also in relation to the amount of temperature contrast between the cooler air above and the warmer surface beneath. Since land is more rugged and has more local temperature variations than water, it follows that turbulence is stronger over the continents than over the oceans. It is equally true that for the same reasons winds will be stronger at sea, because on land the roughness of the terrain reduces the effective wind speed.

Because of the vulnerability of shipping to changes in wind velocity, it is not surprising to discover that it was a British seaman, Admiral Beaufort, who developed the well-known scale of wind speed that bears his name (Figure 62), although it will be seen that certain specifications have been added for use on land.

Pressure differences in a horizontal plane can be denoted on a map by the use of lines known as *isobars*, which are analogous to the contours of a topographic map. Thus, just as we speak of a slope gradient between areas of high and low relief, the meteorologist uses the term *pressure gradient* to describe the change in pressure with horizontal distance, and frequently refers to the 'steepness' of the pressure gradient. It is easy to understand that the steeper the pressure gradient, the more closely spaced will be the isobars and the stronger the wind which blows across those isobars – down the pressure gradient from high to low pressure.

It has long been known that the earth's atmosphere divides itself into constantly changing patterns of high and low pressure cells, which are depicted on weather maps by roughly circular or elliptical isobaric configurations known as *anticyclones* (highs) and *cyclones* (lows). Such pressure systems generally cover tens of thousands of square kilometres and move

Beaufort Force	Velocity (miles per hour)	National Weather Service Terminology	Specifications for use on Land
0	< 1	Calm	Smoke rises vertically
1	1–3	Light air	Wind direction shown by smoke, but not by vanes
2	4–7	Light breeze	Wind felt on face; leaves rustle, vane moves
3	8–12	Gentle breeze	Twigs in constant motion; wind extends light flag
4	13–18	Moderate breeze	Raises dust and loose paper; moves small branches
5	19–24	Fresh breeze	Small, leafy trees sway; wavelets on inland water
6	25–31	Strong breeze	Large branches in motion; whistling in telegraph wires
7	32–38	Near gale	Whole trees in motion; resistance felt in walking
8	39–46	Gale	Breaks twigs off trees; generally impedes progress
9	47–54	Strong gale	Slight structural damage (chimney pots, roof tiles)
10	55–63	Storm	Trees uprooted; considerable structural damage
11	64–72	Violent storm	Rarely experienced inland; widespread damage
12	73–82		
13	83–92		
14	93–103		
15	104–14	Hurricane	Very rare occurrence except in tropics;
16	115–25		catastrophic structural damage;
17	126–36		heavy loss of life

Fig. 62. The Beaufort Scale of Wind Velocity.

at varying speeds across the earth's surface. For a high-pressure area to be maintained air must descend vertically within it, thereby warming, tending to become dry and clear, and flowing outwards at the surface (Figure 63a). Conversely, for a low-pressure area to be maintained air must rise within it, thus becoming cooled, tending to form clouds and precipitation and drawing air inwards to the low-pressure centre (Figure 63b).

At first glance it would appear that air should flow directly down the steepest part of the pressure gradient, very much as a stream flows directly down a slope, normal to the contours. Instead of flowing directly inwards, parallel to the gradient, however, it will be seen from a study of Figure 63b that the wind blows obliquely across the isobars because it is governed by

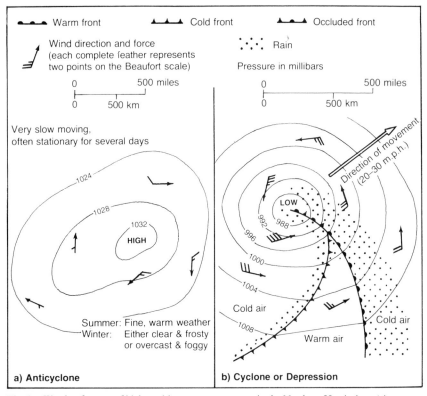

Fig. 63. Weather features of high- and low-pressure systems in the Northern Hemisphere (air movement in the Southern Hemisphere is in the opposite directions) (a) Anticyclone; (b) Cyclone or Depression.

deflective (Coriolis), centrifugal and frictional forces, as well as by the pressure gradient. In the Northern Hemisphere the earth's rotation causes the wind to be deflected to the right, resulting in a counterclockwise spiral around the low-pressure centre – whilst in the Southern Hemisphere the situation is reversed, causing a clockwise spiral. Such circular motions as these are termed *vortices*, which vary in size from the smallest *dust devils*, through the *tornadoes*, upwards to the larger *hurricanes* and *cyclones*. Most of the world's severe-weather disasters are associated with vortices in some form or another, and it is generally true that the magnitude of the disaster depends very largely on the amount of energy available within the revolving storm system. Figure 64 illustrates the different degrees of kinetic energy

Storm type	Kinetic energy (Joules)
Dust devil	4.10^7
Tornado	4.10^{10}
Thunderstorm	4.10^{12}
Hurricane	4.10^{16}
Cyclone	4.10^{17}

Fig. 64. Energy of severe-weather phenomena (after L. J. Battan).

associated with various types of vortices and explains in part the devastation caused by hurricanes and tropical cyclones.

Dust Devils, Tornadoes and Waterspouts

The least powerful and therefore least destructive of the atmospheric vortices is the *dust devil*, which is a small-scale tornado-like whirlwind originating from severe localized heating of the earth's surface. On hot summer days most people have witnessed the sudden miniature whirlwind which sends dust and litter swirling spirally upwards, although the phenomenon usually lasts for less than a minute. The spiral movement may be generated as the air flow is deflected around obstacles such as buildings or even groups of trees, whereupon the hot spinning air concentrates into a columnar vortex. Air particles spinning tangentially around the column prevent external air from penetrating the vortex walls, although buoyant air is drawn in at its base. The ascending hot air eventually reaches an altitude (generally less than 1000 metres) at which it mixes with cooler non-rotating air, rotation is lost and the vortex top gradually retreats towards the ground as the dust devil dies away.

Laboratory experiments have shown that the mechanisms of the smaller vortices, described above, are very similar to those which generate the more fearsome *tornadoes* and *waterspouts*. Figure 65 illustrates the idealized vertical flow of buoyant air within a tornado vortex and demonstrates how tornadoes are often associated with thunderstorms. Waterspouts are the counterparts of tornadoes but are confined to oceans and lakes where their less vigorous rotation and the sparsity of human occupancy means that they are less destructive (Plate 33). Nevertheless, there are numerous records of small boats being overwhelmed by such phenomena and there is a particularly vivid account of a waterspout causing considerable damage in

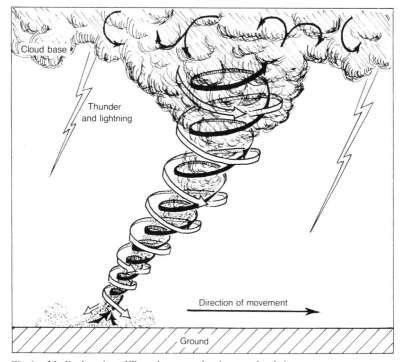

Fig. 65. Idealized section of Tornado vortex, showing postulated air movement.

Swansea, South Wales, in September 1886. Having travelled across the sea the waterspout struck the coast at Kelvey Hill (200 metres), whereupon it released great volumes of sea-water. The torrents rushed down the slopes, bursting through a row of houses, washing people and their belongings far down the hill. Forty families were rendered homeless and some 8,000 tonnes of earth and rock dumped at the foot of Kelvey Hill.

Although it is known that tornadoes occur during periods of severe ground-surface heating which gives rise to strong thermal convection and thunder-storm activity, the exact mechanisms of these destructive vortices is improperly understood. Meteorologists are uncertain whether the theoretical vertical movement of buoyant air in the funnel of the idealized tornado shown in Figure 65 can provide enough energy to maintain the intense spiralling action of the vortex. Because of its frequent association with thunderstorms, for example, it has even been suggested that the tornado may be partly energized from electrodynamic sources, whereby current

33. *right* A spectacular waterspout approaching the Costa Brava, Spain, in September 1965.

flowing to the ground by way of lightning-flashes through the core could provide substantial heating to rising air within the vortex. But whatever its dynamics the tornado is a frightening instrument of destruction, for in certain parts of the world tornadoes, or 'twisters' as they are colloquially termed, carve broad swathes of death and devastation across the landscape.

Tornadoes occur in many parts of the world, having been reported from Japan, Australia, Europe and North America. Among these regions that of the Midwest in the U.S.A. is by far the most tornado-prone; on average more than 200 people are killed there annually. The infamous 'twister' of 18 March 1925 appears to have been the most destructive on record for along its 352 kilometre track through Missouri, Illinois and Indiana it killed some 690 people in three hours and devastated a total area of 425 square kilometres. And yet this killer moved through an area outside the zone of maximum tornado frequency (Figure 66).

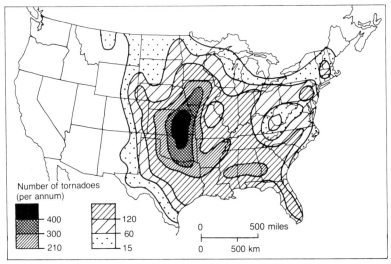

Fig. 66. The distribution of reported Tornadoes in the U.S.A. over a forty-year period (after K. Hindley).

The 1925 tornado was notable not only for the length of its track and its high casualty rate, but also for the velocity of its rotating winds. The amount of damage caused by a tornado is known to have a high degree of correlation with the maximum wind velocity occurring within the vortex. A scale of tornado damage, very much along the lines of the Mercalli scale of

Fig. 67. The Fujita Scale of Tornado damage.

Number	Maximum Wind Velocity		
	m/sec	km/hr	m.p.h.
0	18	65	40
1	33	120	74
2	50	180	111
3	70	252	155
4	93	335	206
5	117	421	260

earthquake destruction (Chapter 2), has in fact been devised by Dr T. Fujita, who has recognized six classes of wind speed (Figure 67) and has published a series of pictures which show the damage relating to each of his classes.

In general the 'twisters' of the American Midwest occur during the late afternoon at the height of the tornado season from April to early July, i.e. when surface heating of the continental interior increases rapidly as the air temperature rises. The widespread convectional activity that results triggers off numerous thunderstorms some of which give birth to tornadoes. A typical 'twister' may start its life rather like a dust devil, but more commonly the updraught first develops within the thundercloud from which a dark, funnel-shaped vortex descends towards the ground as the pressure falls in the narrow core (Plate 34). As the vortex develops it gradually widens and begins to advance along the ground at speeds approaching 55 kilometres per hour, gathering strength as it begins its unpredictable rampage of destruction. The almost random march of the tornado is one of its most terrifying aspects, for it can swing either left or right for no apparent reason, double back on itself or even travel round in circles. The accompanying roar of the rotating wind, which can be heard several kilometres away, adds to the frightening spectacle, whilst the spiralling air, shooting upwards at 100 metres per second, generates an enormous degree of suction. This vacuum cleaner effect at the centre of the vortex is so great that an American expert has described how:

> . . . bark has been peeled off trees, harnesses have been stripped off horses, and clothing has been stripped off people leaving them completely naked. Dead sheep have been found shorn of their wool, feathers have been plucked off chickens . . .

These strong updraughts have been known to carry people, livestock and man-made structures high into the air and lift heavy railway carriages from

34. (a–d) This sequence of photographs demonstrates the stages in the formation of a tornado during May 1970 in Kansas, U.S.A.

their tracks. In Minnesota a 1931 tornado raised one such 85-tonne carriage, together with its 117 passengers, some 25 metres off the ground!

The accompanying downdraughts are equally strong and have produced spectacular instances of driving baulks of timber half a metre into the ground and punching splinters of wood right through metal posts. Significantly, the intensity of the down-draught has convinced some meteorologists that the simple model of a thermal vortex of rapidly rising air is an insufficient explanation of a tornado; after all, the funnel cloud can be seen to dip *down* from the clouds to the ground.

As the tornado moves across the ground, the devastation within its 500 metres to 1 kilometre wide swathe is virtually absolute, for only reinforced concrete or steel structures are able to withstand the extraordinary change of pressure which takes place as the whiplash tail of the tornado strikes. Measurements have shown that the pressure in the 'eye' of a tornado may be more than 100 millibars below that of the surrounding air. When it is realized that on a global scale the total range of pressure between the deepest depression (cyclone) and the highest anticyclone is about 100 millibars,

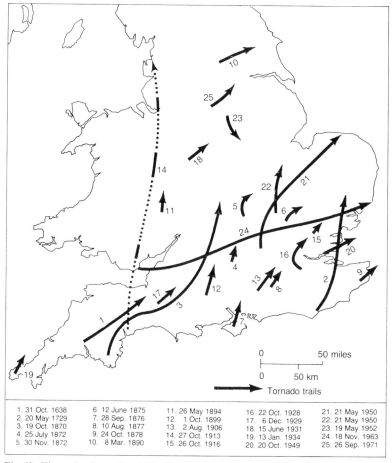

1. 31 Oct. 1638	6. 12 June 1875	11. 26 May 1894	16. 22 Oct. 1928	21. 21 May 1950
2. 20 May 1729	7. 28 Sep. 1876	12. 1 Oct. 1899	17. 6 Dec. 1929	22. 21 May 1950
3. 19 Oct. 1870	8. 10 Aug. 1877	13. 2 Aug. 1906	18. 15 June 1931	23. 19 May 1952
4. 25 July 1872	9. 24 Oct. 1878	14. 27 Oct. 1913	19. 13 Jan. 1934	24. 18 Nov. 1963
5. 30 Nov. 1872	10. 8 Mar. 1890	15. 26 Oct. 1916	20. 20 Oct. 1949	25. 26 Sep. 1971

Fig. 68. The tracks of tornadoes in England and Wales (based on work by H. H. Lamb).

spread across thousands of kilometres, it puts into perspective the incredible pressure gradient of the tornado and explains the ferocity of its winds. Little wonder that timber-framed buildings explode in the partial vacuum thus created, that mature trees are snapped off by the violent twisting motion and that most casualties result from debris flying at phenomenal velocities. There is even a bizarre record of a house hitting a car in Arkansas!

Tornadoes of such severity are uncommon in Britain although less destructive examples occur about once every two years. In contrast to that of the American Midwest the British loss of life is negligible, despite the sixty casualties incurred when a tornado and its associated lightning caused the church spire to collapse onto the congregation at Widecombe-in-the-Moor, Devon, in 1638. Analysis of tornadoes during the period of 1963–66 has demonstrated that in Britain, contrary to expectation, there were more tornadoes in winter than in summer. A search of meteorological records showed that few of the tornadoes were associated with violent summer thunderstorms, but were linked mainly with cool, windy, showery weather. Thus, not only are British tornadoes much less severe than their American counterparts, but they also appear to be spawned in rather different weather conditions. Nevertheless, some notable British tornadoes have created sufficient havoc for their trails of destruction to be recorded and these are illustrated in Figure 68. One of the most severe appears to have been that of 21 May 1950 (No. 21 in Figure 68) which left a 160 kilometre trail of damage from Berkshire to Norfolk, during which maximum wind speeds in the vortex were estimated at about 100 metres per second (360 kilometres per hour, 223 m.p.h.), placing it very high on the Fujita scale (see Figure 67).

It is noteworthy that one of the earliest descriptions of a tornado has been discovered in the *Chronicle of Melrose Abbey*, which refers to a whirlwind in August 1165 near to Scarborough in Yorkshire, England:

Many people saw the old enemy taking the lead in that tempest; he was in the form of a black horse of large size, and always kept hurrying towards the sea, while he was followed by thunder, lightning, fearful noises and destructive hail. The footprints of this accursed horse were of a very enormous size, especially on the hill near the town of Scardeburch (sic), from which he gave a leap into the sea; and here for a whole year afterwards, they were plainly visible, the impression of each foot being deeply graven in the earth.[3]

The phenomena of crater-like imprints on soft ground have been described frequently in the literature, for it is known that the skipping action of the tornado's funnel cloud produces this type of intermittent scouring as it touches down – thus creating the 'footprints of this accursed horse' quoted above.

Hurricanes and Typhoons (Tropical Cyclones)

If tornadoes are regarded as the 'Light Brigade' in Nature's elemental assault on the earth's surface, then tropical cyclones must surely be the 'Heavy Brigade'. It has been calculated, for example, that a tropical cyclone releases energy equivalent to a hydrogen-bomb explosion every minute of its existence! Known in the Western world as *hurricanes* and in the Orient as *typhoons*, these gigantic vortices are responsible for more death and destruction than any other natural event.

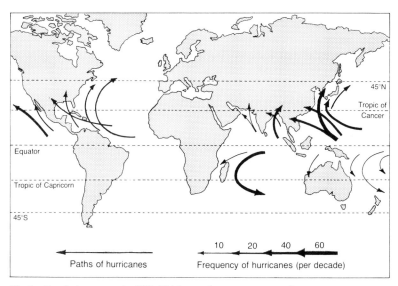

Fig. 69. Tropical storm tracks. N.B. Thickness of arrows represents frequency.

Tropical cyclones start their journeys in mid ocean in low latitudes, often travelling along parabolic-shaped courses following first the Trade Winds and then the Westerlies as they move slowly away from the equator (Figure 69). It appears that a copious supply of warm, moist air is essential for their formation, and it is this which provides sufficient energy to generate and maintain the hurricane or typhoon over lengthy distances. Tropical cyclones are always associated with extremely heavy rainfall and it is in fact the heat released by the condensation of the water that supplies this continuous energy source. Only the tropical oceans can provide this initial input of warm, moist air and it has been shown how hurricanes generally dissipate as they move into continental interiors and into higher, cooler latitudes.

233

A clear distinction must be made between the tropical cyclones outlined above and the cyclones of the temperate zones. Although these extra-tropical cyclones, often termed 'depressions' or 'lows' in West European weather forecasts, are themselves composed of swirling vortices of moisture-laden air, they rarely achieve the high wind velocities of the tropical hurri-canes or typhoons and are therefore less destructive.

Modern satellite photography from above the level of these atmospheric storms has enabled us to have a fairly clear picture of the characteristics of a typical tropical cyclone (Plate 35). One of its most remarkable features is the so-called 'eye' of the storm, about 20 kilometres in diameter, which is characterized by light winds and almost cloudless skies. It is noteworthy that extratropical cyclones do not exhibit such a feature. Around this central core, bands of thick cloud extending out for some 150 kilometres can be seen

35. A satellite photograph from space illustrates the spiral movement of the cloud/wind pattern of a typical tropical cyclone. Note the 'eye' of the storm.

to be spiralling, similar in appearance to a pyrotechnic catherine wheel or pinwheel. These mark the direction of the spinning air as it converges towards the central funnel and this movement, of course, gives rise to the very strong winds (blowing at speeds of up to 70 metres per second or 155 m.p.h.) which are a feature of the tropical storm.

Damage and loss of life caused by hurricanes and typhoons are related to three main causes: first, the high wind velocities, secondly, the river flooding which results from the heavy precipitation and thirdly, the coastal flooding from storm surges, erroneously termed 'tidal waves'.

Despite their very high wind velocities it will be seen that tropical cyclones rarely generate the exceptionally high wind speeds of the tornado. Consequently, the degree of wind-impact damage in a hurricane may, in some instances, be less than in a tornado. Furthermore, the latter's explosive effect on houses is not so marked in the case of hurricanes, because of their slower variations in atmospheric pressure, thus giving time for equalization of pressure on the inside and outside of buildings. Although it is true that some loss of life results from flying debris, the lack of exploding buildings and the somewhat lower wind speeds of a hurricane or typhoon mean that the terminal velocities of airborne missiles is rather less than those of a tornado. Consequently, the greatest destruction of life and property during a tropical storm appears to result not so much from the winds, but from the effects of flooding, either by rivers or by storm-induced 'tidal waves'. The latter were certainly responsible for the greater part of the death-toll in Bangladesh (1970), in India (1977) and in Texas (1900) when, in the United States' worst storm disaster, a storm surge claimed 6,000 lives in Galveston alone.

It is tempting to make a comparison between the relative degrees of damage resulting from hurricanes and tornadoes, although reliable figures exist only for the U.S.A. (Figure 70).

Fig. 70. Losses of life and property in the U.S.A. from severe weather phenomena (after E. Kessler).

Phenomenon	Average Annual Deaths	Average Annual Property Damage
Tornado	125 (1955–69)	$75 million
Lightning	150 (1959–65)	$100 million
Hail	— (1958–67)	$284 million
Hurricane	75 (1955–69)	$500 million

36. The catastrophic flooding of the Bangladesh coastlands during the 1970 cyclone ranked as one of the world's most severe disasters.

One interpretation of the statistics in Figure 70 might suggest that a tornado claims more lives because of its unpredictability, its greater frequency, and the fewer chances of giving advance warning. In contrast, the slower advance of a hurricane allows a greater degree of evacuation following a more reliable advance warning. Nevertheless, because of its greater size and its slower trajectory, a hurricane tends to affect a larger area for a lengthier period of time, a fact which, taken in conjunction with the flood devastation, probably explains the very much higher costs of property damage.

The cyclone disaster which devastated Bangladesh in 1970 has often been referred to as the world's worst twentieth-century natural disaster, not so much in terms of absolute numbers of dead (cf. the Chinese floods and earthquakes) but in the virtual totality of the destruction. The *official* death-toll has always been given as 300,000 but observers have noted that there were vast numbers of migrant labourers in the region at the time, to help with the harvest, so that the *unofficial* figure has been placed as high as one million – equivalent to about one sixth of the population of the affected deltaic area. This higher figure probably includes those who died subsequently from disease and famine during the aftermath. All this resulted from a 10-metre 'tidal wave' which completely inundated several of the low-lying islands (Plate 36). There is a record of an even higher storm surge (12 metres) in the 1737 disaster, when 300,000 perished along the neighbouring coastline of the Hooghly river delta.

It will be seen from Figure 69 that Asia's offshore islands in the Pacific Ocean have to contend with the bulk of the typhoons of that hemisphere. Rarely a year goes by without either the Philippines, Taiwan or the Japanese archipelago suffering from storm destruction. In July 1977, for example, the most powerful typhoon in Taiwan's history devastated the island, bringing many of its factories to a standstill and seriously retarding its economic growth rate. It was reported that one quarter of the island suffered severe damage when 190 kilometres per hour (120 m.p.h.) winds swept away houses and hundreds of steel pylons supporting Taiwan's main power supplies.

The Japanese have calculated that their own islands experience an average of four typhoons each year, creating annual damages of some $400 million. During the post-Second-World-War period Japan has suffered from five very severe typhoons (in 1945, 1947, 1954, 1958 and 1959), the last of which, the Ise Bay Typhoon (1959), brought the country's highest recorded storm surge (5.10 metres) and one of its greatest typhoon casualty rates. Whereas most of the earlier typhoon tracks had missed Japan's major urban areas, the storm of 1959 passed fairly close to a major city, that of Nagoya. Here, an unprecedented storm surge inundated the port and in Nagoya alone caused 42,400 casualties, of which about 2,000 were dead or missing. It was the likelihood of a typhoon of similar ferocity running onshore in Tokyo Bay that spurred the Japanese Government into a detailed research project on storm surge prediction and protection (see p. 134). As in the cases of Bangladesh and India, the majority of the deaths appear to have resulted from 'tidal wave' flooding rather than directly from the winds themselves. Thus, since most of the typhoons approach Japan from the south the greatest hazard zones are located around the south-facing Tokyo, Ise and Osaka bays, because the storm surge will be funnelled into constricted waters (Figure 71). In this disaster-prone group of islands it is not surprising to find that a considerable amount of research has been directed towards

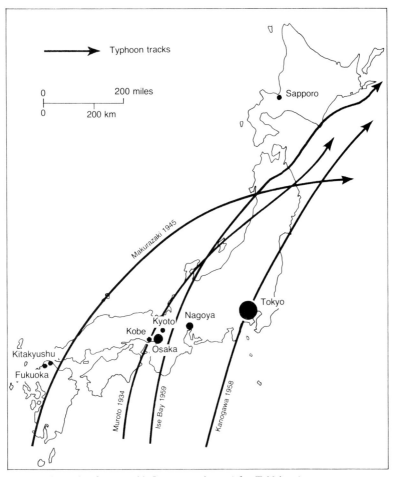

Fig. 71. The tracks of catastrophic Japanese typhoons (after T. Nakano).

hazard prediction and to the costs of the catastrophic events in terms of both life and property. From a study of the post-Second-World-War period it has been decisively shown that typhoons are the most destructive of Japan's natural hazards (Figure 72), although a future earthquake of the severity of the 1923 Kwanto earthquake (see p. 56) could alter the entire statistical picture. Nevertheless, it is significant that whilst typhoons account for only 15 per cent of Japan's natural disasters they result in some 75 per cent of the structural damage.

Fig. 72. Damage caused by natural hazards in Japan (1946–70) (after T. Nakano).

Phenomenon	No. of Events	Deaths	Houses Destroyed	Houses Flooded
Typhoon	59	13,745	576,378	4,479,665
Heavy rain from extra-tropical cyclone	77	7,372	60,877	3,681,042
Strong winds from extra-tropical cyclone	12	784	4,941	16,487
Earthquake	11	5,490	113,339	81,654
Landslide	5	86	143	—
Hail and Thunderstorm	4	28	847	23,482
Heavy snow	2	242	1,734	7,062
Volcanic eruption	1	12	12	—

On turning to an examination of tropical storm damage in the western hemisphere it is noteworthy that hurricane frequency in the Caribbean and in the United States is less than one fifth of that in eastern Asia and approximately one half of the cyclonic activity in the Bay of Bengal. When one also takes into consideration the contrast in population densities between the American Gulf region and the Asiatic nations, it is little wonder that oriental typhoons and cyclones take a much greater death-toll than Atlantic hurricanes. One major exception appears to have been the 'Great Hurricane' of 11–12 October 1780 which devastated some of the West Indies' islands. Six thousand people were killed in Barbados, where a British fleet was entirely destroyed. A convoy of French ships was also overwhelmed and four thousand of the troops which it was transporting perished. On the near by island of Martinique some nine thousand people lost their lives. Nevertheless, when a tropical storm, such as Hurricane Camille (1969) or Hurricane Fifi (1974), strikes, no one is particularly concerned with former records or with global statistical comparisons – the problem appears to be a purely local one.

Hurricane Camille was one of the fiercest hurricanes ever to strike the shores of the United States. With wind speeds estimated at 300 kilometres per hour (190 m.p.h.) this terrible storm moved from the Gulf of Mexico into southern Mississippi, bringing a 6-metre storm surge into the vulnerable coastal areas and sweeping three huge freighters on to the land (Plate 37). Despite the early warning system and the well-planned evacuation programme the hurricane tore across the southern states on 17 August, killing 235 people and making 200,000 homeless in Mississippi and Louisiana alone. Several coastal towns were wiped off the map and others so badly

37. These three large freighters were swept ashore by the winds and high seas of Hurricane Camille when it tore into the Gulf Coast of the United States in August 1969.

damaged that both states were declared disaster areas by the Government. Generally speaking, as a hurricane moves inland its power abates, because the energy derived from condensed moisture lessens as it moves away from the ocean's water supply. Hurricane Camille proved to be an exception, however, for during the next three days it confounded the United States meteorologists as it gained fresh energy and carried on its rampage through the states of West Virginia and Virginia. Exceptional rainfall caused widespread flooding, with the city of Richmond being flooded to record depths. Not until it moved offshore in Massachusetts on 20 August did the devastation cease, leaving the federal government to count the cost of the disaster (256 deaths and one and a half billion dollars worth of damage). The relief effort was the biggest ever staged by America for a single disaster but, paradoxically, the relief work sometimes exacerbated the social and racial tensions of the southern states, with both blacks and whites claiming that the other was being given preferential treatment. One of the basic problems appears to have been whether to use the opportunity to give those in dire economic need a fresh start, or whether to merely return them to the depressed living conditions which they had experienced prior to the disaster.

When Hurricane Fifi struck the Central American state of Honduras on 18 November 1974 some observers wryly commented that Honduras was virtually a disaster area before the hurricane arrived. With the average worker earning a mere £160 a year this tiny country is probably the poorest in the Americas. It has been claimed, therefore, that in terms of environmental impact on a single nation, this was the world's most severe disaster. Half of Honduras's foreign exchange comes from its export of bananas and one entire year's crop was wiped out in a matter of minutes. Those buildings which were not flattened by the winds were swept away by raging floodwaters and in San Pedro Sula, the country's second city, 400,000 were left homeless and a prey to disease and starvation. The United States Ambassador to the stricken country bitterly retorted to newsmen:

> You ask how people can starve in just three or four days, but these people were hungry even before the disaster.[4]

As far as disease was concerned, the Government became so afraid of a typhoid epidemic sweeping through the survivors that it ordered the mass burning of many of the 8,000 victims – in one town alone 2,700 were incinerated where they lay, a scene generally reserved for disease-ridden livestock or wartime atrocities. Because of the inability of its own government to organize a proper rehabilitation programme, the Honduras relief effort was based mainly on overseas help. One of the saddest aspects of the whole affair was the way in which political corruption and inefficiency interfered with the relief work and so diluted the overseas aid that very little reached the stricken areas. Stories were rife of troops battling with Red Cross workers in attempts to plunder the medical supplies, but eventually order was restored and the work of rehabilitation begun. Amongst the many nations sending aid it is interesting to note that the British contribution was coordinated through a newly formed branch of the Ministry of Overseas Development. Termed the Disaster Unit, this was the first occasion on which it was called upon to help.

It is rare for tropical cyclones of this violence to visit the shores of Britain, which in the main is affected only by the storminess of extratropical cyclones. Occasionally, however, a North American hurricane gets caught up by the Westerlies, travels swiftly across the Atlantic and gives to Britain one of its most severe storms. According to Professor H. H. Lamb, a British weather expert, the great storm which swept across southern England on 6–7 December 1703 (referred to as the Channel Storm) still ranks as the most destructive gale ever reported in these islands, when 8,125 people perished. The majority of the casualties occurred around the coasts where hundreds of ships were sunk at their moorings or were blown out to sea to subsequent destruction. Some hundred churches and four hundred windmills were destroyed and the first Eddystone lighthouse swept away without trace. The storm which caused great damage in Ireland on 16 September 1961 was apparently of this type as was the Scottish storm of 1955.

Leaving aside the storm surges of 1953 and 1978 which have already been described in Chapter 4, the most severe casualties and damage from high winds in Britain this century were associated with the gales of 1927, 1957, 1962, 1968 and 1976, all of which related to extratropical cyclones.

The storms of 1927 and 1968 caused the greatest amount of death and destruction in Scotland, especially in Glasgow where brick and stone tenement buildings collapsed and tramcars were overturned. During the 1927 gale the Scottish death-toll reached twenty-six, whilst in the 1968 repetition nine people died in Glasgow alone. The aftermath of this second disastrous storm saw the authorities of Scotland's largest city having to deal with fifty-two collapsed buildings and over 100,000 substantially damaged houses. In addition, shipping had sunk in the river Clyde and high-tension cables spanning the waterway had fallen into the river as their 120-metre pylons had been blown down. The same 1968 gale was also responsible for setting adrift the oil rig *Sea Quest* after it had dragged its anchors in the mountainous waves of the North Sea. It was a grim reminder to Britain's offshore oil prospectors of the extreme weather hazards to be faced in these grey, northern waters, for three years earlier a similar North Sea oil rig had foundered during a gale, carrying with it thirteen victims. Because of the harsh physical conditions North Sea drilling platforms have been designed to withstand the occasional statistically possible wave of 30 metres in height. During winter months wave heights exceed 6 metres for 40 per cent of the time and 2.4 metres for 90 per cent of the time, thus making it difficult for boats to discharge their supplies on most winter days, since materials and stores can only be transferred with waves of less than 2 metres in elevation. Furthermore, helicopters can only operate when North Sea winds are blowing at less than 16 metres per second, so that oil platform crews can often be stormbound. Significantly, insurance companies insist on complete evacuation when weather forecasts predict winds of more than 31 metres per second and waves greater than 6–8 metres in height. Severe weather conditions of these magnitudes have already caused several casualties and resulted in the loss of five North Sea drilling rigs. When the B.P. Forties Field pipeline was completed in 1974 it was more than twelve months behind schedule owing to bad weather – one single squall succeeded in rupturing the oil pipeline itself.

Severe damage from gales occurred locally at Sheffield in 1962 and in Hatfield in 1957, whilst more widespread damage and twenty-eight deaths occurred throughout Britain in January 1976 after which insurance claims approached the £100 million mark, causing insurance shares to fall sharply on the Stock Exchange. But one of the most spectacular examples of wind destruction in Britain took place on 1 November 1965 when three of the giant cooling towers at Yorkshire's Ferrybridge power station collapsed even though the wind velocity was not exceptionally high (Plate 31). Although models had been tested in wind tunnels during the design stage, it was revealed during the subsequent inquiry that insufficient allowance had been made for the effects of gustiness created by turbulence amongst the closely grouped towers. A British Standard Code of Practice for the design of buildings and structures has subsequently been introduced and this includes advice on stress from wind impact, which enables the engineer to choose a design relating to a variety of wind speed probabilities. Thus it is important not only to know the range of wind extremes, but also the significant thresholds beyond which particular types of structural damage have occurred in the past. Only in this way will it become possible to predict the likelihood of future structures being able to withstand different degrees of gustiness or very severe wind impact, known to the engineer as *wind loading*.

Weather forecasting and hazard modification

The type of weather prediction described above is termed *probability fore-casting*, which is part of the so-called empirical approach to general weather forecasting. Such an empirical approach is based upon the hypothesis that observation of past weather patterns and changes should enable us to predict both future weather developments and the probability of their recurrence. In this way the much maligned Long-Range Forecast has been produced by the British Meteorological Office. It is based partly on simple extra-polation of past trends into the future and also on the use of analogues, whereby a search through past records produces the nearest approximation to the current synoptic situation; this should then enable inferences to be drawn as to the probability of future weather trends. Unfortunately, the degree of success attained by this method has been only moderate, largely because of the lack of reliable meteorological data from earlier centuries and also because of the enormous variety of past weather phenomena.

The other major method of general weather prediction includes the field of hazard warning, when severe weather phenomena are identified and their probable behaviour calculated mathematically. This is known as *numerical forecasting* in which equations expressing the physical laws of the atmosphere are solved. This theoretical approach is the one on which most short-term twenty-four-hour forecasts are based, generally with a high degree of success. Because of the tremendous amount of mathematical computation involved in this method, its increasing success is related largely to the introduction of sophisticated computers. Nevertheless, in spite of the con-siderable progress made in weather forecasting by this development and the allied growth of radar and satellite photography, the British forecaster has learnt to be cautious because, unlike his American and Russian counterparts, he is faced with more complex short-term problems, owing to Britain's marginal location between continent and ocean in the restless middle latitudes. Thus it is the uncertainty of the timing and the exact future tracks of the vortices which lead to the greatest errors of prediction. That is why many of the British forecasts are often hedged around with expressions of probability rather than greater degrees of certitude.

A closer look at the field of *severe* weather prediction reveals that the same uncertainties are prevalent here also, but it will be realized, of course, that in many instances the accuracy of the forecast will be a matter of life and death for some communities. Consequently, the more hazard-prone the region the more imperative it becomes for both the timing and the course of the vortex to be predicted with a fair measure of accuracy. But all too often the killer storm is the one which defies the experts' forecast and ploughs its relentless furrow through an unsuspecting landscape.

In the case of American tornadoes, for example, it has been found that many of their most disastrous effects have been caused by a handful of 'rogue' storms, some of which were found to have travelled outside the main tornado belt. For this reason it is often difficult to provide a statistical probability of their likely occurrence at a particular location, although tornado 'risk maps' (see Figure 66) and tornado seasons suggest that certain areas of the U.S.A. are more hazard-prone than others at a given time. In general, tornado warnings can only be made with any degree of certitude once a 'twister' has been spotted. To this end, the Severe Local Storms Warning Service was set up in Kansas City, Missouri, during the 1950s and this soon became known as the Tornado Watch. It was intended that having sighted a tornado, the service would monitor its progress and warn citizens who lived in its projected track. Despite a number of miscalculations and setbacks the number of United States tornado fatalities has shown a marked decrease, even though some severe examples have torn through large urban centres, such as Topeka, Kansas, in 1966. Within the tornado belt of the American Midwest, the annual death-toll from tornadoes has been virtually halved since the inception of the warning service, largely because of the urban alarm systems and the local radio broadcasts which have enabled people to take refuge in their specially prepared shelters.

On turning to the question of hurricane prediction, we find that because of its larger size it is generally possible to discover the malefactor during the vital early stages. As soon as the ominous cloud-spiral has been picked up by satellites or radar it can be tracked across the Atlantic and the Caribbean with some exactitude. Once the hurricane approaches the coastline of Central America or the Gulf states, however, it becomes more and more difficult to predict its behaviour and in particular to pinpoint its exact land-fall. Statistics show that at the twenty-four-hour prediction level the fore-caster cannot give a landfall for anything less than a 240 kilometre stretch of coastline. It is true that as the hurricane gets nearer, its landfall probability can be made with more precision, but by this time the warning period has been cut to a few hours and the chances of an orderly evacuation of the coastal settlements have virtually disappeared. To overcome this uncertainty most North American coastal authorities broadcast hurricane warnings for a broad zone extending many kilometres beyond the computed limits of the storm track. In the United States public warnings are issued at 24-, 12-, and

6-hourly intervals as a hurricane approaches, whilst in Australia cyclone warnings are given first at 6-hourly intervals and subsequently every three hours as the storm closes in.

In order to combat severe weather phenomena there has been a great deal of international cooperation in recent years culminating in the so-called World Weather Watch under the auspices of the World Meteorological Organization. In addition to 8,500 land stations and numerous weather ships this global network depends on meteorological satellites, aircraft and automatic weather stations, all of which transmit their data to some 140 national weather centres. There are also more specific short-term projects designed to investigate particular weather hazards, one of which, termed the Global Atmospheric Research Programme (1974–78), has linked hurricane research with an investigation into the West African drought (see Chapter 9) by monitoring cloud formation over the tropical North Atlantic ocean.

Numerous studies have shown that as far as severe wind hazards are concerned there are basically two ways in which mankind can adjust: first, one can either do nothing and bear the loss, or secondly, one can take some kind of measure to reduce the potential loss. In the less developed countries of the world there is usually little alternative except to bear the loss, but even in the United States a survey of householders from the vulnerable eastern seaboard illustrated that over 50 per cent of them had borne the cost of storm damage over the years. On turning to an examination of the alternative response, that of reducing the loss, we find that mankind is capable of following any of three courses: first, people can adapt their own behaviour by moving away or by improving the hazard-warning system; secondly, they can stay put and strengthen their environment by building protective works, as in the case of the Midwest tornado shelters; or thirdly, they can attempt to modify the storm itself. Let us conclude by looking at some of the ways in which man has attempted to moderate the severity of revolving storms.

Very few efforts have been made to ameliorate the force of a tropical storm anywhere except in the United States. It is true that the Japanese have made a feasibility study of 'typhoon busting', but since these phenomena bring no less than one quarter of their country's rainfall nothing of great significance has yet been attempted. American efforts to ameliorate hurricanes began in 1961, when attempts were made to modify Hurricane Esther. In 1963 similar efforts were made on Hurricane Beulah, but it was not until 1969 that the same technique, known as *cloud seeding*, had any significant results. Then, as part of the hurricane research exercise called *Project Stormfury*, the experiment appeared to weaken the wind velocity of Hurricane Debbie.

Cloud seeding is a device invented in the 1940s by two American meteorologists, Irving Langmuir and Vincent Schaefer, and consists of dropping particles of dry-ice (solid CO_2) or silver iodide pellets into the tops of particular cloud formations. First used in an attempt to produce rainfall, it was later discovered that five seedings at two-hourly intervals could bring about some 20 per cent reduction in the wind speeds of a hurricane. Even though the wind velocity appeared to pick up again later, a further seeding resulted in a similar reduction. It seems that the supercooled particles cause rapid condensation, which drains off reserves of latent heat from the walls of the vortex, thereby de-energizing the storm. There remains, however, a major uncertainty in this technique, relating to the manner in which a redistribution of the hurricane's energy might affect the accompanying storm surge in the ocean. It has been suggested, for example, that a decrease of wind speed at the centre may only result in an increase at the hurricane's perimeter, thus generating a potentially more dangerous storm surge.

As far as tornadoes are concerned, there is currently little hope of our being able to control, or even significantly modify, these severe revolving storms.

8. Floods

After many hours of incessant rainfall the swollen waters of Italy's river Arno finally burst their banks on 4 November 1966, sweeping through the streets of Florence and creating not only one of the country's greatest natural disasters but also a sense of profound shock to countless numbers of people throughout the world for whom this beautiful Renaissance city represented the epitome of Western culture.

It is now known that Tuscany received one third of its annual rainfall in twenty-four hours, causing the rivers to rise at an unprecedented rate of 1 metre per hour and the floodwaters to inundate Florence to depths of more than 5 metres (18 feet). In the surrounding countryside 127 lives were lost, 12,000 families made homeless and hundreds of bridges destroyed, but it was in Florence itself that the damage was most catastrophic (Plate 38). The tumultuous floodwaters, channelled by the narrow streets, raced at speeds of up to 130 kilometres per hour (80 m.p.h.), destroying some 10,000 motor vehicles, ruining the contents of over half the city's shops and inundating the homes of 5,000 of its citizens. The major utilities of electricity, water and sewage were completely disrupted and few of the outside telephone links survived. In addition, half of the city's industries were devastated and it was their ruptured oil tanks, together with the oil from central-heating systems, which added a slimy, odorous veneer to the offensive layer of half a million tonnes of mud which finally blanketed central Florence.

It was the oily mud which proved to be the most damaging feature of the disaster, for it infiltrated every nook and cranny and ruined many of the city's priceless art treasures. The final count demonstrated that among the affected works were 300,000 rare books, 730,000 unique letters and manuscripts and 1,300 paintings and drawings. When viewed in more detail the damage was heart-breaking: much of the renowned Cimabue crucifix, from the thirteenth-century church of Santa Croce, was destroyed; the famous Ghiberti doors of the Baptistery, called by Michelangelo the 'Doors of Paradise', were torn down and badly damaged; the soaked Giotto frescoes in

38. The Arno river overflowing its banks in November 1966 as it brings disastrous floods to the historic Italian city of Florence.

the Medici Chapel began to blister and peel from the walls. And so the sorry catalogue of devastation continues: the lower floors of the Uffizi Art Gallery had to be rapidly evacuated; the National Library on the banks of the Arno was completely inundated, as was the Bardini Museum of musical instruments; the floodwaters tore through the Cathedral Museum, overwhelming its illuminated manuscripts, before flooding Buonarroti House, famed for its Michelangelo drawings. Many of the damaged paintings were ultimately sent for gradual drying to the hothouses of the Pitti Palace, whilst the books and manuscripts which could be salvaged by the vast army of student volunteers from all over the world were distributed to brick kilns and tobacco-curing sheds throughout Italy.

Despite the gravity of the cultural and aesthetic damage, the magnitude of the disaster was to be measured not so much in the loss of the art treasures nor even in the loss of life (surprisingly, there were only thirty-three deaths) but in the loss of livelihood for the survivors and in the enormous reconstruction costs which totalled more than $700 million (£300 million) at 1966 values. One of the few redeeming features in the disastrous flooding was the provision of an opportunity to undertake long-needed schemes of urban renewal. These included the installation of a new sewage system and widespread modernization of numerous buildings behind their crumbling but picturesque exteriors. But reconstruction is only one part of a rehabilitation programme: it is equally important to discover the causes of a disaster and to take steps to ensure that there will be no repetition of the event.

Although investigations soon made it clear that the opening of the sluices at the high dams in the neighbouring Valdarno Hills (ostensibly to avoid dam bursts) had accelerated the rising floods of the Arno, it was necessary to measure the scale of the rainfall and run-off against previous flood records. Such a survey showed that this phenomenal rainfall intensity had been matched on only two previous occasions in the city's history – in 1333, when it was probably of equal severity, and in 1844, when the floods were some 2 metres lower. In view of these findings it became clear that it was not an isolated event and that remedial measures would have to be implemented; in the case of Florence itself five major recommendations were made. First, the Arno flood-warning system must be updated; secondly, the river embankments should be completely rebuilt; thirdly, there would have to be a reversal of the careless land-use policy on the neighbouring Apennines where indiscriminate grazing and tree-felling had led to increased soil erosion and run-off; fourthly, there should be better cooperation between the civic authorities and the hydro-electric boards whose precipitate action had exacerbated the situation, as described above; finally, that an increased number of reservoirs needed to be constructed in order to store the seasonal rains.

Florence provides a spectacular example of a flood disaster but, viewed on a global scale, there are many instances of even greater devastation induced by flooding, for, of all the natural hazards, floods are the most widespread and the type which causes the greatest loss of life. Between 1947 and 1967,

Fig. 73. Historic flood disasters in the world (1642–1972).

Date	Place	Deaths	Property Damage
1642	China	300,000	
1786	Japan	30,000+	
1828	Japan	10,000+	

1864	Sheffield, England	250	Dam collapsed
1887	Honan, China	900,000+	Yellow river overflowed;
1889, 31 May	Johnstown, Pa., U.S.A.	2,000+	Dam collapsed
1903	Heppner, Ore., U.S.A.	250+	Town destroyed
1911	Yangtze River, China	100,000	
1913, 25–27 Mar.	Ohio and Indiana, U.S.A.	700	
1928, 13 Mar.	Santa Paula, California, U.S.A.	450	St Francis Dam collapsed
1931, Aug.	Hwang Ho, China	3,500,000+	
1939, Jul.–Aug.	Tientsin, China	1,000	Millions homeless
1950, 14 Aug.	Anhwei Province, China	500	10 million homeless; 5 million acres inundated
1951, 2–19 Jul.	Kansas and Missouri, U.S.A.	41	200,000 homeless, $1 billion
1951, 28 Aug.	Manchuria	5,000+	
1952, 15 Aug.	North Devon, England	34	
1953, 31 Jan.–1 Feb.	Northern Europe	2,000+	Coastal areas devastated
1954, 1 Aug.	Kazvin District, Iran	2,000+	
1955, 4 Oct.	Pakistan and India	1,700	5.6 million crop acres at loss of $63 million
1959, 2 Dec.	Frejus, France	412	Malpasset Dam collapsed
1961, May	Midwest U.S.	25	
1962, 27 Sep.	Barcelona	470+	$80 million
1962, 31 Dec.	Northern Europe	309+	
1963, 9 Oct.	Belluno, Italy	2,000+	Vaiont Dam overtopped
1963, 14–15 Nov.	Haiti	500	
1964, 8–9 Jun.	Northern Montana, U.S.A.	36	
1964, Dec.	Western U.S.	45	
1965, 18–19 Jun.	Southwest U.S.	27	
1966, 11–13 Jan.	Rio de Janeiro	300	
1966, 3–4 Nov.	Arno Valley, Italy	113	Florence art treasures lost
1967, Jan.–Mar.	Rio de Janeiro and Sao Paulo	600+	
1967, 26 Nov.	Lisbon	457	
1968, 29–31 May	Northern New Jersey	8	$140 million
1968, 8–14 Aug.	Gujarat, India	1,000	
1969, 25–29 Jan.	Southern California	95	
1969, 4 Jul.	Southern Michigan and Northern Ohio, U.S.A.	33	
1969, 23 Aug.	Virginia, U.S.A.	100	
1970, 11–23 May	Oradea, Rumania	200	225 towns damaged
1972, Jun.	Eastern United States	100+	$2 billion
1972, Jun.	Rapid City, S.D., U.S.A.	215	(est.) $100 million

for example, more than 250,000 people died from natural hazards, of which 64 per cent were attributable to deaths from flooding. Rarely a year goes by without a major flood disaster being reported from somewhere in the world (Figure 73) and, despite the increasing amount of money being spent on flood-alleviation works, the damage sustained from flooding continues to rise. This is the price that mankind has to pay when attempting to compete with rivers for the use of their floodplains or when building too close to coastal margins. Many of our earliest civilizations chose to live on riverine lowlands by virtue of the fertility of the alluvial soils and the constancy of the water supply. Availability of water, both for drinking and for irrigation, has always been of paramount importance in the world's arid zones, so it is no surprise to discover that seasonal flooding was welcomed by the peoples who dwelt on the banks of the Nile, Tigris, Euphrates and Indus rivers. Even in the less arid plains of China the annual refurbishment of the rich silts by the far-spreading waters of the Hwang-Ho and Yangtze-Kiang was regarded as a distinct bonus rather than a hazard, notwithstanding the lengthy records of Chinese flood disasters.

It is important to realize that before the eighteenth century, world population was relatively small, so that our pre-industrialized ancestors were often able to adapt their life-styles to periodic flooding. Their responses ranged from extensive but rudimentary flood-protection schemes, as in China, to simple seasonal migration away from the hazard, as in parts of Africa. When world population increased, however, such options were not always available, as riparian settlement became more concentrated and more permanent, not only for the reasons noted above, but also because waterways could provide sources of energy, transportation and food supply. Consequently, with increased industrialization there came changes of attitudes which saw the rejection of some of the traditional adjustments to potential hazards and their replacement by short-sighted obduracy, often in the mistaken belief that man's technical ability would solve most hazard problems. A continuing succession of flood disasters, however, has demonstrated to modern man the folly of his massive urban expansion onto flood plains, deltas and low-lying coasts. Thus, many nations are now adopting a more enlightened approach and some are introducing comprehensive programmes of river-basin planning and coastal protection. To be able to implement such schemes it is important to understand the principles of the hydrological cycle in order to determine the factors involved in flood hazards.

The Hydrological Cycle and Flood Classification

It is generally accepted that the primeval earth had little or no atmosphere, no precipitation and therefore no surface-water bodies. How then did the oceans evolve and how was the hydrological cycle set in train? From a study of igneous rocks it has been shown how tiny quantities of water are sometimes found contained within the crystals of these rocks. Such water is termed primary or magmatic water and is thought to have been derived from the evolving magma of the earth's mantle. Anyone who has visited geysers in New Zealand or Yellowstone Park, U.S.A., for example, or who has witnessed a volcanic eruption, will have noted the great quantities of geothermal vapour generated by such phenomena. Some of this may be genuine primary water, although it is only fair to point out that much of the steam may have been generated by surface water which had penetrated deeply enough to be affected by subterranean heating. Nevertheless, the very earliest release of this primary water vapour by vulcanicity was to initiate the earth's atmosphere, which in turn created reserves of what is termed meteoric water. At some point in the earth's history solar-energy replaced geothermal-energy as the principal agent responsible for heat control at the surface of the earth and from then onwards the systematic circulation of the atmosphere was set in motion. The dynamic atmosphere released its meteoric water in the form of precipitation, thereby creating water bodies on the global terrain. Thus the world's oceans, lakes and rivers were born and water began to move in a regular cycle, termed the *hydrological cycle* (Figure 74). From this we can see how water from the seas and oceans (which contain no less than 97.2 per cent of the circulatory water) is evaporated as vapour into the atmosphere from which it is subsequently precipitated. It is finally returned to the oceans directly by surface run-off, or indirectly by an underground route. But it will also be seen that where direct

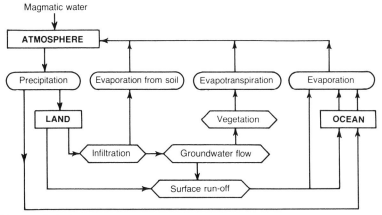

Fig. 74. The hydrological cycle.

evaporation from the soil or evapotranspiration from the vegetation occurs the water follows a different route within the hydrological cycle (Figure 74). It will be realized, of course, that the magnitude of the 'throughput', or volume of water within the cycle, will vary according to one's position on the landsurface; thus the world's deserts will have a considerably lower amount than the equatorial rain forests. But that is not to say that the desertlands will never experience floods, for it is when they undergo a significant positive deviation from their average precipitation, albeit an infrequent occurrence, that they will become flood-hazard zones. Paradoxically, it is often these arid and semi-arid regions, where flood-protection schemes have been thought unnecessary, which experience some of the world's most devastating floods (see p. 261).

Flooding results from a variety of causes, most of which relate to fluctuations within the regime of the hydrological cycle. It is possible, therefore, to recognize the following classification:

(a) Fluctuations within the hydrological cycle
(1) Rainstorm-river floods
(2) Snowmelt floods
(3) Coastal floods due to meteorological conditions and seismic sea-waves
(b) Other causes
(1) Dam or levee failure floods
(2) Floods due to the rupture of a glacial lake
(3) Floods resulting from landslides and volcanic events
(4) Floods induced by land subsidence along coastlines (see Chapter 4)

Rainstorm-River Floods

The most commonly experienced floods are those which fall into the category of rainstorm-river floods, when excessive precipitation leads to a greatly increased surface run-off, as in the case of the Arno and the Florence floods described above. But why is it that in one region a given volume of precipitation will cause negligible damage and little cause for concern whilst the same amount falling elsewhere may lead to devastation? The answer lies in a number of factors, such as steepness of slopes, character of soil and subsoil, presence or absence of vegetation and the degree of man's modification of the river regime.

A contrast is at once recognizable between, on the one hand, a region of steep terrain where run-off will have a high velocity and, on the other, a region of gentler slopes where run-off will be of a lower velocity; in the first instance the capability of the streams and rivers to erode will be considerable, whilst in the latter case their erosive ability will be reduced accordingly. The character of the soils in a region will also dictate the degree to which precipitation is able to infiltrate into the ground surface and soil type is, therefore, a fundamental factor controlling run-off. Infiltration of water depends on the character of the soil pores and fissures, upon the stability of the soil and upon the nature of the underlying geology. Soils with large pores and fissures, such as sandy gravels, allow the maximum infiltration, as do underlying sandstones and grits. Clay soils are the least permeable, although even these can permit rapid infiltration when broken by desiccation cracks. The character of the subsoil is equally important, however, for in some instances highly permeable soils may be underlain at shallow depths by relatively impermeable rocks. In such cases the groundwater may be able to move down slope at a velocity comparable with that of the surface run-off, an underflow of this type being known as *sub-surface storm flow*. The latter is particularly common in coarse-scree slopes where it may considerably exceed surface run-off. Similarly, where the underlying geology is composed of very permeable rocks, such as limestone, high velocity sub-surface flow will take place, leading to complex subterranean river systems.

In all but desert regions a proportion of the precipitation will fall on a vegetation cover, the density of which will play an important part not only in controlling the amount of run-off, but also in regulating the degree of evapotranspiration. In tropical rain-forests, for example, some of the rainfall is intercepted by the leaves, whence it is evaporated directly back into the atmosphere, thus never reaching the ground surface – light showers may be almost entirely intercepted in this way. But heavier rainfall will ultimately reach the ground, where some of it will return to the atmosphere by the process known as *evapotranspiration*, after having passed through the roots, stems and leaves of the plants. It is easy to envisage how destruction of vegetation will not only decrease the amount of interception and evapo-transpiration, but may also lead to an increased surface run-off with conse-quent soil erosion, once the binding action of the roots has been removed. It is not surprising to find that in areas which have been denuded of their vegetation by overgrazing, burning or wanton tree-felling, the incidence of serious flooding has often shown a marked increase (see p. 262). Equally, surface run-off will rise when the soil's infiltration capacity is reduced as a result of urban building. Roofs, pavements, roads and other solid surfaces will have the same effect as an impermeable rock layer, causing water to move laterally, often at an increased velocity. Calculations have shown, for example, that the built-up area of the American city of Jackson on the

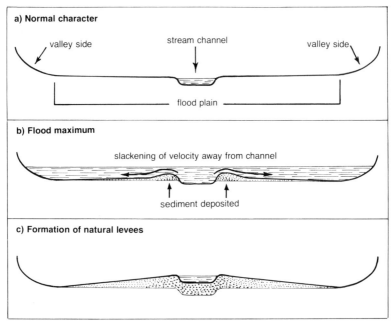

Fig. 75. Flood-plain hazards resulting from river levees; (a) Normal character of river valley (b) Flood maximum conditions (c) Formation of natural levees.

Mississippi has increased the mean annual flood flows by 4.5 times in comparison with those of stream basins in surrounding rural areas.

Surface run-off is ultimately conveyed to the oceans by stream channels and since these are of paramount significance in the hydrological cycle, as far as rainstorm flood hazards are concerned, it is important to know something of their character (Figure 75a). Generally speaking, a river will be capable of eroding material from one part of its catchment, transporting it downstream and ultimately depositing it, as its capacity for carrying its so-called 'load' decreases, partly as a function of its gentler gradient. Rainstorms in a river catchment will increase the volume and velocity of the stream in addition to its carrying capacity, so that floods are damaging not only for their ability to inundate, but also for their ability to wreak havoc from their suspended 'load' which, during maximum flow, may consist of boulders, trees and numerous man-made artifacts such as bridges and vehicles.

During periods of excessive flow, there must come a time when the river will burst its banks once it has exceeded the capacity of its channel. At this stage the floodwaters will occupy the flood plain, which may be up to tens of kilometres wide, and this will act as a temporary storage reservoir until the flood subsides. As the excess water escapes from the stream channel, however, its velocity is immediately checked, whereupon much of its suspended 'load' will be dumped on the flanks of the now-submerged channel (Figure 75b). In this way rivers which are frequently affected by flooding tend to build up an accumulation of sediment along their banks to form natural levees. Ultimately, the accumulation may become so great that the stream channel itself will become elevated above its surrounding flood plain (Figure 75c). Since this poses an even greater threat, man has frequently increased the height of the levees, as on the Mississippi, in order to protect his property and livestock. Naturally, if the artificial levees themselves are overtopped the catastrophe will be greater than before, since the river will now be descending from an even higher elevation. In some cases, once the levee has been breached, the river may find it easier to follow an alternative route to the sea rather than return to its former course. Studies have shown that when left to themselves stream channels are constantly moving laterally, both locally within the flood plain and occasionally shifting into a different river system altogether, so long as the intervening drainage divides are sufficiently low and indistinct. In 1852, for example, the Hwang-Ho in China broke through its levees and changed course a matter of 600 kilometres to the north, where it is now emptying into the Gulf of Chihli instead of the Yellow Sea.

In addition to our understanding of the stream-channel characteristics it is also important for us to know something of the river-basin system of which the channel forms only a part. This is because differences in the make-up of river basins, such as geology and slope gradients, will lead to contrasting stream flows and flood patterns, as illustrated in Figure 76. Here it is shown how two streams with different networks produce different types of flow during flood conditions. Stream network X allows water from the tributaries to pass down the trunk stream successively, thus releasing the floodwaters over a longer period and producing a flatter curve in the associated hydrograph X. In contrast, stream network Y is such that excessive run-off is equally distributed over the catchment area, thus reaching the trunk stream almost simultaneously and producing a sharp but short-lived flood peak as demonstrated by hydrograph Y. The study of river networks and drainage characteristics is known as *hydrology* and is clearly of great significance in the field of flood prediction; thus we shall return to an examination of its utility later in the chapter. It is now time, however, to investigate some examples of rainstorm-river floods, in the light of the foregoing explanations, in an attempt to account for their vicissitudes.

Let us look first at an example of floods in an area of high relief and steep

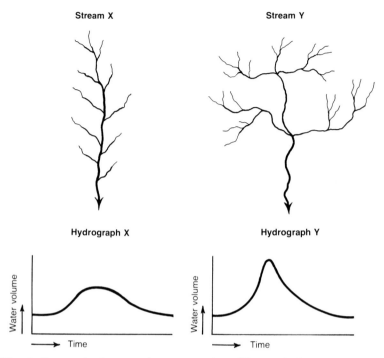

Fig. 76. Contrasts in river-network patterns to show differences in flood magnitude and duration.

slopes which will engender excessive river gradients and high velocity run-off. The first case study is that of Lynmouth where, in August 1952, a river flood devastated the little holiday town. Built amidst the picturesque coastal scenery of North Devon, England, this attractive resort straddles the mouth of the combined East and West Lyn rivers, which here unite after having drained the steep northern slopes of Exmoor. Lynmouth is tucked in beneath the thickly wooded slopes of this precipitous coastline on the only flat land of the area, an excellent example of man's folly, for this happens to be the delta of the steeply tumbling torrents of the Lyn drainage system.

The first fortnight of August 1952 had already witnessed a rainfall of 115 millimetres (4.5 inches), which was equal to the entire August precipitation on Exmoor, but there then followed a torrential downpour of a further 386 millimetres (15.2 inches) in a mere thirty-six hours. Since the moorland soils were already waterlogged, the excessive rainfall ran straight into the swollen rivers. Because of the steep gradients, the floodwaters achieved an incredible velocity, enabling them to carve great chunks of boulder-studded earth from their upper stream courses and cut swathes through the thickly forested river banks. The debris of rocks and tree trunks stampeded into the unsuspecting town, smashing into any obstruction which impeded the river's attempt to disgorge its excessive load across its natural flood-plain/ delta and thence into the sea (Plate 39). Piling up against the river bridges this debris built up temporary dams which broke one by one, to send further surges into the stricken town. The West Lyn altered course, leaving the Lyndale Hotel and its 150 occupants marooned all night. The cataract demolished the Beach Hotel, ninety-three houses and shops and swept more than one hundred vehicles out to sea. When daylight came it was found that thirty-four people had lost their lives and that 200,000 tonnes of boulders choked the devastated town. Although services were soon restored, it was many months before the debris was cleared and the bridges and houses rebuilt.

39. The raging torrents of the Exmoor floods of August 1952 sweep 200,000 tonnes of boulders and splintered trees through the shattered streets of Lynmouth, Devon.

An investigation into the causes was immediately started and it was soon discovered that the chances of a repetition of this event were fairly high, since both of the greatest rainfall intensities ever recorded in Britain had occurred in this region; viz:

28 June 1917, 243 millimetres (9.57 inches) in 24 hours Bruton (Somerset).
18 August 1924, 238 millimetres (9.37 inches) in 24 hours Cannington (Somerset).

By comparison the Lynmouth figures were as follows:

15 August 1952, 228 millimetres (8.98 inches) in 12 hours.

The Dobbie Committee made a list of recommendations in an attempt to avert future disasters, and these included the prohibition of riparian building, the widening of the river courses and the lengthening of the bridging spans, the provision of storage dams and the construction of artificial flood-relief channels. Paradoxically, such remedial measures were viewed with some dismay by many local people who believed that their implementation would destroy the picturesque nature of the town, discourage tourism and create an unwarranted financial burden. In a compromise solution, the majority of the measures were accepted, including the artificial channelling of the West Lyn into a less hazardous course and the smoothing of the river banks to ensure easier passage for flood debris. On 8 October 1960 the new defences were tested by a deluge of similar proportions when a torrent of trees and boulders again swept down the river channel, the flood increasing the height of flow by more than 6 metres (20 feet), but the banks were equal to the test and a disaster was averted.

Disastrous rainstorm-river floods of the Lynmouth variety have also been recorded in other parts of Britain; amongst the most notable were those of 1829 in north-east Scotland, when the rivers Spey and Findhorn ran more than 5 metres above normal, and the 'cloud burst' generated floods of 1770 and 1886 which brought record levels to England's River Severn.

On turning to examine the flood disasters of the River Thames in London we can distinguish two different categories of flooding: first those inundations which were induced by storm surges as described in Chapter 4 and, secondly, the simple rainstorm floods. Prior to the notable tidal flood of 1953, described above, London appears to have been most seriously inundated by storm-surge flooding in A.D. 9, 1555, 1663, 1703 and 1928. The rainstorm flooding, however, seems to have resulted largely from prolonged precipitation over the Thames catchment area, but since the watershed slopes are not very steep and the river gradients relatively gentle we are now dealing with a different type of flood from that which devastated Lynmouth. Thus, the notable Thames floods of A.D. 48, 1242, 1682, 1852, 1872 and 1894 were all associated with excessively wet periods during which the incessant rainfall caused systematic inundation of the river's flood plain. Although the record flood-height upstream from London was achieved in 1894, the flood of A.D. 48 seems to have been the most disastrous for it is reported that the death-toll reached 10,000. The 1852 flood appears to have been notable for the fact that the torrents upset the hearse and horses of the Duke of Wellington's funeral on the Bath Road at Maidenhead! Of London's 1682 flood the following quotation from the Rutland Papers gives a graphic eye-witness description:

> Never was such flodds known as has bine here, howses drowned and pore children drowne in theare cradels swimen up Fleet Bridge [the Fleet was then a navigable river], and there taken up, and tables and hogeds full of beare and all washed away, and peoppele getting up to theare uper lofts and hole heards of hogs drowned.[2]

The second type of rainstorm-river flood may also be illustrated by the phenomenal deluge which devastated many parts of Australia in January 1974 for, as in the case of the Thames floods, the main damage was done not from 'load' battering but by simple inundation. The so-called Great Dividing Range of eastern Australia is really no more than a series of plateaux which front the Pacific as steep escarpments but whose western flanks descend gently into the semi-arid interior of this vast continent. Two distinct drainage systems can therefore be recognized – an east-flowing system of steep, short rivers on which the towns of Grafton, Lismore, Kempsey and Murwillumbah are liable to frequent flooding of the Lyn-mouth type, described above; and a west-flowing system of lengthy rivers whose gentle gradients carry them into the so-called 'dead heart' of Australia, where aridity and drought prevail and where many of the rivers, such as Cooper's Creek, fade away into inland deltas without reaching the sea.

A lengthy period of rain-bearing north-easterly winds, culminating in cyclone Wanda, was sufficient to produce abnormally high rainfall in eastern, central and northern regions and to create Australia's greatest natural disaster. The east coastal towns, including Brisbane, are used to frequent flooding, but not so the towns on the banks of the west-flowing rivers which created new flood records for the 'Outback' of Northern Territory, Queensland and New South Wales. Rises of river level of over 6 metres (c. 20 feet) in twenty-four hours were commonplace as twenty-four-hour rainfall totals passed the 300 millimetres (12 inches) mark. Towns such as Wee Waa on the Namoi river were inundated to depths of 1.5 metres where the thriving cotton-growing district of north-west New South Wales suffered some $15 million (Australian) worth of damage, whilst in this state alone some half-million sheep were lost. In neighbouring Queensland the Outback rivers also broke their banks, flooding thousands of acres of farmland and isolating scores of towns for several days. Because their coal supplies were halted, the Mount Isa copper mines were forced to halve their production in order to conserve supplies. Farther west Alice Springs was completely cut off and had to be supplied by air, whilst the basin of interior drainage around Lake Eyre became a vast inland sea, completely drowning an area some three times the size of Ireland, and this in a region where the total annual rainfall rarely exceeds 100 millimetres (4 inches)!

It is a sobering thought that in Brisbane, where 10,750 homes were destroyed or damaged, hydrologists have calculated that floods of the 1974 magnitude can be expected once in every thirty years. Previously, in 1893, similar flooding had drowned thirty-five people and washed away the city's major bridges, and yet subsequently both housing and industry had been allowed to proliferate on the Brisbane River's floodplain, natural creeks and gullies had been carelessly infilled and woodland felled remorselessly on the surrounding watershed.

Snowmelt Floods

Widespread zones in the polar and sub-polar latitudes of the globe experience heavy snowfalls every year, so that their inhabitants are used to seeing the rivers swollen with meltwater as the warmer spring weather arrives. Thus, to Canadians of the Arctic provinces and to Russians on the banks of such mighty rivers as the Ob, Yenisey and Lena, snowmelt floods are commonplace. Occasionally, heavy winter snowfall occurs in lower, more temperate, latitudes and since these often correspond with zones of greater population density, it is in these zones that the greatest snowmelt disasters are found to occur. It is not merely the quantity of fallen snow, although this is important, but the rate of its melting which increases the magnitude of the hazard – the quicker the thaw the more dangerous the consequences are likely to be. Another important contributory factor relates to the state of the ground during the melting phase, for if the ground is frozen to a great depth then there is little chance of the meltwater percolating into the soil, there to be held for gradual release as groundwater. Frozen ground has the same effect as a city's concrete and tarmacadam, as far as the run-off of the catchment is concerned, i.e. the precipitation will move rapidly across the surface to the stream channel. In the central United States the stream channel will be, as likely as not, part of the far-spreading network of the Mississippi-Missouri system. Disastrous snowmelt floods have been recorded, for example, in the Ohio River basin in 1936, in the Missouri River basin in 1952 and in the Upper Mississippi basin in 1965. In each of these cases the snowmelt floods were amplified by rainstorms when a sudden warm spell began the melt and later continued the precipitation in the form of rainfall. Rainfall not only contributes to the volume of the run-off but also helps to thaw the snowpack, usually at a greater rate than by direct sunshine, because much of the heat of the sunshine is reflected by the surface of the snow. Calculations have shown that, on average, snow will thaw at the rate of about 250 millimetres per day due to a combination of rainfall and warm air; at about 175 millimetres per day under sunshine and warm air; and at about 65 millimetres per day under the influence of warm air only.

In Britain the worst snowmelt floods on record were those which terminated the severe winter of 1946–47. From mid January to early March 1947 prolonged periods of snowfall, combined with strong easterly winds and frost, provided most of the ingredients for a snowmelt flood in the spring. On level ground 2 metres of snow had accumulated in North Wales and the Pennines, for example, whilst in some areas drifts of 5 metres were reported. When it is realized that 1 metre of snow is equivalent to 83 millimetres of rainfall it will be realized how much potential floodwater was being stored up awaiting a sudden thaw. Since the snowfall was so widespread, every part of the country was at risk, unlike the more localized effect of a torrential rainstorm (see p. 258). A warm air mass moved into Britain from the Atlantic on 10 March and, by the following day, flooding was reported from all the counties in southern England (Plate 40). From sub-zero temperatures the thermometer had climbed to 7° or 10°C in a few hours, and because of the added complication of frozen ground and the accompanying rainfall, most rivers burst their banks within a few days. In southern England the Thames caused catastrophic flooding everywhere along its course, except in London, reaching almost record flood-levels in the Oxford-Reading reach, where it was more than 1 metre above its normal springtime level. (The record Thames flood was in November 1894, due to excessive rainfall.) In Wales the Dee, Clwyd, Conwy, Severn & Wye caused severe flooding in their upland valleys which drowned thousands of sheep and newly born lambs. The loss of lifestock was almost as severe elsewhere as the sudden thaw spread from the West Country, through the Midlands to Yorkshire and the Fenlands. Towns as far afield as Bath, Tewkesbury, Shrewsbury, Reading, Tonbridge, Nottingham, Rotherham, Doncaster, Gainsborough

40. River-side dwellers are rescued by an army tank during the 1947 snow-melt floods in the Thames valley near Windsor, England.

and Goole were inundated and thousands of houses flooded to varying degrees. In south Yorkshire catastrophic flooding of some coalmines was only narrowly averted but the East Anglian and Fenland farmers were not so lucky, for hundreds of thousands of hectares of Britain's prime agricultural land disappeared beneath the floodwaters, many areas not being effectively drained until June 1947. The reason for the widespread flooding of the Fenlands was because of the bursting of the dykes and river levees which carried the rivers at levels higher than the surrounding farmlands. This was a result of the shrinking of the peaty soils following their draining and reclamation by Cornelius Vermuyden in the seventeenth century, since when the land surface has declined in elevation by more than 3 metres (see Chapter 6). Large tracts of the Fens between Ely and Wisbech are now below sea level, so that they carry the additional risk of possible inundation from the North Sea, should the coastal defences ever be breached or over-topped.

In Chapter 4 we have already witnessed some of the far-reaching results of this type of catastrophe, such as that which devastated the coasts of eastern England during the 1953 storm surge. Furthermore, Chapter 7 has highlighted the ways in which winds generated by revolving storms can drive ocean waters far inland to create frightful flood havoc along coastal margins. But in the majority of cases coastal flooding by ocean waters follows a steady build up of tide level so that in some countries flood warnings can at least alleviate heavy loss of life. One type of coastal flooding, however, is often unpredictable, either in timing or in magnitude, so that it is the most devastating of all – it is associated with the phenomenon known as the *tsunami*.

The tsunami is not initiated by meteorological storms, nor is it a 'tidal' wave – a very widespread misconception. It is not caused by lunar tidal action, as in the case of normal ocean tides, but is in fact a sea wave generated by submarine earthquakes or by certain volcanic eruptions (see p. 59 and p. 94). Little wonder that the name *tsunami* is derived from the Japanese who, more than most, suffer from these types of natural hazards.

Apart from the historic volcanic eruptions of Thera (Santorini) and Krakatoa, Figure 77 illustrates how the majority of tsunamis are related to seismic events. Studies of Pacific tsunamis have further demonstrated that the type of earthquake is more significant than the Richter magnitude when we are trying to understand seismic sea-wave generation. The 1906 San Francisco earthquake, despite its high intensity and its lateral displacement of 6 metres along the San Andreas Fault, did not produce a tsunami. Yet earthquakes along the shores of Japan, Alaska and Chile have generated substantial tsunamis and coastal flooding. The answer appears to lie in the distinction between transcursion faulting (or tear-faulting), where movement is *horizontal* (as in California) and subduction faulting (or thrust-faulting) where movement is *downwards* into the crust (see Chapter 2). Thus, where part of the ocean floor is moved vertically it displaces water and forces it into a wave-like turbulence.

Such turbulence expresses itself in the open ocean as a series of seismic sea waves of large wave-length (sometimes 100 kilometres between crests) but of low wave height (generally less than 1 metre) so that they remain indistinguishable from storm waves as far as ocean shipping is concerned. In the deeper oceans the wave will travel at speeds in excess of 600 kilometres per hour, but as it reaches shallower water the tsunami not only slows down but increases in wave height or amplitude very substantially, hence its destructive capability on open coastlines. We have seen how earthquake magnitude can be measured on the Richter Scale and Figure 78 illustrates a magnitude scale for tsunamis devised by the Japanese, who propose a relationship with the Richter Scale. Although the record tsunami wave run-up

Fig. 77. Great tsunamis of the World (after B. A. Bolt).

Date	Source region	Visual run-up height (m)	Report from	Comments
15 B.C.	Santorini eruption	?	Crete	Devastation of Mediterranean coast
1707	West Pacific	?	Japan	Osaka Bay 4,900 drowned
1755, 1 Nov.	Eastern Atlantic	5–10	Lisbon, Portugal	Reported from Europe to West Indies
1812, 21 Dec.	Santa Barbara Channel, Calif.	Several metres	Santa Barbara, Calif.	Early reports probably exaggerated
1837, 7 Nov.	Chile	5	Hilo, Hawaii	
1841, 17 May	Kamchatka	<5	Hilo, Hawaii	
1868, 2 Apr.	Hawaiian Islands	<3	Hilo, Hawaii	
1868, 13 Aug.	Peru-Chile	>10	Arica, Peru	Observed New Zealand, damaging Hawaii
1877, 10 May	Peru-Chile	2–6	Japan	Destructive Iquique, Peru
1883, 27 Aug.	Krakatoa eruption	>30	Java	Over 30,000 drowned
1896, 15 Jun.	Honshu	24	Sanriku, Japan	About 26,000 people drowned
1923, 3 Feb.	Kamchatka	About 5	Waiakea, Hawaii	
1933, 2 Mar.	Honshu	>20	Sanriku, Japan	3,000 deaths from waves
1946, 1 Apr.	Aleutians	10	Wainaku, Hawaii	
1952, 4 Nov.	Kamchatka	<5	Hilo, Hawaii	
1957, 9 Mar.	Aleutians	<5	Hilo, Hawaii	Associated earthquake Magnitude 8.3
1960, 23 May	Chile	>10	Waiakea, Hawaii	
1964, 28 Mar.	Alaska	6	Crescent City, Calif.	119 deaths and $104,000,000 damage from tsunami
1967, 28 Feb.	Eastern Atlantic	>1	Casablanca.	
1976, 17 Aug.	West Pacific	About 5	Philippines	3,000 drowned

height is thought to be the 30-metre wave associated with the volcanic eruption of Krakatoa in Indonesia most tsunamis do not exceed 10 metres in their coastal run-up.

The Philippines earthquake of 1976 is reported to have initiated tsunamis which swept thousands to their deaths, although within recent centuries the greatest loss of life from tsunami flooding has been in Japan, where phenomenal 20-metre waves drowned almost 30,000 people in two similar disasters in 1896 and 1933. The great Lisbon earthquake of 1755 also had an associated

Floods

Fig. 78. Table of tsunami magnitude and run-up (after B. A. Bolt).

Earthquake magnitude	Tsunami magnitude	Maximum run-up (m)
6	Slight	
6.5	−1	0.5–0.75
7	0	1–1.5
7.5	1	2–3
8	2	4–6
8.25	3	8–12

tsunami, since the epicentre was off-shore, but of the 60,000 casualties it is impossible to know how many died from drowning. Because of their situation in mid Pacific the islands of Hawaii are particularly prone to tsunami damage (Plate 41), so that the recording station at Hilo has experienced seismic sea waves of various amplitudes that were generated along the coasts of Asia, North America and South America (see Figure 77). It is ironic, perhaps, that despite escaping tsunami deaths in the 1906 earthquake, Californian coastal cities have been swamped by seismic sea waves which originated several thousand kilometres away. In 1964, for example, the great Alaskan earthquake tsunami, in addition to devastating the local coasts (Plate 42), caused about $10 million worth of damage along the Californian coast, including $7 million at Crescent City alone, where thirty city blocks were flooded.

The Crescent City tsunami can be used to illustrate two further points; first, the fact that seismic sea waves occur in series not singly, and, secondly, that the establishment of an international tsunami early-warning system is beginning to produce results. Warnings of the impending 1964 tsunami enabled the United States Civil Defence authorities to carry out some evacuation of the waterfront at Crescent City so that the first two waves caused no loss of life and only minor flooding. Unfortunately, as in other cases elsewhere in the world, many inhabitants returned to the flooded waterfront only to be overwhelmed by the next waves in the series which, in Crescent City, were much more destructive and caused some loss of life.

The Seismic Sea Wave Warning System (S.S.W.W.S.) was inaugurated after the 1946 Aleutian earthquake had caused many tsunami drownings in the Hawaiian Isles. Although the system relates only to the Pacific Ocean, most of the Pacific coastal countries collaborate in the enterprise and its tsunami alerts have undoubtedly avoided even greater losses of life. As in

267

42. Part of the town of Seward, Alaska, flattened by the tsunami which swept inland during the Good Friday earthquake in 1964.

the case of other hazard-warning systems, however, there are certain drawbacks. One is related to the difficulty of predicting the magnitude of the wave, so that although tsunamis actually occur they may be so small as to warrant the accusation of a 'false alarm', thus making many coastal inhabitants too blasé. The other snag in the advance warning system relates to the phenomenon of the sensation seeker who, instead of taking heed, will be drawn by curiosity to the hazard zone. The predicted arrival of the Alaskan 1964 tsunami, for example, is said to have attracted no less than 10,000 sightseers to the coast in San Francisco!

Other Causes of Flooding

The most sensational flood disasters in the world have been examined above, but we must not forget that many lives are lost, albeit infrequently, from less common causes such as dam or levee failure, rupture of a glacial lake and

41. A giant wave, or tsunami, hits the coast of Hawaii and threatens to engulf the onlookers.

from those landslides and volcanic disturbances which influence lakes and rivers.

Dam and levee failures are largely attributable to human error, such as that which caused the 1928 St Francis Dam failure in California when five hundred people died, although it is often a change in geological, atmospheric or hydrological conditions which triggers off the disaster. On 5 June 1976, for example, the almost completed Teton dam on the Snake River, Idaho, U.S.A., was ripped apart by a breach which sent a wall of water roaring downstream. In addition to scores of deaths more than 30,000 people were left homeless and $500 million worth of damage resulted. Thought to have been located in the vicinity of a geological fault and where soils lacked stability, the Teton dam had long been the centre of a major controversy, because of its unusual earth-filled construction, wherein basalt rubble was utilized. This, it was claimed, had allowed water to seep through and finally undermine the structure. Thirteen years previously, on 14 December 1963, a dam built across a minor branch of the San Andreas Fault system had fractured in the Baldwin Hills, Los Angeles. Although great loss of life was avoided by evacuation, the damage in this intensely urbanized area totalled $15 million. Subsequent investigation has suggested that it was not move-ment along the fault itself which caused the rupture, but differential compac-tion of soil on either side of the fault, thus allowing gradual seepage and undermining of the retaining wall.

Neither of these events is the worst-recorded dam burst in the United States for that in Johnstown, Pennsylvania, in 1889 resulted in 2,209 drown-ings (Plate 43). Equally, the Dolgarrog disaster described below is by no means the worst dam failure in Britain (cf. the Bradfield Reservoir rupture, near Sheffield, Yorkshire, which caused 250 deaths in 1864) but it con-tinues to illustrate the folly of man in some of his engineering works. The tiny Welsh village of Dolgarrog is located on the floor of the Conwy valley, Gwynedd, and is the site of a hydro-electricity generating station utilizing the very high precipitation of the mountains of eastern Snowdonia. To harness the run-off, the mountain lake, Llyn Eigiau, was enlarged in 1907–10 by building a concrete dam along a ridge of unconsolidated glacial moraine which impounds the lake. The water is subsequently allowed to run normally to a smaller second reservoir at a lower elevation and thence by pipeline over the precipitous cliffs, which overhang Dolgarrog, and into the power station itself. By November 1925, following a prolonged period of rainfall, the water in the reservoir succeeded in undermining the insecure founda-tions, causing the dam to collapse and releasing over 3 million cubic metres of water across the upland plateau. It has been shown how these floodwaters

43. Johnstown, Penn., U.S.A., was devastated by floodwaters after a dam burst in 1889, culminating in America's worst flood disaster.

tore out scores of boulders, up to 500-tonnes in weight, on their helter-skelter journey and it was these which bombarded the unsuspecting village on the valley floor beneath. The village church and a dozen houses were inextricably buried beneath the enormous debris fan which stands today (now partly forested) as a grim epitaph to those who lost their lives. To understand the magnitude of the disaster it is necessary to compare the scale of the flooding with that of a better-known river. Thus, calculations have demonstrated that during the first hour the velocity of the Dolgarrog flood-waters was 28,300 cubic metres per second which is almost exactly half the discharge of the Mississippi floodwaters during the catastrophic floods of 1973. It must be remembered, however, that the Mississippi floods maintained their peak discharge of 56,800 cubic metres per second for several weeks, during which scores of levees were breached or overtopped and more than five million hectares flooded. By comparison, the peak discharge of the Thames at Teddington Weir is a mere 1,065 cubic metres per second.

The enormous velocities achieved by the floodwaters described above are related to the hydrostatic head of pressure that had been artificially attained behind the dams and levees built by mankind. We shall now examine the relatively few instances when natural events can produce the same potential flood hazards. The first of these relates to the phenomenon known as the *jökulhlaup*, an Icelandic term for the rupture of an ice barrier, leading to the sudden release of an impounded lake. The world's first record of such an outburst comes from Skeidararjokull in 1201, having been described in the Icelandic Sagas. Fortunately, the majority of the world's glacially dammed lakes are located in areas of sparse settlement so that jökulhlaup disasters of the magnitude of artificial dam failures are rare occurrences.

It is possible to recognize five broad categories of ice-dammed lakes: (1) lakes on the ice surface, (2) lakes within the ice mass, (3) lakes dammed in tributary ice-free valleys by a glacier or ice-sheet, (4) lakes impounded by a glacier against its valley wall, (5) lakes created by ice avalanches across a valley. The mechanism which culminates in the draining of a lake is not fully understood, but some scientists believe that the impounded water builds up a hydrostatic head of pressure sufficient to force open a tunnel in the ice-barrier. Others maintain that the deepening lake waters cause the frontal zone of the ice-barrier to lift by flotation, thus allowing the warmer lake waters to escape by enlarging the honeycomb of existing internal pipes and passages within the glacier. This sudden escape will occur during the peak of the summer melting season, but at the beginning of the following winter the ice-barrier will reform as the glacier settles back on the rock floor and dams the meltwaters once more. Alternative means of releasing glacier-dammed lakes include: simple overflow across the ice-barrier; subglacial melting by volcanic heat, which is especially important in countries such as Iceland, where such an event occurred beneath the Vatnajökull ice-cap in March 1934; and weakening of the ice-barrier by seismic events. Needless to say, in these latter instances the glacier-dammed lake release can occur at any time of the year, since it is not related to seasonal weather patterns. Thus, these types of jökulhlaups are the most hazardous of all because of their unpredictability. But even in the cases of seasonally emptying lakes it is not always possible to forecast a flood hazard, because the hydrological characteristics of the impounded lake can change rapidly in response to fluctuations of the run-off in its catchment area, as well as to changes within the ice mass itself. Even the regular summer draining of ice-dammed Lake George on the Knik River, Alaska, ceased abruptly after 1966, a disappointment for numerous tourists and scientists alike, for whom this had been a major attraction for almost fifty years. Elsewhere in Alaska, however, the jökulhlaup is seen as a major hazard to roads, railways and some riverside settlements, for along the Pacific coastal mountain ranges alone, no less than

750 glacier-dammed lakes have been recorded. One of them, Berg Lake, on the Bering River, is a notable future hazard, for an ice-dam failure is forecast to occur at any time, with a predicted flood velocity far exceeding 30,000 cubic metres per second.

The damming of water bodies to create flood hazards may also be the result of landslides and lava flows, one of the worst being that known as the Vaiont Dam disaster, already referred to on page 149 and shown in Figure 42 and Plate 19. It is now time to examine some of the ways in which people respond to the hazards of flooding and to outline the various flood-prediction studies and the remedial measures which have proliferated in recent years.

Human Response to Floods

The majority of studies relating to flood-hazard perception show that in general people have very short memories. In the Hunter Valley, eastern Australia, for example, very few folk were able to say what degree of flooding they could expect in the next decade, despite the prolonged record of flood disasters in the coastal zone of New South Wales. It is claimed by some writers that they may have been lulled into a false sense of security arising from the use of statistical averages rather than extremes in weather research and forecasting. This lack of awareness by the general public is again high-lighted in a British study of 1971, carried out in Shrewsbury, Shropshire, where no less than 190 houses are located on the flood-plain of the River Severn. More than half of the residents questioned were unaware that it was a hazard zone and a similar number did not expect a flood in the future. When asked to outline the major disadvantages of living in that particular location the great majority cited 'social hazards' of traffic noise, vandalism, etcetera rather than the natural hazard of flooding, as being of foremost importance in their lives. When the potential hazard was explained to the residents a great majority claimed that they would merely move upstairs and sit it out, rather than evacuate the area, whilst more than 11 per cent said that they would do nothing. This type of fatalistic approach to flooding was even more marked in a 1971 survey carried out amongst villagers on the Ganges flood plain in India. Here, in a zone which experiences some of the world's most devastating floods, the communities, whilst acutely aware of flood hazards, were not very enterprising, preferring to bear the loss of housing, crops and livestock rather than migrate to another area. There appeared to be a very marked tendency to leave everything to the will of God, whilst they saw any remedial measures against flooding, such as embank-ments, river control, and boat hire for evacuation, as being entirely the responsibility of the State. Finally, American studies carried out at Rock Island, Illinois, confirm the very close attachment of residents to their riverside locations. In these cases too, large percentages of the respondents were uncertain what their responses would be in the face of a flood hazard, and they were largely ignorant of the government agencies who would be able to assist them in the event of a flood emergency.

Despite these case studies, cited above, there is good evidence to support the contention that in general the greater the frequency of flooding '. . . the more accurate is the perception of the hazard by floodplain occupants and the greater is their willingness to consider a wider range of adjustments, including alternative sites for their activities'.[1] But flood frequency is a difficult parameter to measure unless there are sufficient gauging stations as well as meteorological and hydrological data available over a lengthy time period. Thus, flood prediction is a notoriously complex subject, for in addition to the flood frequency it is also important to be able to forecast the rate of rise together with the magnitude and duration of the flood, for only then will it be possible to plan flood-warning systems and flood-alleviation schemes. Partly to this end, in 1976 the British Geomorphological Research Group sponsored the creation of a so-called Floods Patrol whose aims are to monitor catastrophic British floods in order to clarify their magnitude and frequency characteristics for engineering and flood-hazard applications. Before implementing expensive engineering measures to mitigate a flood hazard, however, many planning authorities have sought the aid of cost-benefit analysis in order to determine their priorities. It may well be found cheaper, for example, to re-house the flood-plain dwellers elsewhere than to build massive flood-protection works. On the other hand, if such works can be utilized within an overall water conservation strategy (as in the Clywedog dam scheme, see below) then the flood-plain settlement could benefit from structural remedies. Figure 79 lists the variety of adjustments which may be made in the face of flood hazards, although their implementation will obviously vary from place to place according to the availability of funds.

Remedial Measures

It will be seen from Figure 79 that the simplest method of dealing with an impending flood disaster is to do nothing, i.e. bear the loss, and it is surprising how many of the developing countries adopt this fatalistic attitude, for a variety of philosophical, psychological and economic reasons. But most societies will wish to alleviate the social and economic losses of flooding and will undertake *corrective* and/or *preventive* measures. A *corrective* flood

Fig. 79. Adjustments to the flood hazard (after W. R. D. Sewell, 1964).

Modify the flood	Modify the damage susceptibility	Modify the loss burden	Do nothing
Flood protection	Land-use regulation and changes	Flood insurance	Bear the loss
(channel phase)	Statutes	Tax write-offs	
Dikes	Zoning ordinances	Disaster relief	
Floodwalls	Building codes	volunteer	
Channel-	Urban renewal	private activities	
improvement	Subdivision regulations	government aid	
Reservoirs	Government purchase of	Emergency measures	
River diversions	lands and property	Removal of persons	
Watershed treatment	Subsidized relocation	and property	
(land phase)	Floodproofing	Flood fighting	
Modification of	Permanent closure of low-level	Rescheduling of	
cropping practices	windows and other openings	operations	
Terracing	Waterproofing interiors		
Gully control	Mounting store counters on wheels		
Bank stabilization	Installation of removable covers		
Forest-fire control	Closing of sewer valves		
Revegetation	Covering machinery with plastic		
Weather modification	Structural change		
	Use of impervious material for		
	basements and walls		
	Seepage control		
	Sewer adjustment		
	Anchoring machinery		
	Underpinning buildings		
	Land elevation and fill		

control programme will include most if not all of the engineering works listed in columns one and two of Figure 79. Here, there will be attempts to regulate the river flow to fit the channel capacity or, alternatively, to restructure the channel to accommodate the vagaries of the river. The other *corrective* measures which are included in columns one and two of Figure 79 include the various aspects of floodproofing together with more enlightened land-use control in the catchment area, such as tree-planting, gully control, terracing or slope. *Preventive* measures are normally taken in zones which will remain liable to periodic flooding, despite any structural adjustments which have been made to the hydrological regime. Column three in Figure 79 demonstrates, therefore, some of the ways in which the impact of the loss burden may be modified and the area returned to normality as quickly as possible. In order to implement many of the planning controls included in this section, both central- and local-government bodies may have to be given sweeping statutory powers of compulsory purchase, relocation, etcetera. In most instances, however, such powers are only applied during an official state of emergency when the region is designated a 'disaster area'. One of the greatest problems involved in flood-control programmes is that of allocating the costs, i.e. whether these should be borne by central government, local government or privately financed. Preventive measures may often fall into the latter two categories, but in most instances flood-corrective programmes are funded by the national or state government.

Amongst the most costly of the corrective measures are the engineering remedies which involve the construction of weirs, river embankments and bypasses, the straightening and smoothing of channels, the provision of training walls to obviate silt accumulation and the installation of pumping schemes and reservoirs. Reservoir construction, albeit the most expensive, has the advantage of serving a multi-purpose role of hydro-electricity production, water supply, and recreation as well as of flood control. The Clywedog Reservoir, on the headwaters of the River Severn, in Britain, is a good example of a multi-purpose reservoir, being utilized as a means of water supply, fishing and sailing. Although helping to control the flood levels in such Welsh towns as Llanidloes and Newtown, it has been shown how its influence farther downstream, in the cities of Shrewsbury and Worcester, for instance, is only minimal, because by then the Severn has been joined by major unregulated tributaries. Unfortunately, multi-purpose roles often lead to conflict, as was seen in the case of the Florence floods (p. 248), for flood-control often necessitates the lowering of the reservoir's waters in order to anticipate seasonal flooding. The Clywedog Reservoir, for example, is 'drawn down' between May and October so that it can contain the winter floods of central Wales for subsequent gradual release. But on some occasions, if there are increased demands for water elsewhere in the catchment, due to external forces, the role of flood regulation may be seen as a subordinate one. Hydro-electricity and recreational purposes are best served by a full reservoir, while flood-control requires that the reservoir remains empty!

Nevertheless, skilfully planned water resource programmes can strike an important balance, as was demonstrated by the operation of the Shasta Reservoir, on the Sacramento River in California during the 1970 floods, which were the river's highest this century. Figures 80a and 80b illustrate the effect of this multi-purpose reservoir (usually assisting with irrigation schemes) during the three weeks of flood hazard at an up-river town (Redding) 15 kilometres from the dam and a down-river town (Ord Ferry) 120 kilometres from the dam. At Redding the regulated flow kept the waters within the desired flow limits, thus avoiding flooding (Figure 80a), but at Ord River there were two flood episodes, but at greatly reduced magnitudes.

Fig. 8o. Effect of flood-control measures on flow of the Sacramento River, California: (a) at Redding (b) at Ord Ferry (after B. A. Bolt).

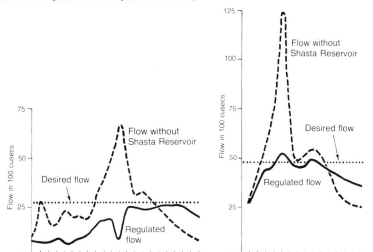

a) Sacramento River at Redding
(15 km downstream of Snasta Dam)

b) Sacramento River at Ord Ferry
(120 km downstream of Shasta Dam)

As in the case of the River Severn at Shrewsbury and Worcester, the Sacramento had received the uncontrolled inflow from major tributaries by the time it had reached Ord Ferry (Figure 8ob).

The redesign of river channels (termed 'river training') is the most common form of remedial measure and most of the advanced nations have developed engineering and research institutes devoted to these types of hazards. In Britain, for example, many of the solutions to major flood problems have been discovered at Wallingford, Oxfordshire, where the Hydraulics Research Station and the Institute of Hydrology are able to simulate the problems by means of both mathematical and working models. As a result of these and other research centres flood-control programmes have been implemented on such important British rivers as the Thames, Trent, Severn, Bristol Avon and the Ouse. That on the Avon has resolved an age-old problem in the city of Bath (Figure 81) which had hitherto suffered serious flooding. In California, the storm drains and flood channels of Los Angeles are no less famous and will be examined in more detail in Chapter 11. As far as the U.S.A. is concerned, however, no less than 73 per

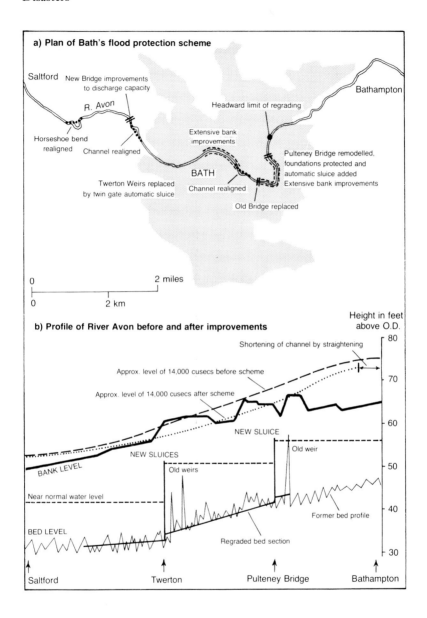

a) Plan of Bath's flood protection scheme

Saltford New Bridge improvements
to discharge capacity

Bathampton

R. Avon   Headward limit of regrading

Horseshoe bend   Extensive bank
realigned   Channel realigned   improvements

Pulteney Bridge remodelled,
foundations protected and
BATH   automatic sluice added

Twerton Weirs replaced   Channel realigned   Extensive bank improvements
by twin gate automatic sluice

Old Bridge replaced

0   2 miles

0   2 km

Height in feet
above O.D.

b) Profile of River Avon before and after improvements

80

Shortening of channel by straightening

Approx. level of 14,000 cusecs before scheme   70

Approx. level of 14,000 cusecs after scheme

60

NEW SLUICE

NEW SLUICES   Old weir

BANK LEVEL   Old weirs   50

Near normal water level

40

Former bed profile

BED LEVEL   Regraded bed section

30

Saltford   Twerton   Pulteney Bridge   Bathampton

Fig. 81. Effect of flood-control measures on the River Avon at Bath, England: (a) Plan of Bath's flood-protection scheme (b) Profile of River Avon before and after improvements (after M. D. Newson).

278

cent of the national funds for river-channel improvement have been devoted to the Mississippi, whose flood problems need no emphasis. In addition, 48 per cent of the American expenditure on embankments and floodwalls is consumed by the Mississippi alone, to say nothing of the Missouri and Ohio, its major tributaries, which together add a further 17 per cent to the claim on federal funds. But such expenditure paid handsome dividends during the 1973 floods, when it was calculated that the remedial measures had prevented some $320 million worth of excess damage in the Mississippi valley, thus recouping almost one fifth of the capital outlay during a single flood.

Flooding which results from causes other than rivers requires very different treatments. In Hawaii, for example, a great deal of research has been carried out into tsunami risks and protective structures against potential damage. Specially designed breakwaters have been suggested at Hilo, costing some $30 million, but a survey has shown that residents in the hazard zone prefer to take the risk of one chance in ten rather than lose their sea view! On turning to the contrasting problem of the jökulhlaup, the engineers are faced with an even greater difficulty. Does the hazard justify costly remedial measures when a slight change in the glaciological regime may render the structures unnecessary? In Alaska, for example, outbursts from glacier-dammed lakes have, in the past, posed only a minimal threat to life and property. In recent years, however, the advent of the Alaskan oil-fields has brought man and his artifacts into previously unsettled zones where the jökulhlaup may become a serious hazard. It is possible that temporary expedient measures may be sufficient in most instances, as in the case of Argentina, where an ice-barrier was bombed by naval aircraft in an effort to prevent the accumulation of a potentially hazardous ice-dammed lake by the Moreno Glacier in the southern Andes. In Norway, another country with many glacier-dammed lakes, the hazard of a jökulhlaup at Demmevatn was in part reduced by carving artificial tunnels in both 1899 and 1938 in order to lower the lake levels. Another ice-dammed lake in northern Norway, on the fringe of the Svartisen ice-cap, was drained by a similar tunnel driven through the mountain side.

9. Drought

Water, like many other elements essential for the maintenance of the world's plant and animal life, is abundantly available on our planet. But, like some of these other necessities, water is an imbalanced resource due to inequalities of geographical distribution. Certain regions of the world have too much, others have too little, whilst some countries are in the curious position of suffering from alternating floods and droughts. China, for example, has suffered a total of 1,029 floods and 1,056 droughts since records began in 206 B.C., leaving one to wonder if any water conservation programme can ever rectify such an apparent anomaly. Historically, water has featured as one of the most important elements in the economic organization of human societies – from the riverine civilizations of ancient Egypt to the commune-based irrigation schemes of modern China. Wars have been waged over water rights in earlier centuries and even today there are heated debates over the control of both international and national water resources. In the developed world of the twentieth century many people have taken for granted the constant availability of water supplies, feeling secure in the mistaken belief that drought comes only to the geographically arid and semi-arid lands of the world. We shall see how in 1976 and 1977 Britain and the United States were shaken out of their apathy when they experienced record droughts.

Droughts and crop failures in the deserts are nothing new, for the annals of history are littered with references to such disasters, but we have to realize that in the present century no less than 14 per cent (630 million) of the world's population live in arid or semi-arid regions. Of these some fifty million people are constantly faced with malnutrition and possible death whenever the rains fail (Plate 44). Such numbers represent those of the desert dwellers whose livelihoods are based entirely on an agricultural economy, as opposed to the oil-rich societies of the Middle East. But observers have noted that in addition to the occasional periods of drought, prolonged years of careless husbandry are resulting in the gradual spread of

44. Drought in the Sahel, Africa, 1974. Starving families sift through corn husks in an attempt to find food in the desiccated landscape.

the deserts – on the margins of the Sahara an estimated 650,000 square kilometres of grazing lands have been lost in the last half century. Thus it has been claimed that the roots of the 1972–74 drought in northern Africa lay as much in land utilization incompatible with the region's environmental limitations as with the rainfall anomaly:

... both the scale of suffering when the rains fail and the scale of destructive human pressures on delicate arid-zone ecosystems are reaching unprecedented proportions in the Sahel and in many other desert regions. As the number of people who rely on the pastures and croplands of the arid zones climbs, once-sustainable social patterns and production techniques begin to undermine the biological systems on which life depends.[1]

Although there are many who subscribe to the belief that man's misuse of the land is the major culprit in the problem of 'Desertification' (as it has

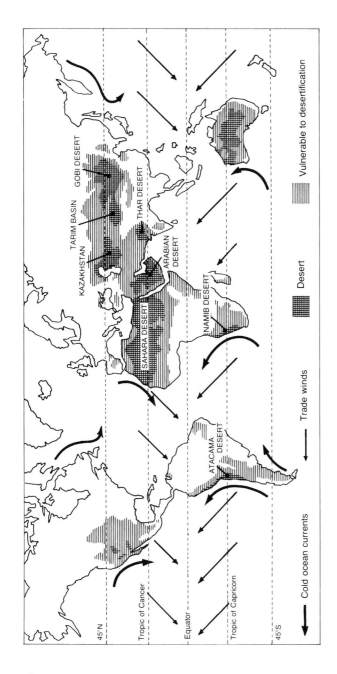

Fig. 82. World deserts and areas liable to desertification.

GOBI DESERT

TARIM BASIN

KAZAKHSTAN

THAR DESERT

ARABIAN DESERT

SAHARA DESERT

NAMIB DESERT

ATACAMA DESERT

45°N

Tropic of Cancer

Equator

Tropic of Capricorn

45°S

Vulnerable to desertification

Desert

Trade winds

Cold ocean currents

come to be called) there are probably an equal number who advocate the importance of climatic change. Here is the dichotomy, so let us examine the evidence that has been used to support such opposing views.

The Causes of Drought

At the outset it is important to delineate the world distribution of deserts and to define the meaning of aridity. Figure 82 illustrates not only the true deserts but the widespread semi-desert areas of the world, all of which can be categorized as the *arid zone*. For statistical convenience the true climatic desert has been defined cartographically by the 100 millimetres (*c.* 4 inches) annual precipitation line (termed an *isohyet*). Calculations have shown that within this zone there is a permanent water deficit, because potential evapotranspiration is so high that it exceeds the total rainfall by a factor of at least ten. The coastal deserts of Chile/Peru and Namibia (South West Africa) are exceptions to the general 100 millimetres rule, for owing to the high humidity of the air in certain seasons the desert margin is marked by the 50 millimetres (*c.* 2 inches) isohyet.

The world's semi-deserts can be defined as those areas lying between the 100–400 millimetres (*c.* 4–12 inches) isohyets, again with the exceptions of north Chile and Namibia, where the limits of 50–300 millimetres apply. These slightly moister parts of the arid zone not only include large stretches of the Middle East and the notorious Sahel belt to the south of the Sahara (see below), but also the Kalahari, Central Australia, much of inner Asia, Patagonia and south-west U.S.A. The widespread range of the arid zone (from 50° latitude to within some 10° of the equator) is sufficient to demonstrate that it is the lack of precipitation which is the dominant climatic element, not the temperature. Thus we can distinguish between the hot deserts of the Sahara and Arabia, on the one hand, and the mid-latitude deserts of Central Australia or the Gobi of central Asia, on the other.

The dearth of rainfall in the arid zone may be caused by one or more factors. In the first place aridity may result from a location in a continental interior, far removed from the moisture-laden oceanic winds, as in the case of central Asia. Secondly, the region may lie in the 'rain shadow' of a major mountain range, so that much of the precipitation from the moist air stream is removed in passage across the mountain zone – the Kalahari and parts of Patagonia fall into this category. Thirdly, we have the coastal deserts, such as the Atacama of Chile, which exist because winds, having blown across a cool ocean current on to a heated land, do not condense their moisture into anything more than mist. Last, but most important, are the major tropical deserts which coincide with large, permanent high-pressure systems, in which air is slowly subsiding before blowing outwards at the surface. In this way rain-bearing cyclones are virtually excluded and precipitation totals are practically nil in wide areas of the central Sahara and Arabia. The driest place in the world, however, occurs near Calama, in Chile's Atacama desert, where no rain has fallen for over four hundred years.

One of the greatest anomalies in the study of deserts has been the discovery of landforms that were undoubtedly carved by running water but have stood virtually fossilized for hundreds of years. The wadis of Arabia, for example, suggest that they were once part of a major system of surface drainage. What other evidence is there that variations in climate during the last million years have caused major shifts in the desert margins?

Careful examination of the world's largest lakes reveals that some of them were once considerably larger than they are today. If this was true of the East African rift-valley lakes, the ephemeral Lake Chad of West Africa and Lake Eyre of Australia, it was equally true of the Great Salt Lake of Utah, U.S.A. It is noteworthy that all of these lie in the present day arid zone, a fact which led early scientists to suggest that during the Pleistocene period, when ice-caps expanded into the temperate zone, a shift in airstreams brought considerably more rain to the deserts. These hypothetical wet phases during the Pleistocene were referred to as *pluvials* and some workers went as far as linking them with glacial advances in higher latitudes. Recent research, however, has demonstrated that this is an oversimplification and that the earth's climate during the glacial maxima was drier as well as cooler than at present. It has been suggested, for example, that at one time during the Pleistocene the southern edge of the Sahara stood 500 kilometres farther south than it does today, whilst in Utah the inland lakes reached their maximum extent when precipitation differed very little from now, possibly because the climate was cooler and evaporation losses smaller than at present.

All of this suggests that during the last million years there have been dramatic shifts of the world's deserts, first equatorwards then polewards, with an accompanying movement of the semi-arid zones also. We can now begin to explain how the Neolithic pastoralists who once roamed what is now the central Sahara drew pictures of their cattle in the rock shelters of the Tibesti mountains, and why ancient Saharan sand dunes are now submerged beneath the waters of Lake Chad. The last major climatic shift of global climate, some five thousand years ago, resulted in a major spread of deserts as aridity was markedly increased. Some anthropologists and demographers have seen the increasing desiccation as the cause of the major nomadic migrations in central Asia, migrations which soon turned into warlike invasions of the more humid regions of Western Europe and China, during the early centuries of the Christian era:

Men do not take their wives and children and move in great masses except under some strong compulsion. I do not need to go into details on the barbaric invasions of Rome. It is enough to point out that they were numerous as long as the climate of Asia grew worse. They spread into each of the southern peninsulas of Europe. They spilled over into Africa. Finally, in the seventh century there came the culminating migration from the desert. The power of the Roman Empire had vanished, and the Arabs surged out under Mohammed. The religious impulse doubtless was of the greatest importance as a unifying factor, but hunger may have been the chief impelling force. So too, in later days, Genghis Khan may have been the unifying factor, but hunger due to a second great period of aridity was perhaps the underlying force that impelled his hordes to surge out of Central Asia.[2]

So much for the evidence of fluctuating climate during the last few millennia, but what of the arguments of those who suggest that man's profligate use of his natural resources has been largely responsible for the spread of desert margins and for placing millions of people on the verge of starvation?

It has been calculated that along the northern fringes of the Sahara about 1,000 square kilometres of grazing land are being converted to desert each year. This is largely because the rapidly increasing populations of Libya, Tunisia, Algeria and Morocco are overtaxing the resources by overgrazing, firewood-gathering, and by pushing arable farming into areas where it cannot be sustained. All of these practices lead to destruction of the vegetation and the spread of desertification. The picture is the same in other parts of Africa such as Botswana, Tanzania and Kenya, whilst the warfare in the Horn of Africa during the 1970s is in many ways an extension of tribal rivalries between Ethiopia and Somalia over water and grazing rights, now dressed up in the garb of international power politics. It will be noted below, as we look at several case studies of drought in the present century, that the majority of the examples are drawn from the developing world. But it is also prudent to note that desertification is not simply a problem of the less developed countries, as the degeneration of the American Great Plains into the infamous Dust Bowl of the 1930s demonstrated only too well. From all corners of the world the message from the ecologists and agronomists appears to be the same:

Instead of the desert being pushed outward by climatic influences, it may be pulled outward by man's mismanagement of the semi-arid zone. Overstocking or inappropriate cultivation may undermine the long-term productivity of semi-arid ecosystems. This process may initially affect only relatively small areas, but it can spread like leprosy.[3]

Drought in the Developing World

Unlike an earthquake, tsunami or avalanche there is no sudden dramatic occurrence which hits the newspaper headlines of an unsuspecting world. Drought is slow and insidious, a creeping death which gradually paralyses entire nations and changes the course of history. Thus, despite contrasting with the cataclysms and holocausts described in earlier chapters drought can still be regarded as a disaster, and in so far as it sometimes persists for years, or even decades, as a major disaster. It is not by chance that we use the word 'desert' as a synonym to describe the horrific aftermath of an earthquake or a tornado. But drought does not knock down buildings, destroy roads and bridges any more than it burns, buries or drowns thousands of people in a few shattering moments. How, therefore, does one communicate the severity of a drought? Perhaps the lingering death implied by Plate 44 is enough, for it illustrates, as numerous Oxfam posters aim to do, that many inhabitants of the developing world cannot help themselves under such circumstances, all assistance must come from elsewhere. If other more fortunate countries cannot help, then millions may die from the ensuing famine. Not all famines are caused by drought, as witness the Irish 'potato' famine of the 1840s (1,500,000 deaths) or the Russian famine of 1920–21 (c. 5 million deaths). But there is good reason to believe that the failure of the rains, and hence the harvests, had a great deal to do with the staggering Asiatic death-tolls of 1770, when tens of millions of Indians died, and of 1877–78, when almost ten million Chinese perished.

One may think it almost inconceivable that such disasters could recur in the 1970s but one has only to recall events in Ethiopia and West Africa between 1972 and 1974 to realize that this is precisely what is happening today. In Ethiopia alone it was finally estimated that 200,000 had succumbed by 1973, after rainfall had dropped considerably below average in the Sahel zone for every year since 1968. From the Atlantic coast to the Red Sea this semi-arid region of Africa, where rainfall is normally between 300 millimetres and 400 millimetres per year, reported almost total crop failures during the fateful years of 1972–74. Since most of the Sahel inhabitants are herdsmen, it was the livestock which suffered first. At the outset, when millet became scarce, the animals were sold, but eventually as the markets became glutted the livestock prices slumped and the animals were often left to starve. Once their means of livelihood had disappeared, their wells had dried up and their supplies of sorghum and millet had been exhausted, the herdsmen tracked south in ever-increasing numbers, flocking into the overcrowded cities to compete with the rest of the landless for food and jobs.

In Nigeria a similar drought had affected the Northern Provinces in 1913 and although things appear never to have reached such dire straits during 1972–74, the early description of the 1913 migration makes informative reading, for this is the type of disaster which struck drought-stricken Ethiopia in the early 1970s:

> The great city of Kano drew the starving thousands from the country in the faint hope of scouring in the streets and markets to pick up what they might, or beg the charity of the townspeople. Not only Nigerians, but thousands from French country drifted down across our borders, passing through villages *en route* all bare of food to offer them. They died like flies on every road.[4]

Although northern Nigeria again suffered badly in the 1972–74 drought the number of fatalities appears to have been negligible in contrast to those in the neighbouring Sahelian states (Figure 83). No official figures are available

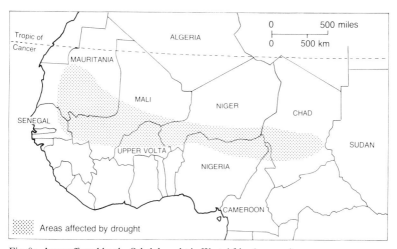

Fig. 83. Areas affected by the Sahel drought in West Africa (1972–74).

for the hardest hit countries of Mauritania, Senegal, Mali, Upper Volta, Niger and Chad, but the death-toll seems to have run into thousands, whilst livestock losses must have totalled several millions, including an 80 per cent loss of cattle. Large-scale relief operations were mounted to bring food to the starving populations and subsequent calculations suggest that in the worst affected areas people received about 100 kilograms of food per head, whilst in the less afflicted parts of northern Nigeria about nine million inhabitants received, on average, about 10 kilograms per head. The Nigerian

Government had proclaimed this region a *disaster area* as early as January 1973 and continued to send aid for several years afterwards, despite the inevitable accusations of inefficiency and lack of coordination. In the drought reports which were finally issued recommendations were made that Nigeria's future National Development Plans should take into account remedial measures against desert encroachment and drought. One further outcome of the 1972–74 famine was the immediate link up of seven of the other drought-affected West African countries to coordinate initiatives taken by their governments to combat the effects of the drought. They agreed upon a scheme, known as *Solar*, in which nomads could drive their cattle into the wetter lands of the south in times of stress.

Between the drought-stricken regions of West Africa and Ethiopia lies the country of Sudan, from which surprisingly little was heard during the critical years in question. It is now known that although the lack of rainfall was just as marked in the Sahelian zone of Sudan as elsewhere, the effect was not as disastrous. There were two main reasons for this apparent anomaly: first, the agricultural economy of the nation depends very largely on irrigation schemes furnished by the Nile which remained unaffected by the drought; and secondly, the nomadic herdsmen of Sudan, unlike their Sahelian brothers farther west, were able to migrate southwards into the more humid tracts of southern Sudan, unhindered by international frontiers. It has often been suggested that because of its high potential for irrigation-based farming Sudan could become the granary of the Arab world, but this has failed to take into account the significant degree of desertification which is taking place within its own boundaries. Land degradation, from over-stocking and poor husbandry, has been monitored over the last two decades and reveals a startling shift southwards of the desert margin in Sudan of almost 100 kilometres in a mere seventeen years! So that even without taking into account any future rainfall deficiency the Sudanese may be unwittingly heading for a disaster of their own making. They have already almost abandoned the traditional system of staple crop rotation in their rush to plant cash crops, and already the results have been disastrous. Within a period of a dozen years peanut and sesame yields have been cut by 75 per cent and millet production has fallen to a mere 12 per cent of its former level. The Sudanese would do well to take note of their neighbours' recent catastrophes and to heed the warnings given by the United Nations Secretary-General, Kurt Waldheim, when referring to desertification: 'Countries could disappear from the face of the map. We risk destroying whole peoples in the afflicted area.'

To offset such threats other nations in the arid zone have already embarked upon ambitious tree-planting programmes. Algeria is creating pockets of trees and is talking about a so-called 'green belt' stretching across the northern fringes of the Sahara from Morocco to Egypt. Since 1963 China has replanted 70 million hectares of trees along the perimeter of the nation's proverbial 'Sand Dragon' – the infamous Gobi Desert – but tree-survival rate has been as low as 10 per cent owing to the inhospitable environment and lack of maintenance. One fears, therefore, for the Algerian efforts and for the hopes of the Sahelian nations who are talking of a similar planting programme along the Sahara's southern margins. China's recent river-harnessing projects, however, appear to have met with much greater success and may finally help to solve the centuries-old problem of alternating floods and droughts referred to on p. 280.

Drought in the Developed World

At the height of the Australian summer in 1977–78 the Outback areas of Queensland, New South Wales and Victoria were gripped by one of the worst droughts on record in this notoriously marginal belt of the arid zone. Empty dams, dried-up waterholes, shrivelled crops and weakening livestock featured in every news report, so that graziers began to shoot cattle in order to foster their slender fodder reserves. In one year this drought had cost Australia over £500 million and the authorities had been forced to declare the worst affected tracts disaster areas. But droughts in this Outback region of Australia are fairly commonplace and many of its rivers, such as Cooper's Creek, frequently fail to operate for several months on end. Serious though it may have been the 1977–78 Australian drought cannot be regarded as a freakish departure from the country's normal weather regime. The British drought of 1976, however, was quite another matter and had it continued for a few more months it seems probable that this major industrial nation would have been brought to a virtual standstill. It is true that no human lives were lost and that in most areas people were able to continue to work normally, but as we shall now see the 1976 drought could have developed into Britain's worst internal disaster since the Black Death.

The British drought really began as far back as May 1975 after which a fairly dry summer was followed by a remarkably rainless winter. During this period the reservoirs became slowly depleted and the ground water table fell lower and lower (Plate 45). Normally, the water resources of this cloudy island are replenished regularly by the succession of Atlantic cyclones or depressions which characterize the humid temperate zone of the

globe. But since the beginning of the 1970s there seem to have been some remarkable changes in the British weather patterns, and the period 1970–75 became established as the lowest mean rainfall total for any five-year period since the 1850s.

Thus, the stage was set for the most rainless sixteen months in the nation's history, when parts of central southern England received less than 40 per cent of their normal rainfall and most of England and Wales averaged only about 60 per cent (Figure 84). The explanation was not difficult to seek, for

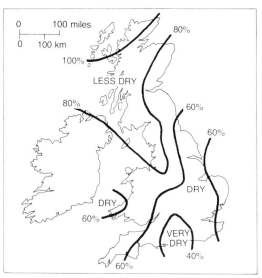

Fig. 84. The British drought of 1975–76. Figures are shown as a percentage of the average rainfall for 1941–70 (after R. A. S. Ratcliffe).

an examination of weather patterns demonstrated that there had been an unusually prolonged shift of the general circulation in the North Atlantic during the 1970s. Instead of the cyclones moving eastwards towards Scotland and southern Norway along their usual paths they were now tracking north-eastwards into the Arctic, carrying with them their moist westerly airstreams and the associated precipitation. This change in circulation had been brought about by an unusually persistent development of high-pressure systems (anticyclones) over the British Isles and the results were soon to prove catastrophic as far as water resources were concerned. By the summer of 1976 the weather pattern illustrated in Figure 85 had become commonplace and southern Britain had begun to scorch as the sun blazed down from cloudless skies, sending the temperature soaring into the nineties (30°C).

45. *left* When some of Britain's reservoirs dried up in 1976, during the country's worst recorded drought, the nation was shocked at the vulnerability of its domestic water supply.

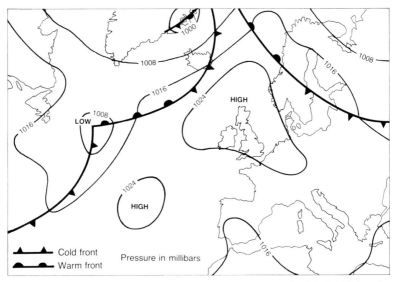

Fig. 85. Weather map of 26 August 1976 to show conditions at the height of the British drought.

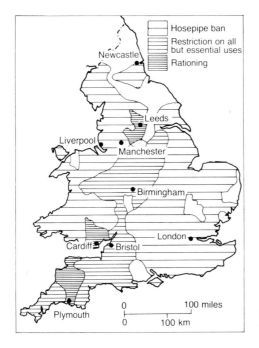

Fig. 86. Water restrictions in England and Wales, August 1976.

The impact was first felt in the domestic water supply, especially in the drier downland areas of southern England where wells soon ran dry. By the end of July road tankers were having to carry emergency supplies to outlying settlements and by early August many towns and cities in West Yorkshire, South Wales and South West England were faced with a total water restriction for many hours of each day (Figure 86). In Cardiff, for example, thirty-five inspectors turned off three hundred street valves daily for a matter of weeks, and all over southern Britain it soon became commonplace to see queues forming at the few official water supply points. The British Government, having set up a Drought Committee, were forced to rush a Drought Act through Parliament which in effect brought water-rationing to the domestic consumer. Non-essential use of water was forbidden so that car washes, swimming pools, golf courses and sports fields were seriously affected. But so far this was little more than a serious inconvenience for consumers – the most important threats to the nation only began to emerge when water supplies to industry and agriculture began to dwindle. For the first time it looked as if large sections of British industry would be faced with total shut down, not from strike action, but from a shortage of essential water. The steel industry in particular was seriously threatened, but British power stations also relied on cooling water from lakes and rivers and this could not be re-cycled indefinitely. Some of the country's Regional Water Authorities began to draw up lists of priorities, selecting the food-processing and agricultural-linked industries to head the lists, but it appeared as though other less essential industries, such as dyeing and tanning, would be severely restricted. Alternative sources of water were examined, including those amounts which had to be pumped out of Welsh coal mines and Cornish tin mines as a safety measure. But these were often contaminated and in any event provided only a minimal addition. The Republic of Ireland offered abundant supplies of free water to the drought-stricken Welsh coalfields, but the transport costs proved to be prohibitive.

By far the most serious effect of the drought was on British agriculture, where crop yields were savagely depleted and thousands of cattle had to be slaughtered prematurely to save fodder. For the first summer ever, the farmers reported an almost zero growth in grasslands over much of southern and eastern England, and this brought a serious depletion in milk supplies. The cereal harvest was catastrophic in some areas and the vegetable crops of East Anglia were decimated, bringing many of the frozen vegetable and canning companies to a standstill and to the verge of bankruptcy. The immediate outcome was a virtual doubling of some food prices, which boded ill for Britain's attempts to escape from its inflationary economic problems.

At the same time farmers were being forced to import expensive feedstuffs for their livestock, leading to a 20 per cent rise in farm expenditure and an annual fall in agricultural output of 10 per cent. When it is realized that this final figure applies to the whole of Britain, most northern parts of which were unaffected, it will be seen how some farmers in southern Britain took a much higher reduction in output.

In recent years it had become a standard practice for farmers to burn the stubble in the harvested grain fields in order to replenish the soil minerals. In August 1976, however, the British Minister of Agriculture and the National Farmers' Union asked the farmers not to burn the stubble, ostensibly because of the shortage of straw for fodder, although in fact the fire risks had become a serious hazard all over Britain. By midsummer the vegetation was like a tinder box with forest and heath fires being reported daily. The public was warned to keep off certain areas, whilst in others the Forestry Commission closed walks and trails by locking access gates, but in vain. In two simultaneous conflagrations, for example, 200,000 trees were destroyed in one South Wales forest whilst in mid Wales a further 150 acres (60 hectares) of conifers were wiped out. Heath fires destroyed property in Sussex and Hampshire, closing main roads for several hours as firemen and troops fought thousands of incidents. The worst situation, however, arose in Dorset, where 346 patients had to be hastily evacuated from a hospital as 30-metre flames from a forest fire swept towards it.

When the final bills were totalled it was discovered that the extra fire-fighting costs alone totalled £2.5 million, to say nothing of the loss of property, crops and trees. And yet in some ways the ecological loss was even greater, for field naturalists have since demonstrated that the fires took a heavy toll on Britain's wild life. Many of southern England's rarest birds, such as the Dartford Warbler, Hobby, Nightjar and Tree Pipit had lost much of their territories and food supplies. The impact was illustrated by one of England's conservation officers who drew attention to the fact that, although 'a bird can fly away from fire it can't take its eggs or nestlings with it'. To make matters worse for the fire-blackened forests, the drought killed off many shallow-rooted trees such as beech and birch and killed five million young seedlings in the Forestry Commission's nurseries.

As some of Britain's rivers dwindled away thousands of fish died from lack of oxygen and from the high water temperatures. This lack of fresh water meant also that bacteria were unable to break up some of the untreated sewage which emptied directly from countless farmlands into the river systems. Before long the Government was warning of serious health hazards to bathers, although thousands were taking to the rivers in order to keep cool

46. By mid August 1976, at the height of the British drought, the River Thames had virtually ceased to flow, leaving these river craft high and dry upstream from London.

and as numerous public swimming pools closed down. On 24 August the sources of the River Thames in Gloucestershire dried up, and shortly afterwards it was reported that a combination of evaporation and leakage from the bed near to Oxford meant that to all intents and purposes the river had ceased to flow (Plate 46). All the Thames locks were closed for lengthy periods, causing serious disruption of holiday boating, but in East Anglia the consequences became even more serious, for cattle began to die after drinking from tidal streams on the Norfolk Broads, because of the increased salinity. In the Fenlands, in attempts to counteract such threats and to replenish agricultural irrigation schemes, all the locks on the River Ouse were closed above Ely and fresh water was pumped back upstream to a reservoir at Grafham, at a cost of £200,000. The restrictions on river navigation and on many miles of the British canal network caused a serious financial loss to some boat-hire firms, but the British Waterways Board were far more concerned about the drought's effect on the clay-lining of the canals and reservoirs. If sections were allowed to dry out the damage caused by cracking and subsequent leakage could cost millions of pounds to repair. This was to say nothing of the potential flood hazard, since some of the canals were constructed on hillsides overlooking heavily populated urban areas. One final effect of the desiccation of the clay soils was seen in the considerable degree of ground subsidence which ensued. Thousands of buildings were affected, suffering serious cracking and disturbance of their structures as their foundations moved by varying amounts. It was estimated that insurance claims would total some £60 million, most of them relating to modern properties which had been built with shallow foundations.

By the autumn of 1976 people were beginning to ask such questions as: Is it just a freakish event? or, Is the United Kingdom weather pattern now locked into drought? The farmers in particular wanted to know the answers for they would have to change their traditional farming patterns very quickly, if disastrous future losses were to be avoided. The weather experts were divided in their opinions. The British Meteorological Office, for example, sees the 1975-76 drought as an unusual departure from normal and as an event which is likely to occur only once in two hundred and fifty years. Academic climatologists, however, take a different viewpoint, arguing that there has been a significant shift in global weather patterns in recent years and that the British drought may not be a freak event after all. They point out that the British rainfall averages have been based on the period 1916-50, which was a time of rapid change in synoptic conditions owing to the very dynamic character of the 'weather machine'. But since 1970 this character has changed and the opposite situation has prevailed. It appears that there has been a marked slowing down of the world's circulatory system, which means that the relative sluggishness has caused high- and low-pressure cells to move more slowly, with a tendency to give intense periodic droughts or floods. Their arguments appear to be borne out by the facts as far as Britain is concerned, for following the driest spell on record the country has endured one of the most prolonged wet spells ever recorded. By the winter of 1976-77 many parts of Britain became inundated by floodwater after months of incessant rain had caused rivers to burst their banks. At Teddington Weir, the largest on the River Thames, 27 million cubic metres of water per day were flowing downstream, some three times its normal flow, in comparison with the mere 225,000 cubic metres at the height of the drought six months previously.

The rainfall anomalies of the 1970s in the Northern hemisphere were not

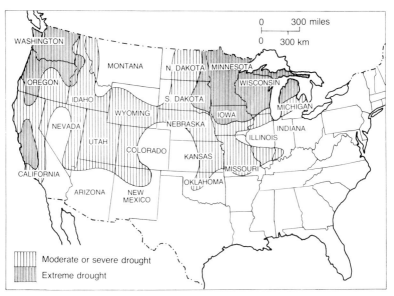

Fig. 87. Drought in the United States, 1977.

yet finished, for by early 1977 it was the turn of the United States to be gripped by drought. The villain of the piece was a vast stationary high-pressure system off the coast of California which effectively blocked the moisture-laden westerlies from reaching the continental interior. Conse-quently, much of the American West and Midwest was soon to be suffering from a prolonged precipitation deficit (Figure 87). By the spring of 1977 the nation was faced with massive crop failures, hydroelectric power shortages, domestic water-rationing and threatened industrial shutdowns. Despite the catastrophic Sahel droughts of recent memory, United States scientists were beginning to talk of the most serious drought conditions anywhere on the globe. Furthermore, because of its threatened impact on the economic well-being of the United States, the drought was seen to have serious repercussions on the developing world, which might no longer be able to look to America to ease its hunger.

The 1977 meeting of the American Association for the Advancement of Science added to the foreboding, for speakers resurrected the spectre of the infamous Dust Bowl of the 1930s as they drew comparisons with the simi-larity of the two sets of weather conditions. There were warnings that the drought and famine conditions, graphically described in Steinbeck's *Grapes of Wrath*, could return to the American West.

The phenomenon of the American Dust Bowl had been a grim warning to agronomists for, after the tenfold population increase of the states of Oklahoma, Arkansas and Texas following the United States' Homestead Act of 1862, the natural grasslands of the Great Plains had become too deeply ploughed in an effort to increase the grain harvests. At first the grain production of the 1920s, coinciding with a rainy period, was prolific enough to earn the appellation of the 'Breadbasket of America', but by 1931 drought had taken these newly won cornfields into its relentless grip. Strong northerly winds began to shift the desiccated and unprotected soils, lifting them into devastating dust storms. These were the fearful 'black dusters' which terrified the homesteaders and brought them to the verge of bankruptcy and starvation (Plate 47). In March 1935 a single storm blew uninterruptedly for twenty-seven days and nights, when an eye witness described how '. . . it just rolled in from the north and you couldn't see your hand before your face at four in the afternoon'. Roofs fell in with the weight of the overwhelming dust, whilst outbuildings became totally buried and roads disappeared.

47. A dust storm approaching a farm in the infamous United States Dust Bowl of the 1930s. Total darkness occurred four minutes after this photograph was taken.

Coinciding, as it did, with the American economic slump, the western drought of the 1930s meant that federal assistance was limited, thus leaving the disaster area to sort out its own remedial measures. With both crops and livestock decimated, the farmers had little alternative but to emigrate – mainly into California. Those that stayed put had to wait until 1941 before the rainfall returned to its former seasonal pattern, allowing the region to become the world's greatest wheatbelt, but this time based partly on irrigation and different ploughing methods.

Little wonder that the modern American farmer was apprehensive during the 1976–77 drought, although this time one of the hardest hit areas was the Central Valley of California, which depended almost entirely on irrigated crop-production for its livelihood. Here, the lack of rainfall rapidly created an economic disaster after the reservoirs had run dry, the irrigation sprinklers had been turned off and the crops had withered away. Farmers' incomes suddenly fell by some 50 per cent and many of them sold up and moved away, bringing the Valley's entire agricultural economy to the verge of collapse. In the state of California alone the crop losses were estimated at $1,000,000,000 and all this in a state which supplies one quarter of America's food. The disaster could not have struck at a worse time, for the United States was battling through its worst economic crisis since the Second World War and the Federal Government had already slashed several national projects in an effort to reduce capital expenditure. Amongst these was the grant earmarked for the Central Arizona Project (C.A.P.), which was a scheme intended to bring sorely needed water supplies to parts of America's arid zone. Arizona had recently become one of the fastest growing states, partly because many inhabitants of the eastern seaboard had fled from some of the harshest winters in United States' history (see Chapter 10). But the threatened cancellation of the C.A.P. led some observers to predict a virtual cessation of Arizona's agricultural production whilst others made gloomy forecasts of renewed desertification overrunning its farmlands and cities within a century.

The states of America's Pacific North West were also badly affected by the 1976–77 drought, especially because falling river and lake levels threatened a shut-down of the large hydroelectric network which provides 90 per cent of the region's power. Furthermore, the dearth of snowfall in the winter of 1976–77 meant that river levels would be extremely low in the following summer, leading to even more severe water shortages and increased forest-fire hazards. On a different note, the shortage of snowfall brought the ski resorts in Idaho, Utah, California and Colorado to an almost complete standstill. With attendances down by 90 per cent, takings decimated and the recreation business virtually ruined, some state Governors were asking for the Federal Government to declare these places as natural-disaster areas.

Meanwhile, in the Midwest the drought threatened not only the grain harvest but also the fodder supplies for the enormous herds of livestock. As in Britain many American beef farmers, faced with unprecedented bills for foodstuffs, sent their herds for early slaughter or sold cattle on an already glutted market. Cattlemen in some regions were reduced to practically giving their stock away as the prices plummeted and were soon staring bankruptcy in the face. Thus, by March 1977 Governors of eleven of the drought-hit states were forced to meet to see what action could be taken. They agreed to ask for a national drought-relief coordinator to be appointed, similar to the post created the previous year in the U.K. They also set up a special task-force to deal with disaster-relief funds and to explore further research into such fields as weather-modification and alternative water supplies. One of the schemes that was costed involved the transporting by rail of 182 million truckloads of water from the eastern states – solely for California's needs. But, like the Irish offer to drought-stricken Wales in 1976, the transport costs proved to be prohibitive – in the Californian case the operation would have cost no less than $437 billion, which was 437 times the actual value of the state's crop losses! Such exercises led one observer to comment cynically that it would be better if people were to live where water was available instead of trucking water to arid areas where they currently wished to live. As far as one of the worst hit areas of California was concerned the same scientist asked a series of very pertinent questions: 'Is it too little water? Or is it too many people? Has the area been developed beyond the capability of its resources to support people?'[5] These questions are of fundamental importance not only to the United States but to all countries faced with desertification and water-resource problems.

Tackling the Problem of Drought

There are basically three alternative methods of facing up to the problem of drought. First, one can bear the loss, i.e. do nothing; secondly, it is possible to move away from the drought-stricken area and settle elsewhere; thirdly, one can reduce the impact of the hazard by adopting remedial measures. Of the first two alternatives little more will be said, because the ability of people to move away from a hazard zone depends on a great number of variables, ranging from their cultural attitudes through to their degree of wealth and their mobility. Thus, we are left with the third of the alternatives, that of undertaking positive action in order to ameliorate the hazard. Again, three possible approaches can be identified, any or all of which may be adopted according to circumstances. The first of these relates to a modification of the hazard itself, i.e. the purely *scientific approach*, including the technique of cloud-seeding, which has been attempted not infrequently. The second alternative might be termed the *behavioural approach*, which involves modifying the behaviour and life style of the arid-zone inhabitants, in order to put less of a demand on the water resources. The third approach we might refer to as the *technological approach*, whereby mankind must seek alternative supplies of water, possibly from outside the arid zone.

Most of these different approaches were discussed at a hurriedly convened Symposium on Drought in Africa, which was held at the University of London in July 1973. Apart from highlighting the ignorance relating to the cause and effect of drought in Africa, one of the most serious conclusions to be drawn from the symposium was the apparent failure of the 'early warning system' to alert the rest of the world to the gravity of the situation until it was too late. This early warning system had been initiated by a branch of the United Nations known as the Food and Agricultural Organization (F.A.O.), which itself planned to coordinate the harvest situation reports from the threatened countries. Unfortunately, both international and national politics had vitiated the machinery of this promising experiment although closer cooperation was to follow in the future. The symposium concluded that to reduce the impact of future drought a combination of behavioural modifications and technological developments would be needed and these included:

> . . . a more careful assessment of water resources and their exploitation; comprehensive land management programmes in conjunction with water resources' development for livestock; coordinated use of surface and underground water and appropriate legislation for its control; complementary development of arable and pastoral sectors; investigation of the possibilities of ranching; and better communications. A more controversial suggestion is the gradual reduction of human populations in areas of extreme and continuing hazard.[6]

In the following year the United Nations' General Assembly called for a world Conference on Desertification and this took place in Nairobi in 1977. If it is possible to summarize the findings in a single sentence then the following may be the most apposite: Droughts appear to be inevitable, therefore land management should be improved. Or, to quote an eminent agronomist; 'To the North of the Sahara it is man who creates the desert; climate is only a supporting factor.'[7]

Not surprisingly, the major emphasis in most of the international symposia has been placed on the alternative which we have termed the *behavioural approach*, probably because it may be cheaper and simpler to manipulate people than to modify the weather or to discover alternative supplies of water. Nevertheless, it would be foolish to believe that by simply changing mankind's behaviour all the problems of the arid zone will be solved. But on the other hand any programme for halting desertification must be based on an understanding of the social and economic predicaments faced by the desert dweller. Desert nomads, for example, own large herds of livestock as a drought insurance, for, if the rains fail, some can be sold off quickly and some will die, but there may not be a total loss. Equally, possessing an over-large family not only ensures a partial survival in times of catastrophe but also provides the labour force necessary for tending herds, fetching water and gathering fuel. Although they appreciate these cultural characteristics most experts now consider that the Sahel zone, for example, carries about twice the number of livestock that it is capable of supporting and that the herders will finally have to accept that quality is more valuable than quantity. Furthermore, the advantages of smaller families will have to be made apparent, for the deserts cannot provide for the present population numbers. The radical transformation of the arid-zone economy, however, need not necessitate the total break-up of the nomadic culture by permanent settlement, as some agronomists insist, but rather a massive reappraisal of the problem largely in terms of a phased biological recovery.

Biological recovery refers to the improvement of a deteriorated ecosystem and may be achieved in a number of ways. By the erection of temporary fencing, for example, vegetation may be regenerated and finally stabilized by means of strict grazing controls which will also allow a return of manure to the soil, leading to an increase in its biological activity. Another method involves the popularizing of new sources of fuel to offset the devastating effect of firewood gathering. The use of the sun's energy for cooking is an alternative which is currently being developed in Israel and Niger. The prevention of bush fires seems an obvious method of conservation, but it has been estimated that the age-old practice of burning removes some eighty million tonnes of forage from Africa's semi-arid zone every year – equivalent to the diet of twenty-five million cattle for nine months!

Turning now to an appraisal of the so-called *scientific approach* we find that there have been many research efforts devoted to modification of the drought hazard itself. Foremost among these has been the technique of cloud-seeding to induce precipitation (see p. 246). Although at a local scale there has been a certain degree of success, whereby rain has been produced in order to fill an empty reservoir, scientists agree that this rain would have fallen anyway, but somewhere else. Furthermore, it goes without saying that cloud-seeding not only requires the presence of clouds, but also a moist atmosphere through which the rain can fall without massive evaporation taking place, and these are features frequently missing from the arid zone. Thus, any attempts to induce rainfall over large tracts of the Sahel are probably doomed to expensive failure. Distance from the moisture supply of the oceans suggests that as far as weather modification is concerned the great deserts of the continental interiors will probably remain desiccated, despite the talk of a 'Sahara internal sea', since evaporation alone would probably negate the results even if the scientific and engineering problems could be solved.

There is also a great deal of scepticism in some quarters for the so-called 'green-belt solution', whereby massive tree- and shrub-planting programmes are designed to influence the overall water balance of a region by increasing its atmospheric humidity. Unfortunately, if the precipitation input is not present in the first instance, then a major link in the hydrological cycle is missing (see Figure 74) whilst groundwater or river sources may not be sufficient to provide an adequate means of irrigation. Nevertheless, where surface water can be made available there are several ways in which the regeneration of the vegetation cover may be artificially assisted. These include the planting of drought resistant trees and shrubs, sand-dune fixation and the creation of shelterbelts.

The provision of a satisfactory basis for large-scale irrigation brings us to the third of the major global alternatives, the *technological approach*, in which twentieth-century man is exploring the means of initiating major changes in the earth's water balance by discovering alternative sources of water.

One of the earliest techniques to be developed was that of *desalination*, in which mineral salts are removed from seawater by distillation. This process produces potable water for human and animal consumption, but is generally too costly an undertaking for crop growing. In certain locations, where water resources are scarce, such as the Persian Gulf, Hong Kong, the Channel Isles and Malta, desalination plants have been established for a number of years, although increasing costs have caused Malta to close down three of its four distillers at the Valletta distillation plant. In this case the power had been supplied by an oil-fired power station, although in other world localities, water has been produced more cheaply in association with nuclear-energy powered plants. But even here the cost of producing 1 cubic metre of water is about $0.10 and since it takes 1 cubic metre of water to generate a mere 2 kilograms of fodder it will be realized that desalination costs will be prohibitive for most agricultural purposes other than luxury products. In any case desalination is of very little use in tackling the problems associated with the vast interior deserts of Africa, Asia and Australia. Two other factors have played important roles in the recent demise of desalination technology: one has been the tremendous rise in energy prices during the 1970s; the other has been the reluctance of Western Governments to allow the proliferation of nuclear power as an alternative source of energy, partly as a result of the recent Indian atomic explosion. Thus, as the prospects of desalination become less certain, alternative sources of water must be found by other means.

In 1976, following the findings of a widespread hydrogeological survey, the Egyptian newspapers proclaimed ecstatically to the world that there was water galore under the eastern half of the Sahara desert. One of the world's largest artesian basins, contained in the aquifers of the Nubian Sandstone, had been discovered, stretching from the Mediterranean shores of Libya and Egypt in the north, deep into Chad and Sudan in the south (Figure 88). The first reports stated that these 6,000 billion cubic metres of water resources were constantly being replenished by subterranean seepage from the Nile and that at least 686 million cubic metres of underground water could be trapped for irrigation annually for an indefinite period. Was this, then, the answer to North Africa's drought problems? Dr E. M. El-Shazly of Egypt's National Academy of Scientific Research remained somewhat sceptical, for he is concerned that there might be a profligate use of this gigantic reserve. One reason for his fears is based on the discovery that the bulk of this underground water was accumulated some 25,000 years ago, during wetter climatic periods, not by current seepage from the Nile. Consequently, if the 'fossil' water is not being replenished, Dr El-Shazly questions the wisdom of establishing major new settlements in Egypt's western desert based on water resources which might be exhausted in a matter of two hundred years. His caution may well be justified; in Libya a major irrigation project has already encountered serious difficulties since the water table has fallen at a rate far faster than was predicted by the theoretical models. In the first instance, therefore, it may be more advantageous for Egypt to explore alternative schemes. One of these relates to the use of the 7.5 billion cubic metres of 'new water' from the Aswan High Dam, not as originally intended for intensification of irrigation along the Nile Valley itself, but rather to be diverted into the so-called New Valley in order to develop fresh agricultural lands (Figure 88). Another scheme envisages flooding the Qattara Depression of northern Egypt with Mediterranean seawater by means of a projected canal. Despite its hydro-electric potential,

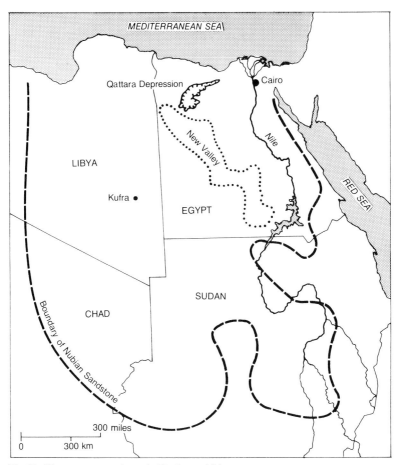

Fig. 88. Water-resources scheme in North-east Africa.

fears have been expressed that the Qattara project may cause pollution of the Nubian Sandstone aquifer by seawater infiltration.

Considerably more ambitious has been a scheme devised to ameliorate Saudi Arabia's ever-present water-supply problem. Currently, Saudi Arabia depends exclusively on desalination for its drinking water, but even one of the wealthiest nations in the world is finding the process too costly, too energy-intensive and too polluting. Thus, the Saudi Government has asked a panel of French experts to prepare a feasibility study on the potential use of icebergs towed from Antarctica. It has been estimated that man's technology is now capable of this gigantic maritime exercise which could supply fresh water at costs some 30–50 per cent cheaper than desalination. The idea, although it smacks of space-age sophistication, was first tried out almost a century ago, before the invention of refrigeration techniques, when small icebergs were towed from Chile's southern glaciers up the coast to Valparaiso. It has long been known that about 99 per cent of the world's fresh water reserves are locked away in glaciers and icecaps, with some 90 per cent occurring in Antarctica alone. Calculations have suggested that existing tugs could tow icebergs of about 1 kilometre in length and that even if 50 per cent of the ice melted in transit, the remaining water would justify the economics of the project (Figure 89). Notwithstanding the mammoth problems involved in protecting the iceberg from melting during its passage through the warm waters of the Indian Ocean, it has been suggested that 70 per cent of the total operational costs would be consumed in slicing the iceberg prior to distribution, after its delivery to the Red Sea port of Jeddah. Despite the scepticism of several other Arab nations the Saudi Government has set up a company, known as the Iceberg Transport International Ltd, to fund the development of the technology.

Fig. 89. The economics of towing icebergs from Antarctica to the Red Sea (after A. Agarwal).

	Large iceberg (One billion cu. m of ice)	Medium-Size iceberg (500 million cu. m of ice)	Experimental iceberg (105 million cu. m of ice)
Daily water production (million cu. m per day)	2.2	1.2	0.2
Investment required (million dollars):			
For water from icebergs	657.5	405.5	88.4
For desalination plants	1,800	1,064	200
Operating costs for oceanic transfer (cents/cu. m of ice):			
Cost of water at Aden	6	7.8	31.2
Cost of slicing	14.2	15.4	21.5
Cost of water at Jeddah	20.2	23.2	52.7

Meanwhile, in the U.S.S.R., schemes are being examined for diverting water from the north-flowing rivers southwards to the nation's arid zone of Central Asia and the Caspian region. Much of the water in Russia's mighty Siberian rivers of the Lena, Yenisey and Ob flows wastefully to the Arctic Ocean, whilst the lands around Lake Balkash, the Aral Sea and the Caspian

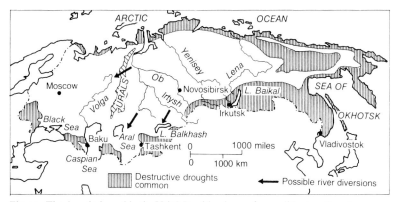

Fig. 90. The drought hazard in the U.S.S.R. with schemes for possible river diversion.

Sea have to endure prolonged years of destructive drought (Figure 90). Indeed, the declining water levels and the increasing salinity of the inland Caspian have given great cause for concern in Russia's southern republics. Feasibility studies have been concerned with two possible schemes: one to divert the headwaters of the Ob-Irtysh system into the deserts of Kazakhstan; and the other to take water from the Ob estuary through the Urals to the Kama and Pechora rivers and thence into the south-flowing Volga. Of the two schemes the latter seems the more feasible and would have the joint advantage of bringing more freshwater to the Caspian and reducing the widespread flooding and swamplands of the Ob river system. To overcome the barrier of the Urals it would be necessary not only to pump water to heights of 150 metres, but also to engineer aqueducts and canals some 113 kilometres in length. Experts claim that parts of the canal:

... would have to be excavated by detonating 250 nuclear charges of up to three megatons each in rows of up to 20 charges. Estimates show that nuclear blasting could slash construction costs to a third or even less, and substantially reduce the time required for the job.[8]

Unfortunately, in view of the enormous possibilities of such a scheme, there are still some reservations being expressed about the nuclear part of the exercise, not only because of radiation hazards, but also because of the possible linkage between nuclear explosions and earthquake triggering (see p. 71).

Measured against the Arabian and Russian schemes, the plans to offset the hazards of a future British drought assume insignificant proportions.

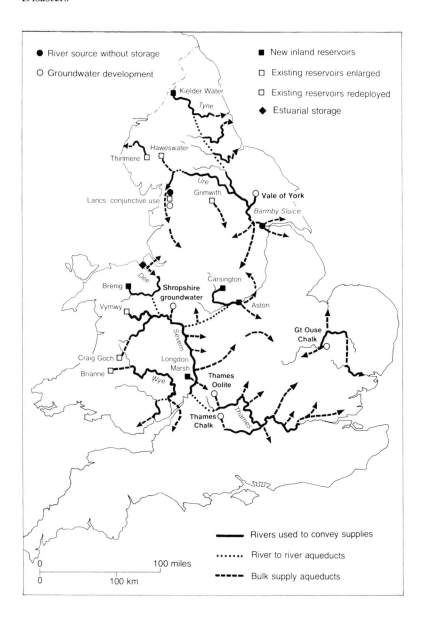

Fig. 91. Water-resource planning in England and Wales.

The water problem in Britain has largely been one of supply and demand, for the heaviest rainfall is in the highland zone of the north and west whilst the maximum demand comes from the lowland zone of the south-east and from the industrial areas. In earlier decades there were grandiose schemes for a national water grid (similar to the existing electricity grid) to offset these geographical disadvantages, but through the inability of the numerous water boards to cooperate no significant action was taken. It was only when the newly created central authority of the Water Resources Board was created in 1964 that some coordinated plans were drawn up, but in place of the water grid the decision was taken to use the existing rivers as ready-made aqueducts. Many of these run in an easterly direction towards the lowland zone and offer excellent opportunities of overcoming Britain's water supply problems. Short man-made aqueducts allied with pumping stations could now be installed to enable water to be transferred from one river system to the next in times of need. The outline of the new scheme is illustrated in Figure 91, which highlights the way in which the existing rivers can be utilized instead of an enormously expensive water grid based on pipelines. The National Water Council, which replaced the Water Resources Board in 1974, is keen to go ahead with this scheme of water reorganization, despite fears that water imported from Wales may be threatened with increasing costs and even insecurity of supply because of the difficulties involved in the political devolution of Wales away from the Central Government in Westminster.

10. Snow and Fog

In reviewing the cultural and technological development of man through time, some observers have suggested that the most advanced societies may have evolved in neighbouring regions which favoured interaction, thus enabling contact to be made with other civilizations. In this way ideas and innovations could be exchanged and spread fairly rapidly in such favourable locations as Europe. Fundamental to this process of interaction is the facility of movement and communication, and it is not without significance that certain scholars have referred to one of mankind's greatest achievements – the Industrial Revolution – as the Transportation Revolution. Consequently, any breakdown in communication or loss of mobility can be regarded as a retrogressive step which, if prolonged, could lead to chaos, decline and ultimate decay of an advanced society. The more dependent a society becomes on transport and mobility the more catastrophic are the effects of any interference with that mobility. This is especially true in the urban areas, which have tended to become less and less self-sufficient and therefore more vulnerable to the vagaries of nature.

Many natural hazards can bring disruption to the traveller, but nothing destroys mobility quicker than snow and fog. Either can reduce visibility within a matter of minutes and bring all motor vehicles, aircraft and shipping to a standstill. Snowfall has the added hazards of inhibiting movement because of drifting or by the accompanying fall of temperature which affects both man and his machines. Nowhere has snow disruption been more severe than in New York, where snow-control programmes currently cost the city some $50 million per year.

Snow Hazards

Snowfall provokes a variety of responses, ranging from the fascination of the child, through the pleasure of the winter sports' enthusiast to the abhorrence of the transport operator and street cleaner. Whereas a sprinkling of snow can add beauty to almost any scene and cause virtually no inconvenience, it has been pointed out that:

> ... the manner in which snow often arrives in a blizzard, or departs by avalanche or thaw flood, means that snow must be considered a treacherous enemy.[1]

It must not be imagined that in order to cause disruption snow must be blown into deep drifts, for even small amounts can cause traffic problems; normal road vehicles are impeded once the level snowfall exceeds a depth of 100 millimetres (4 inches), whilst railways are affected by a level fall of 150 millimetres (6 inches). When the snowfall is driven by a high wind, it has little chance to settle on the ground, except in the lee of an obstruction, where severe drifting takes place. Thus, it is common to experience the apparently anomalous combination of snow-free windswept fields and totally blocked rural roads in the lee shelter of their bounding walls or hedgerows.

In polar latitudes most of the precipitation falls in the form of snow, whilst in the temperate zone snowfall is generally experienced only in the winter months except in the higher mountains, where it may occur at any season. In the less populated countries which fringe the Arctic Ocean snowfall is no major problem, as the communities are usually prepared for the inconvenience and have adapted their way of life accordingly. In addition, it must be remembered that in these countries such as Canada and Russia, which border the almost permanently frozen Arctic Ocean, there is very little vapour in the cold air, so that there is considerably less snowfall on their northern coasts than there is farther south (Figure 92). The greatest depths

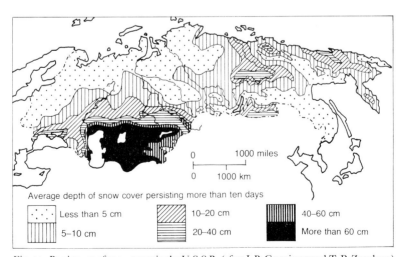

Fig. 92. Persistence of snow cover in the U.S.S.R. (after I. P. Gerasimov and T. B. Zvonkova).

of snow cover in the U.S.S.R. are to be found not in Siberia, as we might expect, but in the southern republics around the Sea of Aral and the Caspian. This is partly the result of continuous transfer by northerly blizzards and redeposition in more southerly latitudes. In North America similar mechanisms exist and the most copious snowfalls occur not in Arctic Canada but in the maritime regions of the Atlantic and Pacific seaboards, where moist oceanic air mixes with the cold continental air masses. Some of the heaviest snowfalls occur in the vicinity of North America's Great Lakes and in New England – one of the most urbanized regions in the world – where damage and disruption from snow often reaches the proportions of a disaster. Not only do severe blizzards cause periodic transport breakdowns but, on average, snow cover persists for some 90 to 140 days per year. Contrast the southern states of the U.S.A. or southern Britain, where average snow cover is a mere one to ten days per annum.

One of the most important factors in determining the degree of disruption in urban areas is the rate at which snow accumulates. Once the rate of accumulation exceeds the efforts of man and nature at clearance and dispersal then a disaster may be generated. Following a snowstorm in 1922 no less than 710 millimetres (28 inches) accumulated in thirty-two hours in America's capital city, Washington. So heavy was the weight of snow that a theatre roof collapsed, killing ninety-six people. Again, a rapid snowfall in Boston caused forty-four deaths in February 1969 and created damage estimated at $150 million. Estimated costs generally include not only structural damage but also the loss of industrial output and the delays to transportation. Loss of mobility means loss of income as people become snowbound, and research has shown that in Toronto, for example, a typical winter's snowfall seriously affected 13 per cent of its workforce of 900,000, causing losses of $3.5 million. Add to these costs the annual bills for snow and ice removal (including salting and sanding roads), which in the U.S.A. average $500 million and in Canada $125 million, and one can begin to estimate the magnitude of the problem in an average year. But average costings became a nonsense when parts of the U.S.A. were paralysed by constant blizzards in the successive winters of 1977 and 1978.

The American Blizzards of 1977 and 1978

By January 1977 it had become clear that the run of six successive relatively mild winters was over and that the U.S.A. was gripped in the most severe winter in the nation's history. Not only were record minimum temperatures being experienced in twenty-six United States cities, including Chicago and

Pittsburgh, but upstate New York was buried for almost two weeks under phenomenal snowfalls. The cause of the big freeze and the extraordinary snowfalls in New England was an unusually persistent high-pressure system in the continental interior, which caused the westerly air-streams to migrate northwards far into the Arctic before sweeping southwards again in eastern America, across the Great Lakes and down as far as Florida to produce unprecedented frost and snow. By the end of January the cold was so intense that states of emergency were declared in New York, New Jersey and Ohio, whilst the Governors of Florida, Pennsylvania and Tennessee asked the President to declare their States disaster areas. By early February two million Americans had been laid off work in attempts to conserve dwindling fuel supplies, especially natural gas, the reserves of which had become almost exhausted. More than one hundred people died in the blizzards, mostly from hypothermia due to the intense cold, but some from traffic accidents and heart attacks in the snow-choked streets as people fought losing battles to clear the snow.

The worst-hit city was Buffalo in upstate New York, which recorded a remarkable 4,651 millimetres (183.1 inches) of snowfall in that notorious winter of 1976-77 compared with its former record of 3,200 millimetres (126 inches). Boonville, New York, surpassed even these statistics with a staggering 7,061 millimetres (278 inches)! The strong winds whipped up the snow into drifts 6-9 metres (20-30 feet) in height and it was these which quickly paralysed the city of Buffalo. Soon the traffic in the streets had disappeared beneath the inexorable white blanket – people marooned in their vehicles sometimes became asphyxiated from carbon monoxide as they kept their car engines running to offset the penetrating cold. The death-toll in Buffalo alone mounted to twenty-five as the County Executive spoke of the '... second coming of the Ice Age ... a disaster in every sense of the word ... We may be witnessing conditions never before seen in a large urban area.'[2] The city was cut off from the outside world and with food and fuel supplies running dangerously low, so a major military operation had to be launched to save it. By the first week in February 1977 more than 2,000 troops had been airlifted into the neighbouring cities of Buffalo and Watertown where over one million people were stranded in the streets, offices, hotels and in their own homes. Heavy-duty snowploughs and rescue equipment took about one week to restore the mobility of the urban area and in order to facilitate clearance all non-essential road travel had to be banned under threat of ninety days jail or $5,000 fine. The same freeze which had caused the neighbouring Niagara Falls to remain in a state of suspended animation had also frozen the snowdrifts so hard that snowploughs broke and bent their blades in an effort to dislodge the burden. Ultimately, many thousands of tonnes of snow and ice were dispatched from Buffalo by freight trains to be dumped in areas where they would not add to the predicted perils of flooding. It must be remembered that such an unprecedented snowfall could have led to disastrous flooding, and the United States' National Weather Service forecast a high flood potential for much of the American north-east during the spring of 1977. Fortunately, the flooding was less catastrophic than was predicted.

The following winter of 1977–78 was to prove equally severe in north-eastern U.S.A. and this time the city of New York was to bear the brunt of the January snowstorms. By February, however, blizzards had also over-whelmed most of the New England states, with recorded undrifted snow-falls of more than 600 millimetres (24 inches) in many places. The February blizzards brought New York's heaviest single day's fall on record (500 milli-metres – 20 inches) and this was sufficient to bring the city's transport system to a total standstill (Plate 48). Cars were completely buried in the deserted streets as gale force winds whipped snow into towering drifts – on

48. In February 1978 the heaviest day's snowfall in the history of New York brought the city's transport to a complete standstill. Cars such as this were quickly buried by the howling blizzard.

the Long Island expressway alone upwards of three thousand cars were abandoned. As more and more vehicles littered the streets snowploughs were unable to make much impact on the piles of snow, leading to an emergency being declared, which meant that no vehicles would be allowed into New York city without snow chains, and that parking was forbidden in most streets. As the few pedestrians took to skis and snow shoes their greatest hazard came from large chunks of ice falling from the skyscrapers. The financial problems of this great city had already meant a severe cut-back in the resources of the street-cleaning department, resulting in numerous complaints against the authorities as New Yorkers grumbled about the tardiness of the snow removal. Some will have recalled the Boxing Day blizzard of 1947 which was followed by freezing rain, when the weight of ice decimated the trees in Central Park and caused several million dollars' worth of damage. Those with longer memories may even have remembered the blizzard of 1888 when some four hundred people died; the 1978 death-toll, by comparison, was less than a hundred, including those who died elsewhere in the U.S.A., but the urban disruption was considerably greater.

Some of the most severe damage occurred due to roof collapse under the accumulated weight of snow and ice: in New York city more than a dozen buildings collapsed, including a 3,000-seat college auditorium; in Connecticut three large buildings caved-in within an hour, including Hartford's $60 million Civic Centre. In New England the Federal Government declared the states of Massachusetts, Connecticut and Rhode Island to be disaster areas on 8 February, with 'disaster-passes' being issued only to essential workers in order to keep people off the streets. This was partly due to the snow clearance problems, but also to the widespread looting, as gangs toured the deserted shops in snowmobiles. Over one hundred arrests were made for looting in Boston and Providence alone. Meanwhile, 11,000 people were forced to leave their homes as snowstorms, high winds and surging tides battered the New England coast.

Snowfall in Britain

By comparison with the North American snow statistics, those for Britain appear fairly insignificant, although it must be remembered that in a nation characterized by relatively mild weather most communities are unprepared for severe winters. This was particularly true in January and February 1978 when, after a decade of mild, snowfree winters, heavy snowfalls whipped up by gale-force winds brought death and destruction to several parts of Britain.

The first to suffer was Northern Scotland at the end of January, when the worst blizzards since 1947 blanketed Caithness and surrounding counties. Thousands of sheep and cattle were killed and whilst the overall loss was 10–15 per cent for the region some crofters lost virtually all their livestock, leading them to consider abandoning their crofts thus denuding the Highlands even more. Highlanders are used to being cut off by heavy snowfall, but this blizzard arrived without warning so that travellers were often caught in open country. A bus with eighteen passengers was snowbound overnight whilst seventy people were trapped in a train between Inverness and Wick. All were eventually rescued by helicopters after many hours in the freezing cold. Four motorists, however, were not so lucky, for they froze to death in their buried cars. The town of Inverness was cut off by road and rail for a few days whilst 85,000 people in the region lost all electricity supplies after cables had been brought down by the blizzard. The severe dislocation of all services gave rise to an official investigation by the police, military and local authorities who called for an improved warning system.

Within a fortnight the south-western counties of England were hit by a similar blizzard as frontal troughs of moist air from the Atlantic became caught up in a bitterly cold stream of air from northern Europe (Figure 93).

Fig. 93. Weather map of 18 February 1978 to illustrate conditions which contributed to the severe blizzards in south west England.

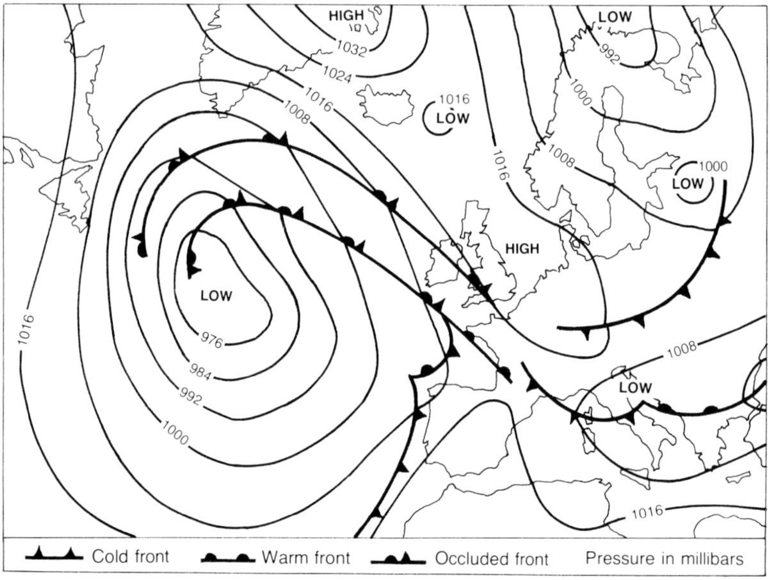

49. *right* The British West Country blizzards of February 1978 left cars totally buried in the deep snowdrifts.

As in Scotland the heavy snowfall was blown into 6 metre (20 feet) drifts by the strong winds, isolating the picturesque villages of Devon, Somerset and Dorset for days. Because of the difficulties involved in road clearance, all but emergency traffic was banned in Dorset, after sightseers had themselves been forced to abandon their cars in the drifts. As in Scotland there were stories of snowbound trains and coaches whilst hundreds of cars were totally buried in the drifted snow (Plate 49). One of the worst hazards was the large number of broken power cables, brought down by snow or falling trees, so that thousands of households were without electricity for several days. The power cuts also halted some pumping stations, bringing a water shortage from Cornwall to east Devon. Paradoxically, in the same region farmers were being forced to pour away thousands of gallons of milk, because no tanker collections had been possible in the snow-choked countryside. This area normally produces one fifth of the milk consumed in Britain and in order to save the lives of the thousands of valuable dairy cattle the Government organized an airlift to distribute fodder at a cost of some £500 per hour. Somewhat ironically, the operation was coordinated by the same Minister of State for the Environment who had taken charge of Britain's drought emergency in 1976. Despite the relief measures, however, there were reports of widespread deaths amongst livestock, with one agriculturalist stating that '. . . Dartmoor is a disaster area with horrifying stock losses'. In fact the south-western counties were declared an emergency region which, like Scotland, were to receive special 'disaster funds' earmarked by the E.E.C. for hardship cases such as these.

By referring to Figure 94 it will be seen how prior to 1978 Britain had experienced a lengthy blizzard-free spell of some twenty-three years during

Fig. 94. The snowiest British winters in the century prior to 1978 (after M. C. Jackson).

Winter	Months with notable falls	Comments
1875–76	N.D.J.F.M.A.M.	600 mm widespread snow, especially in South England.
1878–79	N.D.J.F.M.A.	3 months cover in North. Blizzards in Scotland.
1880–81	O. J.F.M.A.	18–20 Jan. Blizzard on South coast. 900 mm level fall.
1882–83	N.D. M.A.	4–8 Dec. Blizzard South Scotland/North England 1200 mm level fall.
1885–86	O.N.D.J.F.M.A.M.	28 Feb.–2 Mar. Blizzard in North England, Scotland, Ireland.

1887–88	O. D. F.M.	11–14 Mar. Blizzard, North East England/ South East Scotland.
1890–91	N.D.J. M. M.	9–13 Mar. Blizzard, Devon/Cornwall. Report of 60 m drift on Dartmoor.
1899–1900	D. F.M.	Widespread snow 600 mm level fall common.
1900–01	J.F.M.	29 Mar. Blizzard North Wales. 2000 mm in Snowdonia.
1908–09	D. F.M.	Feb.–Mar. Widespread snow. 600 mm level fall common.
1915–16	N. F.M.	Pennines and South Wales mts 3000 mm falls reported.
1916–17	D.J.F.M.A.	1–3 Apr. Cheviot blizzard, South and West Ireland.
1923–24	N.D.J.F.M.A.	29 Feb. Blizzard in North Scotland.
1927–28	N.D.J. M.A.	25–26 Dec. Blizzard on South Coast. 600 mm level fall.
1928–29	D.J.F. A.	16 Feb. Dartmoor 1800 mm in 15 hrs.
1932–33	O.N. J.F.	23–26 Feb. Blizzard, Ireland, Wales, England.
1936–37	D.J.F.M.	11–13 Mar. Blizzard, North Ireland, South Scotland, North England.
1939–40	D.J.F.M.	27–28 Jan. Blizzard, Scotland, North England. 600 mm general.
1940–41	D.J.F.M.	18–20 Feb. Blizzard, North East England/South East Scotland.
1941–42	J.F.M.	19–20 Jan. Blizzard. Scotland, North England.
1944–45	N.D.J.	22–25 Jan. South Wales, South West England. 750 mm in places.
1946–47	D.J.F.M.	Snowiest since 1814. 1500 mm in mts of Wales and England.
1950–51	O.N.D.J.F.M.A.M.	Snowiest of century at high levels (> 100 days snow lying).
1954–55	D.J.F.M. M.	Widespread snow, especially North Scotland. 17 May 50 mm South England.
1962–63	N.D.J.F.	26–29 Dec. Blizzards South England. Widespread falls.
1974–75	J.	The only recorded June snowfall at low levels in England. Snow held up cricket matches in Derbyshire and Lord's cricket ground, London.

which only the notable winter of 1962–63 broke a remarkable period of comparatively mild winters. Prior to the 1950s, however, the table demonstrates that snowy winters, accompanied by blizzards, were fairly commonplace, especially during the nineteenth century, when Britain was less dependent on road traffic and therefore suffered less disruption. Nevertheless, rail traffic was often disrupted in the snowy winters of those earlier years and two of these incidents led to major railway disasters. The first of these caused fourteen deaths when a multiple collision took place near to Peterborough, England, on 21 January 1876, between a goods train and two expresses (including the famous 'Flying Scotsman') which, with the driver blinded by the blizzard, overran all signals. Because of the weight of frozen snow on the cables and arms, the signals had all been forced into the 'all clear' position. The second rail disaster occurred near to Arbroath, Scotland, on 28 December 1906, when frozen snow again brought down telegraph wires and blocked signals. An Edinburgh express ran into the rear of another passenger train stranded in the blizzard, partly because of the poor visibility, resulting in a death toll of twenty-two.

If, as some climatologists have suggested, we are returning to a climate more akin to the severity of the nineteenth century, then Britain will have to take steps to prepare for more frequent snow emergencies and to avoid the almost total breakdown in communications which characterized the 1978 blizzards just described. To remind us of the conditions that we may have to face more regularly in the future, it may be useful to recall some remarks made about the notoriously cold and snowy winter of 1962–63:

> By any standard the winter of 1962–63 was one of the hardest Great Britain has ever had . . . Even the most conservative estimates for the country as a whole conclude that it was the coldest since 1829–30. It was a winter in which cars were driven across the Thames, pack ice formed a quarter of a mile outside Whitstable Harbour, a family was marooned on a Dartmoor farm for 66 days. It killed at least 49 people.[3]

Obviously, the British Isles has experienced more severe snowstorms than those recorded in Figure 94, and it has been pointed out that in the period 1370–90 all of northern Europe suffered from:

> . . . strong blizzards and extreme cold in winter (including record storm flooding of the Dutch lowlands) and heat and drought in summer. The consequences in famine and plague reduced the population of the British Isles by two-thirds.[4]

The similarity of the juxtaposed droughts and blizzards in Britain in the late-fourteenth century with those of the late 1970s may be more apparent than real, but climatologists such as Dr John Gribbin have drawn attention to the significant correlation that exists between periods of maximum and minimum sunspot activity and this erratic variation of the global climate. The same author suggests that we might be faced with significantly lower temperatures in western Europe during the 1980s and 1990s. After a short alleviation around the millennium, it has been predicted that temperatures will then decrease dramatically during the twenty-first century, returning, perhaps, into conditions even more severe than those of the so-called Little Ice Age, which gave some savage weather conditions between 1430 and 1850 A.D. It is easy to imagine the strain that will be placed on world food production, if this predicted deterioration of climate actually materializes.

Several climatologists believe that the warning signs are there to see and that we should not be lulled into a false sense of security by the relative mildness of the British climate during the 1950s, 1960s and early 1970s, for it now looks as if this period, upon which we base most of our weather 'norms', was in fact a period of abnormal climate. Not only is research needed to decipher the reasons for the climatic fluctuations but steps must also be taken to devise a strategy to offset the likelihood of severe snow and frost disruption in future winters. After all, by a comparison with the winters of 1947 and 1962–63 the scale of future disruption can be forecast. Early in 1947, for example, upwards of two million workers became temporarily unemployed and the index of industrial production fell by 25 per cent (Figure 95). At the same time British agriculture was severely hit as crop yields were devastated and 20 per cent (four million) of the nation's sheep

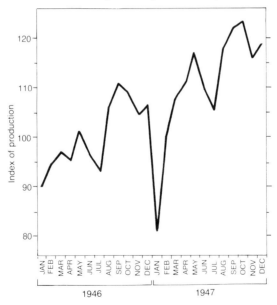

Fig. 95. Graph to show the slump in British Industrial Production due to the heavy snowfall and severe cold of January–February 1947.

were killed. Some highland flocks were wiped out and the country's sheep population did not fully recover until 1952.

In the United States the harsh winter of 1976–77 made an even greater impact on the nation's economy, for the record snowfalls of the East and the freak frosts of Florida were combined with a prolonged drought on the Pacific Coast. In addition to the $6,000 million spent in repairing the physical damage it has been calculated that the United States lost about $9,000 million in unproduced and unsold goods and services and a further $6,000 million in income and profits. Such is the economic price of a weather-triggered disaster, to say nothing of the death toll which can sometimes be quite high as, for example, in Boston when a single blizzard in February 1969 took forty-four lives, or in Japan when two recent blizzards accounted for no less than 242 deaths.

Fog Hazards

It has been seen that snowfall can cause disruption and sometimes disaster partly by its sheer weight, sometimes by its accompanying cold and sometimes when the driving snow of a blizzard causes loss of visibility. On turning to fog hazards we find that lack of visibility is the factor most likely to trigger a disaster but, in addition, there is the menace of air pollution, which can also be a killer. Not only the cost in lives has to be considered, however, for the economic cost of disruption is also heavy. The loss of revenue by a single fog at a major airport can rise to $500,000, whilst fog-induced road accidents cost the United States upwards of $300 million per year.

It is surprising how many changes in visibility occur in one day at a given place, although most people will only notice when their mobility becomes impeded. Obviously, the degree of visibility depends largely on the opacity of the air, resulting from the number of particles held in suspension. The particles can be of three types: first, minute particles of dust or smoke which will produce a *haze*, and minute particles of water which will create a *mist* or *fog*; secondly, there are the coarser particles of dust or snow, large enough to be kept in suspension only by very strong winds – these produce the dust storms and blizzards; thirdly, the worst visibility depends on a large number of suspended particles during a period of heavy precipitation of rain or snow.

Most mists and fogs are created when air comes into contact with a cool surface, thus causing an increase in the relative humidity of the air until it reaches the point at which water vapour starts to condense and become visible. At first the drops of moisture are small enough to create only a mist, but if cooling continues the drops will increase both in size and in number and a fog will result – usually defined when visibility falls below 1 kilometre. The two most common weather situations likely to produce fog are: first, when a clear, cloudless night allows the ground surface to lose heat rapidly, thus cooling the lower layers of air and forming *radiation fog*; and secondly, when air flows from a warm region to cover a cold surface (often the sea) it will produce *advection fog*. An important fact to remember is that normally air is warmed by radiation from the earth's surface and, as everyone knows, gets progressively cooler with increasing altitude. Under certain circumstances, however, this situation can be temporarily reversed in the case of those lower layers of the air which remain in contact with a very cold landsurface. Consequently, it is possible to experience what is termed an *inversion of temperature* (Figure 96) near to the earth's surface, usually within a maximum height range of about 250 metres. Below the *inversion* the air

Fig. 96. The principles of a temperature inversion: (a) Normal temperature gradient (dry air) (b) Inversion conditions.

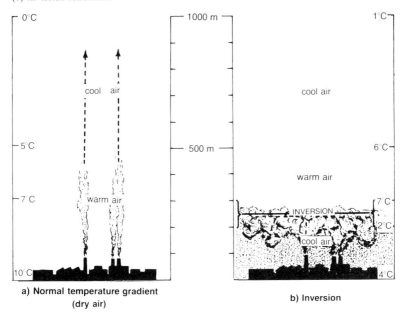

a) Normal temperature gradient (dry air)

b) Inversion

will become cooler than the overlying layers and this is the zone of radiation fog. Above the *inversion* the air remains clear, so that tall buildings or high relief will rise above the fog layer. Such conditions will only exist when a

Fig. 97. Distribution of the World's fog belts.

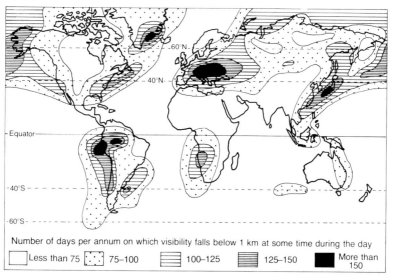

Number of days per annum on which visibility falls below 1 km at some time during the day

| | Less than 75 | | 75–100 | | 100–125 | | 125–150 | | More than 150 |

lack of high winds or turbulence allows the stratified air to remain undisturbed, so that fog is generally associated with certain high-pressure systems or anticyclones. Increases of wind speed (above 5 m.p.h. – 8 kilometres per hour) quickly break up the stratification, thus destroying the inversion and dispersing the fog layer.

From the foregoing account it will be seen that fog will form most readily near rivers and lakes which provide extra moisture and most frequently in valleys and basins into which cold air drains. In industrial areas the presence of numerous dirt particles will facilitate condensation and exacerbate any natural tendencies for fog formation. In general fog is most persistent during the winter months when the low altitude of the sun above the horizon is usually insufficient to counteract the cooling effect of the long winter nights. In certain locations a combination of all these circumstances has produced notorious fog-prone areas (Figure 97) and it is in these that some of the world's worst fog disasters have occurred. Two types of disasters can be identified – those due to lack of good visibility and those resulting from air pollution.

Poor Visibility Disasters

It will be shown how foggy weather most commonly causes a considerable increase in the number of road traffic accidents, but above all it is the mariner who regards fog as his greatest hazard, despite the introduction of radar. Probably the world's worst fog disaster involved a collision at sea when, in May 1914, the *Empress of Ireland* sank in the St Lawrence estuary some two hundred miles below Quebec with the loss of 1,078 lives and a total of only 397 survivors. More recently, another sea-fog collision took place off the American coast near to the Nantucket Lightship, Massachusetts. On 25 July 1956 the Swedish liner *Stockholm* (12,000 tonnes) was sailing eastwards in clear moonlight when the Italian luxury liner *Andrea Doria* (29,000 tonnes), moving westwards towards New York, appeared suddenly out of a fog bank. Unable to avoid a collision the *Stockholm* rammed the *Andrea Doria*, ripping her open and causing her to founder with the loss of fifty-two lives (Plate 50).

50. The tragic end of the Italian luxury liner, the *Andrea Doria*, in July 1956, after it had been rammed by the *Stockholm* in thick fog off the east coast of the United States.

51. The world's worst air disaster at Tenerife airport in March 1977, when two jumbo jets collided, was due partly to navigational error in the mist and drizzle.

Most of the world's air disasters can be explained by mechanical failure or by human error, and even air collisions in the clouds cannot be considered as true fog-generated catastrophes, since fog is strictly a ground-surface phenomenon. When aircraft collide on the ground, however, it is a different matter. This was the case on 27 March 1977 at Tenerife airport, Canary Isles, which witnessed the world's worst aircraft disaster. Two Boeing 747s, the largest passenger-carrying aircraft of the time, belonging to Pan American and K.L.M. airlines, were both preparing for take off with full fuel tanks when they collided on the runway. The ensuing explosion and fire left only seventy-two survivors and a frightful death-toll of 574 passengers and crew. Although a great deal of human error was involved, the lack of radar at the airport meant that the air-traffic controllers in the control tower were forced to rely on visual sighting. Thus the aircraft passed out of sight in the mist which covered the airfield:

While officials insisted that visibility at the time of the accident was not at a minimum, they did agree that it was far from perfect and that it was misty and drizzling.[5]

Each of the aircraft was insured for about $40 million, whilst it has been estimated that passenger liability claims will finally total several hundred million dollars when the insurance procedure is ultimately concluded (Plate 51).

A much more bizarre aircraft disaster took place on 28 July 1945 when a United States bomber pilot, completely blinded by a New York fog, crashed into the Empire State Building, killing fifteen people. The plane ploughed into the seventy-ninth floor, slicing through the elevator cables and causing the passenger lift to plunge straight down to the basement. The irony of the situation was that the top of the fog bank was a mere 5 metres (16 feet) above the point of the accident so that the top few floors of the skyscraper were bathed in sunshine at the time.

Reports of road-traffic accidents due to fog are so commonplace that they rarely make headline news, except on motorways where the speed and volume of traffic often result in a multiple pile-up once the first vehicle has come to a standstill. Although mechanical breakdown may precipitate the accident it is more likely to be caused by a vehicle passing rapidly from normal visibility into a patchy fog bank (Plate 52), applying the brakes and causing a rear-end collision. In Britain the two most devastating motorway pile-ups due to fog occurred within a few weeks of each other: the first was on 13 September 1971 when two hundred vehicles collided on the M6 near Thelwell, Cheshire, killing eleven people and injuring sixty others; the second occurred on 30 November 1971 on the M1 near Luton, Bedfordshire, when seven lives were lost and forty-five were injured during a fifty-vehicle pile-up. In Italy, a serious motoring accident occurred in fog on the Rome-Naples autostrada on 4 January 1977, causing eleven fatalities and twenty-six seriously injured victims. Fog disasters on the railways are less frequent, due to modern automatic working. In Britain only one major accident has been caused by fog: on 26 November 1870 a Liverpool-bound express ploughed into the rear of a stationary goods train at Harrow due to poor visibility and resulted in a death toll of seven.

Air Pollution Disasters

Whilst the disasters caused by poor visibility are usually instantaneous and appalling, those which result from air pollution are slow, insidious affairs but are no less alarming since their long-term effects may be considerably more devastating. There are many types of air pollution ranging from natural events such as coastal salt haze and duststorms to the much more

serious smog and photochemical pollution induced by man. Since smog is the greatest killer this phenomenon will be examined in most detail, although it will not be possible to examine all of its more technical aspects.

Anyone who has lived in an industrial town or city will be aware that the urban air is generally more polluted with impurities than that of the surrounding countryside, despite the various attempts in different countries to introduce clean air legislation over the years. It has long been known that there are certain thresholds beyond which polluted air can become toxic to human beings and the maximum concentration of impurities allowable for prolonged exposure is shown in Figure 98. It will be seen that the concentrations differ as between town and country and also between winter and summer, but it must be remembered that these toxic levels are unlikely to occur at ground level unless a weather abnormality develops. An inversion of temperature which produces a layer of fog and blankets down all vertical air movement is such an abnormality; where the fog persists for several days, trapped beneath an inversion, the air will rapidly become increasingly poisoned by the type of impurities listed in Figure 98, until the danger level is exceeded. At that point we have a smog disaster, although the term (coined from a combination of 'smoke' and 'fog') fails to indicate the presence of such toxic gases as sulphur dioxide and carbon monoxide, most of which are generated by the burning of coal and oil.

Fig. 98. Impurities normally present in the atmosphere (after A. R. Meetham and A. C. Monkhouse), showing maximum allowable concentration before human health is endangered.

	Maximum concentration allowable for prolonged exposure mg/cm^3	On a hazy winter day		In Summer	
		Town mg/cm^3	Country mg/cm^3	Town mg/cm^3	Country mg/cm^3
Sulphur dioxide	26	1.2	0.15	0.2	0.03
Combustible solid and liquid particles		1.0	} 0.24	} 0.2	} 0.05
Incombustible solids		0.2			
Carbon monoxide	120	10.0		2.0	
Sulphur trioxide	3	0.01*		0.001*	
Ammonia	60		0.01*		
Hydrogen chloride	15				
Hydrogen fluoride	2				
Hydrogen sulphide	28				

* Orders of magnitude only.

52. *left* Patchy fog often leads to disastrous vehicle pile-ups on motorways and similar high-speed roads.

During the first week of December 1930, one of the usual winter fogs closed in on the deep and narrow valley of the Meuse in Belgium. Here, in the 24 kilometres between Huy and Seraing, lay a great industrial complex of blast furnaces, coke ovens, steel mills, power plants, glass factories, lime furnaces, zinc reduction plants, a sulphuric acid plant and a fertilizer factory. Each of these continued to pour out great quantities of pollutants so that, while the fog persisted, the trapped noxious air on the valley floor was unable to escape from beneath the inversion. The deadly pall eventually caused people to collapse and ultimately led to sixty-three deaths, mainly from fluoride poisoning, a mortality rate more than ten times greater than normal.

In a similar topographic situation, on the narrow plain of a river, some 48 kilometres south of Pittsburgh, U.S.A., the small town of Donora is also hemmed in by hundred metre hills. It too is an industrial area, based on a large steel and zinc reduction plant. During the last week of October 1948 a temperature inversion, associated with anticyclonic conditions, occurred so that the fog, which enveloped the urban area for a period of four days, became permeated with noxious industrial emissions and turned into a fatal layer of polluted air at street level. The incidence of respiratory illnesses rose sharply, as people suffered bouts of coughing, choking, vomiting and severe headaches. No less than 42 per cent of Donora's population were taken ill, largely from sulphur dioxide poisoning, with nineteen of the more elderly victims finally succumbing.

The third of the world's major smog disasters was the worst, not only because it hit one of the most famous cities but also because it caused the largest number of fatalities. The eight million inhabitants of London would not have been surprised when, on 5 December 1952, a typical winter fog slowly enveloped their city, for was not this the venue of the notorious 'pea-soupers' whose thick yellow colour reflected the degree of smoke pollutants present? But as the inversion persisted for another four days the light winds were unable to mix or replenish the 150 metre layer of poisoned surface air. It has subsequently been calculated that on each day during the great London smog of 1952 the following impurities were emitted: 1,000 tonnes of smoke particles (hydrocarbons); 2,000 tonnes of carbon dioxide; 140 tonnes of hydrochloric acid; 14 tonnes of fluorine compounds; and, most danger-ously, 370 tonnes of sulphur dioxide which were converted into 800 tonnes of sulphuric acid. It was the latter which proved to be the greatest killer and despite the introduction of 'smog masks' upwards of four thousand people died in excess of the normal death rate (Figure 99a). All ages shared in the increased mortality but Figure 99b, which illustrates the mortality in relation

Fig. 99. The London smog disaster of 1952. (a) Death rate with concentrations of smoke and sulphur dioxide. (b) Registered deaths by age: comparison of seven-day period before the 1952 episode with the seven-day period that included the episode (after Logan).

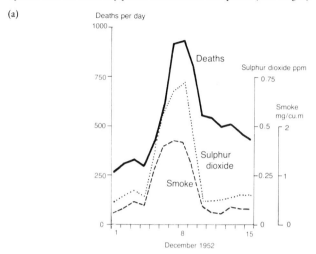

(a)

(b)

Age	7–day period preceding the episode (A)	7–day period that included the episode (B)	Ratio of (B) to (A)
All ages	945	2484	2.6
Under 4 weeks	16	28	1.8
4 weeks to 1 year	12	26	2.2
1–14 years	10	13	1.3
15–44 years	61	99	1.6
45–64 years	237	652	2.8
65–74 years	254	717	2.8
75 years and over	355	949	2.7

to pollution increases, also shows how the younger and older age groups fared worst.

The irritants mainly responsible were probably those derived from the combustion of coal and its products and their lethal effects were almost wholly exercised in persons already suffering from chronic respiratory or cardiovascular disorders.[6]

There had been previous toxic smogs in London (December 1873, January 1880, February 1882, December 1891, December 1892 and November 1948

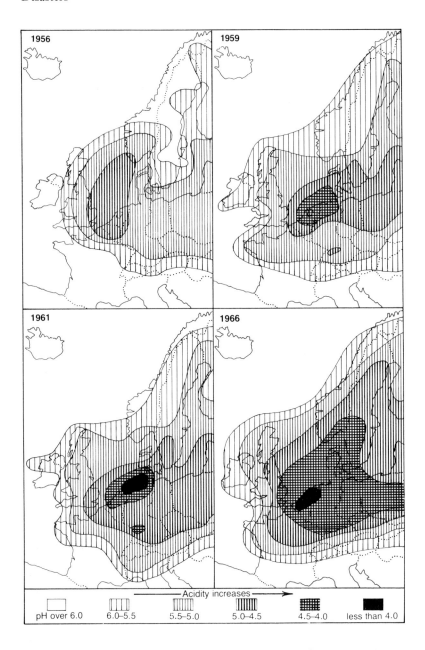

Fig. 100. The increasing acidity of precipitation in western Europe (after G. E. Likens).

– 300 deaths) and despite the passing of the Clean Air Act in 1956 there were to be others (1956–1,000 deaths; 1959; 1962–750 deaths) but nothing as daunting as the 1952 disaster.

Following the wave of post-war legislation to control air pollution, there has been a marked improvement in the smokiness not only of British cities but elsewhere in the world. Nevertheless, there is a continuing plea for even greater vigilance in relation to other sources of pollution, including those from nuclear reactions and from petrochemical industries. There still remains the question – if large numbers died in the Meuse Valley, Donora and London smog disasters in a mere five days of dense pollution, how many people are being affected in the long-term by 'normal' pollution? The increasing hazard of acid rain in Western Europe, for example, is illustrated in Figure 100, and although not a threat to visibility this is likely to prove as severe a health hazard as smog in years to come, unless restrictive measures are introduced.

One of the most severe urban hazards to affect certain world cities in post-war years is that known as *photochemical smog*. Although it has been possible to measure the smoke particles (*hydrocarbons*) and the sulphur dioxide emissions of a true smog of the London variety, the same cannot be said of the petrochemical smog. The latter is very much a product of the age of the internal combustion engine, for its 'witches' brew' is composed of a fast-changing mixture of: *hydrocarbons*, largely from partly burned petrol from vehicle exhausts; *nitrogen oxides*, produced from the air by the heat of car engines, power plants, etc; *oxygen*, also from the air; and most importantly, *sunlight*, which acts upon these constituents to induce a photochemical reaction. The end-product is a foul-smelling, yellowish haze composed of *ozone* and another oxidant termed *peroxyacetyl nitrate* (P.A.N. for short), which together generate severe eye irritation, nasal secretion, coughing, severe fatigue and occasionally death. Unlike true smog, the photochemical variety has only a small proportion of sulphur dioxide. Because of this and because it is not produced by smoke or by fog the name 'smog' is a misnomer in the photochemical context. Nevertheless, it is not only a serious health hazard in such world cities as San Francisco, Washington, New York, Tokyo and Milan, but its haze severely disrupts normal visibility. Photochemical smog is usually associated with the Californian city of Los Angeles whose inhabitants are not only annoyed by the daily irritation and inconvenience but are also concerned about its long-term effects on their health and are worried that one day there might be a major disaster paralleling that of London, 1952. But, since we shall be examining the hazards of Los Angeles in more detail in the following chapter, it will suffice to look at other photochemical incidents which have recently occurred in two cities not normally prone to true photochemical pollution – those of London and Sydney.

During the hot British summer of 1976, the ozone levels in the air of south east England reached the highest levels ever recorded and the London area experienced its first-ever major photochemical smog. In late June and early July the ozone levels reached a maximum of 250 p.p.b. (parts per billion) and remained above 100 p.p.b. for at least eight hours a day over a period of a week. The guideline safety level set by the Greater London Council is 80 p.p.b. so it is little wonder that there were many cases of eye and nose irritation reported at the time. To keep these results in perspective, however, it is noteworthy that maximum concentrations in Los Angeles have reached 490 p.p.b., in which city public warnings are given when the ozone levels exceed 200 p.p.b. Results have shown that when the ozone levels are high in London they are also high elsewhere in Western Europe, which has led scientists to suggest that the greater incidence of winds from an easterly direction, that has characterized British weather patterns in the late 1970s, may be adding continental pollution to that produced by London itself.

No deaths have as yet been attributed directly to ozone. The death rate did rise dramatically during the hot summer of 1976 but that might simply be the effect of the high temperatures. The warning signs are there, however, and for once there is time to evaluate the problem and take action in plenty of time if it proves to be necessary. It is an ideal area for the E.E.C. to take the initiative.[7]

The latest city to report severe doses of photochemical smog is Sydney, Australia. In the normally clear and sunny city thick layers of orange-coloured smog brought respiratory distress and traffic disruption on two occasions in early May 1978. In addition to the sudden increase in road accidents all the ferry and hydrofoil services on Sydney's famous harbour were brought to a standstill and the international airport was forced to suspend its flights. Visiting Americans described the smog as worse than anything experienced in Los Angeles and yet, unlike Los Angeles and Tokyo, there is no early warning system in Sydney, since some local officials contend that there is no smog problem. Although no deaths have been reported there is a record of a group of children collapsing on a Sydney sports field during a similar photochemical smog in 1976.

One final major physical phenomenon which causes severe interference with visibility is that of the *dust storm*. In the previous chapter we have seen how the infamous American Dust Bowl of the 1930s was characterized by dust storms due to inefficient farming methods, illustrated by graphic eye-witness descriptions of the accompanying loss of visibility. Dust storms still occur in the United States, particularly in the arid south-western state of Arizona and have been responsible for several fatal road accidents on the state highways. Thus, expensive signs and warning lights, similar to the fog warning lights of motorways, have been installed on 130 kilometres of interstate highway between Phoenix and Tucson, Arizona, to inform drivers of the impending dangers due to reduced visibility. A dust storm of great physical extent can be termed a *haboob*, after the Sudanese phenomenon, and there are descriptions from Arizona of a seemingly con-tinuous wall of dust 2,500 metres in height, stretching for 100 kilometres, and moving at an average speed of 50 kilometres per hour.

Dust storms of this magnitude are commonplace elsewhere in the arid lands of the northern hemisphere and have serious implications not so much from the temporary inconvenience of restricted visibility as from the per-manent loss of valuable surface soil, because of the long-term effects on agriculture and food supply. Thus, there are numerous reports of air pollution due to dust storms over central China, where crop failures in the interior desertlands are an all too familiar picture. Even more extensive is the atmospheric dust blanket stretching from North Africa to South East Asia which has been monitored by satellite photography. The deepest and densest part of this dust layer hangs over the Rajputana Desert of Pakistan, parti-cularly during the pre-monsoon dry season. There seems to be a fairly clear correlation between the degree of desertification in Pakistan and the thickness of the dust veil. Furthermore, it has now been established that by decimating the vegetation man has caused a rapid deterioration of soils in this region and strong winds have completed the soil destruction. One of the problems facing the Pakistan Government, therefore, is whether much needed agri-cultural land can be reclaimed by controlling the dust source and thereby modifying the climate. This could only be achieved by means of an extensive programme of grass-planting to stabilize the soils. By reducing the magni-tude of the dust veil more solar energy would then reach the ground surface by day and the surface would cool more at night. It is believed that two meteorological consequences would result – more convectional air move-ment by day could generate much needed rainfall, whilst the lower ground temperatures at night should result in dew formation on the grass. In this way the desert might be slowly reclaimed, very much after the fashion of the Chinese arid-land reclamation programmes noted in Chapter 9.

The costs of a soil-stabilization programme in order to offset air pollution and increase national food production could, of course, prove prohibitive to many of the world's developing countries, so that financial assistance would have to be sought from the wealthier nations. But they have serious air-pollution problems of their own, which involve considerable expenditure. Statistics relating to costs involved in the reduction of air pollution are notoriously difficult to obtain and are often hard to interpret, but the following examples may give some idea of the magnitude and the complexity of the problem. In a 1968 report it was estimated that specific 'dirty' industries in Britain had spent £325 million during the previous decade in attempts to control air pollution. Following the Clean Air Act of 1956, when British local authorities were given wide powers to counteract domestic smoke, London alone spent £20 million in the first ten years. During the same period France was reported to have expended 240 billion francs in a single year (1957) whilst the financial estimates for the state of California included $100 million per year for the control of air pollution. It was claimed that the county of Los Angeles alone was suffering an annual crop loss due to pollution amounting to $3 million. But these figures relate only to remedial measures and to certain crop damages and give no real indication of the actual economic and social costs of air pollution on a global scale. How, for example, do we cost the effect of air pollution on world vegetation, of the structural damage caused through corrosion and above all the effect on human health? A frightening commentary on future pollution hazards is provided by the World Health Organization's conclusion:

The W.H.O. 1964 Expert Committee on Human Genetics has emphasized that such environmental factors as ionizing radiation and atmospheric pollution may increase the frequency of mutations.[8]

Is this, then, to be the greatest disaster of all?

Public Attitudes and Remedial Measures

There seems little doubt that by changes in machinery, fuels and industrial processes and also by stricter ordinances relating to site selection and zoning of specific offenders, it will become possible to combat most air-pollution problems. Man's current technological expertise means that it is now feasible to deal with most air pollutants, but it is beyond the scope of this book to describe the complex technical details of low-pollution combustion engines or dirt-free industrial plant, for example. Therefore, the problem is not so much concerned with the mechanical elimination or control of fog, smog or dust as with the question of whether the public is prepared to pay the cost involved. Studies have shown that as far as fog and smog are concerned most people are fairly fatalistic. Smog problems persist in Los

Angeles and are beginning to develop in Sydney but these do not appear to deter the large numbers of people who flock to live in these cities. Public attitudes in Britain have been summarized as follows:

The problems of air pollution in any town or conurbation grow slowly and insidiously, so that the inhabitants become accustomed to them and fail to notice gradually worsening conditions. Environmental standards, such as those of amenity and even cleanliness, become degraded and unpleasantness of towns becomes accepted as natural and inevitable. The cleanliness of the countryside may be envied but it is regarded as something peculiar to rural life.[9]

But the question still remains of whether this attitude should be allowed to prevail, for on a global scale this could ultimately lead to environmental disaster. The majority of national governments have decided that wholesale destruction of the atmosphere in this way should be stopped and that stricter legislation should be enacted and more widespread cooperation and coordination introduced.

In the United Kingdom legislation for smoke abatement is nothing new for proclamations had been issued by Edward I and Elizabeth I, prohibiting the burning of coal in London whilst Parliament was in session, but these seem to have had little effect on the city's degree of pollution through the succeeding centuries. Despite the Public Health Acts which became law between 1875 and 1936, smoke abatement was generally ineffective in British cities until the Clean Air Act of 1956, which followed in the wake of the great London smog disaster of 1952. This latest Act, operated by local authorities, made it an offence to emit dark smoke for longer than a specified period in any of the newly designated *smokeless zones*. The 1956 Act was not only responsible for the introduction of smokeless fuels but also specified the minimum height for chimneys and intensified the regulations relating to metallurgical, chemical and coal-mining industries. Electricity generating stations also became subject to stricter control but the Act does not apply to motor vehicles; consequently, while British cities can now be regarded as almost smoke-free the rate of pollution from motor vehicle exhausts continues to rise, suggesting that in future photochemical smog problems may become more serious.

There has been a great deal of anti-smoke legislation in the United States, where law-making is generally left to the individual states and cities rather than the Federal Government. Ordinances were first introduced in St Louis in 1937 and other major cities quickly followed suit: Kansas City (1943), Pittsburgh (1947) and Los Angeles (1947–49). Almost every American city now has a smoke or air pollution regulation of some kind, although the

increasing hazard of photochemical smog, shown to be closely correlated
with vehicle exhaust emissions, remains a major problem in certain urban
areas (Plate 53). This is particularly true in Los Angeles where, although
virtually no coal is consumed, larger quantities of petroleum are used in
relation to the size of population than in almost any other part of the world.
Occasionally, however, atmospheric conditions in America's Midwest are
such that smog pollution is not simply confined to a single city. Following in
the wake of Hurricane Camille in 1969, for example, an extensive anticyclone
developed across the Midwestern states east of the Mississippi where its
high-level temperature inversion (see Figure 96) soon acted as a 'lid' on all
the pollutants of the region. The gradual increase in the smog levels was
monitored by the National Meteorological Centre and a *high air pollution
potential* (H.A.P.P.) warning was issued for what became known as Episode
104. Figure 101 illustrates the extent of the affected area and also the length

53. Heavy photochemical smog swirls about New York's skyscrapers in November 1966, when
the toxic levels approached danger point.

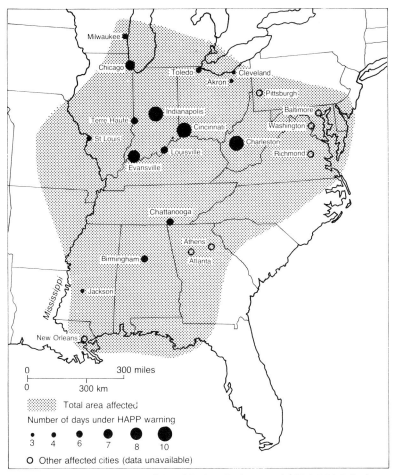

Fig. 101. Map to show the extent of the High Air Pollution Potential (H.A.P.P.) Episode 104 during August–September 1969 in the United States (after V. Brodine).

of the hazardous episode at certain badly polluted cities. By 25 August the smog was so severe in such cities as Chicago and St Louis that the pollution alert system was called into operation, whereby certain industries could ultimately be closed down until the pollution levels had decreased (in fact this closure was not enforced in August 1969). On 27 August it was reported that:

. . . the smog was so thick in St Louis that motorists were driving to work with their lights on and public viewing through the planetarium's telescope was cancelled because the planets and stars were obscured.[10]

Just as the smog levels were reaching thresholds which called for a second-stage (yellow) alert, with its mandatory restriction of emissions, the pall of dirty, poisoned air moved away from St Louis as the winds freshened. A major disaster was only narrowly averted by this atmospheric change, but it must be remembered that the entire episode was being carefully monitored and suitable action was being taken to curb motor vehicle use, waste incineration and some industrial operations. Nevertheless, it is prudent to remember that in America high-air pollution potential (H.A.P.P.) had been forecast on no less than 114 occasions in the ten years prior to 1970 (thirty-nine in western U.S.A. and seventy-five in eastern U.S.A.), as illustrated in Figure 102, and that any of these episodes might have inadvertently developed into a disaster.

Fig. 102. The total number of days during which high air pollution potential (including the number of episodes) was forecast in the United States. Compare Figure 101 (after V. Brodine).

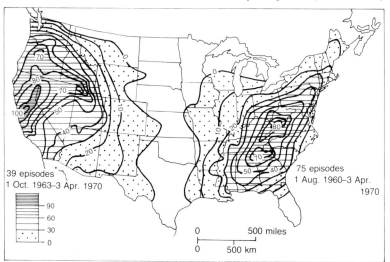

Several major technical advances have been made in the field of fog dispersal, including the use of five different techniques: first, that of fog-seeding by silver iodide crystals to cause precipitation (see p. 247); secondly, the so-called evaporation method in which crystals of hygroscopic material, such as sodium alginate or ammonium chloride, are dropped into the fog to remove the water vapour, since the crystals are capable of absorbing several times their own weight of water; a third method involves the use of ultrasonic sound waves to cause coalescence of fog particles; fourthly, there is the technique of dissipating fog by the use of large fans at ground level or by helicopters hovering above the critical area; finally, there is the method of ground-based heating (similar to the F.I.D.O. technique used by the British airforce during the Second World War). At Orly airport, Paris, for example, twelve large jet engines, known as the Turboclair system, have been installed in underground bunkers alongside the main runway at an expenditure of $3 million and an operating cost of $3,400 per hour. The cost effectiveness of all these various measures can be judged from the increased efficiency of both civil and military flying. In the 1969–70 winter, for example, the United States reported a $1 million reduction in revenue losses at commercial airports thanks to fog dispersal operations. Similar operations were 80 per cent successful at Moscow Airport during the period 1964–67.

The international exchange of technological ideas relating to fog dispersal has not been matched by world-wide cooperation on matters of air-pollution control, despite the pleas of the World Health Organization and a series of United Nations conferences on world environmental problems (viz. Stockholm, 1972). Many of the European Communist countries, under the aegis of the Council for Mutual Economic Assistance (C.M.E.A.), have co-ordinated their thinking on air-pollution control, but in general Western nations continue to act unilaterally. In the developing world there is little inclination to think about air-pollution control or fog dispersal, for their lives are governed more by hunger, disease and poverty.

Turning now to an examination of snow hazards and public attitudes we find that, generally speaking, most people tend to underestimate the danger, considering snow to be more of a nuisance than a serious problem. Consequently, as distances separating urban dwellers from their offices, factories and schools have lengthened, so the traffic chaos and urban disruptions due to snowfall have increased. Research in the United States has demonstrated that snow cover is cited as a hindrance to transportation more often than any other meteorological phenomenon. We have already noted that in addition to causing severe loss of life, blizzards also bring heavy financial losses in their wake. Attempts have been made to classify the various degrees of disruption based on an economic costing, and a hierarchy of snow impact is illustrated in Figure 103. In general it can be concluded that the most severe first-order disruptions cost more than second-order ones and so on.

The work of Dr J. F. Rooney in the United States has highlighted an interesting contrast in snow disruption patterns between the American east

Fig. 103. Hierarchy of Snow Disruptions: Internal and External Criteria (after J. F. Rooney).

Activity	1st order (paralysing)	2nd order (crippling)	3rd order (inconvenience)	4th order (nuisance)	5th order (minimal)
INTERNAL					
Transportation	Few vehicles moving on city streets City agencies on emergency alert, Police and Fire Departments available for transportation of emergency cases	Accidents at least 200% above average Decline in number of vehicles in central business district Stalled vehicles	Accidents at least 100% above average Traffic movement slowed	Any mention Traffic movement slowed	No press coverage
Retail trade	Extensive closure of retail establishments	Major drop in number of shoppers in central business district Mention of decreased sales	Minor impact		No press coverage
Postponements	Civic events cultural and athletic	Major and minor events Outdoor activities forced inside	Minor events	Occasional	No press coverage
Manufacturing	Factory shutdowns Major cutbacks in production	Moderate worker absenteeism	Any absenteeism attributable to snowfall		No press coverage
Construction	Major impact on indoor and outdoor operations	Major impact on outdoor activity Moderate indoor cutbacks	Minor effect on outdoor activity	Any mention	No press coverage
Communication	Wire breakage	Overloads	Overloads	Any mention	No press coverage
Power facilities	Widespread failure	Moderate difficulties	Minor difficulties	Any mention	No press coverage
Schools	Official closure of city schools Closure of rural schools	Closure of rural schools Major attendance drops in city schools	Attendance drops in city schools		No press coverage
Highway	Roads officially closed Vehicles stalled	Extreme-driving-condition warning from Highway Patrol	Hazardous-driving-condition warning from Highway Patrol	Any mention for example 'slippery in spots' warning	No press coverage

		Accidents attributed to snow and ice conditions	Accidents attributed to snow and ice conditions		
Rail	Cancellation or postponement of runs for twelve hours or more Stalled trains	Trains running four hours or more behind schedule	Trains behind schedule but less than four hours	Any mention	No press coverage
Air	Airport closure	Commercial cancellations	Light plane cancellations Aircraft behind schedule owing to snow and ice conditions	Any mention	No press coverage

and west, regardless of the snowfall magnitude. It appears that most of the Western cities experience fewer snow disruptions and this has been attributed to the lower water-content associated with most of the western snow-falls. Thus the 'wetter' snowfalls of the eastern cities may be regarded as a major factor in the greater degree of disruption which they experience. But Dr Rooney has also shown how snow hazard perception varies between eastern and western cities. The urban dweller in the west:

> ... regards snow as an element that must be coped with by the individual [producing] a much more comprehensive range of personal adjustments than are commonly found farther east. Western perception, on the other hand, has contributed to the pathetic ineptitude of public adjustment in the region. This inability of the public sector to react has created a greater vulnerability to severe snow conditions than exists in the East.[11]

One of the consequences is that western American cities, although not suffering the initial inconvenience of very 'wet' snowfalls, often take considerably longer to recover from blizzard disruption than do eastern cities. Nevertheless, in both regions, despite the increased volume of individual complaints which follow a severe snowfall, memories are very short and the average rate-payer becomes less prepared to pay for the costs of an effective snow-emergency and snow-clearance programme, once a series of warm summers and mild winters erase the inconvenience of the blizzards from his mind. When it comes to snow removal:

> Our attitudes are simply reflected in our actions. If demand existed for real innovations in snow control, they would be forthcoming. Most of the improvements developed thus far (radiant heat, snow melters, street flushing devices) have been rejected owing to their high cost and to the lack of knowledge concerning the losses attributable to snow.[11]

Part Five

Will We Ever Learn?

11. Hazard City
A Case Study of Los Angeles

When observers write about Los Angeles they often display a divergence of opinions – they appear either to love it or to hate it. There is almost always a polarization of views, for Los Angeles is not a city which provokes indifference because it is unique – a uniqueness that attracts or repels:

> ... It is immediately apparent that no city has ever been produced by such an extraordinary mixture of geography, climate, economics, demography, mechanics and culture; nor is it likely that an even remotely similar mixture will ever occur again.[1]

An examination of its geography and its climate will illustrate why Los Angeles has another claim to fame, for no other world city exhibits at one and the same time an environment in which the highest quality of urban life can be achieved and yet one which is fraught with the highest number of physical hazards. Of the thirteen hazards described in Chapters 2–10, Los Angeles suffers periodically from eight, some of which culminate in disasters. Only volcanoes, avalanches, hurricanes, tornadoes and blizzards are missing from this formidable list and it will be shown how the strong Santa Ana winds often exacerbate another serious hazard, that of brush fires.

Los Angeles has grown rapidly outwards from its original site on the coastal lowland to infill the surrounding flat-floored basins of San Fernando, San Gabriel and San Bernadino. Rising abruptly from these low alluvial plains and valleys are a series of substantial mountain ranges crowned by the seasonally snow-capped peaks of the San Gabriels and the San Bernadinos. The mountain chain forms an effective topographic as well as climatic barrier to the remainder of California so that Los Angeles is physically isolated in its basin-like setting. Its semi-desert climate of rainless summers and very mild winters combined with its sandy beaches, its subtropical vegetation and its backdrop of snow-capped peaks creates a strikingly attractive environment, conducive to the leisure-orientated, good life. And yet some people have dismissed the city as an environmental

disaster: 'In and around Los Angeles man has meddled with his environment – he has polluted the air, the sea, and the scenery and he has attempted
to destroy agriculture.'[2] Although there are many who will dispute this
contention we shall examine some of the ways in which man has triggered-
off or accelerated some of the disasters in Southern California by thoughtless
development or profligate use of the natural resources in this very delicate
environment. In other instances the ten million Angelenos are powerless in
the face of natural hazards over which they have no control, so it would be
true to say that Los Angeles will remain a hazard zone notwithstanding any
future environmental policy.

Earthquakes

The most serious and the most devastating of the hazards is the threat of
seismic disturbance. Ever since the 1906 earthquake in San Francisco the
seismic activity of California has made headline news and there are few
people in the Western World who have not heard of the San Andreas Fault.
The recent development of the scientific study of plate tectonics has tended
only to highlight the problems of California which sits astride the margins of
two separate plates (see Figure 11). The gradual movement along the plate
margins has built up stresses which are occasionally released with seismic
jolts, some of which have resulted in catastrophic earthquakes (see Figure
12). The San Andreas Fault, which marks the plate boundaries, is not by any
means the only fault in Southern California, for the whole of Los Angeles is
underlain by a fault mosaic which itself has played an important part in the
topographic configuration of its hills and valleys. Thus, not only have the
major mountain ranges been carved from uplifted, fault-guided tectonic
blocks but the basins themselves have been etched out from down-faulted
zones in which younger sediments have subsequently accumulated.
Figure 104 illustrates the large number of faults in the Los Angeles region,
almost all of which are active. It also gives a fair indication of the topographic grain and shows how several of the more exclusive foothill communities, such as Beverly Hills, Hollywood and Pasadena, are located
perilously close to the faults. The San Andreas Fault itself enters Los
Angeles County near the Tehachapi Mountains at the point where a major
earthquake occurred in 1857 (Fort Tejon, magnitude 8.5) and where a 320
kilometre segment of the fault was shifted. From there it runs east-south-
east through Palmdale, to the north of the San Gabriel range, through the
Cajon Pass and along the south side of the San Bernadino Mountains
(Figure 104).

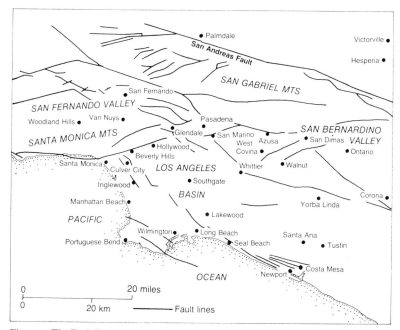

Fig. 104. The Fault Pattern of the Los Angeles region (after H. J. Nelson and W. A. V. Clark).

Recent studies have identified areas of contrasting seismic behaviour along different segments of the San Andreas Fault zone, in which the sections corresponding to the great surface ruptures of 1857 (Fort Tejon) and 1906 (San Francisco) now appear to be 'locked'. This is to say that slippage, or fault-creep, is very small, that strain energy is not being released and that these segments are therefore potential locations for sudden and violent earthquakes within the near future:

> If this pattern of contrasting seismic behaviour is valid, it is clear that both Los Angeles and San Francisco are vulnerable to severe earthquake damage in the future.[3]

Los Angeles, in fact, did not have to wait very long, for within two years of this prediction the peaceful world of the inhabitants of the San Fernando Valley, in the city's northern suburbs, was rudely shattered by a violent earthquake (magnitude 6.7) which ripped through the built-up area, when one of the San Andreas Fault's minor offshoots ruptured just before dawn on 9 February 1971.

In a mere ten seconds the tremors demolished or severely damaged more than one thousand buildings in the San Fernando Valley, brought down

54. During the 1971 earthquake in the San Fernando Valley of Los Angeles a newly constructed freeway was severely damaged.

several overpasses in the city's freeway system (Plate 54) and ultimately claimed sixty-five lives; total damages exceeded the $500 million mark. One of the most worrying aspects of the earthquake was the complete destruction of the Olive View Hospital which had only recently been completed to meet the most stringent earthquake engineering regulations. Though severely damaged, the near-by Van Norman Dam survived the jolt, giving an unsuspecting 80,000 inhabitants a miraculous escape from possible drowning.

Experts shudder to think what might have been the outcome if the earth-quake had struck just a few hours later when the freeways would have been crowded with rush-hour commuters.

Because it had occurred in one of the world's most seismically-conscious cities, the San Fernando earthquake has also become one of the most inten-sively studied. Amongst the findings was the illuminating fact that the crustal surface had been gradually forced up into a dome around the San Fernando region prior to the earthquake. It was also noted how minor earthquake tremors had increased in the area between 1969 and 1971, and these must obviously have been foreshocks. Because of the Japanese records, where crustal uplift had been confirmed as a precursory event in both the 1923 Tokyo earthquake and the 1964 Niigata earthquake, it is now becoming increasingly clear to the Californian seismologists that crustal uplift fre-quently precedes very destructive earthquakes. Imagine the concern, there-fore, when it was reported from the Mojave Desert segment of the San Andreas Fault, just to the north of the San Gabriel Mountains, that a new crustal bulge had begun to appear, centred around the town of Palmdale. Reference has already been made to the notorious Palmdale 'Pimple' (p. 67) which began to rise in May 1959 not far from the epicentre of the devastating Fort Tejon earthquake of 1857 (Figure 105). By 1975 the bulge had risen by 25 centimetres, thereby uplifting more than 1 billion tonnes of rock over an area of 60,000 square kilometres – one of the world's greatest crustal deformations ever to be monitored.

A carefully selected team of some 320 scientists and technicians is keeping a close surveillance on the region for this is a section of the San Andreas Fault which appears to be 'locked', since there is virtually no strain release. Yet the seismologists know that elsewhere in California the tectonic plates are grinding past each other along the line of the San Andreas Fault, at an average rate of 5 centimetres per year. Thus, the strain that is building up in the Palmdale region must be enormous and it appears to be only a matter of time before the fault will move again to produce an earthquake of very great magnitude. Computer-based predictions have already indicated that an earthquake of similar intensity to that of the 1906 event in San Francisco (magnitude 8.3) would cause devastating shaking within a radius of 65 kilo-metres from the epicentre. As Figure 105 illustrates, this suggests that a major proportion of the city of Los Angeles lies within the seismic hazard zone. Nevertheless, earthquake prediction studies are sufficiently advanced for a reasonable warning to be given prior to a Palmdale earthquake, in which case certain precautionary measures could be undertaken. In addition to the evacuation of high-rise buildings and hospitals, nuclear power plants

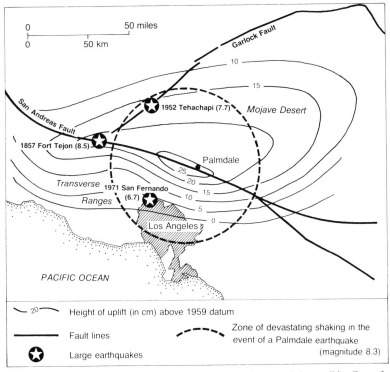

Fig. 105. The ground-surface uplift around Palmdale, California, and the possible effects of a major earthquake on Los Angeles.

could be disconnected, industries halted and oil pipe lines turned off, whilst water levels in local dams could be lowered. General evacuation would probably be unnecessary as the San Fernando earthquake demonstrated that the majority of single-storey, timber-framed houses, favoured by many Angelenos, came safely through the 1971 shaking. Although some taller buildings suffered badly, the very strict building codes, introduced after the Long Beach earthquake of 1933, mean that Los Angeles has fewer sky-scrapers than most American cities. The housing units at greatest risk will be those located on the alluvial areas, where quickclays could liquefy (see p. 147), or in the foothills where landslides could be triggered off by the shaking. The artificially 'made land' could also suffer, especially on the steeper slopes of the Santa Monica Mountains, where building land has been at a premium in this highly sought-after location above the smog level. Despite the gloomy forebodings of the scientists, however, the inhabitants of Los Angeles are remarkably fatalistic, with few of them taking out earthquake insurance. The general attitudes may be summarized by the entrepreneur who considered erecting spectator stands to the north-east of the San Andreas Fault in order that Angelenos could witness the great event if and when it happens.

Tsunamis

In chapter 8 it has been shown how giant sea waves, generated by submarine earthquakes or specific volcanic eruptions, have been termed tsunamis. The Pacific Ocean coastlines are particularly prone to this type of hazard and although the 1906 San Francisco earthquake does not appear to have provoked a seismic sea wave the great Alaskan earthquake of Good Friday 1964 certainly did. Running down the Californian coast the tsunami created havoc along the low-lying shorelines, particularly at Crescent City in the northern part of the state. Although no damage was reported from Los Angeles in 1964 there seems little doubt that the coastal fringes of the city, from Malibu to Redondo Beach, could be regarded as a tsunami hazard zone. This contention is based on the fact that the Pacific floor off California is scarred by a number of major transcurrent faults, known as fracture zones, relating to the gradual northward slippage of the Pacific Tectonic Plate in relation to the main North American Plate. We have already seen how this slippage is taking place along the San Andreas Fault system, and it must now be realized that the submarine fractures are all part of the same complex fault mosaic. During the period 1953–73 no less than fourteen submarine earthquakes were recorded just offshore between San Francisco and Los Angeles. Paradoxically, this high seismic-activity pattern suggests that the fault stresses were being periodically released, thus alleviating the likelihood of a major earthquake. As in the case of the San Andreas Fault, however, there is reason to believe that there remain sections of the undersea faults which may be 'locked' and these are building up strain energy which may suddenly be released as a major submarine tremor. A sizeable tsunami generated in this fashion would strike the Los Angeles beaches with virtually no warning.

Some geomorphologists have claimed that the high coastal cliffs of Pacific Palisades were probably fashioned by seismic sea waves prior to the urban development of the area. Today, however, not only does the Pacific Coast Highway follow the cliff foot but a considerable residential development has mushroomed at beach level between Santa Monica and Malibu. Furthermore, the luxury homes of Pacific Palisades have spread to the very verge of the clifftops, despite the periodic landslips in the poorly consolidated sedimentary rocks (see p. 155). Houses located in such positions would be regarded as hazard-prone even in tectonically stable areas, as the winter storms of 1978 were to prove (see p. 360). but in a seismic zone as active as that of Southern California their siting is remarkably precarious.

Sinking Coastlines

As if the threat from potential tsunami flooding is not enough, the Long Beach stretch of the Los Angeles coastline has become a flood-hazard zone as a result of the considerable degree of crustal subsidence due to the extraction of oil. The greatest sinking was associated with the exploitation of the Wilmington oilfield where parts of Terminal Island behind the harbour descended by as much as 9 metres (29 feet) in the space of forty years (Figure 106). In addition to the extensive damage to the wharves, buildings, streets, bridges and pipelines the area remained for several years in serious danger of disastrous marine flooding. This was especially true during the

Fig. 106. Land subsidence at Long Beach, California (1926–68), due to oil extraction.

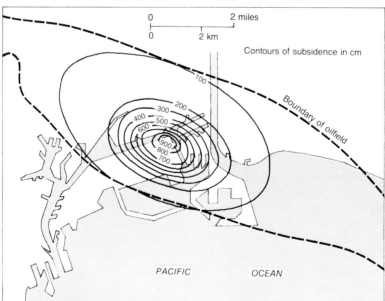

Fig. 107. Subsidence rate, shown before and after water-injection scheme, compared with oil-production figures in the Wilmington Oil Field, Long Beach, California (after M. N. Mayuga and D. R. Allen).

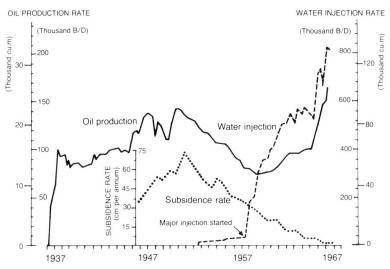

decade from 1948 to 1958 when, in places, the surface was sinking rapidly at the rate of 71 centimetres (26 inches) per year. Considerable financial expenditure of some $100 million was incurred both in repairs and in surface filling, including the ingenious method of raising all the harbour warehouses by jacking. Nevertheless, subsidence caused by withdrawal of oil or other fluids can be halted by injecting water or repressurizing the underground reservoir to achieve crustal equilibrium. By 1968 the Long Beach subsidence had been checked by the introduction of such measures (Figure 107), but not before large tracts of the harbour area had sunk below sea level, necessitating the construction of major sea walls. Until these remedial measures were undertaken the port of Los Angeles remained in dire peril of severe coastal flooding and it was fortunate that no tsunamis affected Southern California during this critical period. Nevertheless, large sections of the Long Beach dockland were periodically inundated at every high tide until the dyking, filling and raising operations had been completed.

In addition to the vertical subsidence the crustal warping due to oil extraction also caused severe shear forces of the landsurface in the horizontal plane. Consequently, not only were railway tracks and pipelines considerably buckled but buildings were so badly cracked and damaged that they had to be rebuilt. The Commodore Heim lift bridge was so severely damaged that the supporting towers were tilted out of position, making it impossible to operate the bridge. The greatest amount of damage, however, occurred in the oilfield itself where the oil well casings were twisted and destroyed, leading to a marked decrease in the oil production figures during the 1950s (see Figure 107). Most of the damage to the oil-well casings resulted from small earth tremors, some 500 metres below the surface, when the underlying shale layers shifted in an attempt to relieve the underground stresses. Certain of the oil wells were so severely damaged that they had to be sealed off and abandoned, but others were fitted with flexible couplings (to offset future horizontal movement) and were lifted several metres into the air before land filling took place.

Landslides

Natural landslides occur within Los Angeles's city boundaries virtually every year, but especially during the winter rainfall periods. The slumping and sliding of the hillslopes in this region result largely from the widespread occurrence of its poorly consolidated and cemented alluvial deposits of gravel, sand and silt, but also from the steepness of the coastal cliffs at Pacific Palisades and the hillsides of the numerous canyons which character- ize its suburbs. When one realizes that the whole area is also criss-crossed with seismically active faults and that man has carelessly over-steepened some of the already steep-walled canyons in attempts to engineer his urban road network, it will be seen that slope instability is one of Los Angeles's major hazards.

Among the most dangerous areas is the coastal zone where 50 metre-high sea cliffs extend along Santa Monica Bay for some 10 kilometres, and where the main Pacific Coast Highway runs beneath the cliff foot on a narrow shelf between the vertical, unstable 'palisades' and the ocean itself. Numerous developments of seashore property have been allowed to take place in this hazardous strip of land, culminating in the well-known resort of Malibu. Furthermore, because of the desirability of the sea view and the cooling influence of the ocean breezes, the cliff-top land has also been extensively urbanized. Here, flat-lying, impermeable Pleistocene gravels and sands with little internal cohesion overlie layers of structurally weak clays and shales which in places dip seawards. Thus, not only have deep-seated bedding-plane slides occurred in the bedrock, but the thin capping of Pleistocene deposits remains conducive to soil-fall from the cliff top, thereby leading to fairly rapid slope retreat. Rarely a winter goes by without a clifftop road or building being sliced away by a cliff fall, so that, in addition to the serious property losses incurred, the safety of motorists on the underlying coastal highway has been repeatedly jeopardized. By far the most serious hazard, however, is posed by the bedrock landslides when millions of tonnes of sedimentary material may suddenly be decanted across the coastal highway (Plate 55). One such landslide occurred between 27 and 31 March 1958 near

55. Landslides such as this sometimes close parts of the Pacific Coastal Highway in Los Angeles County.

to Flagg's Restaurant when, after several days of exceptionally heavy rainfall, an enormous slump of saturated bedrock completely blocked the Coast Highway for a distance of some 300 metres. Because the removal of the landslip would have caused even greater cliff top instability and threatened many expensive residential properties (resulting in major compensation claims), the highway authorities decided to by-pass the slip by relocating the coast road. This was done by rebuilding the highway on the beach itself, having taken care to stabilize the foreshore by constructing massive stone groins out into the sea. From an economic point of view the re-opening of the Coast Highway was of vital importance, so that the cost of relocating the highway was thought to be cheaper than entering into a lengthy phase of litigation concerned with possible compensation claims resulting from the slide removal.

The most serious case of slope failure in Los Angeles is that of Portuguese Bend in the exclusive Palos Verdes residential area. Like those of the Pacific Palisades suburbs the seaward slopes of Palos Verdes exhibit many characteristics of former slope failure, but despite the potentially unstable terrain the planning authorities allowed the construction of housing estates during the 1950s. By 1956 a large section of the newly developed area had begun to slide seawards, opening up a major fault scarp along the upper perimeter of the slump. Within a year certain portions of the landslip had moved some 10 to 15 metres downslope and new fissures and slips had appeared (Figure 108). By the mid 1970s the major slide had moved by more than 70 metres, with its forward movement being accelerated by excessive groundwater which had accumulated in the slippage zone during a spell of abnormally rainy weather. Because the average rate of movement is currently of the order of 3.5 metres per year, it is little wonder that the effect on houses, roads, water and drainage pipes has been catastrophic. As the mass continues to creep slowly downwards along lubricated slide-planes in the shaley bedrock at least 150 homes have already been destroyed at an estimated cost of $10 million. Because it was claimed that the landslide had been triggered by overloading of the headslope with debris from road construction, the property owners have successfully sued the Los Angeles authorities for compensation, despite the fact that this area of Palos Verdes has long been recognized by geologists as a landslide hazard zone in which earlier slippages must have been commonplace. Only a few residents have remained in the area, and it seems unlikely that major remedial measures will be undertaken, for their estimated cost would be a further $10 million.

In Los Angeles's northern suburbs, where the Hollywood hills are dissected by steep-walled canyons, the Highland Park community is one of the

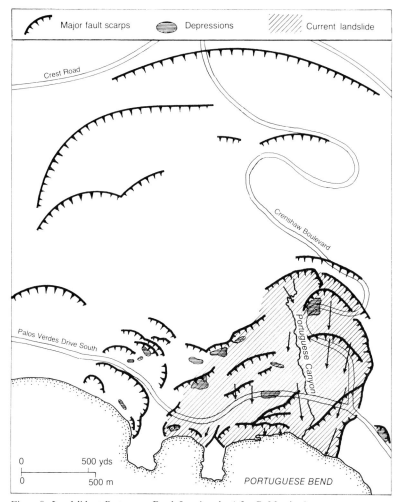

Fig. 108. Landslide at Portuguese Bend, Los Angeles (after R. Merriam).

city's oldest suburbs. The houses have been constructed not only on the canyon floors but also on their slopes in an effort to utilize every metre of valuable building land. What the residents did not know, however, was that the dip of the shaley rocks was outwards towards the valleys and that layers of montmorillionite clay (see p. 199) made the entire area a potential hazard zone. Thus, during a severe winter storm in January 1969 the heavy rainfall

359

created a raging torrent in the canyon floor and this succeeded in under-cutting one of the potentially unstable slopes. Once the supporting footslope had been removed gravity was sufficient to move gigantic masses of the unsupported slope downwards along the lubricated bedding planes. Even-tually the entire hillside slumped down into the floor of the canyon, carrying with it scores of homes, although miraculously there were no casualties.

Exceptionally heavy rainfall in January and February 1978 again triggered off the latest series of landslides and mudflows within the city boundary, whilst neighbouring Ventura County was declared an official disaster area. Ten people lost their lives as landslips crushed their homes in the Woodland Hills area and the Pacific Coast Highway was closed along a 30 kilometre stretch owing to cliff falls and landslips.

Geologists have pointed out that many of the recently constructed residential suburbs in Los Angeles have been built on potentially hazardous quickclays (see p. 159). The saline minerals of these marine clays normally act as a sort of adhesive which holds the clays in a stable form. Once these sodium minerals are flushed out by freshwater percolation, however, the clays become progressively unstable, with a tendency to liquefy and collapse during an earthquake. Judging by the behaviour of the analogous Bootlegger Cove quickclays at Anchorage, Alaska (see Figure 43 and p. 158), the result of a Californian seismic tremor could be catastrophic in a built-up area. And yet the saline minerals are being systematically washed out of the Los Angeles quickclays by a combination of lawn sprinklers and leakage from the large number of swimming pools and other artificial water bodies (Figure 109).

Fig. 109. A schematic illustration depicting the hazardous effects of groundwater seepage on a typical Los Angeles housing development located on quickclays (after Q. A. Aune).

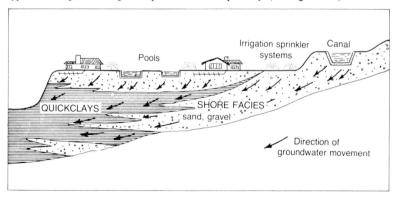

High Winds and Brush Fires

During the period of severe storms which lashed the coasts of California in March 1978 a considerable amount of damage was caused to the famous beach resort of Malibu. Whipped up by gale-force winds the ocean waves tore into the expensive beach homes of this coastal community and smashed them to matchwood. Among those who suffered losses or severe damage were the Hollywood stars Burgess Meredith, Rod Steiger and Merle Oberon, while Malibu itself was cut off from the rest of Los Angeles by landslides which sent cliff-top properties tumbling down the slopes.

Although Los Angeles rarely suffers damage of this magnitude from high velocity winds such as hurricanes or tornadoes, the desiccating local wind known as the Santa Ana is often responsible for the increasingly widespread brush fires which have swept through the surrounding hill country on countless occasions (Figure 110). Sometimes the consequences are disastrous, as in the case of the Bel Air–Brentwood conflagration from 6–8 November 1961 which resulted in an insured property loss of $24 million. In September 1970 an even more catastrophic blaze roared across the Santa Monica Mountains, its fireline extending a distance of 56 kilometres, all the way to Malibu. Upwards of 72,000 hectares of brush were burnt, 295 houses destroyed and three people killed as the fires raged through the hill-top properties.

The brushwood, known as chaparral, becomes highly flammable every autumn when the dry Santa Ana winds drive the small fire outbreaks rapidly across the hills until they combine as a major conflagration, often beyond the capability of the Los Angeles fire-fighting departments (Plate 56). Because of its rapidly expanding population the city's property developments have been pushed farther and farther out into the surrounding hills and mountains where the terrain is not conducive to residential settlement. Consequently, houses have become strung along the narrow ridge-crests or along the canyon floors:

> To reduce erosion, lower costs, and retain the natural feeling of the setting, the slopes between canyons are left in brush. This intimate juxtaposition of brush and residence in hilly terrain sets the scene for disaster.[4]

Dense banks of chaparral become especially dangerous on canyon slopes below houses, because the up-draught situation which is created will act like a chimney flue and spur the flames rapidly upwards. Therefore, Californian law now requires that all brush be cleared within a minimum distance of 10 metres around all structures, and in extreme hazard zones for a distance

Disasters

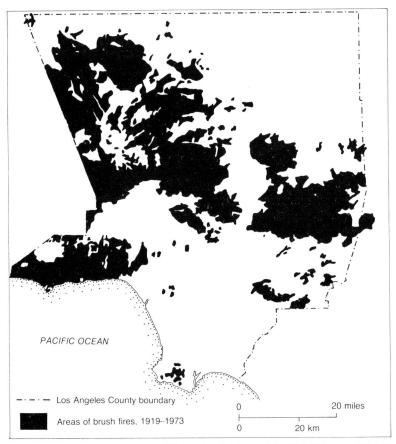

Fig. 110. Areas of brush fires (1919–73) in Los Angeles County (after H. J. Nelson and W. A. V. Clark).

of some 20 metres. Although it has been claimed that the chaparral should be replaced with 'fire-resistant' vegetation, the agronomists of the University of California have pointed out that when the Santa Ana reduces the humidity to as little as 4 per cent, in combination with air temperatures of 30°C, virtually all plants will burn. Thus, they recommend, among other things, that in order to reduce fire hazards high-pressure sprinkler systems should be widely introduced in order to irrigate the vegetation cover. They are aware, of course, that in the watered landscape, problems of soil erosion and

362

slope instability must be carefully monitored, although on certain of the quickclay terraces the introduction of sprinkler systems may create more problems than it solves, for the reasons outlined above.

56. The Californian brushwood, known as chaparral, becomes highly flammable at the end of every summer when the dry Santa Ana winds drive the flames across the hills.

363

Floods

Brush fires are not only a devastating hazard in their own right but they also serve to denude the hillslopes of their protecting vegetation cover, so that until the chaparral is able to re-colonize in about three to five years time, some of the Los Angeles hillslopes will exhibit extensive areas of bare soil. This denuded soil, often overlying friable and easily eroded bedrock, remains extremely vulnerable to rainfall erosion, so that vast quantities of sand and mud are likely to be washed down into the valleys and plains during periods of winter rainfall. At best, the natural vegetation of Southern California is relatively sparse, reflecting its semi-desert climate, so that any interference with the critical stabilizing ground cover is likely to increase the rate of surface water run-off. Add to this the phenomenal development of urbanization, with its hundreds of square kilometres of impermeable roofs and paved streets, and one begins to realize how the run-off must have been greatly accelerated in recent decades. Finally, the surrounding mountains and hills abut onto the heavily populated alluvial basins of the city with such steep gradients that the descent of run-off to the valley floors takes place very rapidly, sometimes in a matter of minutes. This discharge of muddy water has sufficient velocity to carry enormous boulders, up to 20 tonnes in weight, and these act as battering rams as the floods rampage through the foothills before pouring out onto the floors of the basins. Thus, the danger areas are not only the canyons themselves but also the flood-plains which fan out from the main stream channels (Figure 111). It is a surprising fact that almost half of the built-up area of Los Angeles can be regarded as lying within the flood-hazard zone, thereby putting some three million Angelenos at risk together with about $10 million worth of real estate.

Periods of time between floods are sometimes long, whereas memory of man is short. Lands which historically have been seriously menaced were purchased by those – especially newcomers – who thought that the climate of Los Angeles was all sunshine and warmth. They farmed or built industries and homes in the foothills at mouths of canyons, along the low river banks, and even in the dry stream beds . . . [Thus] the metropolitan region of Los Angeles County has probably been subject to a greater potential flood hazard – mainly from flash floods – than any other area of similar size and population density in the United States.[5]

Records show that floods have damaged Los Angeles on twenty-one occasions between 1811 and 1954, with those of 1914 and 1916 causing a combined bill for damages of $14 million. In 1934 a raging torrent devastated the small valley of La Canada, destroyed roads, villages, vineyards and citrus groves, and left forty people dead and damages of $5 million. An even more dis-

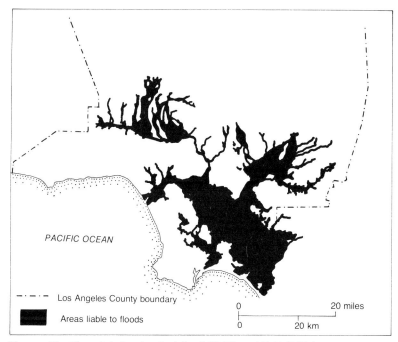

Fig. 111. Flood hazards in Los Angeles (after C. W. Eliot and D. F. Griffin).

astrous flood occurred in 1938, when the entire flood-hazard area was affected, with this time fifty-nine lives being lost and $62 million worth of damages being incurred. In 1969 further flooding swept through the city, killing ninety-two of its residents, making 10,000 homeless and resulting in physical damage estimated at upwards of $60 million. Finally, during the winter storms of February and March 1978, Los Angeles was again severely damaged by widespread flooding, when more than twice the annual rainfall fell in a matter of weeks. The canyons spewed out their debris-laden flood-waters into the streets of Hollywood, washing away scores of hillside homes and carrying cars down into the channels themselves. Following the collapse of a dam in Big Tujunga Canyon further damage was caused when a wall of water swept down onto the residential areas below. In the final count some two hundred homes were severely damaged or destroyed and more than six hundred people evacuated from the hazard zone, some of them by helicopter from rooftops.

Organized flood control in Los Angeles commenced after the 1914 disaster, but it was not until 1936 that the Federal Government became involved in the city's flood problems, after which the United States Army Corps of Engineers was financed and authorized to restructure the city's flood-control measures. Their programme included massive remedial works on the city rivers, straightening and paving the channels, strengthening the embankments, constructing storage reservoirs and check dams, together with a considerable amount of vegetation planting to control run-off and soil erosion. At the same time much stricter ordinances were introduced in order to discourage speculative building in flood-hazard zones. But it must be remembered that in most cases the flood hazard remains localized and that most people soon erase the horrors of the more extensive flooding from their memories. After all, statistics have shown that an overwhelming flood on the scale of the 1938 disaster is only likely to occur once in a hundred years; that a large flood, which inundates only the flood-plain valleys and coastal plain, may occur only six times per century; whilst the localized moderate flood (similar to that of 1934) may strike about once every decade.

Drought

It is paradoxical to think that a city which experiences such devastating flash floods should also be faced with the constant problem of drought. In the deserts and semi-deserts of Southern California, however, water shortages are the rule rather than the exception, because low rainfall and high evaporation combine to produce a total run-off of a mere 12.5 centimetres (5 inches) per year. And yet seven million residents of Los Angeles County have all the water they need for drinking, bathing, car washing, irrigating and filling the thousands of swimming pools. Probably few Angelenos give much thought to this anomalous situation, despite the fact that current plans to transfer water from the wetter northern part of California have led to considerable intra-state resentment. Furthermore, because of this rapidly growing demand for water in the semi-arid areas of Southern California, there has also developed an increasing threat to the traditional water resources of adjoining states, which can only lead to inter-state controversy. Today, Los Angeles receives the bulk of its water supply from the Owens Valley, on the east side of the Sierra Nevada (within the state of California), and from the Colorado River on the borders of Arizona. It was the latter scheme that led to a decade-long legal battle between California and the state of Arizona which ended in 1963 when the United States Supreme Court decreed that Southern California should restrict its supplies from the rapidly dwindling Colorado River. Consequently, Los Angeles has been forced into seeking its extra requirements from the northern part of California by means of a new aqueduct and it is this latest north-south water transfer that has renewed the state controversy. This stems partly from ecological concern and partly from the potential adverse effects that water diversion could have on San Francisco Bay. A National Water Commission, which was established in 1968, has thrown serious doubts on the possibility of future water-transfer schemes. If it is accepted the Commission's 1973 report:

> ... signifies the end of the view that continued agricultural and urban growth in arid areas can be sustained by unlimited interference with natural water cycles in more humid areas. If such a change in policy occurs, and this appears increasingly likely, no State would be more affected than California.[6]

Although there has been no serious water shortage in Los Angeles in living memory, the previous generation of Angelenos knew what it meant to their livelihood when the rivers ran dry, the underground water levels dropped perilously low and wells had to be drilled deeper and deeper into the parched earth. That was eighty years ago, but it is possible that without an enormous amount of expenditure and a great deal of technological ingenuity Los Angeles may be facing an increasingly waterless future. At present virtually all its water is utilized, with only a very small percentage reaching the ocean via the city's surface drainage channels.

Smog

If the majority of the Los Angeles's residents regard water resources as one of the least important of the city's problems then the same cannot be said of the smog question. It is true that smog is by no means confined to Los Angeles but in a comparison with other American cities it is easy to see why Los Angeles has gained its reputation, for it is significantly more smog-prone than most other United States cities (Figure 112).

Los Angeles	115	St Louis	6
San Diego	19	San Francisco	4
Denver	13	Washington	3
Philadelphia	8	Chicago	1

Fig. 112. Number of days per annum when 50 per cent of the population experience eye irritation from photochemical smog in selected American cities (after Patterson and Henein).

It is ironic that the high incidence of sunshine which has made Los Angeles so famous is also responsible in part for the formation of photochemical smog. There seems little doubt, however, that the major culprit is the internal combustion engine, for photochemical smog is generated by the action of sunlight on hydrocarbons and nitric oxides present in vehicle exhausts. Most of the eye irritation results from the smog constituent known as peroxyacetylnitrate (P.A.N. for short) but ozone and aldehydes are also produced by the chemical interactions. Since it has been estimated that almost 90 per cent of the city's hydrocarbons and nitric oxides are generated by vehicle exhausts, it will follow that photochemical smog pollution is only a daytime phenomenon in Los Angeles. Most nights and early mornings are crystal clear, but soon after sunrise, as the millions of vehicles take to the freeways during the morning rush-hour, so the photochemical reaction begins to operate. Nitrogen dioxide, brownish in colour, initiates the process for it is turned into nitric oxide and highly reactive oxygen atoms, once it has captured the sun's energy. In the windless conditions which generally obtain in Los Angeles the contaminants are not easily dispersed so that by 8 a.m. both nitrogen dioxide and nitric oxide are being accumulated in substantial amounts (Figure 113). By the end of the morning rush-hour ozone is also beginning to appear in large quantities, replacing the nitric oxide, since the two cannot coexist in appreciable concentrations. It is known that high concentrations of ozone and nitrogen dioxide are damaging to human respiration, for not only do they cause coughing, but also a severe swelling

Fig. 113. Photochemical smog in Los Angeles during a typical pollution day.

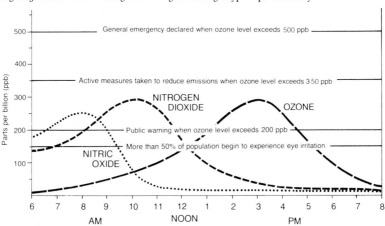

of the mucus membrane, thus restricting inhalation. Add to this the gradual build-up of lethal carbon monoxide from vehicle exhausts, and it will be realized that heavy traffic concentrations can seriously endanger human health under certain climatic conditions. When the mountain-girt basin of Los Angeles becomes influenced by temperature inversions (see Figure 96), as it frequently does during summer, then the photochemical smog will be trapped in the form of a dirty yellow blanket over the city centre for most of the daylight hours.

It is usually on these windless days of anticyclonic temperature inversions that the Angelenos suffer the worst effects of smog pollution. Eye and nose irritation are fairly widespread, especially in the city centre, but during very high concentrations, sufferers from asthma and bronchitis find it advisable to stay indoors. The Los Angeles Public Health Service constantly monitors the amount of pollution, and first-stage warnings are given over radio and T.V. when the ozone level reaches 200 parts per billion (Figure 113). When ozone levels exceed 350 parts per billion (second-stage alert) active measures can be taken to control emissions and when the critical 500 parts per billion level is passed a full-scale emergency would be declared, during which industry could be closed down and traffic brought to a standstill. A general third-stage alert of this sort has yet to be called in Los Angeles but records show that on average between one and six first-stage alerts have occurred every year since the 1960s.

On 14 July 1978 the Los Angeles authorities issued one of their rare second-stage alerts as the smog pollution rose to its highest level of the year. This was the first occasion on which they had been able to predict this stage-two alert and were in a position to take steps to lessen the impact. Consequently, all companies with more than a hundred employees were told to ask them to share car transport on their journey to work; all industries which created hydrocarbons and nitrogen oxides were required to cut their operations by 20 per cent. This meant that the city's oil-burning power stations, the greatest culprits, were forced to switch to imported electricity or to depend on natural gas as a means of power production. In addition, to lighten the demand for electricity, all householders were requested to switch off electrical appliances, including the air-conditioning, despite the 35°C temperatures. In the worst affected parts of the city the public health authorities suggested that children should avoid strenuous outdoor exercise.

As early as 1947 Los Angeles had set up an air-pollution control body in an attempt to avoid incidents of this kind and within a decade they had succeeded in banning all domestic refuse burning. Courts are now empowered to impose $600 fines or six-month jail sentences for offenders.

Despite this increased control of noxious emissions, however, the July 1978 incident demonstrated that the problem remained unsolved, especially while upwards of four million vehicles continue to burn some eight million gallons of petroleum every day.

Nevertheless, it would be wrong to suggest that all of the city suffers from photochemical smog, since the ocean breezes generally keep the heaviest pollution away from the coastal suburbs, whilst the surrounding hills and mountains emerge above the smog level. In general, the sea breeze concentrates the worst smog around the central business district during the middle of the day, but by the afternoon it has succeeded in driving the pollution into the city's eastern suburbs of the San Gabriel and San Bernadino valleys, from whence it occasionally overflows the mountain passes and streams out across the Mojave Desert. During autumn and winter, when the easterly Santa Ana winds blow, the position is reversed, for then the beaches and coastal areas may become smoggier than the inland parts of the city.

In conclusion, it can be said that for the majority of its citizens Los Angeles remains an epitome of the sunshine state of California – a place of both challenge and opportunity. There are those who believe that it mirrors the face of Western civilization where twentieth-century man has achieved the most advanced urban society on earth and has tamed his environment on the way to these achievements. There are others who see such a society merely as a brittle veneer in an environment where hazards have proliferated in response to man's interference with the natural order of things.

12. Disaster Research

Natural hazards have always posed a formidable threat to mankind but it appears that in the twentieth century the world is becoming a more dangerous place in which to live. Whether or not there are currently a greater number of disasters is debatable, for many believe that the modern catastrophe is better reported than in the past, so that a larger number of people are aware of its occurrence. Yet, one aspect is becoming increasingly clear – that the character of the threat is changing within the present century from one in which there is an expectation of a severe death toll to one where there is an expectation of a significant loss of property. At least, this appears to be true of the more prosperous developed countries where this reversal of the life-property loss relationship has resulted from their cultural advances. Thus, whilst the continuing trend towards urbanization has led to greater agglomeration in terms of both property and population, the latter, on the one hand, remains mobile and can therefore escape certain hazards if sufficient warning is given. On the other hand, the greater the massing of urban structures the greater will be the target for the violent acts of God. Compare, for example, the American Gulf Coast hurricanes of 1900 and 1961 (Hurricane Carla), the first of which claimed 6,000 lives in Galveston, Texas (see p. 235) and caused property loss of $30 million, whilst the second killed only forty-six people but wrecked property at a cost of $400 million. Because of the excellent United States forecasting and communications in 1961, thousands of people had been able to leave the hazard areas in good time.

On turning to the world's developing countries, however, the picture seems to be quite a different one, for here the badly housed, poorly informed and virtually immobile rural populations are partly unaware of the natural hazard risks which they frequently face. Even if they are aware of the threats to their lives and livelihoods, there is probably very little that they can do about them, and at first glance this may account for the general air of fatalism which surrounds these poorer populations. By comparison with the expensive real estate of an American city, for example, the value of a South American hill village or a Bangladeshi shanty town may be insignificant, so that the magnitude of any disaster which may occur in the latter cases will be measured largely in terms of deaths rather than in property losses. This is why an urban disaster, such as the Bucharest earthquake (Chapter 2) or the Florence floods (Chapter 8), makes such a profound impact on the developed nations of the world, whilst the Honduras hurricane (Chapter 7) and the Sahel drought and famine (Chapter 9) tend to be soon forgotten in many quarters, even though by 1978 the drought was beginning to recur:

> Since the tragic struggle seems to be the poor versus nature, experts have taken the role of umpire. Some judge that it is mostly the poor themselves who are to blame, by reproducing themselves too frequently; by choosing to live in hazardous places like the Bangladeshi coastal inlets or steep Honduran hillsides; by thoughtlessly unbalancing local ecology in their attempts to farm. Other umpires blame nature; for long-term climatic shifts resulting in *desertification*; for a short-term series of exceptionally wet years in the 1960s that encouraged peasants and nomads to push their luck in lands usually too dry to support them.[1]

To answer these problems satisfactorily much more is needed in the way of disaster research, for a recent investigation conducted at the University of Bradford, England, has revealed the disturbing claim that there appears to have been a decided increase in the frequency of 'large-scale' disasters, i.e. those which involve large surface areas and have long-term impacts on the world's ecological balance. At the same time the investigating team found no significant scientific evidence for major changes in the earth's climate or structure, which led them to the conclusion that:

> The physical and social hazard defences of the rich countries have become more effective, but at the same time the poorest people in the poor countries have become increasingly vulnerable to disaster.[2]

If this is the case, then it is high time that world governments devoted more time and money to research into the cause and effect of disasters and how they can be mitigated. This is not to say that disaster research has been ignored, for in certain countries, such as the U.S.A., U.S.S.R. and Japan, funds have long been available to investigate such fields as: disaster perception; explanation; prediction; prevention and control; corrective measures (including building codes); human adaptation and adjustment (sociological studies); and finally disaster relief. It would be instructive to review some of the major developments which have taken place in these various fields of research, although little will be said about the physical explanation of disasters in order to avoid duplication, since this aspect has been thoroughly covered in earlier chapters.

Perception Studies

A great deal of the early research on human perception of natural hazards was carried out in North America in the Universities of Chicago, Toronto, Clark and Colorado by such distinguished scholars as Ian Burton, Kenneth Hewitt, Robert W. Kates and Gilbert F. White. Their interest lay primarily in discovering how people viewed the occurrence or magnitude of the hazard and how they would perceive the alternative opportunities available to them in coping with the hazardous event. Many of their findings have already been incorporated in earlier chapters, so that only a summary will now be necessary.

In the case of earthquakes, it is remarkable how few Californians, for example, regarded seismic hazards as sufficient reason to change their place of abode. This attachment to the cities of San Francisco and Los Angeles has proved to be an over-riding theme, despite the fact that large numbers of respondents had experienced an earthquake and were fully aware of the fact that they lived in an earthquake hazard zone. Somewhat surprisingly, social and economic disadvantages were often judged to be of greater significance in this perceptual minimization of personal vulnerability to the seismic threat.

On turning to perception of volcanic hazards by the citizens of Hawaii, over 90 per cent of those questioned thought that the advantages of living and farming on the fertile soils of the volcano's slopes far outweighed the hazard potential. Almost half of the respondents claimed that they were not worried by the threat and, of the remainder, a large proportion said that they did not fear for their lives but only for their property and their possessions. It is interesting to speculate whether the Hawaiians, accustomed mainly to threats from lava flows, consider that they have plenty of time to escape. A similar perception exercise in a region threatened by ash fall-out or *nuées ardentes* (cf. Martinique) may produce a different result.

Research into perception of hazards due to slope failure – landslides and avalanches – appears to conclude that people avoid the threat once they are aware of it and are less prepared to take a fatalistic attitude than in the case of seismic and volcanic events. This is probably due to a combination of the higher frequency of the hazard, especially in the case of the seasonal avalanche, together with the extreme rapidity of the event. Thus, the inability to evacuate in some instances probably plays a large part in the fears expressed by many respondents. We find, therefore, that relocation of settlement is a frequent manifestation of avalanche hazard zones, whilst in the case of landslides there is often considerable public expenditure involved in remedial measures to allay the fears of the threatened inhabitants, as in the case of Aberfan (Chapter 5) where the National Coal Board undertook the removal of all the offending colliery spoil heaps.

Responses to the dangers of coastal flooding due to storm surges or tsunamis appear to vary according to the wealth of the community involved, for we have already seen how American Gulf Coast dwellers do not relocate their homes but remain in their towns feeling safe in the belief that the United States storm-forecasting system is sufficiently reliable to give them prior warning of danger. In the crowded deltas of Bangladesh, however, people remain for different reasons, partly because of their family ties and strong communal feelings, partly because of land fertility and income from fishing, but largely, one suspects, from the fact that most of them have no choice but to remain in the hazard area. This fatalistic approach was common in more than 90 per cent of the Bangladeshi sample, despite the widespread expectation of further catastrophic cyclones in the near future.

The flood hazard has been shown to be the most destructive event of all in a global context and as long as mankind continues its riparian-settlement behaviour, the hazard will remain. Probably more perception research has been conducted on flood disasters than on any other of the natural catastrophes. It is significant how the individual studies bear out each other's findings that people regard riverside dwellings as remarkably advantageous and are prepared to put up with the occasional disadvantage of an infrequent flood. Indeed, as was shown in Shrewsbury, England, some flood-plain dwellers are either unaware of the threat, or, in other instances, are prepared to forget the hazard, although the majority expect their homes to be flooded again within their lifetime. In one American case study, less than one quarter of the inhabitants of the hazard zone had saved money to deal with a flood contingency, whilst the majority had only started to worry about safety, damage and inconvenience when the actual flood approached. We have already noted (Chapter 8) how virtually the entire population of the frequently inundated Ganges flood-plain regards the devastation as an act of God, about which very little can be done – certainly not by the individuals themselves. In contrast, there are the reactions of Americans who live in the Midwest tornado belt, many of whom are prepared to spend money on structural modifications of their homes (including the building of shelters) in order to protect both life and property. Almost all of these Americans had taken out insurance against wind damage, but it must be remembered that insurance policies against Ganges flooding, even if they were available, would be at prohibitive costs in relation to the average income of the Indian peasant farmer.

We have returned, therefore, to a recognition of the different abilities of rich and poor countries to bolster themselves against hazards, and one final example will serve to illustrate the way in which perception studies highlight this dichotomy. Investigations of the impact of drought in northern Nigeria have demonstrated that in this area drought is not regarded as the most important of the environmental hazards. Shortage of good farming land, damage from locusts, debilitating and fatal diseases and lack of drinking-water wells were together regarded as being of much greater significance to the poor communities, so that one wonders whether preoccupation with problems of the social environment always takes precedence over natural hazards in all the case studies conducted in the developing countries? But the problem is not a simple one, for it has also been suggested that in certain of the world's most advanced urban societies environmental hazards are viewed primarily in terms of traffic noise, aircraft noise, water pollution, industrial and traffic dirt, together with visual intrusion of the built environment, rather than in terms of flooding, storm damage, etcetera. Only when it comes to the question of air pollution do we find that the publicly expressed concern of the urban dweller matches his concern for the other social hazards, and, as we have already seen in Chapters 10 and 11, air pollution is of our own making and is only regarded as a quasi-natural hazard.

Before turning to the problems involved in predictive, preventive and corrective studies, it is instructive to examine briefly the question of over-use of natural fuels in our present global economy, for this falls within the field of air-pollution research and is now thought to threaten severe catastrophic consequences. Such arguments have recently been advanced by American geophysicists who believe that the continued burning of fossil fuels such as coal and oil is likely to produce a warmer climate. They claim that within the space of two hundred years the average global air temperature may be raised by some $6\,^{\circ}C$ ($11\,^{\circ}F$) if carbon dioxide continues to be emitted into the atmosphere at increasing rates. Since the start of the Industrial Revolution the amount of carbon dioxide in the atmosphere has reputedly increased by 13 per cent and this will ultimately have the long-term effect of trapping the sun's heat at the earth's surface – the so-called *greenhouse effect*. In addition to raising sea level about 1 metre, by virtue of the expansion of surface sea-water volume under increased solar heating, it is claimed that substantially increased snowfall in Greenland and Antarctica would generate ice-cap surges into the surrounding oceans, thus raising sea level by a further 5 metres. The effects of such a rise on all the world's coastal cities, including London, New York, Tokyo, Amsterdam and the like, would be disastrous. Whether or not such claims will support the advocates of alternative energy sources remains to be seen!

Predictive, Preventive and Corrective Studies

Research into disaster prediction and mitigation has progressed in different countries with varying intensities over the years, both at local and at national levels. Much of the research has been closely linked with university institutions, although many of their projects have been funded from government sources. In a few instances countries have established their own centralized research centres for disaster prevention and, not surprisingly, the national centre in the hazard-prone islands of Japan was one of the first to be inaugurated. Founded in the early 1960s, Japan's National Research Centre for Disaster Prevention (N.R.C.D.P.) involved several government agencies and was intended partly to collect, coordinate and disseminate information on disaster research and partly to pursue the research itself. Although much of its work has necessarily been involved with earthquakes it has also been concerned with tsunamis, heavy snowfall and river-flood research.

In the United States and Canada disaster research has remained largely in such university institutions as Chicago, Colorado, California and Toronto, although there has been an increasing involvement by their central governments, which has led, for example, to the United States Flood Control Act of 1936 and the United States National Flood Insurance Act of 1968. On the whole, however, the Federal Governments of both Canada and the United States have tended to leave the responsibility for research and preventive measures at the local or regional levels, and it has been demonstrated in fact that there are instances in which, despite the national Government's assumption of responsibility for disaster prevention, there has been no significant improvement in the disaster strategy planning – in some cases the magnitude of the hazard impact has actually increased, largely because the initiative has been taken away from the local authorities (e.g. snowfall hazards in the United States, see Chapter 10). But in the case of particular hazards where the damage potential is extremely high, the Government may be the only agency capable of funding and coordinating the disaster research, so it is often the federal authorities who take control – as in the United States where the National Weather Service is intimately involved in hurricane and tornado prediction. Furthermore, the newly created United States Office of

Emergency Preparedness, which has its organization within the President's Executive Office in Washington D.C., bears overall responsibility for national-disaster contingency plans.

The Soviet Union's disaster strategy, not unexpectedly, is a good deal more centralized than that of most other nations, although it divests some authority to the twenty-nine regions which have been recognized on the basis of various combinations of the expected hazards. These regions have been classified into four groups depending on the magnitude of the combined impact of the hazards: Group 1 includes catastrophic natural hazards that may cause loss of life and great damage to the economy (earthquakes, volcanoes, tsunamis); Group 2 includes destructive natural phenomena that seldom cause deaths, but result in significant damage to the economy, especially industry (earthquakes, avalanches, mudflows, floods and hurricanes); Group 3 includes economically dangerous natural processes (droughts, floods, hurricanes, landslides); Group 4 includes local hazards which can cause damage mainly to agriculture (high winds, rainstorms, frosts, snowstorms).

The British interest in disaster research is a relatively recent phenomenon, although the establishment of a government Disaster Unit and the creation of a ministerial post with responsibility for United Kingdom disaster planning was a significant step taken during the 1970s. Nevertheless, Britain by virtue of her widespread Commonwealth links has always attempted to participate in international ventures of cooperation in matters of disaster relief, prediction and prevention. In recent decades this type of research and knowledge has been coordinated through United Nations agencies who have given much needed technical advice and assistance, especially in the fields of drought and flood hazards, through the auspices of their Food and Agriculture Organization (F.A.O.). In general, however, despite the continuing advice given by the World Meteorological Organization (W.M.O.) and U.N.E.S.C.O.'s assistance with earthquake research, much of the United Nations' past efforts have been concerned with disaster-relief organization *after* the event, rather than with research into predictive and preventive measures. Nevertheless, this failing was in part corrected when, in 1971, the United Nations created a Disaster Relief Office whose job is to investigate disasters and coordinate research into preventive measures in addition to its normal function of organizing relief.

By far the greatest proportion of funds for disaster research has been allocated to seismic investigation, particularly in the fields of prediction and earthquake-proof building design. Recent advances in earthquake research were reviewed in a U.N.E.S.C.O. conference of 1976 in which the theme was the *Assessment and Mitigation of Earthquake Risk*. This followed the inauguration in 1962 of U.N.E.S.C.O.-sponsored earthquake reconnaissance missions to collect data on catastrophic seismic events. During the period 1962–76 no fewer than twenty missions were undertaken to study the aftermath of particularly disastrous earthquakes which killed a total of 116,000 people and caused property damage amounting to $2,550 million. The findings of these field exercises were summarized in the 1976 international conference noted above and it was further reported that the United Nations Development Programme had meanwhile supported the establishment of several international and regional centres for data handling and for training in seismology and earthquake engineering. Much of this training has been received at the special seismic institutes in Tokyo and Skopje, Yugoslavia. Although it recognized that there was an urgent need to move forward from theoretical principles into the actual practical applications of earthquake-resistant designs, the 1976 U.N.E.S.C.O. conference also noted that to date most research had centred primarily on major urban structures. Thus, there was an urgent demand for future research to be aimed more at reducing earthquake damage in (a) rural dwellings constructed by their inhabitants using local materials; and in (b) dwellings for which low incomes had precluded the participation of seismic engineers. For, after all, in the developing countries few if any could afford the expense of specially engineered structures in their house design, and well over half of the earthquake missions referred to above had been involved in seismic disasters in the poorest of the world's countries.

Because of the enormous expense involved in adequate earthquake-proofing of structures it is no surprise to discover that only a handful of nations have taken advantage of the recent advances in earthquake engineering. Foremost amongst these have been the United States and Japan. In the former country two government agencies share earthquake research – the National Oceanic and Atmospheric Administration and the United States Geological Survey – each competing for funds supplied, very largely, by the Federal Government. In President Ford's last budget the 1977 funding for seismic research was doubled for the 1978 fiscal year ($54 million) and was planned to increase to $70 million during 1979. By this time earthquake engineers had reached the stage at which theoretical studies and experimental work:

. . . allow us to build certain configurations of structures in particular materials on selected soils with a fair degree of confidence and without excessive extra cost. The last proviso in that heavily-qualified sentence provides the nub of the question: what degree of security will a building owner pay for? Provision of earthquake-resistance can be divided into two broad issues: deciding on the degree of earthquake risk to accept, and providing the structural performance appropriate to that degree of risk.[3]

The random behaviour of earthquakes, however, makes it almost impossible to assess with any confidence the degree of seismic risk for a particular building. But this is precisely what the customer would like to know, especially if the structure concerned is a hospital, school or major public building. Nevertheless, unless there is a legal ordinance to provide a minimum strength, it is generally too costly to produce buildings which will withstand earthquakes without any structural damage. It is significant that one of the few buildings in the world constructed to withstand an earthquake of magnitude 8.4 on the Richter Scale is a sixty-storey Los Angeles bank. This particular building was built in steel, probably the most suitable for high-seismic-risk zones, but reinforced concrete is another material with good earthquake resistance. Lower degrees of confidence are expressed for precast concrete, masonry walls and finally adobe, which is the most hazardous material of all. Unfortunately, adobe, mud and stone buildings are commonplace in the poorer developing countries so that loss of life from building collapse is proportionately heavier.

An illustration of the contrasting damage resulting from the differences in behaviour of seismic waves was tragically illustrated in the Bucharest earthquake of 1977 (Chapter 2), in which the greatest structural damage was caused to old multi-storey reinforced concrete buildings. Although these had been built long before modern research had had any effect on earthquake engineering design principles, it is now clear that strength requirements in the East European seismic zone which might have been based on Californian research and experience would probably have been dangerously misleading. This is because Californian earthquakes are mainly shallow, with a source only a few kilometres from the surface, whilst the Romanian shock emanated from a source almost 100 kilometres within the crust. As a result, the Romanian earthquake shook most strongly at low frequencies, for which building ordinances are less stringent. Conversely, the high-frequency shaking, which is common in California, and which therefore requires a high degree of earthquake proofing, appeared to create less damage in the Bucharest disaster.

A final note of warning on earthquake engineering serves to demonstrate that we still have a long way to go before complete safety can be guaranteed. In 1978 a Japanese earthquake (magnitude 7.7) caused the concrete walls of so-called earthquake-proof buildings to collapse into the streets of Miyagi, thus being responsible for several of the twenty-two fatalities. Perhaps, being rather too complacent of their very advanced technological expertise, the local authorities had allowed the building of modern, multi-storey blocks, influenced by the fact that an earthquake of similar magnitude in 1936 had caused virtually no damage in the low-rise buildings of the same urban area. In Britain some experts have pointed out that the majority of the high-rise buildings in the United Kingdom would be vulnerable to an earthquake of the magnitude of that which devastated Colchester in 1884, and they further believe that Britain can expect an earthquake of this scale about once every hundred years.

This leads us on to the question of earthquake prediction studies, in which considerable progress has been made in recent years. Many amateur and professional scientists have spent an inordinate number of hours grappling with the statistical periodicity of natural disasters, particularly with those involving earthquakes. As early as the nineteenth-century attempts were being made to link these catastrophic events with astronomical periods, for it was recognized that tidal forces may be a significant trigger mechanism. Apart from tidal effects on the triggering of both volcanic eruptions and minor seismic tremors, however, it has ultimately been found that the correlations are very poor. Thus, by the mid twentieth century, the astro-nomical periodicity correlations had been virtually abandoned after it had been demonstrated that the larger, and therefore the most devastating, earthquakes were quite random in time. Nevertheless, this did not mean that research into earthquake prediction had come to an end, and in 1965 there came a plea that readings should continue to be taken:

... of measured strain, measured stress, atmospheric pressure, tide potential, sea level, microearthquake activity, everything down to the mating habits of fish in the nearby harbour.[4]

These types of measurement were, of course, the ones that had proved so successful in recent Chinese seismic predictions, but during the 1960s a far more scientifically based methodology was beginning to be devised – this was to become known as the *Dilation theory* (see p. 68). First described by two Russian seismologists, A. M. Kondratenko and I. L. Nersesov, the significantly different behaviour of seismic-wave velocities in the period immediately preceding an earthquake soon become the single most import-ant means of earthquake prediction. This was particularly true in so far as the empirical relationship between the total duration of the anomalous wave-travel-time ratio and the magnitude of the resulting earthquake was found to be highly significant. Unfortunately, for the dilation theory to have any chance of success as a predictive tool, it would require an extremely large array of expensive seismic stations, a requirement beyond the means of all but a handful of countries. Furthermore, it has subsequently been discovered that the dilation principle probably doesn't work below depths of 15 kilometres so that many of the deep-focus earthquakes in the Mediterranean, Asia and South America could not be predicted in this way. Thus, apart from a few special cases, such as the San Andreas Fault in California, it seems that the dilation theory as a means of seismic prediction has only a limited value, partly because of its narrow geographical effectiveness and partly due to its high capital-investment costs. Among the countries which suffer catastrophic earthquakes only China, Japan and the United States have the capacity to mount the necessary technological and logistic operations demanded by seismic predictions of this sort.

In Japan predictive research has concentrated on measurement of ground-surface elevation changes in an attempt to establish seismic uplift patterns similar to those of the notorious 'Palmdale Pimple' in California (see p. 351). This involves repeated instrumental levelling and triangulation surveys in which sophisticated laser-beam measurement techniques in electro-optical instruments, known as geodimeters, have been introduced. Additionally, some use is made of seismic tiltmeters and strainmeters which are installed in underground vaults in order to measure crustal deformation. An earthquake prediction programme, under the auspices of the Tokyo Earthquake Research Institute, was funded to the extent of 4,000 million yen ($13 million) for the period 1965–72 – a great deal of money by Japanese research standards – but since an earthquake of the 1923 Kwanto magnitude has been forecast statistically for the Tokyo area in the 1980s any possibility of more accurate predictions would be welcomed wholeheartedly by the Japanese public.

Unlike hurricane, tornado and flood warnings, which are normally issued only a matter of hours or days in advance, earthquake predictions might be published several years ahead. But, paradoxically, the longer the warning the greater are the chances that an ensuing economic and sociological disaster will exceed the costs of the earthquake disaster itself. These are the findings of a research team from the University of Colorado, headed by J. Eugene Haas and Dennis S. Mileti, who point out that seismic prediction may prove to be very beneficial in saving lives and reducing structural damage, but:

. . . it may prove harmful, enabling false alarms to be sounded, causing widespread economic disruption, or encouraging a false sense of security and diverting attention and resources from such loss-reducing strategies as earthquake engineering and land-use planning.[5]

In the threatened area there would be a strong possibility that unemployment would rise dramatically as businesses closed down, whilst property values would fall drastically. Research has also shown that under the seismic threat unscrupulous speculators would move in to buy property at bargain prices, making it impossible for many people to return to re-settle the disaster area at their former living standards. A further complication in earthquake prediction relates to the Government's critical decision on whether to certify a particular prediction in view of the legal liabilities involved. Who, for example, would be responsible for economic losses generated by a false alarm? Furthermore, are the local authorities liable to pay compensation if they ordered the closing of a business or the demolition of a dangerous building before the event? Even in California, where earthquake prediction studies are the most advanced, these questions remain to be answered.

It has already been seen in Chapter 3 how people are attracted to the rich soils of a volcanic terrain, largely because of their high agricultural potential, but also by virtue of population pressure and land hunger elsewhere. This is not only true in the poorer developing countries but also in more prosperous countries such as Italy, where farmers continue to dwell on the hazardous slopes of Vesuvius and Mt Etna. If, however, prediction techniques could be improved and corrective measures be implemented on a larger scale there is no reason why people should not be able to live in volcanic areas with only a modicum of danger.

To date five methods of predicting volcanic eruptions have been employed: topographic surveys; geothermal monitoring; geomagnetic measurements; seismic investigations; and studies of the periodicity of eruptions. One of the most reliable indicators of an impending volcanic outburst is the slow doming or uplift of the land surface, known as *tumescence*, resulting from the accumulation of molten material within the crust. First observed in Japan, more than sixty years ago, this phenomenon can now be measured with a great deal of accuracy by utilizing tiltmeters and geodimeters, just as in the monitoring of seismic doming (p. 381). The presence of magma within the crust can also be detected by measuring the heat which it generates. Recent advances in remote sensing, using infra-red photography obtained from satellites, has had considerable success in recording thermal changes of the ground surface due to subterranean lava injection. This arrival of magma near to the surface also disturbs the geomagnetic properties of the crustal rocks and these, too, can be successfully monitored, as long as the magma reaches to within 2 kilometres of the surface. The eruption of a Japanese volcano, O-Shima, was successfully predicted in this way in 1950, but the method cannot be used in places like Hawaii where the magma remains at considerably greater depths until the actual eruptive phase. The fourth predictive method is one that has been known for centuries, for slight seismic tremors are easily discernible even to the layman. In general, these precursory earthquakes have been found to increase in frequency and magnitude as the eruption approaches, thus leaving no one in doubt that an explosion is about to occur. At least, this was true in the cases of the world's greatest eruptions, such as Vesuvius in 79 A.D. (where seismic tremors persisted for sixteen years prior to the event) or Krakatoa, but in one recent example the seismic activity did *not* lead to an eruption. More is the pity, therefore, that the large-scale, well coordinated evacuations of the population from the hazard zone of La Soufrière in the West Indies in 1971 and again in 1976 were both false alarms (see p. 101). Fully aware that in earlier years failure to take action in good time had precipitated the volcanic disasters of Mt Pelée (1902) and La Soufrière itself (also in 1902, when mud-flows and *nuées ardentes* killed 1,350 inhabitants), the local authorities were taking no chances. One wonders what the island people's reactions will be if a third warning is given in future years, for any hazard prediction must be seen to be reliable if it is to be taken seriously. This is why the fifth and final predictive method – that of forecasting eruption dates from a statistical study of former events – has proved to be fairly unreliable. Vesuvius, for example, is already considerably overdue in respect of its so-called 25–30 year eruptive cycle.

On turning to the problem of mitigating the volcanic hazard, we find that man is about as powerless to influence the event as he is in the case of earth-quakes. The major policy has always been one of evacuation, providing that the warning is given in sufficient time, but generally there is little that can be done to save property. The building of walls or earth barriers to divert lava flows has had a limited success, but oftentimes it merely diverts the hazard onto someone else's property, as in the case of Catania, Sicily (see p. 103). On turning to the more serious menaces of *nuées ardentes* and mudflows, any of the former attempts to build protective embankments have usually been wasted effort, since the speed and fluidity of the 'flow' have overwhelmed every obstacle as if they had been non-existent. The only possible way of minimizing these risks by corrective measures appears to be one of a highly accurate aerial bombing of the vent in order to divert the *nuées* and mudflows into safer escape routes.

In Chapters 4 and 6 it has been seen how deformation of the ground sur-face, either by natural tectonic forces or by the vagaries of mankind, has often resulted either in triggering existing hazards or producing a new set of hazards of a different kind. Changes of level in a landsurface may sometimes have no serious effect on a community, except in the case of a sudden seismic rupture which is almost certain to cause casualties and severe property damage. In other instances, however, even a gradual long-term change of level may pose a threat to the continued existence of a community, especially if this happens to be located on or near to a coastline. Centuries of slow isostatic sinking, in such regions as the southern North Sea and the Po delta, have placed in jeopardy many of the ancient urban settlements which have grown up along their shores. But it must also be remembered that coastal areas have always been zones of natural hazard and yet people continue to be lured to the shore for a variety of socio-economic reasons. In America, for example, more than one third of the United States population are coastal dwellers, despite the contention that:

... shorefront residents must come to terms with a number of serious physical problems. In addition to coastal erosion these include wind damage, flooding, tsunamis, landslips and surface instability, fragile vegetation associations, high levels of soil and atmospheric salinity, salt water encroachment into aquifers or brackish lagoons and readily polluted substrata.[6]

In the Netherlands the Dutch have long been aware of these hazards and have spent heavily over the centuries on coming to terms with them. In Britain, an awakening to the increasing threat of coastal flooding and an imminent disastrous inundation of London itself has taken a great deal longer, so that large-scale remedial measures were not undertaken until the 1960s and 1970s. In Venice too, both the local authorities and the national Government have been slow to act, in the face of mounting international criticism. But in the coastal communities of Bangladesh and India, who face the persistent hazards of flooding from violent cyclones, the problem of remedial measures is so vast that it is virtually impossible to resolve. Even in the wealthier nations of the world coastal defence works that have any likelihood of significant success have been built only in a few localities and even then at a phenomenal financial cost. Nevertheless, a large number of adjustments are available to modify the hazards of coastal flooding and coastal erosion and these are illustrated in Figure 114. In the majority of cases these will suffice to modify all but the most severe storms or tsunamis and will probably prevent considerable loss of life even if not of property. In recent years substantial advances have been made in the world's storm-warning communication systems whilst a recent discovery has helped scientists to predict more accurately the direction and timing of tsunami sea waves. It has now become possible to monitor the low-frequency sound waves sent up into the air by earthquakes thereby disturbing the ionosphere.

Adjustments to loss	Modifications of loss potential	Modifications of erosion hazard	Adjustments affecting hazard cause
Loss bearing	Storm warning and evacuation systems	Regulations against destruction of dune vegetation	Prohibition of beach excavation and harbour dredging
Public assistance	Public purchase of threatened land	Emergency filling and grading	Reduction in soil conservation activities
Insurance		Beach nourishment	Storm track modification
	Zoning for open space and low density uses	Dune stabilization	Removal of dams on rivers
	Planning maps	Grading slopes	Biological control of erosion-causing fauna
		Sluices, Bulkheads, seawalls, and revetments	
	Subdivision regulations, building codes, orders and ordinances	Breakwaters, tetrapods, artificial seaweed, bubble break-waters	
	Moving endangered structures	Groynes	
	Installing deep piling		
	Landfill		
	Planned unit developments		

Fig. 114. Adjustments to the hazards of Coastal flooding and erosion (after J. K. Mitchell).

Since these sound waves travel faster than the tsunami itself, a study of the ionospheric disturbance patterns has speeded up the forecasting process.

Deformation of the ground surface by man's activities is, in general, something which can be arrested or at least alleviated once the cause of the problem has been recognized. Thus, subsidence from water or mineral extraction can usually be dealt with once it can be demonstrated that public security and interest is more important than the economic return in the cost-benefit equation. In some instances, of course, if abstraction is not halted the hazard which has been generated may destroy the mining operation itself – as was threatened in parts of the Long Beach section of the Wilmington oil field, California (Chapters 6 and 11). In recent years the environmental lobbies in various countries have achieved significant success in pressurizing their governments into introducing stricter mining ordinances, in the belief that the social and cultural benefits are of more importance than the value of the abstracted resource. Unfortunately, in a few instances the policy change came too late to safeguard property.

Studies of mass-movement have led some authorities to the conclusion that:

> Landslides and related phenomena such as mudflows, earthflows, rockfalls, snow or debris avalanches, and subsidence are natural events that would occur with or without human activity. However, human use and interest has led to both an *increase* in some of these events . . . and a *reduction* of landslides by stabilizing structures or techniques on naturally sensitive slopes . . .[7]

The above quotation makes it quite clear that in the opinion of some experts the majority of disasters related to slope instability are natural events and that man has probably exacerbated the process only in a number of critical areas. Disaster research in the field of slope stability probably occupies more people than in the case of all other hazards except floods, for landslides and avalanches are fairly commonplace both in time and space. A knowledge of soil mechanics, rock structures, hydrology and even meteorology is a requirement of the modern civil engineer, who now finds it essential to understand not only crustal and surface processes but also the vagaries of the atmosphere as well. As in the other fields of disaster research, experts have: first, to understand the principles involved; secondly, to identify the areas at risk; thirdly, to design where possible structures to prevent the occurrence of the disaster; fourthly, to develop policies to control or ameliorate the hazard if prevention is impossible; and, finally, to attempt to predict the magnitude and timing of the threat itself.

Risk maps for landslide hazards have become increasingly important planning tools in land-use zoning studies, so that in most instances modern building development plans have avoided high-risk areas. Alternatively, remedial measures have been undertaken in order to eliminate the risks, and since most of these measures have been described in Chapter 5 repetition is unnecessary. The same is true in the case of avalanches, although there are, as yet, no avalanche zoning ordinances in Canada and the United States, in contrast to Switzerland where the avalanche risk is proportionately greater. Thus, the Swiss have spent considerable sums of money not only on settlement relocation but also on protective measures such as snow barriers in order to safeguard their communications and property. But permanent structures such as these are extremely costly and are only likely to be implemented on rare occasions in less affluent countries even though their avalanche hazards are equally severe. In the Andean countries of South America, for example, it is quite unlikely that even temporary corrective measures (e.g. explosives for avalanche triggering) will be adopted on a large scale. It is significant, perhaps, that avalanche research in both Europe and North America has been closely geared to the seasonal activity of winter sporting activities such as skiing.

On more than one occasion we have noted that floods are the greatest killer of all the environmental hazards currently under investigation. In past centuries mankind has sought riverine situations for his livelihood and settlement for a variety of economic reasons, and as a result has often suffered the disastrous consequences. In earliest times man was able to develop a strategy whereby he moved to higher ground during threats of flooding and it is only in recent centuries that we have witnessed a reversal of this policy of temporary migration. Paradoxically, this change has largely been the result of technological progress in which modern man, more concerned with effects than causes, has placed undue reliance on flood-control structures, has therefore been encouraged to re-settle the flood-plain and has virtually ignored the root of the flood hazard:

> In the main the real cause of damage is faulty land management and unwise governmental programmes, which in turn usually result from a failure of decision-makers to understand or apply rational planning precepts about riverine and estuarine systems.[8]

From this it follows that to mitigate future flood hazards it will be necessary to rethink our piecemeal strategy more in terms of multiple-purpose river-basin planning, along the lines of the much publicized 1969 United Nations report on *Integrated River Basin Development*. In order for it to be successful, flood prediction must depend on a very wide integrated knowledge of hydrological, meteorological and pedological information covering the entire catchment area, which in turn calls for a considerable amount of field observation and measurement. Because there is usually greater human occupancy in the lower reaches of large river systems, at first sight it would seem imperative that flood forecasts for these reaches should be of greater reliability than for the sparsely peopled headwater zone. Nevertheless it is this critical upstream zone where the flood is usually spawned, so that it is equally important to have an accurate understanding of headwater conditions. As we have seen in the case of other environmental hazards, only the more prosperous countries can afford first, to monitor the stream system effectively enough to provide all the necessary data; secondly, to pay for the technical expertise; and finally, to install the essential communication system to transmit the flood warning. Conversely, the less developed countries will have to suffice on incomplete data, poorer interpretation and a generally unsatisfactory flood-warning system. But even in the most advanced countries ineffectual watershed management, such as over-grazing or indiscriminate forest clearance, combined with poor operational control of the existing remedial structures can culminate in a disaster, as shown by the catastrophic Arno floods in Italy in 1966 (Chapter 8).

It was seen in Figure 79 that there is a wide range of possible adjustments to the flood hazard, including a long list of engineering works to modify the flood. It is undue reliance on these flood-control devices, however, which appears to have exacerbated the problem in the United States, where investigations have demonstrated that since the Federal Government adopted a structurally orientated flood-control programme in 1937 the endangered population is at greater risk than before – and this after an expenditure of some $12,000 million! Although remedial structures give short-term local relief, flood research has suggested that the dams, channels and levees may have caused more long-term problems than they have solved. Levee construction on the Mississippi, for example, may actually have worsened the flood hazard. Critics of the so-called 'flood-structure strategy', where it is used without any other form of river-basin management, have used four principal arguments to justify their case: first, it encourages human occupation of the flood-plain; secondly, it causes unnecessary loss of valuable resources; thirdly, it discourages economic land use; and finally, it is not cost effective. In any future development there seems little excuse to build houses or factories on high-risk flood-plains even where there has been great expenditure on flood-protection schemes, for this will merely postpone the day of reckoning and make the inevitable disaster more severe. In the case of existing settlements, however, these arguments are inapplic-able so that in most of the world's older riparian towns and cities there must be a continuing attempt to modify the urban susceptibility to damage from flooding. Where relocation of buildings is impossible it may be essential to adopt any number of flood-proofing measures (see Figure 79). Otherwise flood-insurance schemes might be the only alternative, and such beliefs were probably instrumental in pressing the United States Government to implement their 1969 Flood Insurance Act, whereby the Federal Government guarantees a flood-insurance subsidy to those who were willing to adopt new flood-plain management practices.

On turning to look at current research into disasters generated by vagaries in weather and climate, it is not surprising to discover that there is a vast amount of investigation going on not only into the forecasting of weather but also into its modification. In the last decade or so great advances have been made in the field of hurricane and tornado warnings, partly as a result of the widespread introduction of computers to aid in rapid interpretation and partly from more sophisticated techniques of communication. Consequently, in countries such as Japan and U.S.A., there have been marked decreases in the number of fatalities from violent storms. Nevertheless, there has been no abatement in either the magnitude or the frequency of the storms themselves, so that property damage has continued to escalate. It is not surprising, therefore, that a good deal of the current meteorological research in hazard-prone countries is being devoted to weather modification.

Hurricanes and related tropical storms remain the most destructive of the atmospheric hazards in view of their widespread and prolonged violence, so that many experiments are being conducted on storm modification by means of cloud seeding (see p. 246). It has been demonstrated that successful seeding tends to lessen the wind speeds, but this is achieved only by increasing precipitation in specific areas. An increase in the volume of rainfall may, of course, create a flood hazard whilst at the same time depriving neighbouring regions of their essential water requirements. Thus, there is a certain amount of reluctance to seed storms, partly through fear of inducing secondary hazards and partly because of the legal liabilities involved. A cloud-seeding exercise carried out in the Sierra Nevada, California, in 1955, for example, was responsible for an important legal action brought by property owners following disastrous flooding of Yuba City, where damage exceeded $65 million. It was claimed by the plaintiffs that the hydro-electricity generating company and their weather consultants had contributed to the magnitude of the flooding by negligence and were therefore liable for damages. Although the judge ruled that these specific organizations were not legally liable he found that the State of California must recompense for damages because of its failure to maintain the river levees. The litigation, therefore, raised important questions of public policy concerning weather modification, and since many experts believe that, contrary to popular supposition, seeding will not destroy hurricanes, nor change their tracks, nor significantly affect rainfall totals, there are those who ask if storm modification is worthwhile.

Nevertheless, it has been suggested that a similar seeding of cumulo-nimbus clouds associated with tornadoes might modify their intensity or at least shorten the tornado's life. Thunder clouds, of the type which generate 'twisters', have in fact been dispersed by downwash created from modified jet aircraft flying through the cloud tops. But in general there remains a feeling that:

Actual modification attempts on menacing tornadoes are probably several years away. In the meantime, we should seek improved building codes and construction practices, and continue research into the actual morphology of convective vortices.[9]

As in the case of hurricanes and tornadoes, there seems to be little hope of making major modifications to the intensity or duration of either snowfall or fog, although we have now reached the stage at which local fog can be dispersed at specific locations, particularly at international airports. Thus, in the general field of transport hazards it might be more realistic to concentrate on more reliable forecasting, allied with continuing attempts to modify the loss burden by improving the safety factor of the vehicles themselves. Already car manufacturers are experimenting with radar-like devices which would enable drivers to anticipate motorway accidents due to fog, since static hazard-warning lights have had only a limited effect.

Any attempt to predict climatic change or to modify climate involves problems of an altogether different scale, and despite the considerable amount of funding for research in these fields it seems unlikely that there will be any significant advances for some time to come. Consequently, it seems likely that permafrost and drought will continue to burden specific climatic zones of the world for the foreseeable future. Even a grandiose scheme such as the Trans-Alaska pipeline (Chapter 6) is still bedevilled with problems of severe permafrost-induced ground movement, whilst desalination projects and plans to tow polar icebergs to the Middle East (Chapter 9) can only be regarded as limited exercises to solve local problems. Despite their remarkably ingenious technology, such exercises are so costly that only a handful of countries could afford to adopt them. Drought is such a widespread hazard in some of the world's developing countries, however, that research efforts have been multiplied in an attempt to avoid the disastrous bouts of starvation which have recently decimated the lives and livestock of Africa's Sahelian population. Chapter 9 includes descriptions of the ways in which various countries have adopted different types of adjustments, ranging from bans on grazing and firewood gathering to monumental water resource programmes, such as the Egyptian New Valley project (see Figure 88). Of the major water-conservation programmes, one in particular is worthy of further comment because of the questions which it raises in the field of environmental pollution. The project has been reported from the U.S.S.R. where Russian scientists are advocating an increasing use of peaceful nuclear explosions in order to create artificial underground water-storage reservoirs. In fact one such reservoir has already been created by *nuclear engineering* in the arid heart of Soviet Asia and it has been claimed that the surface evaporation has been virtually eliminated whilst at the same time valuable land has been retained for agriculture. Needless to say, fears have been voiced outside the Soviet Union that not only groundwater but the atmosphere itself will be seriously contaminated if this programme is continued, to say nothing of the earthquakes which might be inadvertently triggered-off. Because of the threat of radioactive contamination most other nations have proceeded with considerable caution in the field of *nuclear engineering* and it remains to be seen whether northern Africa's problems can be solved by these means. It is significant that the United States, after conducting a series of experiments of its own, has abandoned its peaceful nuclear testing programme, largely because of the difficulties of containing the radiation hazard. We have already seen how mankind has created more than enough air-pollution problems without adding to them in this manner.

Research into Human Response and Adjustment in the face of Disaster

During a recent U.N.E.S.C.O. conference on mitigation of earthquake risk there was a concerted call for the strongest degree of interdisciplinary co-operation between the natural, human, social and engineering sciences, and this plea can be extended into the broader field of geography, which studies, amongst other things, man's behavioural response to all environmental hazards. Perhaps spurred on by the plethora of disaster studies which appeared during the holocaust of the Second World War, research into the social-behavioural aspects of catastrophic events has mushroomed in post-war years. Foremost amongst the research workers in this field of the sociology of disasters have been Professors E. L. Quarantelli and R. R. Dynes of the Disaster Research Center at the Ohio State University, who have attempted to differentiate the specific research areas. The following are included in their impressive list of topics already being pursued: decision-making in crises; the operation of civil defence in natural disasters; the functioning of expanding organizations in community disasters; community functions under disaster conditions; warning systems in disasters; community conflict in natural disasters; looting behaviour; panic behaviour; and medical services.

Amongst the findings from all this research into human response and adjustment to catastrophic events Quarantelli and Dynes were able to identify a number of myths. One of the most common is the widely held belief that when faced with a hazardous situation most people will panic, but this was found to be generally untrue, since one of the greatest difficulties appears to be getting people to move rather than having to prevent disorderly flight in a panic situation. Studies have shown, furthermore, that the people who do leave tend to be visitors and tourists, as the majority of the inhabitants do not wish to be evacuated. One result of this mistaken belief is the suggestion that local authorities are loath to issue disaster warnings until the very last moment, fearing that an irrational panic may be almost as catastrophic as the disaster itself. This type of argument has frequently been quoted with reference to the predicted high mortality rate of freeway traffic accidents in Los Angeles or San Francisco in the event of an earthquake warning. A second myth is thought to be the common belief that:

> . . . shock leaves the victims dazed and disoriented, unable to cope with the immediate task of recovery, dependent on outside help from the Red Cross. They are also supposed to suffer permanent emotional damage from the trauma of the disaster. The evidence suggests that this image is false.[10]

Research has revealed that only a small minority of people exhibit a shock reaction after a catastrophic event and that this so-called *disaster syndrome* (largely in the form of apathy) does not last for long. Two further myths, that post-disaster looting may be a serious problem and that outside relief agencies underestimate the basic food and clothing resources that still remain available in the stricken area, may only be true of more affluent countries such as the United States. It is arguable, however, that in most nations looting and loss of possessions may still pose major problems, in so far as human response to a disaster will vary according to the degree of social organization and the availability of wealth (Plate 57). Even in the Communist world, where community discipline is of paramount importance, the impact of flooding or severe drought in China, or an earthquake in Romania (see Chapter 2), can nevertheless become a major setback to the national economy:

> These blows are hard to accept psychologically for governments, scientists, managers and all those who have become accustomed to applying a powerful technology with a confidence that problems can be solved.[11]

Broadly speaking, national governments' reactions to a disaster can be divided into two types of adjustments: first, those who are able to cope with the aftermath and, secondly, those who are unable to recover without international aid, though political ideology sometimes blurs the boundary. In general, it has been the policy of the Communist world to deal with all disasters internally, spurning offers of external assistance, as was the case in the devastating 1976 Chinese earthquake. Individual adjustments, however, differ considerably, depending on such variables as the magnitude and swiftness of the disaster, together with all the contrasts in sociological, economic, religious and cultural backgrounds.

57. A policeman stands watch against looters during flooding in Cambridge, Ontario, Canada.

One of the most significant behavioural responses to a disaster is that which sees a change in the ethics of the society in question. Disaster research has shown that in some instances previously unaccepted practices such as theft, prostitution or even cannibalism become acceptable, or in other instances the trauma brings out remarkable feats of heroism. Some cases of antisocial behaviour in the aftermath of disasters (such as widespread looting, or the murdering and robbing of Japanese victims by Korean urban gangs after the 1923 Tokyo earthquake) have been explained as the unleashing of the grievances of underprivileged minority groups. Conversely, there are numerous records of generosity and unselfishness, as was the case after the 1953 Waco tornado disaster in the United States when injured people carried on helping others for several days. There are also many examples of unscrupulous exploitation by a few individuals who aim to capitalize on the disaster. This is frequently true in the case of famines induced by drought or floods, when starving people are forced to buy food at inflated prices. The report of the Commission of Enquiry into the 1943–44 Bengal famine, for example, revealed that for every death due to starvation some 1,000 rupees excess profit was made by the grain dealers. Regrettably, one is forced to conclude that following in the wake of every disaster there will continue to be reports of corruption, selfishness and inefficiency.

Disaster Relief

There is no doubt that disaster relief is now a well-organized, large-scale phenomenon, dealing with scores of catastrophic situations annually. Equally, despite their magnificent assistance, rendered in all types of stressful situations, it would be wrong to disguise the fact that the world's disaster-relief organizations have also come in for a certain amount of criticism. The newly formed research-oriented International Disaster Institute has recently joined the ranks of those who believe that some of these organizations not only fail to comprehend the true requirements of disaster relief in general but sometimes duplicate the efforts of other agencies in particular situations:

. . . the voluntary agencies, like everyone else, must start becoming accountable, not only to their donors, but also to the people they are helping. The sad irony is that in all major disasters there are surplus supplies of unused materials and money.[12]

It has been claimed, for example, that after the 1976 Guatemalan earthquake, though the Red Cross sent in thousands of tents, less than ten of them were occupied, thus revealing an underestimate of the victims' rate of recovery and their ability to construct temporary dwellings. In fact some 50,000 makeshift shelters had been constructed within twenty-four hours of the earthquake. Such provocative statements will, of course, continue to inflame the relationships between the experienced and long-established relief organizations and the innovative, newly formed disaster-research units, many of which are headed by groups of academic scientists and economists. The Directors of Oxfam, Christian Aid and the Save the Children Fund quickly refuted the recent criticisms, pointing out that the coordination and cooperation between British voluntary organizations was much better organized than is generally known. There is, for instance, a Disasters Emergency Committee, on which there are representatives from the six major voluntary agencies, and which exists solely to coordinate and implement the British relief efforts, once their field mission has sent back a balanced assessment of the aid required in the disaster-stricken area.

It is not generally realized that there are two types of disaster-relief operations – those which deal with the short-term problems during the *recuperation phase*, and those concerned with the more laborious process of rebuilding in the longer-term *recovery phase*. During the immediate post-disaster period the agencies are primarily concerned with problems of disease, injury, food and clothing shortages and with insufficient shelter. This recuperation phase is generally hampered by an inadequacy of information and communication and occasionally by anti-social behaviour (looting, etcetera) or by ghoulish throngs of sensation seekers. The long-term recovery phase is the one which endeavours to bring the stricken community back to its former level of existence. Thus, although immediate post-disaster assistance will always be rendered, a much greater proportion of the aid is normally reserved for this second, recovery, phase during which attempts are made to re-establish schools, health clinics and community centres and to inaugurate redevelopment schemes and job-training programmes. Despite the theoretical distinction between the two relief phases, in practice there is a certain amount of overlap, as in the case of housing renewal which, although part of the long-term recovery programme, effectively begins with the clearing of the debris.

Much of the confusion and apparent inefficiency which follows in the wake of a disaster often stems from lack of information and a breakdown in communication systems due to damage or destruction. Hence the criticism of the relief organizations, who are often hindered by wrong information and the throng of well-meaning but badly organized volunteers who swamp the hastily organized emergency centres. Because of the great variety of the requirements which may exist, it would be wise for any community in a hazardous area to have a range of contingency plans already prepared:

By preparing a post-disaster plan in anticipation of an extreme event, search procedures can be considerably improved over the makeshift operations that generally exist today.[13]

Nevertheless, many of these local-government plans may be thwarted by events, not least of which may be the arrival of foreign aid. Paradoxically, if some of the voluntary agencies from overseas refuse to work within the guidelines already laid down by the local officials they can actually make things worse. After the 1976 Guatemalan earthquake, for instance, so much food was imported that local farmers were almost bankrupted by the fall in the price of corn. Furthermore, so many of the drugs which had been flown into the stricken area were either out of date, totally unsuitable or simply not required, that many of them had to be destroyed by the Guatemalan medical authorities. This problem of unrequested and unwanted aid is one that is constantly being deplored by the United Nations Disaster Relief Organization, in its attempts to coordinate international aid and to avoid wholesale dumping of rubbish or duplication of resources. But in practice foreign governments often act unilaterally, sometimes inspired by altruistic motives, and at other times by political ideology.

On turning to the field of housing reconstruction in the aftermath of a disaster, we discover that here, too, the efforts of relief agencies are sometimes found to be misplaced. There appears to be a general unawareness that in the developing countries most survivors are normally capable of providing adequate temporary shelter whilst they rebuild their shattered homes. Furthermore, house building in such countries is much more rapid than in the developed nations, because of the more acceptable lower standards of construction. It has been suggested, therefore, that the role of relief organizations should be related to the provision of low-technology tools and materials, together with a re-training of the local tradesmen in the techniques of safer building. In earthquake-prone areas, for example, the continued use of stone and adobe as building materials must be discouraged, but only if *suitable* alternative building materials can be made available. Already, there are records that ill-fated polyurethane huts were being supplied by relief agencies following recent disasters and that they were almost totally rejected on cultural as well as on practical grounds. Furthermore, these pre-fabricated homes were found not only to be too costly, but also incapable of generating local employment. Because of this type of evidence, and because it is now being realized that many of the disaster survivors deplore the overt paternalism which sometimes generates apathy, bitterness and unrest, there have even been suggestions that external aid should be rejected and all effort concentrated on self help, as in the case of China, Mexico and the Philippines. Such beliefs have been summarized as follows by Professor Otto Koenigsberger:

There are really four principles. 1. Relief is the enemy of reconstruction. Therefore minimize relief. 2. Even the minimal relief operation stretches the public-sector executive capacity to the utmost. Therefore avoid paternalism. 3. Under the immediate impact of a disaster people are ready to change. Therefore act quickly to introduce improved construction methods and bye-laws. 4. Quick action means planned action. It is no good making plans after the event.[14]

Man, as a rational being, has the capability of anticipating environmental hazards, measuring the degree of their impact and alleviating their consequences. He also has the ability to create a different set of hazards in addition

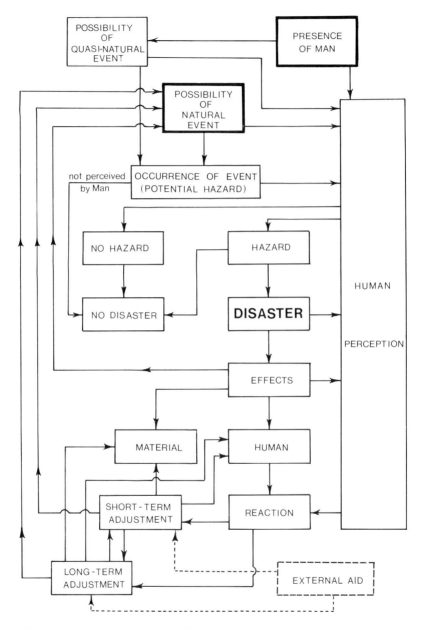

Fig. 115. A general systems model to illustrate the effect of environmental hazards and the possible adjustments to a disaster.

to provoking disasters by his careless exploitation of natural resources. As far as the majority of environmental stresses are concerned, however, man has virtually no control and it would seem logical, therefore, that he should avoid the most severe hazard zones. But due to population pressure, to a demand for mineral wealth and new sources of energy, or even to a desire for a spectacular view, people will continue to encounter hazards so that disasters will still occur. And so the toll of life and the costs of property destroyed by these catastrophic events climb steadily upwards when taken on a global scale, although we have seen that in the developed world there is a pattern of declining deaths but escalating property-loss rates. Overall, the absolute costs of disasters are usually heaviest for those least able to pay so that the human response to a hazard is not only a function of the hazard itself, but is also related to the prosperity of the particular nation or group. Consequently, there will be varying adjustments to the hazard, ranging from attempts to modify the natural process itself, through a variety of remedial measures aimed at ameliorating the loss burden, down to the fatalistic option of doing nothing. Thus, although the human response to environmental hazards is flexible, it is possible to distinguish a *general systems model* which illustrates the complex relationship between man and the natural systems (Figure 115). It will be seen from this how a natural event may or may not produce a disaster, depending upon the different degrees of magnitude of the perceived hazard. The model also depicts how human reactions to the disaster are followed by adjustments, either short-term or long-term, both of which can be affected by disaster relief from external sources. It will also be seen how the long-term and short-term adjustments are often designed to lessen the impact of future hazards, which leads back through the circuit to the initial possibility of the occurrence of a natural event.

Whatever the nature of the environmental hazard and whatever the cultural or political nature of the society, a model of the sort illustrated in Figure 115 may help to give a greater understanding of the complexities involved in mankind's eternal struggle with his hazardous environment on planet Earth.

References

Chapter 1: Environmental Hazards

1. Kates, R. W. (1976) in: Wapner, S., Cohen, S. B. and Kaplan, B. (1976), *Experiencing the Environment*, Plenum Press, New York, p. 140.
2. Scheidegger, A. E. (1975), *Physical Aspects of Natural Catastrophes*, Elsevier, Amsterdam, p. 2.
3. Tucker, Anthony (1976), *Guardian*, 18 May 1976.
4. Davies, D., editor of *Nature* (1976), letter to *The Times*, 21 August 1976.
5. Tucker, Anthony (1978), *Guardian*, 22 February 1978.
6. International Disaster Institute (1978), publicity material issued from 85 Marylebone High Street, London W1M 3DE.

Chapter 2: Earthquakes

1. *Report of the State Earthquake Investigation Commission on the California Earthquake of April 18th 1906.*
2. Oxburgh, E. R. (1974), 'The Plain Man's Guide to Plate Tectonics', *Proceedings of the Geologists' Association*, **85**, p. 353.
3. *Henry IV*, I, iii, 1.
4. Brodie, Ian (1976), reporting an interview in Los Angeles with Dr C. F. Richter for the *Daily Telegraph*, 16 August 1976.
5. Anderson, D. L. (1976), *Frontiers of Knowledge: Earthquakes, Volcanoes, Climate and the Rotation of the Earth*, paper presented to the 56th Annual Meeting of the International Geophysical Union.

Chapter 3: Volcanoes

1. Mrs Prentiss (1902) in: Francis, P. (1976), *Volcanoes*, Penguin, Harmondsworth, p. 84.
2. Thompson, Assistant Purser (1902) in: Bullard, F. M., *Volcanoes, In History, in Theory, in Eruption* (1962), University of Texas Press, Austin.
3. Arnoux, R. (1902), in: Francis, P. (1976), *Volcanoes*, Penguin, Harmondsworth, p. 86.
4. Dion Cassius in: Bullard, F. M. (1962), *op. cit.*, p. 146.
5. Francis, P. (1976), *op. cit.*, pp. 207–8.

Chapter 4: Sinking Coastlines

1. Buckland, D. (1820), *Vindiciae Geologicae*, Oxford, p. 24.

2. Steers, J. A. (1964), *The Coastline of England and Wales*, Cambridge University Press, second edition, p. 401.
3. Jansen, P. Ph. ed. (1972), *The Tide Goes Out*, Zuid-Nederlandsche Drukkerij N. V., p. 5.

Chapter 5: Landslides and Avalanches

1. Erickson, E., and Plafker, G. (1970), in: *Keesing's Contemporary Archives*, 1–8 August 1970, p. 24112.
2. Casaverde, M. (1970), in: Bolt, B. A. *et al.* (1975), *Geological Hazards*, Springer-Verlag, Berlin, p. 39.
3. Brock, R. W. (1910), extract from a letter addressed to Canadian Coal Consolidated Ltd in: Coates, D. R., ed. (1974), *Environmental Geomorphology and Landscape Conservation*, Vol. 2, Urban Areas, Dowden, Hutchinson and Ross Inc., Stroudsberg, p. 226.
4. Brock, R. W. (1910), in: Coates, D. R., ed., (1974), *op. cit.*, p. 227.
5. So, C. L. (1971), 'Mass Movements associated with the Rainstorm of June 1966 in Hong Kong', *Transactions of the Institute of British Geographers*, **53**, p. 64.
6. Ward Lock Guide (1926–27), *A Pictorial and Descriptive Guide to Folkestone, Sandgate, Hythe, etc.* eighth edition, Ward, Lock & Co., London, p. 43.
7. Leggett, R. F. (1962), *Geology and Engineering*, second edition, McGraw-Hill, New York, p. 425.
8. Report of the Tribunal Appointed to Inquire into the Disaster at Aberfan, in: Bolt, B. A. *et al.* (1975), *op. cit.*, pp. 184–5.

Chapter 6: Ground Surface Collapse

1. Vitruvius (first century B.C.).
2. Leggett, R. F. (1973), *Cities and Geology*, McGraw-Hill, New York, p. 206.
3. Brackett, W. R. (1964), in 'Foreword' to: *Mining Subsidence: A Survey*, College of Estate Management, London, p. 1.

Chapter 7: High Winds

1. White, Anne (1974), 'Global Summary of Human Response to Natural Hazards: Tropical Cyclones', in: White, G. F., ed. (1974), *Natural Hazards, Local, National, Global*, Oxford University Press Inc., New York, p. 257.
2. Wigg, Richard (1977), in: *The Times*, 25 November 1977.
3. English translation by the Church Historians of England (1856).
4. Sanchez, P. (1974).

Chapter 8: Floods

1. Beyer, J. L. (1974), 'Global Summary of Human Response to Natural Hazards: Floods', in: White, G. F., ed. (1974), *Natural Hazards, Local, National, Global*, Oxford University Press Inc., New York, p. 267.
2. Reported in Brooks, C. E. P., and Glasspoole, J. (1928), *British Floods and Droughts*, Ernest Benn, p. 83.

Chapter 9: Drought

1. Eckholm, E., and Brown, L. R. (1977), in: American Geographic Society, *Focus*, **28**, No. 1, p. 2.

2. Huntington, Ellsworth (1917), 'Climatic Change and Agricultural Exhaustion as Elements in the Fall of Rome', *The Quarterly Journal of Economics*, **31**, p. 200.

3. Elkington, John (1976), 'Desertification: a Leprosy of the Soil', *New Scientist*, 14 October 1976, p. 108.

4. Hastings, A. C. G. (1925), *Nigerian Days*, John Lane, p. 111.

5. Miewald, Robert (1977), *Time*, 7 March 1977, p. 55.

6. Mortimore, M. (1973), in: Dalby, D., and Harrison-Church, R. J., eds., *Report of the 1973 Symposium on Drought in Africa*, Centre for African Studies, Society of Oriental and African Studies, University of London.

7. Le Houerou, H. N. (1975), *Nature and Causes of Desertization*, Paper presented at a Symposium in the University of Cambridge, September 1975, p. 14.

8. Belitzky, Boris (1976), 'Atomic Blasts to Save the Caspian', *New Scientist*, 15 January 1976, p. 122.

Chapter 10: Snow and Fog

1. Holford, I. (1976), *British Weather Disasters*, David & Charles, Newton Abbot.

2. Regan, Edward (1977), reported by Ian Ball in the *Daily Telegraph*, 2 February 1977.

3. Moorhouse, Geoffrey (1963), *The Long Winter 1962–3*, A Guardian Pamphlet, Manchester Guardian & Evening News Ltd.

4. Willett, H. G. (1976), 'The Sun as a Maker of Weather and Climate', *Technology Review*, January 1976, p. 47.

5. Debelius, H. (1977), in: *The Times*, 29 March 1977.

6. G.B. Committee on Air Pollution (1953, 1955), in: Heinemann, H. (1961), *Air Pollution*, World Health Organization, p. 173.

7. Nature–Time's News Service (1977), referring to *Nature*, **269**, p. 569.

8. World Health Organisation (1964).

9. Marsh, A. (1959), International Clean Air Conference, London, *Proceedings of the Diamond Jubilee International Clean Air Conference (1959)*, Published by the National Society for Clean Air, 1960.

10. Brodine, V. (1971), *Air Pollution*, Harcourt Brace Jovanovich Inc., New York, p. 16.

11. Rooney, J: F. (1967), 'The Urban Snow Hazard in the United States: An Appraisal of Disruption', *Geographical Review*, **57**, pp. 550 and 557.

Chapter 11: Hazard City - A Case Study of Los Angeles

1. Banham, Reyner (1971), *Los Angeles: The Architecture of Four Ecologies*, Allen Lane, The Penguin Press.

2. Robinson, W. W. (1968), *Los Angeles, A Profile*, University of Oklahoma Press, Norman.

3. Pakiser, L. C. *et al.* (1969), 'Earthquake Prediction and Control', p. 103 in: Tank, R. W. (1976), *Focus on Environmental Geology*, second edition, Oxford University Press Inc., New York.

4. Nelson, H. J., and Clark, W. A. V. (1976), *The Los Angeles Metropolitan Experience*, Ballinger, Cambridge, Massachusetts, p. 16.

5. Biggar, Richard (1959), *Flood Control in Metropolitan Los Angeles*, University of California Press (Publications Political Science), Berkeley, **6**, pp. 2–3.

6. Wilcock, D. N., Birch, B. P., and Cantor, L. M. (1977), 'Changing Attitudes to Water Resource Development', *Geography*, **62**, p. 136.

7. Patterson and Henein (1972), 'Urban Development', *Ecology and Environmental Planning*, p. 38, Table 3.1.

Chapter 12: Disaster Research

1. Wisner, Ben, Westgate, Ken, and O'Keefe, Phil (1976), 'Poverty and Disaster', *New Society*, 9 September 1976, p. 546.
2. *op. cit.*, p. 547.
3. Dowrick, David (1972), 'Must Earthquakes Always Win?' *New Scientist*, 28 December 1972, p. 735.
4. Press, Frank (1965), quoted in: Brander, J. (1976), 'When do Earthquakes Occur?' *New Scientist*, 12 February 1976, p. 343.
5. Aaronson, S. (1977), 'The Social Cost of Earthquake Prediction', *New Scientist*, 17 March 1977, p. 634.
6. Mitchell, J. K. (1975), 'The Rush to the Shore', *Landscape Architecture*, April 1975, p. 170.
7. Keller, Edward A. (1976), *Environmental Geology*, Merrill, Columbus, Ohio, p. 97.
8. Arnold, M. (1974), 'Floods as Man-made Disasters', reprinted in *Ecologist*, 6, No. 5, p. 169.
9. Davies-Jones, R., and Kessler, E. (1974).
10. Quarantelli, E. L., and Dynes, R. (1972), 'When Disaster Strikes', *Psychology Today*, February 1972.
11. Hewitt, K., and Burton, I. (1971), *The Hazardousness of Place*, University of Toronto Geography Department Res. Publications.
12. Moorhead, Caroline (1978), *The Times*, 16 August 1978.
13. Dacy, C. D., and Kunreuther, H. (1969), *The Economics of Natural Disasters*, Free Press, New York, p. 63.
14. Davis, I. (1978), 'Charity Begins with Homes', *New Scientist*, 6 July 1978, p. 17.

Further Reading

Adams, W. M., ed., (1970), 'Tsunamis in the Pacific Ocean', *Proceedings of the International Symposium on Tsunami Research*, East-West Science Center, Honolulu.

Arey, D. and Baumann, D. (1971), *Alternative Adjustments to Natural Hazards*, United States National Water Commission, Washington, D.C.

Armstrong, R. L., La Chapelle, E. R., Bovis, M. J. and Ives, J. D. (1974), 'Development of methodology for evaluation and prediction of Avalanche hazard in San Juan Mountain area of southwestern Colorado', *Institute of Arctic and Alpine Research, University of Colorado, Occasional Paper. No. 13.*

Battan, L. J. (1961), *The Nature of Violent Storms*, Doubleday Anchor, New York.

Bell, F. G. (1975), *Methods of Treatment of Unstable Ground*, Newnes-Butterworths, London.

Bolt, B. A. (1976), *Nuclear Explosions and Earthquakes – The Parted Veil*, Freeman, San Francisco.

Bolt, B. A., Horn, W. L., Macdonald, G. A., and Scott, R. F. (1975), *Geological Hazards*, Springer-Verlag, Berlin.

Bullard, F. M. (1962), *Volcanoes: In History, in Theory, in Eruption*, University of Texas Press, Austin.

Burton, I., Kates, R. W., and White, G. F. (1968), 'The Human Ecology of Extreme Geophysical Events', *Natural Hazards Research Working Paper No. 1.*, University of Toronto.

Burton, I., Kates, R. W., and White, G. F. (1978), *The Environment as a Hazard*, Oxford University Press Inc., New York.

Campbell, D. (1968), *Drought: Causes, Effects, Solutions*, Cheshire, Melbourne.

Coates, D. R., ed. (1972, 1973, 1974), *Environmental Geomorphology and Landscape Conservation*, Vol. I (1972), Vol. II (1974), Vol. III (1973), Dowden, Hutchinson & Ross Inc., Stroudsburg, Pa.

Dacy, D. C. and Kunreuther, H. (1969), *The Economics of Natural Disasters*, Free Press, New York.

Davison, C. (1924), *A History of British Earthquakes*, Cambridge University Press, Cambridge.

Dunn, G. E. and Miller, I. B. (1964), *Atlantic Hurricanes*, Louisiana State University Press, Baton Rouge, La.

Flawn, P. T. (1970), *Environmental Geology: Conservation, Land-Use, Planning and Resource Management*, Harper & Row, New York.

Flora, S. D. (1953), *Tornadoes of the United States*, University of Oklahoma Press, Norman, Okla.

Francis, P. (1976), *Volcanoes*, Penguin Books, Harmondsworth.

Fraser, C. (1966), *The Avalanche Enigma*, Murray, London.

Funnell, B. M., ed. (1974), 'Prediction of Geological Hazards', *Miscellaneous Paper of the Geological Society London*, 3.

Gribbin, J. (1978), *The Climatic Threat*, Fontana, Glasgow.

Grieve, H. (1959), *The Great Tide*, Essex County Council.

Hess, W. N. (1974), *Weather and Climate Modification*, Wiley, New York.

Holford, I. (1976), *British Weather Disasters*, David & Charles, Newton Abbot.

Hoyt, W. G., and Langbein, W. B. (1955), *Floods*, Princeton University Press, Princeton, N.J.

Kates, R. W. (1962), 'Hazard and Choice Perception in Floodplain Management', *University of Chicago, Department of Geography Research Paper*, No. 78.

Keller, E. A. (1976), *Environmental Geology*, Merrill, Columbus, Ohio.

Lane, F. W. (1966), *The Elements Rage*, David & Charles, Newton Abbot.

Lamb, H. H. (1957), 'Tornadoes in England', *Meteorological Office Geophysical Memoirs* 12, No. 99, H.M.S.O., London.

Legget, R. F. (1973), *Cities and Geology*, McGraw-Hill, New York.

Lomnitz, C. (1974), *Global Tectonics and Earthquake Risk, Developments in Geotectonics* No. 5, Elsevier, Amsterdam.

Lynn, D. A. (1976), *Air Pollution: Threat and Response*, Addison-Wesley, London.

Meetham, A. R. (1956), *Atmospheric Pollution – Its Origins and Prevention*, Pergamon, Oxford.

Nakano, T. (1970), 'Lands below sea level due to land subsidence in the urban areas of Japan', *Association of Japanese Geographers, Special Publication*, No. 2.

Nelson, H. J., and Clark, W. A. V. (1976), *The Los Angeles Metropolitan Experience*, Ballinger, Cambridge, Mass.

Newmark, N. M., and Rosenblueth, E. (1971), *Fundamentals of Earthquake Engineering*, Prentice-Hall, Englewood Cliffs, N.J.

Newson, M. D. (1975), *Flooding and Flood Hazard in the United Kingdom*, Oxford University Press, London.

Oakeshott, G. B. (1976), *Volcanoes and Earthquakes, Geologic Violence*, McGraw-Hill Earth Science Paperback Series, New York.

Perla, R. I., and Martinelli, M. (1976), 'Avalanche Handbook', *United States Department of Agriculture Forest Service. Agriculture Handbook* No. 489.

Quarantelli, E. L., ed. (1978), *Disasters: Theory and Research*, Sage Studies in International Sociology No. 13, Beverly Hills, California.

Richter, C. F. (1958), *Elementary Seismology*, Freeman, San Francisco, California.

Riehl, H. (1954), *Tropical Meteorology*, McGraw-Hill, New York.

Rikitake, T. (1976), *Earthquake Prediction, Developments in Solid Earth Geophysics*, No. 9, Elsevier, Amsterdam.

Scheidegger, A. E. (1975), *Physical Aspects of Natural Catastrophes*, Elsevier, Amsterdam.

Seckler, D., ed. (1971), *California Water*, University of California Press.

Sharpe, C. F. S. (1938), *Landslides and Related Phenomena*, Columbia University Press, New York.

Stanissi, P. C. (1972), *Disaster Analysis*, United Nations Disaster Relief Office, Geneva.

Tank, R. W., ed. (1973), *Focus on Environmental Geology*, Oxford University Press (second edition, revised, 1975).

Tannerhill, I. R. (1956), *Hurricanes, their Nature and History*, Princeton University Press, Princeton, N.J.

Taylor, K. K. (1967), *Florence – Ordeal by Water*, Hamilton, London.

United Nations Department of Economic & Social Affairs (1955), *Water Desalination, Proposals for a Costing Procedure and Related Technical and Economic Considerations*, New York.

United Nations Economic and Social Council (1971), *Assistance in Cases of National Disaster: Comprehensive Report of the Secretary-General*, New York.

U.N.E.S.C.O. (1970), *Annual Summary of Information of Natural Disasters*, Paris.

U.N.E.S.C.O. (1971), *The Surveillance and Prediction of Volcanic Activity*, Paris.

United States Senate (1963), *Federal Disaster Relief Manual*, Committee on Government Operations, United States Government Printing Office.

Wapner, S., Cohen, S. B., and Kaplan, B. (1976), *Experiencing the Environment*, Plenum Press, New York.

White, G. F. (1964), 'Choice of adjustment to floods', *University of Chicago Department of Geography Research Paper*, No. 93.

White, G. F., ed. (1974), *Natural Hazards: Local, National, Global*, Oxford University Press Inc., New York.

White, G. F., and Haas, J. E. (1975), *Assessment of Research on Natural Hazards*, M.I.T. Press, Cambridge, Mass.

Woodford, V. L. (1960), *Tornado Occurrence in the United States*, United States Department of Commerce, Weather Bureau, Washington, D.C.

In addition to the books listed above there are a large number of disaster and hazard articles in a variety of journals, of which the following are of particular importance: *International Journal of Disaster Studies and Practice; Environmental Geology;* and *Ground Engineering*. Of particular note are the six articles on volcanic hazard prediction in: *The Journal of the Geological Society*, Vol. 136, 3, 1979.

Index